Justice after War

"Dr. Kwon gives us a book that is systematic in its treatment of lineages of arguments and schools of thought in just war theory, comprehensive in its analysis of classic and contemporary scholarly sources, erudite in its depth, and wise in its conclusions. His *Justice after War* is at once a fine introduction to its subject matter and a robust thesis about it."

—Paulo Barrozo, Associate Professor, Boston College Law School

"This is an excellent book—David Kwon illuminates the extensive theological and philosophical debate about *jus post bellum* by carefully and critically examining the main proposals in the literature, and he argues for primary attention to human security in the immediate aftermath of war along with political reconciliation. I recommend it with enthusiasm."

—James F. Childress, Professor Emeritus, University of Virginia, and founding Director of the Institute for Practical Ethics and Public Life

"David Kwon masterfully approaches the great thinkers of just war, postwar justice, and peace theory with his own well-researched and well-reasoned understanding. David not only understands the just war thinkers, peace scholars, and justice after war writers theoretically, but importantly he has a grasp on and recommendations for practical applications for a kind of rapprochement between these areas. This is a must-read for anyone interested in justice, peace and reconciliation, and war and its aftermath as well as ethical approaches to these issues. It is also an incredibly important work for all of us who want to learn more about just war, human security, peace, and justice after war, along with helpful reconciliation efforts and how to be an agent of transformation in these areas."

—Drew Christiansen, SJ (1945–2022), was Distinguished Professor of Ethics and Human Development, Walsh School of Foreign Service, Georgetown University

"What is justice in the horrific aftermath of war? David Kwon's lucid interpretation of the philosophical and theological issues at stake in this question enables him to engage the concrete decisions of foreign policy and religious mission that confront the contemporary world. *Justice After War* incisively evokes the reader's ethical deliberation of a global crisis."

—W. Clark Gilpin, Margaret E. Burton Professor of the History of Christianity, emeritus, The University of Chicago Divinity School

"In this substantial and resourceful study, David Kwon advances our understanding of justice after war. Though mainly concerned to develop postwar justice from a Christian theological point of view, Kwon draws broadly from various contributors to the literature, and articulates both theoretical and applied insights into today's problems—with policing, punishment, and political reconstruction—inherent in post-conflict situations. Well-organized, erudite, and enjoyable, this is an important contribution to the crucial discourse surrounding what to do as societies move from war to peace."

—Brian Orend, Professor of Philosophy and
Director of International Studies, University of Waterloo, Canada,
and author of *The Morality of War*

"Traditional Just War theory has focused on two aspects of warring: justice before and during war little has been said about the third aspect: justice *after* the war (*jus post bellum*). David Kwon's *Justice after War* is a superb study of this third aspect. Deeply rooted in the classical tradition and well-informed in its dialogue with contemporary ethicists and moral theologians, it promises to be a classic in the field. Kwon does not limit himself to theoretical consideration; he also discusses after-war just policing and just punishment. With this book, Kwon establishes himself as one of the foremost experts on the Just War tradition. I most enthusiastically recommend it to both students of moral theology and national and international policymakers."

—Peter C. Phan, The Ignacio Ellacuria, SJ,
Chair of Catholic Social Thought, Georgetown University

"How to transit from war to peace while keeping justice intact is a crucial question for our day. Drawing insight from moral theology and the experience of practitioners, this book adopts a holistic approach toward navigating the competing demands of postwar peacebuilding. In so doing, it provides superb guidance in this challenging domain."

—Gregory M. Reichberg, Peace Research Institute Oslo (PRIO),
and author of *Thomas Aquinas on War and Peace*

"David Kwon offers a welcome and much needed contribution to the development of postwar ethics. He carefully and charitably engages the preliminary attempts of others, including myself, as he constructively provides a more systematic and coherent account of *jus post bellum*. Bridging theology, ethics, and other disciplines—as well as theory and practice—Kwon's work is to be commended."

—Tobias Winright, Professor of Moral Theology,
St Patrick's Pontifical University, Maynooth, Ireland,
and author of *After the Smoke Clears*

Justice after War

Jus Post Bellum in the Twenty-First Century

David Chiwon Kwon

Foreword by
Kenneth R. Himes, OFM

The Catholic University of America Press
Washington, D.C.

The paper used in this publication meets the minimum requirements of
American National Standards for Information Science—Permanence of
Paper for Printed Library Materials, ANSI Z39.48–1984.

∞

Cataloging-in-Publication Data is available from the Library of Congress
ISBN: 978-0-8132-3-6513
eISBN: 978-0-8132-3-6520

Contents

Foreword xi
Kenneth R. Himes, OFM

Preface and Acknowledgments xv

Introduction 1

PART I
DEVELOPING A THEORY OF *JUS POST BELLUM* FOR
MORAL THEOLOGY

1. **Common Issues and Themes in the Early Foundational Literature**
   Introduction 13
   Foundational Sources That Made the Case for *Jus Post Bellum* . . . 13
      Aristotle 13
      Thomas Aquinas 19
      Michael Walzer 26
      Brian Orend 31
   Discerning *Jus Post Bellum* Foundational Themes 41
      Finding Common Issues: *Jus Post Bellum* as a Third
         Element of Just War Theory 41
      Distilling Core Themes: Three *Jus Post Bellum*
         Foundational Themes 45
      Reconstructing Questions: Three Foundational Questions for
         Jus Post Bellum 47

2. **Moral Philosophy of *Jus Post Bellum***
   Introduction 49
   The Liberal Foundation of *Jus Post Bellum* 50
      A Shift of Norm Focus from *Right* to *Responsibility* 50
      The Responsibility to Protect 51
   Minimalist and Maximalist Approaches 54
      Alex Bellamy's Minimalist and Maximalist Positions 54
      Redefining Minimalist and Maximalist Positions 56
   Three *Jus Post Bellum* Foundational Themes 68
      Reconstruction of Just Policing 68

Reconstruction of Just Punishment 73

Reconstruction of Just Political Participation 77

3. **Moral Theology of *Jus Post Bellum*: Human Security**

Introduction: Movement toward Theological Reflection from
Philosophical Analysis 81

Human Security: Why and How Does Theology Matter? 85

The Church's Response to the Norm of R2P 85

Michael Schuck's Augustinian *Jus Post Bellum* 94

Kenneth Himes's Thomistic *Jus Post Bellum* 99

Mark Allman and Tobias Winright's Niebuhrian
Jus Post Bellum 108

Conclusion 119

4. **Moral Theology of *Jus Post Bellum*: Political Reconciliation**

Introduction 121

Political Reconciliation: Distinguishing Transitional Justice
and Postwar Justice 121

Does Political Reconciliation Matter to *Jus Post Bellum*? 124

Daniel Philpott's Ethic of Political Reconciliation 124

Anna Scheid's Consistent Ethic of Reconciliation 137

A Way Forward for Christian *Jus Post Bellum*: The
Maxim(um) of Ethical Minimalism 143

A Recap of Two Moral Visions: Human Security and
Political Reconciliation 143

The Maxim(um) of Ethical Minimalism: The Norm of the
Common Good 147

The Common-Good-Seeking Justice: Social Charity and
Political Prudence 154

Conclusion 157

PART II
POLICY-ORIENTED AND PRACTICAL CONCERNS IN
JUS POST BELLUM

5. **Reconstruction of Just Policing**

Introduction 161

From Theory to Practice 161

Just Policing: Refreshing and Refining the Theoretical
Ground for Practice 161

Just Policing for Dealing with Present Injustice 163
   Classical Just Actors: Peacekeeping and Nation Building 163
   Challenges of Just Policing 175
   Conclusion 187

6. Reconstruction of Just Punishment
Introduction 189
   From Just Policing to Just Punishment 189
   Just Punishment: Refreshing and Refining the Theoretical
      Ground for Practice 189
Just Punishment for Amending Past Wrongdoings and
      Securing the Rule of Law 191
   The Fundamental Sources of International Law for Just
      Punishment 191
   Occupation Law: Just Punishment for Securing the Rule
      of Law 197
   International Criminal Law: Just Punishment for
      Amending Past Wrongdoings 206
   Defining the Scope of *Jus Post Bellum* for Just Punishment
      Practices 210
   Conclusion 222

7. Reconstruction of Just Political Participation
Introduction 225
   Just Political Participation: Refreshing the Theoretical
      Ground for Practice 225
   Just Political Participation: Refining the Theoretical
      Ground for Practice 226
Just Political Participation for Peacebuilding and Reconciling
      Future Hostility 227
   Civil Society Peacebuilding 227
   Refining the Niebuhrian Approach to *Jus Post Bellum* for
      Civil Society Peacebuilding 246
   Conclusion 258

Conclusion: Lessons Learned and Future Challenges 261

Selected Bibliography 271

Subject Index 287

Foreword

Kenneth R. Himes, OFM
Boston College

"You can win the war but lose the peace" has become an adage in contemporary international studies. Indeed, the United States, a military superpower, has known the bitter aftertaste that comes with a lost peace. As a result, thinkers representing a variety of disciplines have wrestled with strategies about how best to secure a peace after war. Among those who have written on the topic are philosophical and theological ethicists who have viewed their work as an extension of the just war tradition, inquiring into the moral dimensions of a process that moves from conflict to restoration of a peaceful social order.

The categories of *jus ad bellum* and *jus in bello* are familiar categories to anyone with even minimal knowledge of the just war tradition. However, the idea that *jus post bellum* should be included as a third element of the tradition has not been endorsed by all who think of themselves as supporters of a just war framework. The idea of *jus post bellum* as an element of a fully satisfactory theory of just war does have some precedent. It is suggested by comments in writings of both Francisco Suárez (d. 1617) and Immanuel Kant (d. 1804). Both men argued that an adequate treatment of the ethics of warfare must include establishing post-conflict justice in order to have a true peace. Nonetheless, many modern just war thinkers are reluctant to include much of what falls under the rubric of *jus post bellum* into their theories. David Kwon's work enters that conversation with an excellent study of why a *jus post bellum* ethic is important for the just war tradition.

A tradition is, of course, a living thing; it is an ongoing conversation not only with one's contemporaries but also with those who have gone before us. After all, as G. K. Chesterton suggested, there is no reason to bar someone from a conversation just because they happen to be dead. Engaging with thinkers like Augustine and Aquinas remains a rich resource for insight on the human condition and human societies. Hence, historical thinkers like Vitoria and Grotius, as well as contemporary ones like Walzer and Hehir, call upon on the insights of those who have preceded them.

The late Jesuit, John Courtney Murray, referred to a tradition as having two ends, one rooted in history, preserving the insights of individuals and communities from the past, and the other end, the growing end of a tradition, that engages in ongoing conversation about new issues, new situations, and new actors. The work of David Kwon is a fine example of someone who cultivates both ends of a tradition: its roots and its development in an evolving environment. His scholarship draws upon the wisdom of classical thinkers in the just war tradition. He also has read widely in the contemporary just war literature that treats the theme of *jus post bellum*.

Like any tradition, that of the just war admits of a variety of theories. Too often people speak of a specific just war theory as if it is the sum and substance of the entire tradition. David Kwon knows better and is well versed in the variety of theories found within the just war tradition. As this study demonstrates, Kwon is a close reader and insightful analyst of those who have been contributors to ethical reflection on the problem of wars and how to end them. He brings a broad and varied educational experience to the conversation that is matched with an open and searching intelligence in his dialogues with thinkers who have examined the daunting task of bringing war to a just conclusion.

Another mistake when talking about the just war tradition is to reduce it to a set of norms. The norms are treated as clear and precise, and their application can be rather mechanical, employed as a checklist to determine the rightness of a conflict. Policymakers and some public officials in recent decades have slipped into this mode of employing just war ideas. People may disagree over exactly how many norms there are, which are basic and which are secondary, and how rigid or elastic the application should be, but the focus is always on norms. Still others treat the just war tradition as primarily an effort to defend certain values vital to human well-being that are at stake in situations of armed conflict on a large scale. The values may generate norms, which can be revised or added to as experience dictates, but it is the values that remain uppermost in the mind. In this study, David Kwon assesses the values a *jus post bellum* ethic ought to serve through its norms and why they are the appropriate values to choose as the crucial goods to be protected and promoted by a *jus post bellum* framework.

Throughout the book, Kwon provides clarity by his use of terms. For example, he carefully distinguishes transitional from postwar justice, as well as explaining what is meant by political reconciliation in a post-conflict setting. Kwon's lucid use of terms helps a reader grasp the differences between various theorists even when they employ the same terminology.

Certainly, the need for ethical reflection on post-conflict resolution has never been more urgent. To wit, the stated aim of humanitarian intervention, or the "responsibility to protect" doctrine, is to improve the lot of people who have been living in extremely oppressive situations. Unlike wars fought to resist another nation's aggression, humanitarian intervention is meant to enhance a victimized nation's well-being. Addressing the actual resolution of a conflict, therefore, is essential. Has life, in fact, gotten better for those people on whose behalf other third-party actors took up arms? Establishing some shared support for fundamental values as well as determining the proper priority to be given to those values in a postwar setting is vital if the aim is to help oppressed people attain a better social order.

Today, the lack of moral guidance for *post bellum* situations has helped create a legal vacuum, heightened political insecurity, and increased the possibility of injustice once the shooting has stopped. In international law the available wisdom for post-conflict settings is found in articles 32–41 of the 1907 Hague Convention. Unfortunately, much of what is found there is outmoded and irrelevant to present times. Guidance about buglers and white flags is manifestly insufficient today. Politically, the lack of assurances about the rights of the defeated can extend conflicts and increase casualties and destruction as both sides jockey for favorable bargaining positions. Morally, the absence of standards may foster inconsistent and disproportionate outcomes that only encourage future outbreaks of aggression. As is widely known, a bad peace can encourage a future war.

Readers of this volume will find much insight as to what should be the goals and the makeup of an ethical framework for the work of post-conflict activity. It is possible that readers will differ with David Kwon on facets of his *jus post bellum* ethic. My strong presumption is that Kwon would welcome such a reaction; he acknowledges the complexity of the task he has taken on and does not assume he has said the final word. What is manifestly evident in this very fine study is that David Kwon offers a constructive word in the ongoing conversation that is the just war tradition. I admire his contribution.

Preface and Acknowledgments

Modern just war tradition can be divided into two main parts: *jus ad bellum* (right to go to war) and *jus in bello* (right conduct in war). Hence, while much has been discussed about determining justifications for waging wars and the proper conduct for fighting wars, much less attention has been paid to the accountabilities of rebuilding and protecting individuals and communities in vulnerable societies devastated by war. However, the latter, namely the concept of *jus post bellum*, or postwar justice and peace, has been added to the recent just war discourse—as there is a growing discussion of the idea of *jus post bellum* across disciplines and what it means as an addition to just war thinking. In this book, the term *jpb*, or the abbreviation for *jus post bellum*, will be used for the sake of brevity and convenience.

Drawing on the work of both *jpb* philosophers and theologians, this book begins with an understanding that in Christian ethics, the definition of *jpb* remains diffuse and underdeveloped. Despite challenges that have faced church and society since the two recent US-led wars in Afghanistan and Iraq, it is yet to say that Christian ethicists and theologians as well as both religious and civil leaders altogether have fully engaged *jpb* issues with a clear respect for diverse positions and perspectives in a fair, balanced, and inclusive way. Further, Christian ethicists and theologians are often better prophets than peacemakers. They need lucidity on strategies that actually can bring peace. On no account, therefore, should Christians ask the question of how best to establish a just and sustainable peace after war. However, the question remains: to what extent can Christians contribute to *jpb*? As a member of a global society, the Church needs to be discreet, and its mission requires political prudence, especially when engaged in human security and political reconciliation practices that are primarily led by the state and the international community. This book is dedicated to these topics.

This book is intended as a theologically inspired introductory text in *jpb* ethics geared primarily toward just war thinkers and peace scholars but is also appropriate for those of the general audience who are interested in the ethics of war and peace. In addition, this book is expected to appeal to advanced undergraduate and graduate students in departments of theology or religious studies of which the curriculum is particularly interdisciplinary, thematic, or fairly praxis-driven. It could also be used for other discipline programs that often teach religion or the role of faith in social life as key subjects, such as philosophy, peace studies, and international relations. My goal in writing this book is to encourage moral discourse and theological reflection on ethical issues in *jpb* rather than resorting to ready-made and prescriptive answers to concrete dilemmas.

I believe this book offers three elements that set it apart from similar writings. First, while deeply rooted in the classical tradition and well-informed in its dialogue with contemporary ethicists and moral theologians, this book does not limit itself to theoretical consideration. Instead, this work presents a unique multidisciplined, yet conversational, approach to the ethics of war and peace that helps readers understand a wide spectrum of today's complex and urgent postwar justice and peacebuilding issues with global awareness, open-mindedness, and respect. These conversations include, but are not limited to, expanding *jpb* to embrace a "Responsibility to Protect" strand of advocacy, promoting strategic peacebuilding practices with a proven tendency to defuse potentially destructive hostilities, reforming the body of international law in compliance with a vision of empowerment to the local community, and casting the Church (and faith-based organizations) as an alternative body politic in the modern, liberal nation-states.

Second, and related to the first, this book employs a wide range of literature to explore how contemporary scholars view the idea of *jpb* and how this relatively new development fits within the Christian tradition of just war, a moral tradition that is historically interdisciplinary. This work employs not only an interdisciplinary approach, but also a constructive approach, because it addresses more than simply situating and understanding diverse *jpb* scholars' thoughts and subjecting them to critical analysis. In particular, with this attempt to construct a coherent cross-disciplinary body of *jpb* theory, this book adopts a holistic approach toward navigating the competing demands of postwar peacebuilding, namely, centering on human security and political reconciliation, proffering three attendant practices: just policing, just punishment, and just political participation. In so doing, this book attempts to clarify the scope of *jpb* practice that requires the establishment of a just peace in the *immediate* aftermath of war, not just any time after war's ending, and provides corresponding practical guidance. If postwar society fulfills human security, at least at a basic level, then that society will require a larger, longer-term-based agenda than what *jpb* proposes. In my book, this agenda calls upon transitional justice, moving from a phase in which armed forces are in charge of human security to a phase in which nonmilitary, civilian forces, namely police, are in charge of human security. This is also critical for my book in that in many other books, both the terms *postwar justice* and *transitional justice* are often used interchangeably, without distinguishing between them.

Third, this work carefully reviews and intersects with current just war and postwar theories and thinking. In many instances new sociopolitical complications, new institutional changes, and new cultural movements have outpaced the Church's capacity to initiate a critical analysis of, or to moderate a meaningful conversation about, such developments. This book engages current responses to questions about if and when Christians can support their nations' efforts to end wars and to what extent they should participate in, or challenge, them. In so doing, this book proposes a fresh and relevant way to our post-Cold War, globalizing contexts in the twenty-first century, especially when the globalizing world is facing increasing political and economic insecurity and widespread violence and conflicts.

My scholarly interests are united by my deep commitment to being a theological and philosophical educator in the service of church and society, as well as a conflict analyst with extensive expertise in war, social conflict, and contemporary cultural and political division, especially in postwar societies. My overarching aim as a Christian just war thinker and peace scholar is to find ways of bridging these divides and work for the common good. This commitment aligns with my conviction: "Blessed are the peacemakers, for they shall be called the children of God" (Mt 5:9).[1]

I am grateful to the team at the Catholic University of America Press for helping me bring this book from an initial big idea from my dissertation to final execution. I feel indebted especially to John Martino, who believed in my idea and helped me focus it. Despite Covid-19 challenges, he was a patient, diligent editor who gave me excellent feedback and kept me on track.

This book is developed from my dissertation. My dissertation advisers, teachers, and friends to whom I owe deep thanks are Kenneth Himes, OFM, Lisa Sowle Cahill, and Stephen Pope. I greatly benefit from each of their expertise while they all share the interest in the ethics of war and peacebuilding. Another reader, Paulo Barrozo, Boston College Law Professor, cannot be left out because of his support and review for the chapter "Reconstruction of Just Punishment."

---

1 This and all subsequent biblical references are to the New Revised Standard Version.

Colleagues at Saint Mary's University and elsewhere provided advice and answers to research questions. These colleagues include Drew Christiansen, SJ, Jean Bethke Elshtain, Erik Owens, Joshua Snyder, Tobias Winright, Mark Allman, Daniel Philpott, James Patrick Burns, IVD, Molly Lohnes, and Stacy Dean; each gave great feedback on a chapter or more in an area of their expertise. I want to thank them as well as my friends and teachers W. Clark Gilpin, Peter Phan, Lubomir Martin Ondrasek, Mike Sohn, Anna Scheid, Eli McCarthy, Laurie Johnston, William Douglas, Lindsay Thompson, Anselm Min, Hakjoon Lee, Ki Joo Choi, Jon Cahill, Kate Jackson, Cristina Richie, Sean Clifford, Peter Park, Carlo Calleja, James Weiss, James Keenan, SJ, David Hollenbach, SJ, James Bretzke, SJ, Andrea Vicini, SJ, Marcel Uwineza, SJ, Jun Nakai, SJ, Damian Park, OFM, Dan Horan, OFM, and the three anonymous reviewers, who gave me much to think about and much to do. Finally, students in my Peace Studies and Conflict Resolution courses gave me great insights as I tested out these ideas and some of the text with them.

Introduction

In times of crisis, especially in the aftermath of war, it is important for Christians and people of good will to return to basic questions and, together, seek renewed moral clarity and conviction. Consider a postwar society where people continue to harm each other for revenge or other reasons, all of which lead to a dysfunctional society and threaten human security. As wounded bodies lie in the streets again and people fear recurring violence, responsible individuals must ask how best to (re)establish a just peace following violent conflict.

The complexity and importance of increasing postwar challenges in the twenty-first century explain a large number of academic disciplines and practical approaches that attempt to analyze the problem from diverse angles and contexts. Nonetheless, perhaps the most accessible perspective from which one can begin to engage in postwar issues is a historical one, since every war and its postwar influence inevitably becomes part of history. Although some have not read postwar literature nor watched postwar films such as James Kent's *The Aftermath* (2019), Christian Petzold's *Phoenix* (2014), or Peter Webber's *Emperor* (2012), most have heard about the horrors of the Second World War and its subsequent postwar tragedies. For example, the Soviet Union suffered the loss of sixteen million civilians during the Nazis' invasion. But when the Nazis were defeated and the Soviet Union occupied Berlin at the beginning of May 1945, retribution had already begun. In Vienna alone, which Soviet soldiers had taken by the beginning of April, eighty-seven thousand women were reported by doctors to have been raped by Soviet soldiers. Throughout 1945, the citizens of Vienna lived on just eight hundred calories per day. It was clear that the postwar period was almost as vulnerable as the war. Further, like many modern wars, this war was not just an armed conflict. The then-warring parties let their fury and resentment be unleashed on their ideological or ethnic enemies whether from the same state or not. To think then that the end of the war means the end of hatred, resentment, and violence is naïve.

However, we have learned lessons from the past. The concept of human security has been developed to protect people in the immediate aftermath of war from traditional (i.e., armed violence) and nontraditional threats (i.e., poverty and disease). Moreover, the Human Security Unit (HSU) was established in 2004 to apply the human security approach to United Nations (UN) activities. At the same time, the international community has gradually succeeded in exploring the political influence and broader implications of the tradition and practice of nonviolence for ensuring human security and long-lasting peace, such as political reconciliation and social healing. Pope Francis also elucidated this request in his 2017 World Day of Peace Message, "Nonviolence: A Style of Politics of Peace," noting that "peacebuilding through active nonviolence is the natural and necessary complement to the Church's continuing efforts to limit the use of force by the application of moral norms."[1]

Nonetheless, without doubt, the recent wars in Iraq, Afghanistan, and elsewhere have pushed church and society to think even further about postwar issues and reassess traditional just war measures. Conventionally, the just war tradition (JWT) has employed two categories, *jus ad bellum* (reasons for war or right to wage war) and *jus in bello* (just conduct in war once it has begun). However, growing attention is being given to the quality of the *post bellum* reconstruction as a crucial factor in determining a war's overall justness. In fact, recent works in just war ethics have developed the concept of *jus post bellum* (*jpb*, postwar justice and peace) as a foundational principle and have placed questions of *jpb* at the front and center of contemporary debates about the ethics of war. Furthermore, in his recent article "Just War in the Twenty-First Century," Drew Christiansen, a Jesuit priest and Georgetown University professor, expects that two vital issues in the *jpb*—the duty of reconstruction and the place of reconciliation in securing a just peace—will be part of a multifaceted terrain of warfare in the twenty-first century.[2]

Plainly, the category of *jpb* is a welcome addition to discussions of the justice of war. The goal of this book is to review the significance of this recent development within the JWT. This project is based on a proposition that just war should aim at just peace; peace does not only mean the absence of armed conflict, but it also requires the establishment of justice. There is no true peace if it exists for the strong but not for the weak, or for the victor

---

1 See Pope Francis, "Nonviolence: A Style of Politics for Peace," Message for the World Day of Peace, January 1, 2017, 6. cf. Drew Christiansen understands this message as in an implication of the tradition and practice of nonviolence for the just war tradition. See Drew Christiansen, "Just War in the Twenty-First Century: Nonviolence, Post Bellum Justice, and R2P," *Expositions* 12, no. 1 (2018): 34.

2 For details, see Christiansen, "Just War in the Twenty-First Century," 37–45.

but not for the vanquished. Accordingly, a just peace is the ultimate goal that any just war should pursue. At the heart of *jpb* is the establishment of a just peace.

With this preliminary proposition in mind, this book endeavors to challenge the view of those who argue that reconciliation, mainly political reconciliation, is the first and foremost ambition of *jpb*. Instead, it proposes that achieving just policing, just punishment, and just political participation is essential to building a just peace, a peace in which the fundamental characteristic must be human security. In the *immediate* aftermath of war there are little or no avenues for policing, punishment, or political participation to protect the civilians of defeated states, especially the most vulnerable individuals and communities. Therefore, this project argues (i) that human security is a neglected theme in the discourse of moral and theological intellectual traditions; and (ii) that a more balanced understanding of *jpb* must pay direct attention to the elements comprising human security in a postwar context as well as the quest for reconciliation.

In this book, I will attempt to accomplish five tasks.

(1) I will examine the theme of *jpb* as it emerges in traditional just war literature.

(2) I will refine an understanding of existing *jpb* literature in order to identify common themes that emerge in this literature survey, which I call the three "foundational" *jpb* themes:
  a) reconstruction of just policing,
  b) just punishment, and
  c) just political participation.

(3) I will analyze and compare the way the category of *jpb* is being discussed in five disciplines: moral philosophy, moral theology, security studies, international law, and peacebuilding work. In this survey, I will concentrate on the articulation of *jpb* in moral theology and refer to the other disciplines as a means to illuminate the ethical and theological discussion.

(4) I will demonstrate that human security is an oft-neglected theme in the recent discourse of moral theologians and that a more balanced understanding of *jpb* will direct attention to the elements composing human security in a postwar context, as well as the quest for reconciliation.

(5) Finally, I will address whether the category of *jpb* ought to be acknowledged as a third element of the JWT, akin to *jus ad bellum* and *jus in bello*.

Through these five tasks, two main agendas emerge. The first agenda intends to explore whether *jpb* is a third element of the JWT and if so, how. For the second agenda, this book attempts to bring two different layers of *jpb* discourse together—that of just war theorists and that of practitioners in *post bellum* settings—while looking for their commonalities, especially with regard to the core issues of human security and political reconciliation. The first agenda will be predominantly discussed in the first half of the book, while the latter will be discussed in the second half. Therefore, this attempt will be distinguished from the work of major *jpb* proponents, such as Michael Walzer and Brian Orend, who remark that it is of no interest for their projects to delve into the different interpretations of *jpb* per se outside just war theory.[3] Instead, this book includes the discourse produced in studies by security policy writers, international lawyers, and scholars of peacemaking, with their emphasis on the viability of *jpb* as a practice.

The basic structure of the book falls into two major segments. Chapters one through four will develop a theory of *jpb* for moral theology. Chapter one will review what might be called the foundational texts that made the case for *jpb*, resulting in the identification of three common themes: reconstruction of just policing, just punishment, and just political participation.[4] Chapter two will examine moral philosophy writings on *jpb*, and chapters three and four will review moral theology writings on *jpb*. Based on these materials, I will first propose an initial articulation of what composes the category of *jpb* and then illuminate the moral theological discussion of *jpb*. In the second half of the book, chapters five to seven, I will turn to the more policy- and practice-oriented discourse. I will present security studies (chapter five) and international law (chapter six) literatures that introduce

---

3 Larry Mary, "*Jus Post Bellum*, Grotius, and *Meionexia*"; and Mark Evans, "At War's End: Time to Turn to *Jus Post Bellum?*," in *Jus Post Bellum: Mapping the Normative Foundations*, ed. Carsten Stahn et al. (Oxford: Oxford University Press, 2014): 15–25; 26–42. Larry May and Mark Evans observe that there are now two different layers that rule *jpb* discourse: one group is conducted by scholars and practitioners of law, security, and peacebuilding; and the other originates with the just war theorists, such as Michael Walzer and Brian Orend. For a more comprehensive introduction of the *jpb* discourse, including May's and Evan's views, see Jennifer S. Easterday, Jens Inverson, and Carsten Stahn, "Exploring the Normative Foundations of Jus Post Bellum: An Introduction," in *Jus Post Bellum: Mapping the Normative Foundations*, ed. Carsten Stahn et al. (Oxford: Oxford University Press, 2014): 1–11, especially 3.

4 As discussed throughout the book, to be clear, the expression "reconstruction" does not simply entail rebuilding or return to the status quo *ante bellum* (the prewar situation). Rather, reconstruction involves dynamic multiple transitions from war to peace: the reconstruction of policing, law, and a civil society with local initiatives.

an array of concerns not fully developed in the work of philosophers and theologians on *jpb*. Finally, chapter seven will draw upon lessons from (primarily faith-based) civil society organizations and their work in peacebuilding to propose a proper integration of human security discourse with reconciliation discourse so as to attain an adequate and balanced approach to *jpb*. I will apply the insights of *jpb* literature from the first half of the book to the three specific areas of just policing, just punishment, and just political participation that are identified in the last three chapters.

This introduction chapter does not contain the summary of each chapter. Instead, each chapter has its own introduction for the sake of clear guidance. This will help readers understand how each chapter connects to another. Further, for the sake of clarity of this project with its multidisciplinary nature, readers are encouraged not to skip the conclusion, "Lessons Learned and Future Challenges." It will not only highlight each chapter's main subjects but also clarify what might have been overlooked.

The methodology employed in this book will utilize and compare different disciplinary perspectives on *jpb* in order to reconstruct a more adequate and comprehensive perspective on the subject. While examining the interrelated challenges of moral and social norms in both political and legal domains, this book proposes an innovative methodology for linking theology, ethics, and social science so that the ideal and the real can inform each other in the ethics of war and peacebuilding. As of yet, there is little consensus between various disciplines regarding how to understand *jpb* and its embedded issues. Therefore, examining the norms proposed by various disciplines on the topic of *jpb* is a valuable contribution to the JWT, *a moral tradition that is historically interdisciplinary*. Although I will make reference to these norms, this is not a book about international law or security/peace studies, nor is it a policy memo about a particular postwar context. Instead, this book explores how contemporary scholars view the idea of *jpb* and how this relatively new development fits within the Christian (primarily Catholic) tradition of just war. At its best, the Christian *jpb* ethics is a collaborative enterprise in which we come to a better grasp of what is good and true *post bellum* by listening to and learning from others. Through such collaboration, we may discover that we do not always agree with another's thought and study, but we should be better at listening humbly and attentively to what the other has to say. In this respect, my hope is that readers will feel invited to this *jpb* discourse and feel welcome to contribute to and continue it.

Further, while other disciplines describe the structure of *jpb* theory and practice with objectivity and detachment, theology seeks the meaning of *jpb* with moral and existential concerns. Christian life, whether at peace, war, or *post bellum*, is not about keeping a set of rules and norms but about engaging a lifelong process to become a disciple of Christ, namely, living in the world in a way by striving for God, or to imitate and represent Christ to others (*imitatio Christi*). To be clear, norms and rules are necessary and useful for refining *jpb* ethics, but without discipleship they lead to nothing but legalism—or at its best, metaphysical speculation. The mission of the Church *post bellum* is to be people of God by working on behalf of God's plans and purposes for the (re)establishment of a just peace on earth. The Christian JWT provides an overarching framework with key touchstones that enhance ethical reflection on the common good. The same is true for *jpb*. In reflecting on why this framework might be an appropriate way for envisioning the Christian moral life, we explore what it means to be called a disciple *post bellum*.

Catholic moral theologians have developed the JWT as states have adopted war as a means to pursue a range of political opportunities. The Church has offered theological insight and moral principles for discerning when and how war can be accepted and tolerated as a necessary evil by identifying possible justifications including *self-defense and protection of the innocent and vulnerable.* In practice, the Church has responded to the reality of war in tandem with international legal treaties and agreements—all of which seek to bind states to appropriate behavior during war. Although the current international law of war, primarily governed by the United Nations, seeks to balance the self-interest of its members with humanitarian ideals, its legal and technical assessments of war reflect the JWT's influence on moral reasoning. However, an absence of *jpb* criteria in international law and the teaching of the Church is a consequence of the absence of moral and theological norms for behavior *post bellum*. The development of norms and criteria of *jpb* is imperative because the reconstruction of a civil society, or a failure to do so, determines future autonomy and stability for human lives *post bellum*. In other words, there is a lack of moral clarity concerning *jpb* efforts in the Christian JWT; nor is there a theological logic, which gives priority to the *post bellum* questions. With no agreed upon norms and criteria of *jpb*, actors are not held substantially accountable for their postwar efforts even when violent conflict and social instability continue.

Plainly, the Christian JWT has contributed theological insights to the sense of justice regarding when and how war can be waged, but the tradition has not made similar contributions to understanding how war should end. Meanwhile, the production of theological thought and discourse on political reconciliation has provided significant contributions to the literature of post-conflict studies but has had little to say about how this scholarship can contribute to the entire body of the JWT. This is surprising because at least from a theological and ethical perspective, political reconciliation seems best suited to challenge the complex and hands-on issues with which *jpb* scholars grapple. Central to these issues is the distribution of all warring parties' postwar responsibilities.

In my view, however, the cornerstone of *jpb* is the norm of human security, not that of political reconciliation—although these two norms are not always distinct. In the wake of both war and postwar events, individuals who were not liable for the harms of war often suffer serious deprivation and pain. This suffering—and suffering alleviation initiatives—must be addressed as a matter of urgency. Further, my version of *jpb* will allow actors to reflect morally upon saving human life *post bellum*, as well as how to better use the resources at their disposal. When a war ceases, the need for the distribution of postwar resources and services raises pressing questions, not only for secular just war theorists and post-conflict scholars, but also for Christian just war thinkers. These two strands of thinking about justice—human security and political reconciliation—have engendered separate lines of theorizing. In this book, I suggest that *jpb* can be developed most effectively if both of these strands *properly* consider the end of war.

In particular, holding a realistic view that war is inherently destructive to people, institutions, and infrastructure, this project focuses on "justice" in reconstruction—reconstruction of just policing, just punishment, and just political participation. This destruction raises questions about the fulfillment of justice in the damaged postwar society. Considering these issues through the lens of human security and political reconciliation theories, I propose my "maxim(um) of ethical minimalism" for *jpb*—*the principle of achieving to the highest extent possible human security, which is the necessary and essential outcome for jpb*. It is the norm for *jpb* to achieve the common good to the highest extent possible, with priority on human security, using nonviolent means insofar as possible and violent means only when necessary. This proposal suggests that the *jpb* norm should be specified to address the damage to relationships that need to be not only restored but also fundamentally transformed in the postwar society to prevent future threats. This book will pay particular attention to civil society peacebuilding, which needs to be considered *only* to the extent that it is an objective of the postwar discussion and to the extent it is affected by *jpb* decisions. Nonetheless, it will also guide that this transformative vision of *jpb* should be distinguished from an *extensive* buildup of a civil society scheme, which requires a wider and longer range of peacebuilding efforts. Instead, it must be tempered by realism in a careful and concrete manner, since the priority should be given to human security in the *immediate* aftermath of war.

Every war is different. Every war has its own unique conditions that influence how justice should be fulfilled in the aftermath of that war. Therefore, it is worth noting the limits of scope in this writing. First, this book will deal with cases of conventional war, namely, interstate warfare. Although I refer to wars that involve a degree of civil conflict (e.g., the Rwandan genocide of 1994), these civil war cases are only employed in comparison to interstate war cases. This also means that recent examples of asymmetric warfare (e.g., the 9/11 terrorist attacks and the ISIS insurgency) are beyond the scope of this book. While they are important topics, for the sake of focus in the traditional just war literature, I intend to avoid investigating political and military responses to insurgency, terrorism, and other forms of irregular warfare.

Second, the concept of *jpb* should be distinguished from transitional justice.[5] Both forms of justice address postwar challenges and are compatible but distinct. In my book, a narrower set of contexts fall under the scope of postwar justice than under the scope of transitional justice, which applies not only to *post bellum* contexts but also post-repression contexts. Additionally, the aim of postwar justice, as part of the JWT, is the establishment of a just peace. In contrast, implicit in the idea of transitional justice is an assumption that a community is transitioning to democracy, or at least toward the political culture of democratic government. As one way of accounting for such matter of fact, in this book the *jpb* discourse is limited to the postwar context and its aim to bring a just peace, not a democratic regime alone. This clarification is an integral part of this book when

---

5 Throughout the book, and especially in chapter four, I will attempt to delineate more clearly the boundary, from a theological perspective, between transitional justice and *jpb*. In my view, the boundary between transitional justice and *jpb* is still murky and underdeveloped in the field of theology, unlike other academic disciplines. In this regard, I will compare the theological literature with that of law, philosophical ethics, and political science.

discussing the three foundational elements of *jpb*—implementing just policing, just punishment, and just political participation.

Third, *jpb* is claimed to be part of the JWT. This means that the military is the main agent conducting *jpb* practices, as in *jus ad bellum* and *jus in bello*. Although there are other actors involved—such as governments, the international community, local communities, and the Church and faith-based organizations—the military force is involved in all of the *jpb* areas in the name of Military Operations Other Than War (MOOTW). This not only applies to arms control and peacekeeping, but also to humanitarian assistance, disaster relief, reconstructing public goods, training local securities, and supporting civilian/business organizations. It is important to distinguish these kinds of forces from those forces in *jus ad bellum* and *jus in bello* and to define who these forces are, what they do, and when they are involved. Most forces in *jus post bellum* are noncombat soldiers such as sappers, medics, trainers, and special units for search and rescue. Importantly, this fact demonstrates that the purpose of the military involvement is for what is called "comprehensive security," which implies both state and human security.

Finally, several of these chapters cover interrelated but diverse bodies of literature, and some of them are quite expansive. With this in mind, I would like to request the reader's patience. This deep engagement is necessary for my argument to fully unfold. Even so, I will be selective in my discussion, exploring only those elements that are most salient to *jpb* surrounding human security and political reconciliation.

Part I

Developing a Theory of
Jus Post Bellum for Moral Theology

Chapter One

Common Issues and Themes in the Early Foundational Literature

INTRODUCTION

Chapter one will focus on the work of the so-called "foundational" *jus post bellum* (*jpb*) thinkers. The authors it will examine are Aristotle, Thomas Aquinas, Michael Walzer, and Brian Orend.[1] The main reason why I refer to them as foundational is that these thinkers' works are widely cited across disciplines of the *jpb* literature: theological, philosophical, legal, and security studies. Each author has contributed important insight to *jpb* thinking: Aristotle's quest for justice in war, Aquinas' systemic outline of the JWT, Walzer's modern attempt to reconstruct the moral norms and practices that constitute the JWT today, and Orend's theoretical foundations for *jpb* in contemporary warfare. This chapter will first articulate each of their crucial theses that inform my case for *jpb*. This review will result in the identification of three common themes of *jpb*—reconstruction of just policing, just punishment, and just political participation—and further reframe them as my foundational questions.

FOUNDATIONAL SOURCES THAT MADE THE CASE FOR *JUS POST BELLUM*

Aristotle

It is not often that Aristotle is regarded as a just war thinker. Thus, one might wonder: Can Aristotle be legitimately given the title of *jus post bellum* thinker? While Aristotle frequently addresses the question of justice, he writes comparatively little about war. Further, his quest for justice in war is

---

1 One might wonder why Augustine is not considered a foundational *jpb* thinker in this book. Although Augustine is noted in history as one of the founders of just war theory, his work has been rarely addressed in the present-day *jpb* discourse, except in Michael Schuck's short piece, "When the Shooting Stops," *Christian Century* 111, no. 30 (1994): 982–84. Therefore, in this book, Augustine is occasionally introduced as a reference in comparison to the foundational *jpb* thinkers; likewise, Schuck's work is visited to clarify Kenneth Himes's Thomistic *jpb* conception.

only limited to *jus ad bellum* considerations—that is, dealing with the moral reasoning that justifies the resort to war, not even to *jus in bello* questions seeking the legitimacy of the means used to wage war. Aristotle, unlike Augustine and Aquinas, is not known as a founder of just war thinking. He believed that war could be fought for the acquisition of property—both monetary and human—so as to maintain a proper hierarchy as one of the requirements for his just *polis*.[2] Most contemporary readers, however, would probably have a hard time considering this view to reflect justice. Indeed, they would see it as pure aggression. In contemporary politics, aggression is the main charge that procures a guilty verdict against defendants, such as in the case of Nuremberg. A different set of norms exists between Aristotle's system of ethical war and contemporary thought on the JWT, and no one can deny that Aristotle's quest for justice in war is different from that of most modern just war thinkers.

Aristotle's quest for the justice *of resorting to war* is not wholly distinct from his quest for justice *after war*. Here, he is similar to other just war thinkers who have acknowledged the relations between these two quests— how one defines *jpb* for a certain context is closely tied to the reasons for going to war. In other words, it may be argued, *jus ad bellum* considerations look to the end of the war and tacitly, if not explicitly, establish certain general requirements for postwar justice. The classical sources of the JWT always demonstrate some concern for the aftermath of war—especially when those sources relate the end of war to the ultimate purpose of war, which is the establishment of a just peace. Aristotle reveals himself as sharing this view when he claims that the ultimate purpose of war is to achieve peace. Hugo Grotius invokes Aristotle's view that "the purpose of war is to remove the things that disturb peace." In his discussion of "the law of war," Grotius explains that one must *not* do what is unjust in order to secure peace, a concept which came to be known as a negative peace approach.[3]

---

2 Aristotle, *The Politics*, trans. Trevor J. Saunders and T. A. Sinclair (London: Penguin Books, 1981), 1256b15.

3 Hugo Grotius, *The Law of War and Peace*, trans. Louise R. Lommis (Roslyn, NY: Walter J. Black, Inc., 1949), 375. To be clear, Hugo Grotius does not use the term negative peace. It is the term which has been used by contemporary scholars. In particular, Johan Galtung refers to negative peace as the "absence of" something, namely war and violence. He refers to positive peace as the "presence" of something, namely the presence of cooperation between people and states and the "integration of human society," including, incorporating social justice, respect for human rights, and elimination of structural violence. cf. Johan Galtung, "Violence, Peace, and Peace Research," *Journal of Peace Research* 6, no. 3 (1969): 167–91.

Plainly, while Aristotle is content to define peace among nations (*poleis*) as simply the absence of war, he maintains that within a *polis* peace is the establishment of an order, a just order that sustains the proper hierarchy inherent in nature. In this regard, fighting for the acquisition of property among *poleis* can be understood as a way of removing what disturbs the peace in a *polis*. For Aristotle, then, fighting for the acquisition of property is simply a means to the establishment of proper leadership and peace. This establishment should, therefore, be the aim of any postwar society. This Aristotelian brand of a peaceful *telos* of war implies a *jpb* vision that appears to help produce clear and realistic postwar goals and forestall postwar problems. However, a question still remains: what does "the establishment of a just order that is in harmony with *nature*" mean?

It is important to note that several of the causes of war, such as war for the sake of enslavement and for wealth, are, Aristotle argues, just by nature. He finds that such policies have a justification in the cosmos. In a way, he returns to a view of justice that is similar to that of Herodotus: humans are part of the cosmos, and the cosmos is just. Aristotle, therefore, seeks to define justice as being in accordance with the cosmos. Because war is necessary for this naturally or cosmologically ordained condition, it is in a sense justified. However, Aristotle does not place the origins of war with fate, as does Herodotus, who believes that the cosmos will establish peace and justice.[4] In contrast, Aristotle argues that humans must make the proper decision in order to attain justice and fulfill their natures in the best way. In other words, he sees nature and the cosmos as the ultimate judge of whether something is just, and he requires that humans follow a particular path in order to achieve this harmony with nature. For him, fighting for the acquisition of property is one of the paths toward that harmony. War, then, is the way to recover the harmony that was lost when an "injustice" occurred through external threats (e.g., foreign invasion) or domestic concerns (e.g., famine, slave riots). Aristotle, therefore, justifies war as a natural practice for survival in human society. However, to be clear, although Aristotle sees war as arising from the need for acquisition of slaves and resources, this acquisition is not about fulfilling some inner desire. Instead, this acquisition is concerned with the establishment of a *polis*, as the need for acquisition

---

4 For an extended discussion of Aristotle's and his ancient Greek interlocutors' views on war and peace, see W. Kendrick Pritchett, *Dionysius of Halicarnassus: On Thucydides* (Berkeley: University of California Press, 1975).

involves taking what one is entitled to by nature. For Aristotle, war is justified if one intends to use these resources, whether objects or (other) humans/labor forces, in accordance with nature. This affirms that some wars cannot be justified when those who initiated the wars are confused about the natural order of human affairs.

This viewpoint emerges from Aristotle's belief that there is a political hierarchy inherent in nature. Just war, as a natural process, is one that establishes or maintains the natural hierarchy of Greeks over non-Greeks and masters over slaves. Hence, waging a war is justified as long as it protects those who, by nature, deserve to acquire, those who deserve to command others, and those who deserve to remain unconquered. Clarifying war as such a natural process made sense for Aristotle, as humans are a distinct type of animal, the *polikon zoon*, who have specific purposes as natural beings; these humans use war to achieve the *telos* that is in accordance with nature. According to him, there are some people whose natures make them destined to be ruled. However, when they become disobedient to the ruling class, war will be waged against them, and "war of such kind is naturally just."[5] For example, in Aristotle's thought, Greeks are entitled to rule over barbarians; and even among the Greek population, some are entitled to mastery while others are slaves by nature.[6] Because Aristotle sees this hierarchical arrangement of life as justified by nature, he approves the use of war, a natural process, to attain this state. This state is a just *polis* for him. In other words, war is waged for the protection of a just *polis* by (re)establishing proper leadership, which includes enslaving those who are slaves by nature as well as protecting the office of ruler over those who are incapable of ruling themselves.

However, it is important to recall that, despite this reasoning, Aristotle writes of war as something that will be justified for its effects only when leading to a just *polis*. In his eyes, therefore, it is imperative to weigh the effects of war before waging war. Even if a cause is just, war can be devastating and debilitating. Hence, it is a nation's duty to consider foreseeable effects of war and to establish a just *polis* after war, as such reflection may curb unnecessary violence. This duty can shed light on one's war objectives and thus better protect those impacted by war. Therefore, taking this insight from Aristotle as a touchstone to guide ethical reflection

---

5 Aristotle, *Politics*, 1256b25.
6 *Politics*, 1255a3.

on war will make explicit the already implicit just war reflection on the postwar situation.

This *jpb* implication in Aristotle's thought affirms that his main concern is with war as a means to an end, with that end being the creation of peace. For him, war that leads to a just *polis* is meant to produce conditions that cultivate virtues in the human soul. In *Nicomachean Ethics*, Aristotle develops the idea that the ultimate purpose of war is peace, and that peace within a *polis* should properly be used for the pursuit of virtue.[7] Plainly, although these virtues require an orderly structuring of the human soul, war has no intrinsic value for a virtuous soul; instead, war is only worthwhile as a natural process for the establishment of peace within a *polis*. This peace is achieved through the common good, which is the purpose of all political practices in a human society.[8] The proper combination of the common good and peace results in the creation of a just *polis* that is capable of establishing a setting for the life for which all strive: a life of virtue consisting of the goods of the body, the goods of the soul, and external goods, such as the wealth necessary to live a good life.[9] Developing virtues is not only the way humans become more ethical but also the way they pursue the good in human life and further the common good in political life. In Aristotle's view, on that account, those who wage unjust wars are unjust not solely because they are doing harm to others or taking resources from them, but rather because they are denying themselves the chance to attain this good life.

Therefore, it is important to note that Aristotle believes that humans are political animals, but they are also beings who seek the good. War is a political means to achieve the common good. This determines that war is a necessity if it helps secure a just *polis* in which humans are able to attain the goods necessary to live a virtuous life. In other words, the virtue of justice results from living within a just community, which is to say a setting that provides one with the opportunity to become a virtuous person. For Aristotle, the virtuous person is the most truly human being, a person who grows in virtue socially, by surrounding himself with other virtuous people and learning from them, and thereby grows in *phronesis* (practical wisdom). War is necessary to found this community, as it requires material resources

---

7 Aristotle, *Nicomachean Ethics*, trans. Terence Irwin (Indianapolis: Hackett Publisher, 1999), 1177b6–11.

8 *Nicomachean Ethics*, 1092a28–b10.

9 Aristotle, *Politics*, 1323a21.

and slave labor, both of which can be obtained through war. War, therefore, is justified insofar as it protects this community.[10] This Aristotelian vision of a just community can be understood within *jpb* contexts. A postwar society as a whole could grow ethically by providing people with an education that trains them in the virtues and in moderating their desires. It is important for this society to provide the necessities for living a safe and healthy life because a certain amount of earthly goods is needed to practice virtues like generosity or even forgiveness, and also because it is difficult to develop these virtues if one is constantly preoccupied with hunger and other bodily needs. This aspect of protecting Aristotle's vision of a just community is related to the primary concern of human security for *jpb* that I will examine throughout this book.

Further, specific *jpb* implications in Aristotle's thought include his concern for people of defeated nations and his rejection of the idea that all the citizens of a defeated nation should be slaves. According to Aristotle, victors need to protect those whose natures are noble from being made slaves even though they have been defeated.[11] This claim that Aristotle makes is not wholly different from the *jpb* principle that encourages the protection of citizens of a defeated nation from being pressed to carry the burdens of war after war—not just the humiliation of defeat but also the pain of enduring the unendurable after war. However, it is true that Aristotle's idea is still quite distant from that of present-day *jpb* contexts, where there is no longer a slave system. Above all, those individuals he refers to as citizens are different than the idea of citizens today. Aristotle does not believe that slaves or women are equal citizens. They and resident aliens are in a different category and are not allowed to rule. Citizens live a life of virtuous activity and ruling, while the working classes (artists and farmers) are *non-full* citizens. Manual labor takes up time and makes people unfit for virtuous activity. These activities should be left to slaves or foreigners.[12] Therefore, it is difficult to expect that his *jpb* implications should work perfectly for today's concepts of justice after war, which applies to all involved in war. Still, Aristotle's quest for justice in war cannot be completely understood without the idea of postwar justice that I have introduced.

---

10 *Politics*, 1334a.

11 For further discussion, see Coleman Phillipson, *The International Law and Custom of Ancient Greece and Rome* (London: MacMillian, 1911), 2:192–93.

12 Aristotle, *Politics*, 1328b33ff.

Thomas Aquinas

Unlike Aristotle, Thomas Aquinas is regarded as a just war thinker. Yet, it is questionable if he can be legitimately given the title of *jpb* thinker. One might argue that Aquinas, like Aristotle, can be understood as a *jpb* thinker according to the *jpb* principles that have the same foundation as those principles underlying *jus ad bellum* (i.e., an establishment of just peace). However, Aquinas's case differs from Aristotle's; while Aristotle is still in the initial stage of questioning about justice in war, which allows for more diverse ways of interpreting his work, Aquinas thoroughly examines and carefully develops the JWT. But it is clear that he does not explicitly address *jpb* principles. Despite this, when one reads Aquinas, it is also clear that Aquinas has an implicit notion of *jpb* in mind as he writes. In this section, I will briefly examine Aquinas's just war theory and whether it is related to *jpb* issues.

For Aquinas, war is a natural means to enact the law of God as it serves the common good and peace.[13] Aquinas begins his examination of war by identifying that "war is not always sinful" through reference to Augustine's reflection on John the Baptist's instruction to the centurion "to be content with your pay" (Lk 3:14).[14] War, he suggests, can sometimes be just. He attempts to ground just war in the common good, stating, "wars are lawful and just in so far as they protect the poor and the entire commonweal from suffering at the end of the foe."[15] Also, drawing from Augustine, Aquinas affirms that just wars are aimed "at peace, and so they are not opposed to peace, except to the evil peace, which our Lord came not to send upon earth" (Mt 10:34).[16] The reference to "evil peace" refers to Jesus' proclamation that he came not to bring peace but the sword, and it points to the idea that there are some forms of "evil peace" that are oppressive, overbearing, and therefore unjust. For Aquinas, this means that war is not opposed to peace, but opposed only to the "evil peace" that comes at the price of justice. A just war, then, is one that combines, in the proper way, serving the common good and peace. By combining them properly, we look for the establishment of a just peace, not just any peace. Aquinas aims at securing a just rather than unjust version of peace. This viewpoint is similar to that of Augustine, who

13 Thomas Aquinas, *Summa Theologica*, trans. Fathers of the English Dominican Province (New York: Benziger Brothers, 1948) II-II, q.40, a.1. (Hereafter cited as *ST*.)

14 *ST*, II-II, q.40, a.1.

15 *ST*, II-II, q.40, a.2.

16 *ST*, II-II, q.40, a.1.

distinguishes between *justa pax* and *iniqua pax*.[17] But it should be noted that "for Aquinas, peace in the political community is accomplished by justice and the rule of law much more emphatically than for Augustine."[18] In other words, for Aquinas, justice is not only a prerequisite for true peace, but is also revealed in a more specific way in the reality of politics. Peace is not just a form of a rightly ordered love, as in Augustine's thought, but is revealed throughout the common good as the product of justice.

Aquinas, like Aristotle, understands the common good in the context of a political society, but he uses the lens of law. His taxonomy of law is wide, and human law has the clearest points of contact with Aristotelian philosophy—due to the direction of all laws toward the common good and in accordance with reason.[19] However, the theological backdrop of Aquinas's view of law must be elucidated before discussing human law. In the *Summa theologiae*, Aquinas defines law as "an ordinance of reason, ordained for the common good, made by one who has authority, and is promulgated."[20] He argues that every law derives from the eternal law, which is in God. Deriving from eternal law is natural law, which is inscribed in the hearts of all persons. The first principle of natural law is "good is to be done and evil is to be avoided."[21] Humans reach this principle through *synderesis*—an immediate, non-inferential (inborn and habitual) grasp of the principle of good and evil. Natural law has several precepts that derive from the first principle. Humans are social and political by nature in order to govern the interests of the common good. Therefore, recognizing the sociability of man and woman, as a result of the precepts of natural law, entails that certain parameters of societal interactions are needed. In the estimation of Aquinas, human law is considered as a set of these parameters. Human law governs actions for the

---

17 Augustine, *The City of God*, trans. Gerald G. Walsh et al. (Garden City: Doubleday, 1958), 19.12.

18 Lisa Sowle Cahill, *Love Your Enemies* (Minneapolis: Fortress Press, 1994), 92.

19 For details, see Thomas Aquinas, *St. Thomas Aquinas on Politics and Ethics*, trans. and ed. Paul E. Sigmund (New York: Norton, 1988), 7–8. For Aquinas, law is the exercise of the rational soul which separates humans from beasts. The proper cultivation of man's rational capacities to order the bodily appetites leads to a life of moral excellence in the *vita activa* within the political order. It should be noted that the highest form of life is not the *vita activa* but the *vita contemplativa*. Moral virtues cultivated in the *vita activa* mold dispositions that enable the individual to be open to the grace of God enabling him to contemplate God's substance. Because this book focuses on Aquinas's political theory on war and the flourishing of the individual within the purview of the sociopolitical order, I limit my discussion to the natural origins and ends of human beings in the *vita activa*.

20 *ST*, I-II, q.90, a.4.

21 *ST*, I-II, q.94, a.4.

common good as it rests upon the natural law; humans participate in the eternal law not only through the natural inclination that God has imprinted upon their natures but also through both the light of human reason and the knowledge of the true good (building toward the common good) that ought to be done, especially the naturally known perceptive principles of the natural law. This law seeks to promote the human pursuit of their proper inclinations. Since Aquinas gives a teleological justification of earthly rule that is mirrored in divine rule, he has a fairly high estimation regarding the human capabilities of constructing law to bring about happiness and harmony in this world. Therefore, the law must serve to secure or recover the order of society, peace among its members, and the overall common good. In this sense, wars can be waged to protect this order from any threat.[22]

In particular, Aquinas's just war framework is one that provides a universal rationality regarding the achievement of the common good. Protecting the common good from any threat is a crucial reference point for his just war theory. While the theory itself does not define the common good, it has been linked to the common good from its inception and thus provides ways to reflect on how the common good is impacted and best achieved.

For example, Aquinas develops the JWT with three key principles—legitimate authority, just cause, and right intention—in order to recover the just order of society for the common good. A just war is one that should be waged with these conditions.[23] I will not go into detail about how Aquinas sees each of these principles. However, what is important for us here is that he proposes them in order to protect the common good. To be brief, legitimate authority is a proper authority legitimated by those who are responsible for the common good. It is the right authority of the sovereign to prevent individuals from declaring war on one another. The principle of just cause prompts the legitimate authority, the sovereign, to think about what he is doing and why. The principle of right intention motivates the sovereign to examine his motivations, keeping them honest and tethered to a just cause and peace. According to Aquinas, this intention should be understood within the framework of his own religious thought as it refers to "the object of our will," which is God—finding out what it involves in itself as "we are in a sense obliged to conform our will to God's and in a sense we are not."[24] In other

---

22 *ST*, II-II, q.40, a.2.
23 *ST*, II-II, q.40, a.1.
24 *ST*, II-II, q.23, a.8.

words, the object of our will, namely, the goodness of God is *regula et mensura* (the rule and measure) of every good; however, since good depends upon the end, our will is called good on the basis of its relation to the reason for willing, which is the end. Our right intention is expected to confirm with God's insofar as we see a relationship between object and end. For Aquinas, God is "the ultimate good," which "we" seek as an end since human beings seek to mirror God's goodness.[25] Just war, then, demands we reflect on the object of our will when we respond to a threat in order to secure the common good. In these ways, Aquinas's just war theory provides a framework with key touchstones that enhance ethical reflection on the common good.

However, the question still remains: can we find *jpb* thinking in Aquinas's understanding of protecting the common good as a reference point for his just war theory? In fact, Aquinas does not specify *jpb* considerations in his discourse on war; the three principles explained above are originally known as the criteria for the judgment of *jus ad bellum*. Nevertheless, Aquinas gives a hint as to the importance of *jpb* in recovering just order in a war-torn society. In particular, the principle of right intention can be understood in *jpb* contexts. It is important to note that the principle of the right intention, as it relates to both *jus ad bellum* and *jus in bello*, implies the existence of norms applicable to the end, and the aftermath, of war. To make this point clearer, the contemporary just war thinker James Turner Johnson's understanding of Aquinas's notion of the right intention should be noted. According to Johnson, Aquinas's right intention is understood in two ways, negatively and positively. "Negatively, he rules out evil intentions, . . . the desire for harming, the cruelty of avenging, . . . [and] the lust of domination. . . . These are the things which are to be blamed in war. Positively, right intention is the purpose of establishing or restoring a disordered peace."[26] By combining them properly, he concludes that Aquinas's notion of the right intention focuses on "the fundamental moral purpose of all uses of force to achieve the peace that comes only with a justly ordered community."[27] This statement demonstrates that the state of mind of the one who properly authorizes the war and those who fight under that authorization "*intend*

---

25 See Brian Davies, *Thomas Aquinas on God and Evil* (Oxford: Oxford University Press, 2011), chaps. 6 and 8.

26 James T. Johnson, "The Just War, As It Was and Is," *First Things* (January 2005), 19.

27 Johnson, 19.

the advancement of good, or the avoidance of evil."[28] Additionally, it shows that their assessment of the principle of right intention involves a state of mind which considers future conditions of their nation. Plainly, the right intention principle prohibits the pursuit of unjust ends *post bellum* since it intends to fight for a just peace and to establish this peace at the end of the war. This peace is achieved through the common good as the product of justice. *Jpb* as a principle, when considering going to war, protects the common good because it demands that the one who authorizes the war and those who fight under that authorization take into account how the people in the war-torn state will cope *post bellum*.

Indeed, one of the main uses of *jpb* as a principle raises the question as to what extent a postwar society suffering the effects of war—loss of life, property, infrastructure, and a sense of defeatism—can be restored or even potentially transformed. Aquinas does not explicitly address these issues, yet his notion of the right intention—including (re)constructing a justly ordered community or restoring a disordered peace—shows the postwar concern. In other words, because the main purpose of *jpb* is (re)establishing a just peace, or "a peace ordered to the common good," it is appropriate to think of it as belonging to the discourse of the right intention. In fact, Aquinas's notion of the right intention ensures that he has a more convincing ground upon which to base *jpb* discourse than does any other classical just war thinker. For example, I characterize the heart of *jpb*, which is the establishment of a just peace, as more closely aligned with Aquinas's notion of the right intention than Augustine's, of bringing by way of "a harsh kindness or punishment, the benefits of peace to the enemy."[29] The contemporary *jpb*

---

28 *ST*, II-II, q.40, a.1. For details, see Thomas Aquinas, "Whether it is Always a Sin to Wage War?" in *St. Thomas Aquinas Political Writings*, ed. R. W. Dyson (Cambridge: Cambridge University Press, 2002), 241. One might wonder whether this view carries a presumption against war or a presumption against injustice. To be clear, if there is no presumption against war, then it does not need any excusing reasons, which just war tradition itself provides; a presumption does not mean that war is always wrong, it means that it requires good reasons; and as Richard Miller argues, it adds nothing to say there is a presumption against injustice, because that is the premise of all ethics. In this regard, I agree with Richard Miller. See Richard Miller, *Interpretations of Conflict: Ethics, Pacifism, and the Just War Tradition* (Chicago: University of Chicago Press, 1991). For another thoughtful discussion, see Gregory M. Reichberg, "Is There a 'Presumption against War' in Aquinas's Ethics?" in *Ethics, Nationalism, and Just War: Medieval and Contemporary Perspectives*, ed. Henrik Syse and Gregory M. Reichberg (Washington, DC: The Catholic University of America Press, 2007). Also see Gregory M. Reichberg, *Thomas Aquinas on War and Peace* (Cambridge: Cambridge University Press, 2019).

29 Mark Allman and Tobias Winright, *After the Smoke Clears* (Maryknoll, NY: Orbis Books, 2010), 32.

thinkers Mark Allman and Tobias Winright emphasize that Aquinas's notion of right intention is more broadly discussed but also more thoroughly focused than Augustine's, especially with regard to defending the common good: "[Aquinas's] just war seeks to undo the harm wrongdoers inflict upon themselves by sinning against their neighbors and against justice, and to address the damage the wrongdoer has inflicted upon the common good of the community."[30]

This emphasis on the common good, primarily drawn from Aquinas's notion of the right intention, would set up further human laws in *jpb* contexts that determine the responsibilities of the legitimate sovereign—we call them the responsibilities of the government today—to provide for citizens. It is important to remember that Aquinas's theology draws heavily from Aristotle's system, especially in its recognition of the basic social orientation of human beings and the orientation of all relationships toward the common good. Aquinas's anthropology begins with the recognition of the integral relationship between human beings and God. Happiness, for humans, is found in their ultimate *telos*—union with God.[31] The virtues, then, are directed toward cultivating habits of mind and heart that move each individual toward this ultimate happiness.[32] Aquinas argues that justice is a general virtue because it directs the rest of the virtues toward the good of others. Yet, justice can be called general in another sense, in that it directs all actions toward the common good of society.[33] For this reason, general justice is also referred to as legal justice due to its role in ordaining individual humans toward the greater whole.[34] For Aquinas, as for Aristotle, a

---

30 Allman and Wright, 32–33.

31 See J. Philip Wogaman, *Christian Ethics: A Historical Introduction* (Louisville: Westminster John Knox, 1993), 85–88.

32 Aquinas gives priority to four cardinal virtues and develops three theological virtues from the Scriptures (cf. 1 Cor 13). The theological virtues, given as God's gift, are faith, hope, and charity; and the cardinal virtues are prudence, justice, temperance, and fortitude. Cardinal virtues have both infused and acquired aspects: we can develop them through our actions but a gift of infusion from God is required for these virtues to be perfected. People who do not have relationships with God, as Aquinas understood it, can still develop the acquired versions of these virtues through their actions, although that alone would not gain happiness (the beatific vision of God) or salvation.

33 *ST*, II-II, q.58, a.1, 11.

34 *ST*, II-II, q.58, a.6; and II-II, q.58, a.7, 8. There are two types of justice: general and particular. General justice indicates that all virtues are directed by justice inasmuch as justice directs the other virtues to the common good. Particular justice has to do with directing one in relation to another and in relation to particular goods.

certain amount of earthly goods is necessary to develop a virtuous life. Therefore, encouraging prosperity and just distribution are ways for societies to become more virtuous. In this sense, human laws should aim to secure a postwar society from potential threats. Consequently, maintaining order is an important goal that extends to people fulfilling their prescribed role in society, so Aquinas further believes that just rulers, enforcing social order more generally, contribute to virtue. In this way, Aquinas's moral theory paves the way for a rich understanding of the importance of the right kind of relationship needed to build a more just society, even in *post bellum* contexts. On that account, therefore, Aquinas would propose a legal framework in a postwar society determined according to his understanding of human law, yet always connected to his overall perspective on law. These laws would thereby be first and foremost determined according to reason. Further, the laws must always be determined according to the common good of the entire postwar community, not the individual good of any specific part to the exclusion of the whole. Finally, the promulgation of law by the lawmakers would play a critical function as the members of the postwar society need awareness of the laws in order to abide by them. For these reasons, the legitimate authority should continue to secure the peace that comes only with a justly ordered community, but for Aquinas, it is also important that all these *jpb* practices must be accompanied with virtues—justice in particular—in order to foster the common good.

Lastly, but most importantly, Aquinas's notion of the right intention, by entailing the avoidance of wrong intention and the positive aim of securing peace, affirms the initial grounds of the foundational *jpb* practices that I will discuss throughout the book, especially from chapters five to seven: reconstruction of just policing that aims to deal with the present injustice, reconstruction of just punishment that aims to correct the past wrongdoing, and just political participation that aims to prevent future violence in the aftermath of war. Both the positive and the negative aspects of the right intention are included when Aquinas quotes Augustine's claim that wars might be peaceful with a pacific intentionality (or that wars might be authorized and with cause, and yet still must have a good intention to be peaceful): "True religion looks upon as peaceful those wars that are waged not for aggrandizement, or cruelty, but with the object of securing peace, of punishing evildoers, and of uplifting the good."[35] Taken together, each

---

35 *ST*, II-II, q.40, a.1.

object—securing peace, punishing evildoers, and uplifting the good—corresponds to each of the *jpb* themes respectively—just policing, just punishment, and just political participation.

Michael Walzer

Unlike Aristotle and Aquinas, Michael Walzer, one of the most well-known contemporary just war thinkers, employs the term *jpb* and explicitly addresses the idea of *jpb*, especially with regard to whether it has a place within the JWT. Therefore, the main topic of discussion in this section is not whether he can be legitimately given the title of *jpb* thinker as it was in the cases of Aristotle and Aquinas. Instead, I will examine Walzer's *jpb* from the perspective of his just war theory. In *Just and Unjust Wars*, Walzer looks at the moral reality of war in two aspects: "War is always judged twice, first with reference to the reasons states have for fighting, secondly with reference to the means they adopt."[36] This distinction between *jus ad bellum* and *jus in bello* is crucial for his reflections on *jpb*, which are also framed within the context of this distinction: those in political office are responsible for crimes of war (*jus ad bellum*), while military personnel are responsible for crimes in war (*jus in bello*). Within these two distinctions, various *jpb* concerns can also be discussed in an attempt to secure peace after the end of war and render it morally permissible. Therefore, it is worth briefly noting Walzer's just war theory of *jus ad bellum* and *jus in bello* before discussing its *jpb* implication.

In the previous section, we reviewed Aquinas's three necessary conditions for a just war (*jus ad bellum*): legitimate authority of the sovereign, just cause, and right intention. According to the Canadian *jpb* thinker Brian Orend, Walzer's modern just war theory adds the following conditions of reflection on *jus ad bellum*: last resort, probability of success, and proportionality.[37] To be clear, in Walzer's just war theory, these new rules are additionally important conditions of *jus ad bellum*, but they do not belong on the same level of importance as Aquinas's, or other classical just war theorists' original formulation of legitimate authority of the sovereign, just cause, and right intention. Walzer also makes clear that all these rules are used as

---

36 Michael Walzer, *Just and Unjust Wars* (New York: Basic Books, 2000), 21.

37 Last resort: a war should proceed only if all else fails. Probability of success: a war that is expected to be futile is an unjust war. Proportionality: a war may proceed only if the estimated benefits of the war are proportional to, or worth, the probable cost of it. For details, see Brian Orend, *The Morality of War* (Buffalo, NY: Broadview Press, 2013).

touchstones to guide ethical reflection on war rather than simply thinking about them as a checklist. In fact, he is aware that the meaning and use of each of these principles in the contemporary political landscape is not as simple as in theory. The debate over the meaning of each of these principles is evidence of the usefulness of just war theory, for implementation of the theory sparks in-depth reflection on issues such as the nature of just cause, last resort, and proportionality. These issues should never become static but should always be reassessed in light of the changing landscape of war, international politics, and other pertinent factors. This prudential observation from Walzer's theory of *jus ad bellum* also applies to his *jus in bello* principles: discrimination and noncombatant immunity, proportionality, no means *mala in se*, and no reprisals.[38] Lastly, but most importantly, for Walzer, the relationship between *jus ad bellum* and *jus in bello* demands greater scrutiny. One main reason is that he aims to make a clear separation between the two; he emphasizes that they are "logically independent," which ultimately allows for a more prudential discretion. For example, even if war was waged for just cause or other conditions that had met *jus ad bellum* conditions, there is no right to commit crimes of using weapons of mass destruction or unnecessary means in order to shorten a war.

It is important to note that Walzer articulates his reflection on just war theory on the basis of the moral reality of war, which is rooted in a long tradition of thought on moral rights in war: the right to resort to armed force and the moral rules governing war itself. It is the idea that a state can defend itself or be defended with help of the defense of a third party or the international community if it is attacked, in the same way an individual can. But also, these moral rights are not restricted to self-defense. The right to defend another state can be legitimate, especially when an aggressive state seeks to crush the attacked nation's citizens. From this point of view, Walzer first contends that just war should be based on the moral reality of basic human rights, or in his terms that of "individual rights to life and liberty."[39] That is to say, war is just if it aims to protect basic human rights, whereas neglect of basic human rights points toward the injustice of war. For him, securing

---

38 Discrimination and noncombatant immunity: combatants are banned from deliberately targeting civilians. Proportionality: soldiers may only use armed force proportional to the end they seek. No means *mala in se*: soldiers may not use certain means, which are traditionally considered to be "evil in themselves" (e.g., genocide, biological agents). No reprisals: just actors must condemn all reprisals against innocent people. For details, see Orend, *The Morality of War*, 40–41.

39 Walzer, *Just and Unjust Wars*, 54.

human rights itself is a universal notion of morality. Second, Walzer also emphasizes "the right of nations to sovereignty"; an act of aggression must be regarded as a breach of the political sovereignty and territorial integrity of the attacked state.[40] This breach, therefore, justifies an armed defense. The right of nations to sovereignty should be respected except in cases of failed states or aggressive regimes, which are either incapable or unwilling to protect their own people and their basic human rights. In this framework of Walzer's political thought, therefore, a war may legitimately commence when these rights of individuals and nations (to sovereignty) are threatened, but also it must cease once these rights are safeguarded.

Understanding the morality of these two rights in Walzer's just war theory—individual human rights and the right of nations to sovereignty—is crucial in that it sheds further light on his *jpb* concerns. In particular, identifying these two rights in *jpb* contexts, as they are related to each other in a political life, is indispensable. This recognition affirms that Walzer's goal of *jpb* is to keep the citizens' basic human rights safe in the occupied zone after the end of war, and to reconstruct a just and legitimate sovereign state so as to take that lead role to coordinate all safety activities in the area. But also, it demonstrates how this goal is to be achieved. Walzer relies on a democratically oriented political theory. The political philosopher Gary Bass understands Walzer's rationale behind the two rights of individuals and nations to be in line with a tradition of democratic thought on one's rights to participate in political life. This rationale affirms that individuals have a right to organize their polities as they choose, and thus that political communities like nations derive their rights from the consent of their citizens.[41] To be precise, Walzer clarifies that (modern) democracy is not merely the best regime for postwar justice, but it has historically been the political system least likely to turn on its own people. Furthermore, this democracy may provide a fair and supportive environment for a postwar society as it is "generally to be preferred for the sake of its inclusiveness," regardless of class, ethnicity, gender, religion, and socioeconomic status.[42]

---

40 Walzer, 123.

41 For Gary Bass's analysis of Walzer's approach to *jpb* and postwar politics, see Gary Bass, *Freedom's Battle* (New York: Alfred A. Knopf, 2008). For Walzer's democratic political theory-based guidelines for the Iraq intervention of 2003 and its *jpb* practices, see Michael Walzer, "Just and Unjust Occupations," *Dissent*, Winter 2004, paragraph 10.

42 Michael Walzer, "The Aftermath of War: Reflections on *Jus Post Bellum*," in *Ethics beyond War's End*, ed. Eric Patterson (Washington, DC: Georgetown University Press, 2012), 44.

In this way, Walzer urges that occupying forces must continue to secure the rights of individuals and, where possible, to adhere to consent of the occupied sovereign state, a state based on a democratically elected government, especially when engaging in postwar reconstructive efforts.

Further, the demand of specific *jpb* considerations arises as war is over. Two concepts in Walzer's moral realism that stand out for *jpb* are local legitimacy (i.e., the goal of reconstruction) and closure (i.e., denying the defeated aggressor the ability to wage future war, while also requiring accountability for war criminals). Walzer's argument for local legitimacy follows his understanding of the rights of individuals and nations; in his view, political reconstruction may follow extreme cases, especially when these rights are threatened. What is important is that the goal of political reconstruction must be local legitimacy. For in Walzer's view, the goal of political reconstruction cannot be achieved without local supports; the new regime cannot survive the withdrawal of the occupying armed forces, which set it up, if it is not supported by local citizens politically (with local agents who provide civil and security services) and economically (with local communities who pay taxes to maintain those public services).[43]

The second concept, closure, can be discussed more practically, as it touches on a wide range of *jpb* practices, such as war crimes trials, compensation, and restoration. Walzer looks into these three war crime issues in detail, while other *jpb* issues do not fully interest him: No trial, no justice.[44] To be brief, for war crimes trials, he opposes bringing only political leaders of the defeated states to account for their decisions. Limiting accountability only to a regime's rulers appeals to the *jus ad bellum*, but not the *jus in bello*. Hence, he makes clear that those who are responsible for the violation of both the *jus ad bellum* and the *jus in bello* are senior leaders, both political and military.[45] However, at the same time, he shows a more balanced view by carefully looking at the cases of war crimes trials; there might be a negative correlation between the success of war crimes trials and the prospect of political reconciliation. Walzer is not one who argues for peace by selling justice, but he is fully aware of the limits of war crimes trials: "Sometimes a clear judicial repudiation of mass murder and the punishment of the murderer is the best way to forge a secure peace. Sometimes security might

---

43 Walzer, 43–44.
44 Walzer, *Just and Unjust Wars*, 288.
45 Walzer, 298.

require amnesties and public forgetfulness. Sometimes the simple exposure and acknowledgment of crimes may be [better than trials in pointing] the way to reconciliation."[46]

While Walzer recognizes the complex nature of war crimes trials, he does not provide such a careful examination for his other *jpb* practices of closure. For example, he asks about who must take responsibility for compensation. Assuming that "nationality is a communal destiny," he argues that every citizen of the defeated state is responsible for compensation.[47] However, according to Orend, this view is essentially flawed, for it ignores the principle of discrimination that distinguishes between governors and those governed. With regard to restoration, Walzer opposes returning to a status quo *ante bellum* because it would put in place the same unfortunate political conditions that led to war. Instead, he argues for "restoration plus" to characterize a more secure and just state of affairs than that which existed prior to the war. This alternative aims to improve political conditions for both state sovereignty and individual human rights as long as the improved conditions prevent any threat.[48] He offers the 1991 Gulf War as an example of restoration plus. This war not only made the original border safe (sovereignty) and liberated Kuwait citizens from the Iraqi occupation (individual rights), but it also extended the imposition of restraints on the Iraqi regime. However, the Catholic writer Robert Royal finds that Walzer's argument for restoration plus lacks explanation as to how "large or small the plus side of the formula needed to be. . . . [Restoration plus] needs other criteria to make it meaningful."[49]

Most essentially, Walzer is hesitant to make a checklist for deciding which *jpb* practices to apply. In his just war discourse, he is fully aware that the defended state or the intervenor state of the third party cannot often stop the massacres without putting even more people at risk than those who are being massacred. It is, therefore, a prudential decision that further needs *jpb* considerations; there have to be various political and diplomatic responses to each case. For this reason, he encourages us to look at the circumstances of each case and to talk to those who are actually making

46 Walzer, "The Aftermath of War," 45.

47 Brian Orend, *Michael Walzer on War and Justice* (Montreal: McGill-Queen's University Press, 2001), 142.

48 Orend, 136–37.

49 Robert Royal, "In My Beginning Is My End," in *Ethics beyond War's End*, ed. Eric Patterson (Washington, DC: Georgetown University Press, 2012), 71.

decisions. But also, he suggests a minimalist approach for both *jpb* practices of local legitimacy and closure. With respect to *jpb* practices of local legitimacy, Walzer notes, "*jus post bellum* is most importantly about social justice in its minimal sense: the creation of a safe and decent society . . . , which is, minimally, nonmurderous."[50] Further, he argues that the rules of sovereignty allow for the right to not intervene, but that once the state acts, it must have the support of the locals. He contends that this support should be understood in terms of *basic* provisions, and that they include such minimum requirements for basic human rights and right of nations to sovereignty as law and order, food, clothing, and shelter. The same argument goes for closure. The minimum-yet-crucial requirement of *jpb* is the preservation of human life; as a means to this end, all *jpb* practices of closure ultimately have to be taken over and sustained by the locals, yet Walzer would still look carefully at the circumstances of each case.

Brian Orend

Brian Orend is the most well-known *jpb* thinker. He is perhaps also the most prolific writer on the topic of *jpb*. Drawing upon Orend's *jpb* discourse, the following issues will be discussed and critically reviewed. First, Orend develops *jpb* differently from Walzer, his former teacher at Harvard. Second, unlike his predecessors, Orend offers a detailed and comprehensive listing of *jpb* criteria. There are six principles that he emphasizes for *jpb* discourse: rights vindication, proportionality and publicity, the principle of discrimination, punishment, compensation, and rehabilitation. Third, unlike most other *jpb* theorists, Orend's primary concern is not the normative discourse itself, but the implementation of his ideas into international law regarding war termination issues (e.g., reinforcing the Geneva Convention).

It is important to compare Walzer and Orend, as the comparison not only demonstrates how differently their primary *jpb* considerations have been developed, but also clarifies which part of their arguments I stand for. Orend's *jpb* theory is distinguished from Walzer's in three aspects. First, Orend argues that if there is an unfair behavior in any of the three stages (the phases of *ad bellum*, *in bello*, and *post bellum*) the outcome will be an unjust war; whereas, for Walzer, an unjust war can lead to a just outcome. Second, Orend's model of a "minimally just society" aims for *human* security, but for Walzer's minimalist approach of *jpb*, *national* security. Finally,

---

50 Walzer, "The Aftermath of War," 37–38, 45.

Orend stands for cosmopolitan ideas, while Walzer stands for communitarian ideas. In this book, I support Walzer with respect to the first point, while for the second point, Orend. As for the third point, I have a mixed opinion colored by both of their theories.

Orend agrees with Walzer (and perhaps Aquinas, as I proposed previously) that how one defines *jpb* for a certain context is closely tied to the reasons for going to war (*jus ad bellum*). Both men appear to subsume the ends of *jpb* under *jus ad bellum* considerations. For example, a state going to war to stop an aggressor state would be more likely to have narrower *jpb* concerns than a state going to war to implement democracy for a regime change or to rebuild a society for the relief of destitute children and women. To be clear, they agree to apply *jus ad bellum* principles to work out *jpb* ethics, but not vice versa (i.e., they do not intend to add *jpb* concerns to *jus ad bellum* reflection). In other words, they believe that a just ending is more likely if the end of the war is taken into account before deciding to go to war. Further, they make clear that this relationship between *jpb* and *jus ad bellum* does not mean the justness of the war can only be determined by its outcome, subordinating *ad bellum* (and *in bello*) justice to *post bellum*.

However, despite this common ground, Orend and Walzer have a different understanding of the relationship between *jpb*, *jus ad bellum*, and *jus in bello*. Orend's understanding of the relationship between *jpb* and *jus ad bellum*, as well as their relationships to *jus in bello*, is that they are tightly bound together, whereas for Walzer, they are loosely tied to one another. In other words, assuming just war theory as one practical body, comprised of all three phases, *ad bellum, in bello,* and *post bellum* justice, Orend argues that if there is an unfair behavior in any of the three stages, the outcome will be an unjust war. The only way to achieve a just peace is that a "potential participant in armed conflict should consider in advance whether it is likely that the requirements of all three sets of just war principles can be satisfied *prior to* engaging in political violence."[51] On that account, he contends that *jpb* be determined on the basis of *jus ad bellum*. In contrast, Walzer believes it is possible to devise a just ending to an unjust war. Recall Walzer's argument that the *jus ad bellum* and *jus in bello* are *logically independent* for the sake of a more prudential discretion. Likewise, Walzer contends that *post bellum* and *ad bellum* (and *in bello*) justice are all independent to one

---

51 Brian Orend, "Justice after War: Toward a New Geneva Convention," in *Ethics beyond War's End*, ed. Eric Patterson (Washington, DC: Georgetown University Press, 2012), 5.

another.[52] Also worth noting is that the concepts in this book coincide with Walzer's view: the belief that a postwar situation never stands still, it always keeps going, and consequently, there is no one linear way to achieve an objective of postwar justice, as Orend argues. Rather, as Walzer points out, the channels are diverse and dynamic to arrive at the goal. His approach thus serves better for the purpose of discerning the fairness of the actors during the *post bellum* phase, characterized as a transitional and flexible time frame in nature.

Another reference point worth comparing between Orend and Walzer is that they are regarded as the advocates of a restricted or minimalist version of *jpb*. On the surface, Orend's "minimally just society" theory looks similar to Walzer's minimalist approach for *jpb*. They agree that dealing with issues of *jpb* has to be flexible enough to find a way between *a just* peace and just *a* peace, as its core is about social justice.[53] However, Orend maintains that Walzer's minimalist approach—aiming to (re)make "a safe and decent society," "which is, minimally, nonmurderous"—does not seem definitive or complete.[54] Orend proposes a more concrete version of his theory than Walzer. For Orend, a minimally just society must satisfy three general principles. First, it should be peaceful and nonaggressive internationally. Second, it should be legitimate both domestically and internationally, and it thus should be freely recognized. Third and most importantly, it must attempt to satisfy the human rights of all of its people. The bottom line is that human rights are genuinely universal values and that there must be a near universal consensus about what kind of human rights people actually have. For Orend, there are five foundational human rights, "[as] the most basic objects of vital human need" for a "minimally good life in the modern world": right to life (i.e., "personal security"), right of personal freedom, right of material subsistence, right of nondiscrimination (i.e., "element equality"), and right of "social recognition as a person and rights-holder."[55]

---

52 For further discussion, see Mark Evans, "Balancing Peace, Justice and Sovereignty in *Jus Post Bellum*: The case of Just Occupation," *Millennium: Journal of International Studies* 36, no. 3 (2008): 535.

53 Walzer, "The Aftermath of War," 45.

54 Walzer, 38, 45. For further discussion, see Orend, *Michael Walzer on War and Justice*, 135.

55 Orend, "Justice after War," (2012), 187. Given this basis of human rights, Orend proposes a new Geneva Convention to *actually* build a minimally just society (details of this are discussed later in this section).

Looking at Orend's more concrete outline of basic human rights, his minimalist model is more convincing than Walzer's. I agree with Orend that Walzer's theory is not complete enough to define his minimalist approach to *jpb* despite the human rights doctrine underlying Walzer's view of just war theory. Further, this book will stand for Orend's model of a "minimally just society," at least as far as the relevance of human security to international law for securing basic human rights is concerned. Walzer's emphasis on the role of the state might dilute his original intention of making the issue of human rights noticeable in the *jpb* discourse. State actors can and ought to protect their people from any threats, but historically, they have sometimes emerged as the major threats to their people. In addition to applying his theory to states, as the only just and legitimate parties, Walzer fails to consider that warring parties are increasingly comprised of both state and non-state actors, a feature of contemporary warfare in which his theory of *jpb* is rendered silent. The rights-based just war thinkers Robert E. Williams and Dan Caldwell note, "in spite of the centrality of human rights in Walzer's account of the war convention, his just war theory . . . is fundamentally centered on the state. His concern, to put it differently, is more with the ethics of national security than with the ethics of what has more recently come to be called human security."[56] Moreover, this tension between national and human security seen in Walzer's just war theory can be reframed for Orend as a tension between state sovereignty and human rights. Orend proceeds to ground all political systems (including institutions endorsed by state sovereignty) in the concept of individual human rights. He privileges human rights over the rights of nations to sovereignty, proposing that "respect for [human] rights is the foundation of civilization."[57]

Given this proposal of human security for human rights, it is worth noting that Orend is a just war theorist inspired by Immanuel Kant. Although Kant is not generally regarded as being a just war thinker, Orend credits Kant as the progenitor of *jpb*.[58] In Orend's view, Kant initiated a *jpb* discourse with his seminal essay *To Perpetual Peace*, a Kantian conception

---

56 Robert E. Williams and Dan Caldwell, "*Jus Post Bellum*: Just War Theory and the Principles of Just Peace," *International Studies Perspectives* 7, no. 4 (November 2006): 314.

57 Brian Orend, "*Jus Post Bellum*: A Just War Theory Perspective," in *Jus Post Bellum: Towards a Law of Transition from Conflict to Peace*, ed. Carsten Stahn and Jann K. Kleffner (The Hague: T.M.C. Asser Press, 2008), 43.

58 See Brian Orend, *War and International Justice: A Kantian Perspective* (Waterloo, ON: Wilfrid Laurier University Press, 2000), 57, 217.

of positive peace that argues for the idea of individual freedom and human liberty as the bedrock of peace. In particular, Kant proposes that the international system ought to be settled by a confederation of republican states (under the law of nations) since this confederation is more likely to secure both the rights of their own citizenry and the laws governing international sovereignty.[59] Moving from this Kantian foundation, political scientists Peter Sutch and Juanita Elias argue that "Kant [projected that] in 1795, the war-weary people of Europe would realize this [the law of nations] and begin to build a conference of republican states with a further cosmopolitan order that would end war between them." They continue: "[The reason why] Kant saw peace through politics was because the injunction to leave the state of nature was not merely instrumental. Rather it was a categorical, moral *ought*."[60] For Kant, peace is not just ending the state of war among nations but establishing the (international) political institutions under which people can live morally, respecting the freedom of all others, and thus eradicating the primary source of war. This approach to positive peace is also employed by Orend. His Kantian brand of peace is contrasted with Walzer, who argues for a more restrained conception of peace.

Kantian thought has been critical since it shapes some of the *jpb* theories that reflect cosmopolitan ideas, which will be an integral part of the argument that Orend makes. In contrast, Walzer can be more closely understood as one whose *jpb* theories reflect communitarian ideas. Walzer emphasizes the ways in which people shape their values in communities, whether national, religious, or ideological. While he stresses the rights of individuals with emphasis on a theory of liberalism, Walzer does not overlook the importance of how rights are formed in the context of a group or community. In the context of interstate wars, individual rights are protected by the legitimate sovereign as long as the rights of nations to sovereignty are respected. In the communitarian idea, the order to be created is that among communities or states; whereas, in cosmopolitan thought, it should be an order based on ensuring the security of the individual. Therefore, state security can be viewed as means to an end, not the end itself. This book

---

59 Immanuel Kant, *Perpetual Peace, and Other Essays*, 1795 (Indianapolis: Hackett Publisher, 1983), 112. cf. Three conditions of Kant's "perpetual peace": (i) the world needs to be made of democratic states; (ii) states must join an international league governed by democratic principles; and (iii) citizens must adopt cosmopolitanism, not national parochialism.

60 Peter Sutch and Juanita Elias, *International Relations: The Basics* (New York: Routledge, 2007), 69.

stands on both sides. Orend's cosmopolitan ideas will be useful for top-down approaches of *jpb*, such as creating an international regulation, and Walzer's communitarian ideas will be insightful for localizing postwar justice during the phase of *post bellum*.

Moving on from this comparative analysis between Orend and Walzer, now we will take a closer look at Orend's *jpb*. Given the basis of a Kantian foundation, Orend proposes a very Kantian, or cosmopolitan, set of six rules or principles for *jpb*.[61] Principally, he believes that there will be no just war if we fail to uphold these six principles. The first principle is "rights vindication," meaning that the crimes that triggered the just war should be justly remedied. For Orend, it does not make any sense for the good guys to win the war and not fix the original problem. The problem that caused the war should be remedied.

Second, Orend argues for "proportionality and publicity." This principle not only emphasizes that the terms of peace must be made by a legitimate authority, and the terms must be accepted by a legitimate authority but also, and more importantly, that settlement should be public; it should be about being proportional to the crimes that were originally committed and should not just be about getting revenge on someone who you have been fighting for a while.

Proportionality also matters for a practical reason. Victors may have the intention of helping defeated states after the end of war, but if being helpful to them demands extreme sacrifice and a high cost, the victors may reconsider the *jpb* requirements.

Third is "the principle of discrimination." What is at stake in this principle is that the victorious state must differentiate between political and military leaders, and combatants and civilians. Civilians should not be punished for the acts of the government. Instead, punitive measures are to be limited to those directly responsible for the conflict. In particular, Orend emphasizes that socioeconomic sanctions are not allowed; there are things that he makes clear are generally not allowed in a just war (e.g., taxes that go directly to the winning side).

Fourth, Orend argues for "punishment." He defines it in two ways:

---

61 See Brian Orend, "*Jus Post Bellum*: A Just War Theory Perspective," 40–41. Orend originally proposed five principles in his earlier writing: just cause for termination, right intention, legitimate authority, the principle of discrimination, and the principle of proportionality. Cf. Brian Orend, "Jus Post Bellum," *Journal of Social Philosophy* 31, no. 1 (2000): 128–29.

Punishment #1. When the defeated country has been a blatant, rights-violating aggressor, proportionate punishment must be meted out. The leaders of the regime, in particular, should face fair and public international trials for war crimes.

Punishment #2. Soldiers also commit war crimes. Justice after war requires that such soldiers, *from all sides to the conflict,* likewise he held accountable to investigation and possible trial.[62]

For Orend, this principle should be understood together with the principle of discrimination. On the one hand, fair punishment should be meted out specifically for leaders who endorsed any war crimes. He emphasizes that the leadership responsible for the war must be differentiated from the populations and that mass punishment should not be imposed. This is because, historically, most leaders of the aggressor states have taken advantage of their power to wage wars for their own private interests, whereas most citizens did not benefit from these wars and were usually isolated from the initial decision to wage war. On the other hand, fair punishment should be meted out for soldiers who committed war crimes, on both sides of the conflict. The victors who committed war crimes also need to be punished. But at the same time, Orend is also aware that truth and reconciliation commissions may sometimes be more important than punishing war crimes, especially when it helps prevent vindictive revenge, but the priority remains that the state and its legitimate authority must seek justice for war crimes committed by all sides.[63]

The fifth principle is "compensation." The victor cannot demand financial restitution from a loser that has no resources left. Orend notes, "there need to be enough resources left so that the defeated country can begin its own reconstruction."[64] For example, the penalties imposed on Germany after WWI kept the country in a weak economic situation; hence the collective anger of Germans paved the way for WWII. He also answers the question of who should be held responsible for financial restitution. He argues that financial restitution should be acceptable from the government, but a tax on civilians should not be allowed. This is because if one leaves a

---

62 See Orend, "*Jus Post Bellum*: A Just War Theory Perspective," 40.

63 For details, see Brian Orend, "Justice after War," *Ethics and International Affairs* 16, no. 1 (March 2002): 43–56.

64 Orend, "*Jus Post Bellum*: A Just War Theory Perspective," 41.

government completely destitute and, therefore, is unlikely to have good relations with that government in the future, it is probable that the destitute government may wage another war.

The sixth and last principle is "rehabilitation." In Orend's discourse of rehabilitation, he emphasizes transformation of the aggressor's regime, demilitarization, human rights education, and other transitional justice issues. Rehabilitation is an important but also hugely controversial piece of the *post bellum* just war. Basically, he argues that if there was a problem with the original government, they need to fix that government and prevent it from waging the same war again. However, in reality, there is potential pushback from the losing state because it does not want someone from the opposing government (or the international community) to change its government. Indeed, Orend is fully aware of this challenge, and he clarifies that rehabilitation is the most controversial principle since it may involve coercive regime change.[65] Nevertheless, Orend makes clear that it is also important for the legitimized authority, whether it be the winner or the international community, to prevent wars from happening in the future.

Orend continuously redefines these six principles, but his guideline for most *jpb* considerations remains rested on them. It is important to note that this paradigm applies to interstate wars but not for civil wars or rogue nations, since Orend's scheme of *jpb* primarily operates within a state-based model. One of the most valuable contributions that he makes is his insistence on the need for these *jpb* principles as a set of consistent normative threads to be run through *jpb* conduct during the phase of *post bellum*. He believes that these *jpb* principles are primarily moral principles that are meant to inform decisions about how international law is best to be established down the road. Consequently, proposing that postwar justice can and must be a concern for international regulation, Orend calls for a brand-new Geneva Convention exclusively devoted to issues arising from the phase of *jpb*. His argument can be understood in two parts: the theoretical part, where he addresses postwar justice in general, and the practical part, where he answers the question of what, if anything, do we still owe Iraq and Afghanistan.

In the theoretical part, Orend's main focus is that we need a new or revised Geneva Convention. For him, if a minimally just society is the kind of society to be sought after by pursuing postwar reconstruction, this draft

---

65 For details, see Orend, *The Morality of War*, 190–217.

to structure a new international treaty will be the most reasonable means to achieve it. Orend offers six reasons. The first reason is that we need to complete the laws of war. Despite the fact that there are a variety of laws about regulating the outbreak of armed conflict (e.g., UN Charter) and regulating conduct in war (e.g., Geneva Convention), there are few laws regulating the endings of wars. Historically, this has been a result of the conviction that to the winners go the spoils of war. Instead, the endings of war should be regulated just as the beginnings of war and conduct during war are. Second, he calls for a new Geneva Convention in order to focus practical attention on the importance of this *jpb* issue; drafting a legal document to construct a new Geneva Convention itself would inspire decision-makers to discuss conduct after war and further develop the discourse in public. Third, such a convention should provide clear guidance both for winners and for losers, as Orend stresses both. In keeping with the guidance provided, the losers would be protected from any draconian measures that the winners might impose. At the same time, even the winners would appreciate being able to point to such postwar guidelines, which would help avoid unexpected cost and time commitment. Fourth, unregulated war endings prolong fighting on the ground because the combatants do not have clear rules or expectations. Fifth, we need such a convention to restrain the winners who have been known to exact draconian terms of peace—World War I is a classic example. The sixth reason is that wars that are wrapped up badly create future wars, so everyone needs guidance in this regard. Orend notes that the examples are the World Wars, the Serbian wars in the nineties, and the Iraq wars; the second wars in each of those pairings would not have happened at all, had the first ones been appropriately concluded.[66]

It is worth remembering that Orend's minimally just society must satisfy three general principles: it should be nonaggressive, legitimate, and focused on human rights. On the basis of these principles, Orend proposes what he calls "a ten-step recipe" that should apply to a new Geneva Convention as a general blueprint. They are as follows:

(1) Adhere to the laws of war during the regime take-down and its occupation.
(2) Purge much of the old regime, and prosecute its war criminals.
(3) Disarm and demilitarize the society.

---

66 For details of the six reasons, see Orend, "Justice after War," (2012), 175–77.

(4) Provide effective military and police security for the whole country.
(5) Work with a cross section of the locals on a new, rights-respecting constitution that features checks and balances.
(6) Allow other non-state associations or civil society to flourish.
(7) Forego compensation and sanctions in favor of rebuilding the economy.
(8) Revamp educational curricula to purge past propaganda and make new values.
(9) Ensure that the benefits of the new order will be (a) concrete and (b) widely, not narrowly, distributed.
(10) Follow an orderly, not-too-hasty [and paced] exit strategy when the new regime can stand on its own two feet.[67]

With the ten-step recipe, Orend argues that "history shows that successful postwar reconstruction has been done [such as in Germany and Japan after WWII], therefore logically it can be done."[68]

A practical question, then, arises: will this successful postwar reconstruction be completed in Iraq and Afghanistan? Orend doubts that this will happen and observes that "it . . . has seen a mixture of both successes and failures."[69] He admits that it seems somewhat evident that the international community, as led by the United States, has been attempting to implement some aspects of the ten-step recipe in both nations. These efforts had some success, such as the replacement of rogue regimes with new governments, the constitutional protection of personal freedom, and the progress of gender equality in some areas. However, despite these successes, Orend offers five reasons why the process of reconstruction has seen critical failures in both nations: "the weight of history," "internal division," "external interference," "[the steady decline of] security," and "[the challenge of] the local economy."[70] I will not go into much detail about each of these five obstacles in this chapter (some of them will be discussed in the second half of the book as a more practice-oriented discourse). However, what is impor-

---

67 Orend, 188.

68 Orend thinks that Germany and Japan post WWII are the exemplary cases for successful postwar reconstruction. For details, see Brian Orend, "Justice after War: Toward a New Geneva Convention," lecture given at *Ending Wars Well: Just War Theory and Conflict's End*, Berkeley Center at Georgetown University, April 22, 2010, https://berkleycenter.georgetown.edu/events/ending-wars-well-just-war-theory-and-conflict-s-end.

69 Orend, "Justice after War," (2012), 189.

70 Orend, 190–93.

tant for us in this section is that Orend believes that postwar reconstruction is a difficult business, as shown by the cases of Iraq and Afghanistan. Further, he believes that structuring a new Geneva Convention about postwar justice would advance the purpose of that discussion.

DISCERNING *JUS POST BELLUM* FOUNDATIONAL THEMES
Finding Common Issues:
Jus Post Bellum as a Third Element of Just War Theory

Through these four thinkers, I will explicate common themes within *jpb*, although it is hard to articulate the common themes because not all of these writers explicitly focus on *jpb*. While Walzer and Orend are fully engaged in the discourse of *jpb*, Aristotle and Aquinas do not address *jpb* concerns in a clear-cut and definitive manner. However, when one reads Aristotle and Aquinas from the perspective of just war theory, they have an implicit notion of *jpb* in mind. Both of their thoughts affirm that their main concern is with war as a means to an end: the creation of a just peace for the common good, whether it be for a "just *polis*" or "justly ordered community." This *jpb* concern is shared through Walzer's "[minimally] safe and decent society" and Orend's "minimally just society." Furthermore, I have noted specific *jpb* implications in the thoughts of Aristotle and Aquinas. For Aristotle, this discussion included his concern for people of defeated nations, namely, his rejection of the idea that all the citizens of a defeated nation should be slaves. It is also important to remember that Aquinas's concern is more critical for the purpose of this book. This is because his three objects of a just war— "securing peace," "punishing evildoers," and "uplifting the good"—correspond to each of the *jpb* themes which will be discussed in chapters five through seven (just policing, just punishment, and just political participation). Consequently, I affirm that calling these writers foundational *jpb* thinkers is valid, and thus that exploring them together does permit common issues to appear. I will therefore first address these issues before delineating common themes within *jpb*.

In particular, there are seven common points that these four foundational *jpb* thinkers have either initiated or at least implied in their writing. I suggest that these issues are shared concerns among these four scholars, but also, and more importantly, that they are seven points which should play a key role in framing future debate about the nature and scope of *jpb*. I will also outline them to affirm a proposition that the category of *jpb* ought to be acknowledged as a third element of the JWT, akin to *jus ad bellum* and *jus in bello*.

(1) A just war should pass three phases of verification—*jus ad bellum, jus in bello*, and *jpb*—all of which must be met for any war to be just or at least considered ethically acceptable. Interstate wars are included in this proposition. The first common point, thus, at least *in theory*, is that a nation cannot claim a just war if it meets only one or two just war criteria. However, to be clear, this point does not mean that the violation of *jpb* always amounts to a violation of *jus ad bellum* and/or *jus in bello*. Rather, this highlights that the state or states that wage a just war in *ad bellum* and *in bello* terms may still be faulted on *jpb* criteria. Winning a just war, thus, does not always guarantee a just peace. Keeping that in mind, this book supports Walzer's argument that the three just war criteria are logically independent for the sake of a more prudent discretion *in practice*. This viewpoint affirms not only that a just war in *ad bellum* and *in bello* terms can lead to an unjust outcome if actors fail to fulfill *jpb*, but also that even an unjust war may lead to a minimally decent—not perfect—just outcome, namely the establishment of just peace, if the actors fulfill *jpb*. The justice of peace is closely associated with the justice of war, but the justice of peace should be evaluated independently of the justice of war. This stance allows for a more careful, dynamic, and comprehensive approach to *jpb* than Orend's rigid version of the linear approach to achieve just peace *post bellum* as *the* necessary condition of just war since this position serves better for its purpose of discerning the fairness of the actors during the *post bellum* phase, characterized as a transitional and flexible time frame in nature.

(2) If the violators of *jus ad bellum* and *jus in bello* should be punished, so should the violators of *jpb*. This statement is made from the common *jpb* concerns that these four thinkers share: What are the potential effects of war? What people will be impacted and how? How will (fair) justice after war be defined (and by whom)? Who will carry out that justice? How will the effects of war impact the victor's ability to end war and thus to further *jpb* practices of policing, punishing, and rebuilding the war-torn areas? For the present I simply note these questions.

(3) Although warring parties usually maintain that their side conducts a just war, in reality, the so-called justice is determined on the battlefield, and in turn, it often results in unfairness. In other words, the systems in place to mete out justice on the battlefield are often unable to successfully render fair decisions in some of the most complex real-world situations, as shown

by numerous international criminal law scholars' work.[71] In addition to these *in bello* situations, a common argument used by the realist critics of international criminal law is that it often amounts to "victors' justice." After winning a war, the victors usually carry out justice on their own terms, applying different rules to judge what is right or wrong to their own forces, rather than to those of their defeated foes. The realist critics argue that the difference in rules leads to injustice. This claim for fair justice on both sides, for both the victor and the vanquished, has also been observed by the foundational *jpb* thinkers, especially in both Aristotle's and Aquinas's moral sensitivity to the idea of fairness for all involved in war and in Walzer's and Orend's careful examination of the complex nature of war crimes trials. Therefore, war crimes by victors should also be punished to realize just peace. Any serious offenses on either side of the war need to be brought to justice all the way down from political leaders to combatants. This punishment for war crimes is a necessary step to reestablishing a just system of governance.

(4) Intention in war should be emphasized in *jpb* as well as in *jus ad bellum* and *jus in bello*. All four thinkers agree that having the right intention in war is the first and foremost criteria to achieving a just peace. Aquinas (the notion of right intention, entailing the avoidance of wrong intention and the positive aim of securing peace), Walzer (respect for individual human rights and the right of nations to sovereignty), and Orend (rights vindication, supporting the idea of rehabilitation over the idea of revenge) have all clearly discussed right intention. Aristotle, however, does not explicitly address the idea of intention. However, his thoughts on intention in war can be found in his belief that all human activities in a just *polis* are intended to cultivate the virtues in the human soul. In his argument, war is justified when it leads to a just *polis*, defined as his just cause to wage a war. Also, he gives a hint that his idea of intention follows this justification. Therefore, for him, the intention of a war leading to a just *polis* is to produce conditions that cultivate virtues in the human soul.

(5) If *jpb* criteria are violated, it often results in oppression and turmoil. In particular, Orend sees that there has arguably been a perceived failure of implementing *jpb* practices in defeated states like Iraq and Afghanistan, followed by ongoing insecure situations and conflicts. Walzer also stresses that violation of *jpb* criteria usually results in victors' peace only (i.e., imperial

---

71 For instance, see Chris Bay, *Court-Martial: How Military Justice Has Shaped America from the Revolution to 9/11 and Beyond* (New York: Norton, 2016); and Richard Falk, "War, War Crimes, Power and Justice," *The Asia-Pacific Journal* 10, no. 4 (January 16, 2012): 1–12.

peace) and oftentimes results in oppression and turmoil for the vanquished, as historically shown in the *Pax Romana*.[72] For Aristotle, victors need to protect only those vanquished whose natures are noble from becoming slaves. This law should be kept not merely for respecting their human dignity, but more precisely for protecting a just *polis* by maintaining proper leadership, which includes enslaving those who are slaves by nature, but not those who are noble by nature. If it is not kept, potential chaos could arise as the natural order of human affairs collapses. Aquinas shares a similar view concerning the (re)establishment of a just order with Aristotle, but not with emphasis on the question of slavery. For him, maintaining order is also a *telos* that extends to people keeping their prescribed role in society, but solely for the common good for all, not for the acquisition of property for some.

(6) The goal of war is for a better peace despite the cost of war. But also, this goal should be approached in a wise manner. For example, Aquinas, as well as Walzer and Orend, emphasize the principle of proportionality.[73] They all are aware that employing disproportionate force causes unnecessary sacrifices, usually including innocent civilian casualties. This principle can be understood in *post bellum* contexts; especially when defeated areas demand extreme sacrifice and high cost, the victor may need to reconsider the *jpb* requirements. This is because a disproportionate demand for postwar reparations would belie the alleged justification of the war. Another concern regarding this proposition is the question of whether status quo *ante bellum* (the way things such as rights, property, and borders were before war broke out) is valid for the goal of war. Both Walzer and Orend oppose it, since those can be the exact same conditions which led to war in the first place. Lastly, security is a major concern in *post bellum* contexts, whether it be human security (Orend) or national security (Walzer). This concern accompanies another: political reconciliation. Further, all of these concerns are related to the following questions, which all of these four thinkers raise: how do we define success in war? What will just peace *post bellum* look like? What should be the political goal for it—protecting human security? Political reconciliation? How will the devastation of war thwart or advance these goals?

---

72 Michael Walzer, "The Triumph of Just War Theory (and the Dangers of Success)," *Social Research* 69, no. 4, International Justice, War Crimes, and Terrorism: The US Record (Winter 2002): 925–44.

73 Aquinas does not explicitly address this *jpb* implication. His use of the principle of proportionality is limited to the contexts of *jus ad bellum* and *jus in bello*. For details, see *ST*, II-II, q.40, a.1.

(7) The international community can be the real victor if it secures the support and appreciation of the vanquished nation or losing party in securing a just peace. All of these thinkers share the thought that there is not a clear line drawn between the moral and the legal. From this standpoint, *jpb* principles are primarily moral principles that are meant to inform decisions about how international regulation should best be established down the road. In particular, Orend encourages the international community to construct a new Geneva Convention, which aims to improve the political conditions of both state sovereignty and individual human rights in war-torn societies. This is more than a peace treaty, as it aims not only to deal with punishment for war crimes and compensation of victims, but also to accomplish the somewhat daunting task of reconstruction in war-torn areas. This is especially true when considering the global influence which the vanquished seeks to (re)establish and the large amount of time, money, resources, and potential human costs involved in reconstruction efforts. However, these international efforts not only include top-down approaches, such as the UN Charter, the Geneva Convention, and other peace treaties, but also should be collaborative efforts within a wide range of locally based agencies, such as NGOs, faith institutions, and other local communities. Fostering the legitimacy of operations is paramount to the success of *jpb* practices, Walzer believes, and recognizing the central role of local actors may help to increase legitimacy. This is because these locally-based agencies are seen as having less historical baggage and place more of an emphasis on overcoming the legacy of conflict than might the high profile international organizations along with the victor state.

Distilling Core Themes:
Three *Jus Post Bellum* Foundational Themes

From these seven points, which should play a key role in framing future issues about the nature and scope of *jpb*, I will refine the *jpb* common themes for the purpose of constructive discourse. The three *jpb* foundational themes I will distill are:

Reconstruction of (1) just policing; (2) just punishment; and (3) just political participation.

In this section, I will briefly touch on why and how I define them as the three core themes of *jpb*. They will be more conceptually articulated in chapters two through four, as they should correspond well to moral philosophical and moral theological reflections on *jpb*. Each of these themes correspond to the three different fields of *jpb* practices—policing in security work, punishment in law, and political participation in peacebuilding activities—that I will further present in chapters five through seven.

In a nutshell, *I propose that establishing a just peace is the main purpose of jpb*. This proposition is understood in accordance with the *jpb* practices as follows: reconstruction of just policing aims to deal with the present injustice, reconstruction of just punishment aims to correct the past wrongdoing, and reconstruction of just political participation aims to prevent future violence in the aftermath of war. In other words, the first theme tells the present aim of *jpb*, for the second, the past, and for the third, the future. In the politically unstable *jpb* context, the primary responsibility should be to keep people safe today while resolving threats from the past to establish a just peace in the future.

The line of reasoning behind these themes presents how to deal with past, present, and future enemies. By doing so, just actors will find a way to move forward to a better peace and a more fulfilling path for a just peace. In fact, these themes are also commonly found in the work of most contemporary *jpb* scholars. In particular, Mark Evans summarizes three dimensions of the *jpb* literature to begin with.

> (a) what they [the victorious states or just actors] may do *to* their former enemies (for example with respect to punishment and reparations); (b) what they may do *for* them (for example with respect to reconstruction); (c) what they may do more widely, beyond their direct relationship to their former enemies, in contributing towards future peace and security (for example with respect to the establishment of international peace-promoting organizations and mechanisms).[74]

Each of these three dimensions of the *jpb* study—focusing on dealing with the past, the present, and the future—corresponds to each of the three *jpb* foundational themes which I present. However, the task for this book is distinguished from these three discrete dimensions of the *jpb* work expounded by Evans in that the three *jpb* foundational themes are employed together as an integrated project of *jpb*. They are independent but correlated. Central to this consideration is that a comprehensive engagement with the morality of just peace building, as the completion of a just war's ultimate

---

74 Evans, "Balancing Peace, Justice and Sovereignty in *Jus Post Bellum*," 535.

goal, necessitates the acquisition by the JWT of a robust understanding of war's causes and the mechanisms for its possible containment and prevention. In this way, the three *jpb* foundational themes will not only overcome the challenge that there is little consensus within the disciplines on how to define *jpb* and its embedded issues but also reveal how these themes square with the Christian tradition of just and unjust wars.

Reconstructing Questions:
Three Foundational Questions for *Jus Post Bellum*

Based on these three themes, I pose three *jpb* foundational questions. In this way, it will more effectively fulfill the purpose of this book, which is to reconstruct the status of *jpb* in the JWT through the weave of a cohesive "interdisciplinary" methodology. The methods employed in this book are most often used in qualitative historical and political science case studies, as well as in both philosophical and theological methods of critical reflection. In this sense, the comparison will be among the various disciplines' approach to the overarching question: what constitutes a just peace? From this principal question, the remainder of this book will seek to answer a limited set of foundational sub-questions to be done comparatively. Again, the three foundational questions for *jpb* that I will investigate are:

(1) How should just policing be established in the tasks of human and national security to deal with the present injustice?
(2) How should just punishment be enforced by both the laws of war and peace to correct the past wrongdoing?
(3) How should just political participation balance the tasks of human security and political reconciliation to prevent future violence in the aftermath of war?

By answering these three questions, the perspective of each discipline's view on *jpb* will emerge. My quest in this book is, in part, to contribute to the academic discourse of *jpb* and further the usefulness of the JWT in the public arena.

Chapter 2

Moral Philosophy of *Jus Post Bellum*

INTRODUCTION

This chapter first examines the *jpb* literature produced by moral philosophers, and then explores the three foundational themes drawn from the work of the foundational school presented in the previous chapter. It encompasses three main sections: first, an introduction to the discourse surrounding the conventional norm of a right to fight (defend or intervene) versus the emerging norm of a responsibility to protect people; second, the *jpb* discourse of minimalist versus maximalist positions; and third, a redefinition of these two positions to shed light on the three foundational themes of *jpb* in this book: the reconstruction of just policing, just punishment, and just political participation.

The first section explores the liberal foundation of *jpb* as it explicates how international moral and political norms have shifted from a *right to fight* to a *responsibility to protect* within the JWT. In the second section, first Alex Bellamy's distinction between minimalist and maximalist approaches to *post bellum* obligations will be considered. He observes that there are two major positions of thought present within the *jpb* debate and that most *jpb* scholars oscillate between them.[1] Then his view will be contrasted with that of Mark Evans who argues, contra Bellamy, for "restricted" and "extended" conceptions of *jpb*. At the same time, the work of other *jpb* scholars will be discussed in order to redefine the minimalist and maximalist positions. In redefining both minimalist and maximalist positions, one should view them as two extremes on either end of a continuum. If we consider the middle ground between these absolutes, we can attain a more balanced and nuanced view of the continuum, with differences that often appear to be of degree rather than type. Lastly, my analysis will include how this redefined minimalist and maximalist framework is related to the three *jpb* foundational themes for the establishment of a just peace.

---

1 Alex Bellamy, "The Responsibilities of Victory: Jus Post Bellum and the Just War," *Review of International Studies* 34 (October 2008): 602.

THE LIBERAL FOUNDATION OF *JUS POST BELLUM*
A Shift of Norm Focus from *Right to Responsibility*

Chapter one discussed the notion of *jpb*, or its related thoughts, from the four foundational *jpb* thinkers to explore whether it belongs as an addition to the JWT. The seven common points that I addressed are strong enough to affirm that the category of *jpb* ought to be acknowledged as a third element of the JWT, akin to *jus ad bellum* and *jus in bello*. In particular, the discourse of *jpb* has been developed through Walzer's model of "[minimally] safe and decent society" and Orend's model of "minimally just society." These two models share an idea that all people involved in war should be protected from further threats after war.

Standing behind this position are the political ideals of liberalism. This liberal perspective is understood as a more modern sensibility to develop a just war theory. The classical JWT focuses on the right to fight (i.e., the right to defend or intervene), but modern just war thinkers such as Walzer and Orend emphasize a responsibility to protect people from life-threatening circumstances. This norm of *responsibility* is added to—not substituted for—the established norm of *right* in the JWT. The classical political liberals, for example, John Locke, believe that humans possess fundamental natural rights to liberty—to preserve themselves, but not to violate the equal liberty of others unless their own rights to preservation are threatened. This means that all citizens have the right to be treated as humans and the responsibility to treat others as human subjects, not as objects or means.[2] This liberal outlook has been expanded into a kind of liberal internationalism—as in the cases of Walzer and Orend—that military intervention can be justified as a last resort but also as a means to protect people from the violations of

---

2 Both Kant and Locke argue for liberal ideas of responsibility, but with different reasons. Kant argues that one should treat others as human subjects, not as objects or means; (i) the fact that we are human has value in itself; (ii) humans are the ones who do the valuing; (iii) and their conscience actions have moral worth. Hence, Kant believes that all of our duties can be derived from one ultimate principle, which he calls the categorical imperative, namely, a rule stating what ought to be done based upon pure reason alone and not contingent upon sensible desires. In other words, he believes only responsible actions performed for the sake of duty have moral worth. Whereas, for Locke, the idea of one's own rights to liberty is central to preserve oneself. This also means that others' rights to preservation should not be threatened. In this regard, like Kant, Locke also believes that the responsibility to treat others as human subjects should be kept. In particular, he believes that people have natural rights simply because they are human beings. However, unlike Kant, Locke emphasizes the role of a state; these natural rights should be protected by the government.

human rights. This calls for international cooperation to protect people from challenges that failed states cannot or are not willing to meet.

The Responsibility to Protect

International society has also noticed that the mission to protect is important, and as a result, international moral norms have emphasized civilian protection in response to humanitarian crises. This practice aimed at protecting civilians has come to replace the commonly shared practice of intervening for self-interested reasons, but it also has shifted norms from *a right to fight*—or more precisely *a right to intervene*—to *a responsibility to protect*, within the JWT. One version of this globally emerging moral norm is the so-called Responsibility to Protect (R2P), which was first articulated and proposed by the International Commission on Intervention and State Sovereignty (ICISS) in 2001 and was unanimously adopted by the United Nations World Summit in 2005. Since then, the ICISS has popularized humanitarian intervention and democracy-restoring intervention under the name of the responsibility to protect human rights—although broad understandings of both humanitarian intervention and democracy-restoring intervention are beyond the R2P's primary agenda. On the one hand, the R2P initiative ought to be bounded by the four mass atrocity crimes: genocide, war crimes, crimes against humanity, and ethnic cleansing.[3] On the other hand, the R2P adopts some concepts from these two interventions, especially the humanitarian one, arguing that sovereignty is not absolute. The R2P and broad theories of humanitarian intervention both aim to protect individuals from life-threatening circumstances beyond borders by conducting a military practice of assistance, with armed fighting as a last resort to relieve or prevent widespread suffering or abuse.[4] However, they put different emphasis on moral and political norms to achieve the goal. While humanitarian intervention sticks to state-centered motivations by focusing on the *right* of states to intervene, the R2P introduces a new way of examining the essence of sovereignty, emphasizing a *responsibility* to protect

---

3 While humanitarian interventions have been justified in various situations, the R2P focuses only on the four mass atrocity crimes: genocide, war crimes, crimes against humanity, and ethnic cleansing. The first three are defined in international law and codified in the Rome Statute that established the International Criminal Court. Ethnic cleansing is not a crime defined under international law, but it is defined as a crime by the UN.

4 For comment and discussion, see Nicholas Wheeler, *Saving Strangers: Humanitarian Intervention in International Society* (New York: Oxford University Press, 2003).

populations at risk to the international community. In fact, in the final version of the R2P document, the use of force as a humanitarian imperative is
not permitted without the authorization of the UN Security Council.[5]

It is important to remember that the norm of the R2P is primarily initiated by the *jus ad bellum* concern, but not limited to it; its concern is
deeply relevant to the violation of human rights, whether it be in the *ad
bellum* or *post bellum* context. This is because the R2P principally aims to
protect individuals from life-threatening circumstances in so far as they are
relevant to the four mass atrocity crimes of genocide, war crimes, crimes
against humanity, and ethnic cleansing. On that account, this norm can also
apply to *post bellum* situations, especially when the people vanquished are
left to suffer under oppression and turmoil. The R2P frames the issue in
terms of *jpb* as it explores a guiding question: once intervention has
occurred, what should be the responsibility of the intervening state(s) and
the international community for those suffering populations of the losing
side? In response, the R2P proposes a more comprehensive sense of responsibility than a mere responsibility toward war-torn societies. It is more than
securing a tranquil order in the aftermath of war. In fact, one of the responsible acts proposed by the ICISS is a "responsibility to rebuild [war-torn
societies]," which includes issues of recovery, reconstruction, reconciliation,
and amelioration of "the cause of harm the intervention was designed to
avert or halt."[6]

The political thinker Alex Bellamy proposes three key propositions for
the R2P. First, states have the primary responsibility to protect their own
people from crimes against humanity, genocide, ethnic cleansing, and war
crimes. Second, the international community has the responsibility to support states in fulfilling their responsibility to protect their people. Third, the
international community has the responsibility to react to human rights
violations if states are unable or unwilling to fulfill their responsibility; this
reaction may include political and economic sanctions, as well as the use
of force as a last resort. Further, Bellamy emphasizes that if the R2P leads
to an armed intervention, it should not be taken unilaterally but rather

---

5 For details, see Mark Notaras and Vesselin Popovski, "The Responsibility to Protect," *United
Nations University*, April 5, 2011, http://unu.edu/publications/articles/responsibility-to-
protect-and-the-protection-of-civilians.html.

6 International Commission on Intervention and State Sovereignty (ICISS), *The Responsibility to
Protect: Report of the International Commission On Intervention and State Sovereignty* (Ottawa:
International Development Research Centre, 2001), 39.

multilaterally. For example, the R2P will require the authorization of the UN Security Council (UNSC). However, Bellamy doubts the council's singular authority and asks whether the UNSC alone can authorize military intervention.[7] For Bellamy, the R2P is an emerging international norm—a collective international responsibility to protect—as it has been discussed in the context of UN reforms aiming to share more authority with a broader range of nations beyond the UNSC in the determination of military interventions.[8] For Bellamy, this is particularly important because he believes that multilateralism prevents great powers from pursuing national interests rather than humanitarian objectives in intervention.

In particular, the ICISS assumes a position akin to another concept, related to the *jpb* norm, subsidiarity. It states in the introduction of the R2P document that sovereign states have a responsibility to protect their own citizens, but again, when they are unwilling or unable to do so, the responsibility must be borne by the broader community of states (with emphasis on multilateralism). In this way, the ICISS respects sovereignty without absolutizing it, while also acknowledging that the limits, bounds, and details of this position are still difficult to determine. Through the use of the phrase "responsibility to protect" over a "right to intervene," the ICISS shifts international focus. This shift focuses attention on those who should be helped, as opposed to drawing attention to discussions over "rights." Furthermore, the R2P expands the purview of international relations to include prevention and rebuilding in *jpb* contexts. It claims that diverse agencies should engage in rebuilding postwar communities both physically and socially in order to ensure the human rights of all citizens are protected.[9] Nations are still responsible to prevent, react, and rebuild in light of catastrophes, with prevention being the primary concern.[10]

---

7 Alex Bellamy, *Responsibility to Protect* (Cambridge: Polity Press, 2009), 198.

8 Examples are the former UN secretary general Kimoon Ban's Implementing the R2P (2009), Early Warning, Assessment and the R2P (2010), and The Role of Regional and Subregional Arrangements in Implementing the R2P (2011). See Kimoon Ban, *Implementing the Responsibility to Protect Report*, UN Document A/63/677, January 12, 2009; Kimoon Ban, *Early Warning, Assessment and the Responsibility to Protect*, UN Document A/64/864, July 14, 2010; Kimoon Ban, *The Role of Regional and Subregional Arrangements in Implementing the Responsibility to Protect*, UN Document A/65/251, June 28, 2011. All the R2P documents are available at https://digitallibrary.un.org.

9 ICISS, *The Responsibility to Protect*, 39.

10 ICISS, viii.

MINIMALIST AND MAXIMALIST APPROACHES
Alex Bellamy's Minimalist and Maximalist Positions

Within this historical background of the R2P, it is worth noting that Bellamy particularly develops his idea of *jpb* by the use of the norms of the R2P. A 2008 article maps out a way to think about the victor's obligations in post-war contexts, especially with regard to moral questions about the winning side's coalition operations during and following the recent wars in Afghanistan and Iraq. Bellamy names two major strands of thought present within the *jpb* discourse: the maximalist and minimalist positions. In a nutshell, the minimalist argues that moral principles derived from both the *jus ad bellum* and *jus in bello* topics must constrain what winners are entitled to do. He defines this position as one in concert with the earlier just war thinker Hugo Grotius: the *post bellum* principles are designed to rein in the excesses of victorious states. That is to say, minimalism defines *jpb* in terms of restraints to be put on the victors, especially with regard to their rights to actions that "protect themselves, recover that which was illicitly taken, [and] punish the perpetrators."[11]

On the other hand, the maximalist position views the *post bellum* principles as imposing duties upon the victors rather than granting them permissions. This concern is opposite to the minimalists, who assume that the victors do too much in victory so that these excesses must be curbed. Instead, the maximalists assume that the victors do too little. As a result, the defeated state remains as a dysfunctional social system that cannot fulfill its citizens' basic human needs. Therefore, the maximalist argues that the victors require additional responsibilities to guarantee the security of the citizens of the vanquished. According to Bellamy, this position is more grounded in liberalism and international law than in the classical JWT.[12] Unlike the minimalist position embedded in the JWT, invoking a way to prevent victors from inflicting harms, the maximalist position aims to bring about the conditions of both political and economic reconstruction under which the people in the vanquished state can lead decent lives.

Bellamy finds both positions on *jpb* problematic. He criticizes the minimalist approach due to the limitations it faces when confronted with the current international law of war, and due to its lack of scope toward restoring

---

11 For details, see Bellamy, "The Responsibilities of Victory," 602–5.
12 Bellamy, 615.

a just society, leaving a gap in how to address cases in which war has completely destroyed a society. Further, he critiques the minimalists for having a tendency to separate morality (drawn from the classical JWT) from legality (such as international laws) and thus to overlook the reality of law that enforces morality. He argues that "if positive law is to play a part in shaping judgments about the peace, it is imperative that the (rather extensive) law relating to occupation, almost entirely ignored by *jus post bellum* writers—be placed firmly within this minimalist account."[13] However, he also criticizes the maximalist position by making five points: first, it lacks a justification of *why* the winners take on additional responsibilities in every type of war. Second, the boundary of the maximalist position to apply in *post bellum* contexts is ambiguous. Who determines it and to what degree? Third, despite the proposition that maximalism is an addition to minimalism, not a substitution, there is the chance that maximalism might violate the requirements of minimalism due to the complex reality of the *post bellum* context. Fourth, the maximalist position is conceptually detached from the classical JWT. Fifth, this position assumes a general consensus on the most desirable form of postwar society whereas it could be plausibly asked whether such consensus actually exists.[14]

In fact, what Bellamy actually opposes by these critiques of both the minimalist and maximalist positions is the proposition that the category of *jpb* ought to be acknowledged as a third element of the JWT, akin to *jus ad bellum* and *jus in bello*. Bellamy sees it as problematic that *jpb* is a distinct area fundamentally apart from the JWT. He emphasizes "[*jpb*] as yet unresolved questions about its connection to the other just war criteria, their applicability in different types of war, their impact upon broader judgments about legitimacy, and relationship with the indeterminacy of the *jus ad bellum* criteria."[15] Although he clearly makes the point that attempts to add *jpb* as a third strand to the JWT are "premature," he is not fully against the development of an idea of *jpb*. Indeed, he proposes his own six-point solution that attempts to take into account the particular situation at hand.

> (1) The justice of the peace should be evaluated independently of that of the war.

---

13 Bellamy, 608.

14 Bellamy, 619–21.

15 Bellamy, 622.

(2) The responsibility to uphold the *jus post bellum* is collective.

(3) Different responsibilities emerge from different types of war.

(4) Rights vindication is a vital constraint but is already a component of *jus ad bellum* and *jus in bello*.

(5) There is an important difference between entitlement and obligation.

(6) Beyond rights vindication, elements of *jus post bellum* must be developed through consensus.[16]

This six-point solution demonstrates that he still believes there is merit in continuing to refine the idea of *jpb*. On the other hand, it also confirms his cautious attitude toward the *jpb* discourse. In this cautious manner, especially shown in his sixth point, he concludes that the idea of *jpb* must be developed carefully and by a consensus as he argues that without a consensus, it will never gain legitimacy. However, I should note that his claim against adding *jpb* as a third strand to the JWT is fundamentally opposed to my main argument in this book.

Nevertheless, his analysis of the minimalist and maximalist positions is worth discussing since it challenges the dominant norm of *right to fight/intervene* within the JWT and shifts to the norm of *responsibility to protect*. And it is also important since this analysis brings more diverse *jpb* scholars into the conversation, including both just war theorists (who believe in adding a *jpb* as a third element of the JWT) and non-just war theorists (who have different interpretations of *jpb* concepts like justice, postwar, or peace than those in the JWT). To recap, Bellamy sees that while the minimalist position is drawn from the JWT, the maximalist position is alien to the JWT, and further it cannot be fully discussed without international law and other practices. His careful examination of the limits of the two positions opens a door for further discussion.

Redefining Minimalist and Maximalist Positions

There are two major positions within the JWT discourse of *jpb*. One approach is the restricted or minimalist position. This view is based on Bellamy's description of the minimalist position. However, I will also include Mark Evans's study of the minimalist position, not just to compare with Bellamy's version, but also to complete the definition of the minimalist position. According to Evans, this approach is primarily concerned with the

---

16 Bellamy, 622–25.

immediate time after war. He states that this minimalist approach is based on a "rectificatory concept of justice."[17]

Another approach is the extended or maximalist position as defined by Bellamy; this approach seeks for a broad comprehension of postwar justice that may include external actors to support reconstruction so as to ensure a just peace that aims for social justice. I will expand the scope of this maximalist position by adding the so-called reconciliation-focused *jpb* approach. This reconciliation-focused *jpb* is based on a consensus-building process that seeks to expand *jpb* beyond the limits of the traditional liberalism or the liberal foundation of *jpb* approaches. The traditional liberal approach primarily deals with both *right* and *responsibility*, whereas the consensus-building approach goes beyond the *jpb* idea of right and responsibility, to seek a broader restoration of right relationships among victims, offenders, and communities.[18]

One of the major exponents of the minimalist or restricted version of *jpb* is Eric Patterson, who is highly skeptical of the maximalists' attempts to call for a new international order, especially with regard to the "Pottery Barn Rule." The punchline of this rule is "you break it, you buy/own/fix it."[19] This rule is certainly in line with the maximalist position that the victorious states or the international community have obligations to the vanquished states. These obligations include repairing what has been destroyed during the war and thus leaving the losing side as a functioning member of international society. Patterson sees the overconfidence that "we can fix things" as hubris, not a moral norm of the international community.[20]

In particular, Patterson cites Thomas Hobbes as providing insights into the realities of the *post bellum* context. The Hobbesian legacy is based on Hobbes's *Leviathan*, which usually underpins the realist position in international relations that states do not recognize each other's right to exist and warfare is constrained by the power of other actors within the system, not by morality. This view is exactly the opposite of liberal calls for reconstructing

---

17 Evans, "At War's End: Time to Turn to *Jus Post Bellum*?," 31.

18 For details, see chapter four. See Daniel Philpott, *Just and Unjust Peace: An Ethic of Political Reconciliation* (New York: Oxford University Press, 2012), 65.

19 The *New York Times* columnist Thomas Friedman coined the phrase originally as "the pottery store rule." For reference, see Thomas Friedman, "Present at . . . What?," Opinion, *New York Times*, February 12, 2003.

20 Eric Patterson, *Ending Wars Well: Order, Justice, and Conciliation in Contemporary Post-Conflict* (New Haven: Yale University Press, 2014), 13.

a new international order. Instead of relying upon the liberal foundation of *jpb*, Patterson develops a model for *jpb* based on a hierarchy of priorities: order, justice, and (re)conciliation. He observes that from reconstructing an order, the space for reconstructing justice is created, and from that justice, the wished-for reconciliation arises. In essence, providing a minimal postwar order aiming at a situation of stability and security is a modest but fundamental goal.

On the one hand, Patterson emphasizes order due to its primary role to provide for a postwar situation of security. In his argument, promoting international security and preserving human life is itself the most fundamental moral good of *jpb*. On the other hand, he believes that (re)conciliation is rare in political life, so he is skeptical of those who call for it. He even clarifies that conciliation is beyond a political realm. In fact, his concern begins with his critical review of *jpb* literature that tends to discuss the goals of order, justice, and reconciliation all at once as they conceptualize *jpb* as multidimensional. In response, he argues that through narrowing the scope of what *jpb* should encompass and thus "elucidating specific mechanisms and structures" for it, the chance for a more just and lasting peace can be raised.[21]

The just war thinker Jean Bethke Elshtain takes a stance similar to Patterson's in many ways. She contends with the relation between the JWT and *jpb* ethics as she argues that *jpb* must be added to the JWT and that "the basic aim of *jus post bellum* is a more just situation than that which pertained before the armed conflict."[22] Like Patterson, she returns to the more holistic approach to war encompassed within the classical JWT, rather than solely relying on either a legal or political paradigm. Both scholars criticize the idea of liberal internationalism, as Elshtain calls it hubris just as Patterson does.

> This form of hubris—seeking power but without the expense and the responsibility—was reinforced by a reliance on courts and lawyers and the proliferation of various agreements. . . . [It] had no tangible effect on . . . [postwar societies]. The vicious cycle of 'poverty, instability, and vio-

---

21 For an overview of the hierarchy of priorities, see Eric Patterson, *Just War Thinking: Morality and Pragmatism in the Struggle against Contemporary Threats* (New York: Lexington Books, 2009), 95–98.

22 Jean Bethke Elshtain, "The Ethics of Fleeing: What America Still Owes Iraq," *World Affairs* 170, no. 4 (Spring 2008): 94.

lence' behaves rather like a perpetual motion machine—it will not stop
unless some countermovement stops it. Those movements must be the
creation of accountable, responsible, states.[23]

She is skeptical of the movement of building the international governance
for *jpb*. Instead, like Patterson, she emphasizes the "countermovement" of
(re)building the state sovereignty through narrowing the scope of what *jpb*
should encompass. In other words, she takes the same stance as the minimalist position that significant investments in national state security will
allow a greater chance for wars to end well. Further, Patterson's priority listing of order, justice, and conciliation is found in Elshtain's argument since
she emphasizes the establishment of a just order to successfully end wars.
She argues that an armed force for policing the war-torn society is capable
of providing a political order in the immediate aftermath of a war.[24] For her,
the goal of *jpb* is to attain this decent peace by ensuring order for security.
She is aware of the importance of a *jpb* that proceeds to (re)build a just political order that promotes the common good.

In addition to this general discourse of the scope of what *jpb* should
encompass, Elshtain discusses an ethics of exit with four criteria. First, the
lesser the degree of responsibility an occupying state has for a war, the lesser
the responsibility it has for ensuring a just peace, usually counted as a "minimally decent state." Likewise, if that state's role is major, its responsibility is
correlatively increased for attaining a just peace, aiming at "sustained stability." Her second criterion is similar to the first one but pays particular attention to an occupying state's military role, so the greater the degree of
commitment the victor has to military operations, the greater the accountability it has for repairing the harm that is a direct result of military activities.
The third criterion is an occupying state must ensure the provision of defense
and security until the occupied state can do so on its own. Fourth, the occupying state must deter the occupied state from reverting to the unjust ways
that caused the deposed regime to be occupied in the first place.[25] Like Pat-

---

23 Jean Bethke Elshtain, *Just War against Terror: The Burden of American Power in a Violent World* (New York: Basic Books, 2004), 170–71.

24 For details, see Jean Bethke Elshtain, "Just War and an Ethics of Responsibility," in *Ethics beyond War's End*, ed. Eric Patterson (Washington, DC: Georgetown University Press, 2012): 125–26.

25 For an overview of Elshtain's ethics of exit with four criteria, see Elshtain, "Ethics of Fleeing," 95–97.

terson, Elshtain is a minimalist. Her minimalism is shown by these four criteria, as she does not place the burdens of reconstruction on every occupying state. She recognizes that the issue of postwar justice is real and that it should be adjudicated on a case-by-case basis using careful moral and political considerations, not that it be based on an adoption of some universal criteria especially endorsed by the international community.

Both Walzer and Orend appear to be *jpb* minimalists. While it seems obvious since each of the names of their ideal models of *jpb* tells about their positions: Walzer's model of "[minimally] safe and decent society" and Orend's model of "minimally just society," it is actually not that obvious. Rather, they are somehow too complex to be categorized as either minimalist or maximalist. On the one hand, some of the minimalist viewpoints are found in Walzer and Orend, as shown by their comparative points in chapter one that the victorious states secure the just cause of the war and deter future aggression by punishing the aggressors. For example, Walzer usually espouses a minimalist stance, but he is also an advocate of governmental or societal transformation under extreme circumstances, such as in the case of Nazism.[26] For him, peace is a restoration of legitimate political order, not a desire to remake a society, which is a very similar view to Patterson and Elshtain. However, he also allows for what he calls "restoration plus," or simply put, transformation, in extreme cases. In most cases, peace represents a return to status quo *ante bellum*, to the degree possible, once the violated rights have been restored. Walzer and Orend, as well as the minimalists, commonly argue that full assumption of the control of the vanquished government should be prohibited.

However, on the other hand, most *jpb* thinkers, including Walzer and Orend, incorporate aspects of both the minimalist and maximalist positions. Bellamy affirms that both Walzer and Orend cannot be defined as occupying either position. Both of them imply that "just belligerents are entitled to do more than simply restore the status quo."[27] Further, while Walzer and Orend support the rights vindication endorsed by minimal-

---

26 Walzer was initially identified as part of the minimalist approach, however, in his 2012 essay "The Aftermath of War: Reflections on *Jus Post Bellum*" supports a more maximalist approach, arguing that *jpb* has to be flexible enough to find a way between just peace and just a peace, as its core is about social justice. See Michael Walzer, "The Aftermath of War: Reflections on Jus Post Bellum," in *Ethics beyond War's End*, ed. Eric Patterson (Washington, DC: Georgetown University Press, 2012): 35–47.

27 Bellamy, "The Responsibilities of Victory," 605.

ists, they also make two maximalist propositions: victors' responsibility (i) to secure people in the occupied lands and (ii) to reconstruct the war-torn society.[28]

I identify Walzer as one who is closer to the minimalist group, despite the fact that he is also seen as a maximalist in some extreme cases. The main reasons why I categorize him as a minimalist are as follows: as discussed in chapter one, he prioritizes the idea of national security over that of human security; second, his communitarian view is opposed to the international governance perspective; and third, the concept of his "restoration plus" is not only underdeveloped, but also not as specific as Orend's conditions to meet that goal. Therefore, I call Walzer a *loose* minimalist, but still a minimalist. In contrast, I regard Orend as a maximalist thinker. Firstly, he privileges human security over national security; secondly, his cosmopolitan view supports the effort of building international governance; finally, his argument for the idea of rehabilitation certainly reflects the maximalist position. In reference to these three points, I name Orend a *loose* maximalist, but still a maximalist.

By way of contrast, Mark Evans's approach is one example of "the maximalist," despite the fact that he uses a different term to describe his position, namely, "the extended." In his study *Moral Responsibilities and the Conflicting Demands of Jus Post Bellum*, he begins his argument by reviewing Bellamy's conception of minimalist and maximalist strands of *jpb*. In fact, Evans contrasts his view with that of Bellamy—he argues, contra Bellamy, for "restricted" and "extended" conceptions of *jpb*. The restricted position is defined as one that takes the norms to govern the immediate aftermath of a war. In order for these norms to be actualized in practice, this position "focuses on the *rights* of just combatants, whereas their *responsibilities* are apparently limited in the sense that they are largely negative in character (specifying what a just combatant is *not* allowed to do)."[29] According to Evans, both of Bellamy's minimalist and maximalist positions tend to offer the restricted stance in their accounts. That is to say, both the minimalist and maximalist views are limited to a short timeframe in the immediate aftermath of the war, and most of their discourse narrows down to the rights of the just combatants versus their responsibilities. Therefore, both of these

28 Bellamy, 609–10.

29 Mark Evans, "Moral Responsibilities and the Conflicting Demands of *Jus Post Bellum*," *Ethics and International Affairs* 20, no. 3 (Summer 2009): 150. Italics added.

views endorsed by Bellamy, which Evans calls "premature" attempts at *jpb*, have fundamental errors due to the condition of their "restriction."[30] Evans sees that the restricted position presents a problematic and weak variant of *jpb* and suggests the extended position, noticing that there are broader post-war requirements pertaining not only to the unjust, but also to the just. The essence of his *jpb* theory is that the extended conception can draw from a broader view of postwar permissions and responsibilities—due to the belief that the restricted position fails to grasp the nuances of postwar scenarios.

Evans further suggests that *jpb* scholars develop an extended conception, which should be manifest in the relatively long timespan envisaged for the discharge by just combatants of their *post bellum* obligations. Further, the extended conception should be manifest in the relatively lofty, elusive, and long-term nature of the postulated contributions to be made by the former combatants in pursuit of establishing a just and lasting peace.

Evans offers four *jpb* criteria that states just combatants must be prepared to:

(1) set peace terms that are proportionately determined to ensure a just and stable peace as well as to redress the injustices that prompted the conflict

(2) take full responsibility for their fair share of the material burdens of the conflict's aftermath in constructing a just and stable peace

(3) pursue those national and international political initiatives for conflict prevention (and/or, sub-optimally, conflict containment and post-conflict reconstruction)

(4) play a full and proactive part in the ethical and sociocultural processes of forgiveness and reconciliation.[31]

Evans also adds a fifth criterion later in his work but does not see it applying only when there is an occupation.

(5) Where just combatants occupy the defeated aggressor, and/or are present in another territory in the aftermath of a humanitarian intervention, they have a duty to restore sovereignty/self-determination to the territory as soon as is reasonably possible.[32]

---

30 Evans, 163.
31 Evans, "Balancing Peace, Justice and Sovereignty in *Jus Post Bellum*," 541.
32 Evans, "Moral Responsibilities and the Conflicting Demands of *Jus Post Bellum*," 157.

Evans emphasizes that this fifth criterion helps to prevent a "mission creep problem," which "occurs when occupying forces find that their responsibilities deepen and expand as time goes by, setting in motion a cycle of ever-lengthening occupation."[33] In fact, all these criteria—especially the last criterion—are drawn from Evans' idea of atonement. Influenced by both Augustine's conception of war and Kant's terms of atonement, Evans explains his basis for the extended obligation in occupied states. He argues that the obligations of the victor extend from the Augustinian just war principle that war is the lesser of two evils. Plainly, war, even a just one, is still evil. This line of reasoning implies that in order to atone for the evil rendered by war, the victor has incurred an obligation to reconstruct the vanquished state or at least restore a legitimate political order through a just occupation. Further, for Evans as for Kant, the evil accompanying every war, even a just one, carries with it inherent obligations; therefore, at the end of war, atonement is always required with the duty being to rebuild the defeated nation, and thus to leave it as a functioning member of the international community.[34] To be clear, for Evans, this concept of atonement is not theologically understood as a form of pleading one's guilt, but it is his political caution against the mission creep problem. This occurs when the victors are tempted initially to adopt a minimalist understanding of postwar obligations, especially given the long-term, systemic injustices, and then belatedly acknowledge festering problems. He argues that these duties should include state building, but as a just war thinker, he also makes clear that this state building mission is only valid insofar as the requirements of legitimate authority and probability of success are concerned.

One can glean an understanding of the major threads of debate and analysis regarding the extended position that Evans proposes. Among them, two points should be made clear. First, unlike Bellamy, Evans argues for the idea of *jpb* as a necessary addition to the JWT. For Evans, this is neither simply a question regarding the rights of the just combatants versus their responsibilities nor a task to be done in the immediate aftermath of war, but instead it is a way to more closely capture the moral and political reality of ensuring peace. This is because just combatants are demanded to fully understand the idea of *jpb* given the changes in the nature of warfare and

---

33 Evans, 158.
34 For details, see Evans, 153–54.

the unanimous adoption of the R2P in 2005 by the United Nations General Assembly. Second, this extended model of *jpb* supports the inclusion of third-party international actors that can help to establish political initiatives for war prevention and encourage just combatants to assume a proactive role in "the ethical and sociocultural processes of forgiveness and reconciliation."[35] Assuming that the conception of forgiveness is characterized as an attitude that allows the process of reconciliation, Evans makes a point that "forgiveness and reconciliation are always required in some minimal form, but that what they actually mean and entail will vary according to circumstances."[36] However, he does not fully explain how and when this should happen.

Two other maximalist *jpb* thinkers, Daniel Philpott and Larry May, pay closer attention to the ethical and sociocultural processes of forgiveness and reconciliation. Strictly speaking, May and Philpott are more inclined to rely on a legal paradigm than they are to return to the holistic approach to war encompassed within the JWT as Evans does. In particular, in one of his *jpb* texts *War Crimes and Just War*, May engages in a philosophical project to lay out the moral and normative justifications of war crimes prosecutions, especially with regard to international war crimes prosecutions.[37] In framing this dialogue, May maps the interplay of influences between *jpb* thinkers in the JWT and modern elements of international criminal law: "My view is that *jus post bellum* principles are primarily moral principles that are meant to inform decisions about how international law is best to be established down the road."[38] Assuming that there is no clear line drawn between the moral and the legal, he believes that "[*jpb*] principles are normative in that they should become law."[39]

Philpott attempts to lead his *jpb* discourse out of the JWT and into the field of peacebuilding, especially with regard to transitional justice. He suggests a less "Western-centric way for a just peace," exploring the monotheistic religious traditions of Christianity, Islam, and Judaism and their

35 Evans, "Balancing Peace, Justice and Sovereignty in *Jus Post Bellum*," 541.

36 Evans, "Moral Responsibilities and the Conflicting Demands of *Jus Post Bellum*," 156.

37 For reference, see Larry May, *War Crimes and Just War* (Cambridge: Cambridge University Press, 2006).

38 Larry May, *After War Ends: A Philosophical Perspective* (Cambridge: Cambridge University Press, 2012), 5.

39 Larry May, "*Jus Post Bellum*: Proportionality and the Fog of War," *The European Journal of International Law* 24, no. 1 (2013): 318.

approaches to restorative justice.[40] He is inspired by advocates of restorative justice, who typically look beyond modern Western law and justice to the *ubuntu* ethic of sub-Saharan Africa, *sulh* rituals in the Islamic tradition, and certain strands of Christian theology, especially the historic peace church tradition. As a result, he obtains a model based on the reciprocal recognition of common political rights aimed at renouncing violence as a means of resolving disputes, encompassing some of the core commitments of the liberal tradition such as human rights and restoration of right relationship. He proposes an ethic of political reconciliation along with an array of matching practices that seek to restore the right relationship. To begin with, these practices are composed of six *jpb* elements: building socially just institutions, acknowledgement of suffering caused, reparations, accountability/punishment, apology, and forgiveness.[41] These elements are independent and complementary. The ultimate intention of the ethic of political reconciliation is to redress a different set of wounds of political injustice in a distinct way but also to restore a dimension of human flourishing and just political order.

It is worth noting that this kind of model is nearer to what Evans qualifies as a "pristine" or idealistic conception of *jpb*—which posits what is just in the ideal world for justice after war. He notes the importance of these pristine concepts since these concepts denote "our fundamental, most ideal normative commitments and inspire . . . us to reflect and act upon how best we might move closer to their realization."[42] In other words, Philpott's six *jpb* elements cannot be understood as a set of required procedural steps to achieve a just peace, but they work as a matter of guidance and inspiration for efforts in a nonideal world.

This kind of pristine concept is also found in May's work, especially with regard to the concept of *meionexia*, or asking less than one's due.[43] For May, this concept is understood as a pristine principle for *jpb* considerations.

---

40 Philpott, *Just and Unjust Peace*, 28. What Philpott means by "Western-centric way for a just peace" refers to two strands of common morality in the West: a natural law strand dating back to Aquinas and a strand dating back to Kant. This understanding of his relies on the argument made by the contemporary philosopher Alan Donagan, *The Theory of Morality* (Chicago: University of Chicago Press, 1977). For further discussion, see chapter four.

41 For comment and discussion, see chapter four. Also, for original reference, see Daniel Philpott and Gerard F. Powers, *Strategies of Peace: Transforming Conflict in a Violent World* (New York: Oxford University Press, 2010), 97.

42 Evans, "At War's End," 31.

43 May, "*Jus Post Bellum*, Grotius, and *Meionexia*," 19–22.

This principle aims not to rectify the wrongdoings of war to the standards of what is due but instead defends an idea of limited restitution as a virtue, a disposition that helps warring parties at the end of their conflict to achieve a just peace, asking the victims and the just actors to compromise for the benefit of the long-term common good. May develops his *jpb* model based on six normative principles with emphasis on the concept of *meionexia*: retribution, reconciliation, rebuilding, restitution, reparation, and proportionality (this last one is especially relevant to the idea of *meionexia*).[44] For him, these six principles are pristine concepts that should govern the postwar situation. These pristine ideals will help *jpb* practitioners succeed by keeping them in view and under review as guides and inspirations, although these ideals will not be fully achieved.

Further, the principle of *meionexia* does not mean to rule out the victor's (or the international community's) obligation to punish both the initial aggression and any subsequent war crimes. Instead, what the principle of *meionexia* argues is that just actors need a forward-looking, or long-term obligation for rebuilding the war-torn societies, not only conducting justice for war criminals, which is a backward-looking model. Central to May's argument is the premise that justice in the *post bellum* context calls for moderation since building a just peace in war-torn societies inevitably involves compromises from both war-parties, the victor and the vanquished. May's concern is not just about ending a war successfully. He defines *jpb* as one which discusses "very little about *bellum termination*," but much about the "justice-based considerations after war ends, *jus post bellum* proper."[45] This viewpoint is different from many minimalist *jpb* thinkers, especially Patterson, who argues that ending a war successfully is all about *jpb*.

While both Philpott and May have their merits, I must challenge their arguments. I believe that their beliefs are beyond the scope of the *jpb* discourse since their ideas of justice serve for transitional justice, which I believe should be distinguished from postwar justice. They might give *jpb* readers a false impression that the *jpb* discourse is valid for transitional justice. For them, the element of *jpb* is used as a tool to produce a better peace that ultimately enters into the fields of law and transitional justice, transforming each of the two thinkers' principles into recipes for a just peace. However, this argument is the opposite of my contention that the *jpb*

---

44 May, "*Jus Post Bellum*: Proportionality and the Fog of War," 316.
45 May, *After War Ends*, 4.

discourse should be valid enough when it serves for postwar justice, not transitional justice. Recall from the introduction and chapter one that transitional justice is *not* identical with postwar justice, and in fact, it is beyond the scope of the *jpb* discourse in this book. In particular, I am cautious of those approaches in which both the terms *postwar justice* and *transitional justice* are often interchangeably used without distinguishing them. As such, these two *jpb* thinkers have fallen into the constraints imposed by peacebuilding practices rather than the *jpb* discourse within the JWT. They are more interested in restoration-oriented practices than preventing possible injustices through the development of a clear frame of moral principles. To be clear, this book does not rule out some of their conceptions as part of the maximalist discourse, but their *overarching arguments for transitional justice* are *not* included. We will revisit their ideas in the next two chapters—specifically Philpott's work in chapter four—for two reasons: one is that both their ethics of punishment and forgiveness are helpful to theological reflections on human security and political reconciliation. Another reason is that the logic of their ethics often relies on theological concepts or their associated philosophical ideas, thus allowing for a channel to enrich the *jpb* discourse through the dialogue of the two disciplines.

By redefining these minimalist and maximalist positions in the work of moral philosophy, I reaffirm that the defining split between these two strands appears to be more in terms of degree rather than type. For example, most minimalist approaches, including the loose minimalist thinker Walzer's model of "[minimally] safe and decent society," might be appropriate for interstate wars in which neither nation-state subjugates or occupies the other. However, even in these kinds of scenarios, victorious states' obligations oftentimes are required to do more than ensure a peace settlement that restores the prewar status quo, especially when the war was originally justified because of long-term and systematic injustice. In those cases, the *jpb* responsibilities must be closely tied to the more holistic approach to war encompassed within the maximalist approaches, including the loose maximalist Orend's model of "minimally just society." Taking these two approaches together, the victorious states and the international community can take concrete steps not only to create a minimally just and decent state, but also to maximize the chance for peace by leaving the vanquished state as a functioning member of the international community. I would say that *this is the establishment of a just peace, or the goal of jpb, leading the war-torn state to be a good neighbor and a good global citizen.*

Therefore, the defining division among major *jpb* scholars is not nec-essarily static in the way of Bellamy's minimalist versus maximalist posi-tions. This does not mean that we need to bring a new frame for defining two or more groups. Neither do we need to pay too much attention to the discourse of how to frame a certain division among *jpb* scholars in this or that way. Instead, what makes the *jpb* discourse more valid today is how we bring it out of the JWT while still appreciating that *jpb* is a part of the JWT. As a first step for this purpose, we will briefly revisit these minimalist and maximalist *jpb* scholars to explicate the three fundamental themes proposed in this book—reconstruction of just policing, punishment, and political participation. This work will be a touchstone for guiding the development of *jpb* discourse toward a central theme of human security and political rec-onciliation in chapters three and four, and to discuss further specific *jpb* practices from chapters five through seven.

THREE *JUS POST BELLUM* FOUNDATIONAL THEMES
Reconstruction of Just Policing

Defining the reconstruction of just policing is not an easy task, and to com-plete it, a more practical knowledge of security issues of *jpb* is required. While we will examine this in depth in chapter five, here we take an initial step to understand the reconstruction of just policing. I borrow from the JWT to examine the idea of reconstructing just policing in relation to the objective of *jpb*. As discussed in chapter one, the goal of *jpb* is the establish-ment of a just peace. Likewise, the goal of reconstructing just policing is to build a just peace. Therefore, the first step necessary is to clarify a just peace. As argued by contemporary *jpb* scholars such as Walzer and Orend, one's definition of a just peace is determined by whether just actors, be they the victor or the international community, seek national security or human security. In general, the norm of national security is traditionally seen as the defense of state borders from external threats, as it emphasizes the role of the state in providing for the protection of its citizens and the rule of law. In contrast, the norm of human security prioritizes individuals' security over national security as it focuses primarily on protecting people and improving the human condition in postwar societies. These two norms often are mutually reinforcing as the idea of national security has to do pri-marily with the protection of its citizens, but national security does not automatically equate with human security. Plainly, while sovereign states attempt to protect human rights, the rights of human beings are often violated during war in the name of national security.

To explain in more detail, the minimalist *jpb* scholar Eric Patterson relies on Thomas Hobbes's understanding of peace; Patterson prioritizes seeking order over justice and conciliation as the way to build a just peace.[46] Patterson refers to a quotation from Hobbes's work *Leviathan*.

> For war consisteth not in battle only, or the act of fighting, but in a tract of time, wherein the will to contend by battle is sufficiently known; and therefore the notion of time is to be considered in the nature of war; as it is in the nature of weather. For as the nature of foul weather lieth not in a shower or two of rain; but in an inclination thereto of many days together; so the nature of war, consisteth not in actual fighting; but in the known disposition thereto, during all other time there is no assurance to the contrary. All other time is peace.[47]

The analogy of war relating to the weather is important because in Hobbes's view, the state of nature is a war of all against all, in which human beings constantly seek to destroy each other in an incessant pursuit of power. In response, the laws of nature are required for human societies. These laws state that human beings must strive for peace, which is best attained by consent to a sovereign authority who is the head, the Leviathan, the maker of laws, and the defender of civil peace. Here, Patterson, speaking for Hobbes, emphasizes the notion of state sovereignty as a key to protecting human life and rights. This is because, in the Hobbesian view, states in anarchy are always in a state of war, therefore, securing the state's sovereignty is always needed to build a just peace.

Patterson seeks to ensure order in the immediate aftermath of war rather than creating conditions in which (future) conflicts would become unlikely. Patterson, therefore, argues for privileging order above justice and reconciliation in the *post bellum* context. He emphasizes that *jpb* obligations are first about ensuring order within the war-torn societies; order consists of stopping murder, rape, and violence, while ensuring governance. Like most minimalists, he does not hesitate to address the term "minimal" in

---

46 Patterson, *Just War Thinking*, 97.

47 Eric Patterson, *Ethics beyond War's End* (Washington, DC: Georgetown University Press, 2012), 6; Patterson, *Just War Thinking*, 42; Patterson, *Ending Wars Well*, 5. For the original source, see Thomas Hobbes, *Leviathan, 1651, With Selected Variants from the Latin Edition of 1668*, ed. Edwin Curley (Indianapolis: Hackett Publishing, 1994), 8.

reference to defining these obligations; promoting a minimal postwar order aiming for stability is a moral imperative, but also, and more importantly, it is a pragmatic instrument for the victor to achieve a peace while facing the postwar reality.

Similar to Patterson, Elshtain emphasizes the establishment and maintenance of a just order. She believes that an armed force is incapable of delivering full peace in the aftermath of war but that it is still capable of providing order in the immediate aftermath of a conflict and that ensuring this order secures people in the war-torn areas. For her, the goal of *jpb* is to attain this decent peace, which consists primarily of the striving for a just order. What she means by striving for a just order is establishing a legitimate political order to secure people from violence. Based on this belief, she proposes a model of "minimal decency." This model aims at not only stopping immediate violent threats but also ensuring national governance and security control, especially through democratic processes, including elections, representative government, and a constitutional document written by the citizens of the vanquished state.[48]

In addition to these security concerns and democratic processes, Elshtain also believes that there are certain minimal standards of moral imperatives that must be applied for her minimal decency model. She argues that all states have a stake in creating a system of "equal moral regard of persons."[49] However, since there is no international sovereignty capable of enforcing that moral imperative, the stake falls to the states with the greatest levels of military capability to undertake the lion's share of armed intervention in oppressive regimes or failed states, whether they be *ad bellum* or *post bellum* contexts.

In contrast to these minimalist positions, Orend has a different understanding of establishing a just peace relating to the issues of just policing.[50] As discussed earlier, it is important to understand Orend's foundational use of Kant's work in his ideas concerning *jpb* and the conception of peace. Kant proposes a positive peace, which requires the transformation of the international system settled by a confederation of republican states (under the law of nations).[51] Orend believes that this international system will facilitate

---

48 For details, see Elshtain, "Just War and an Ethics of Responsibility," 125–27.

49 For details, see Elshtain, "International Justice as Equal Regard for the Use of Force," *Ethics and International Affairs* 17, no. 2 (September 2003): 63–75.

50 As discussed earlier in this chapter, I put Orend as a loose maximalist thinker despite the language that he uses for his "minimally just society."

51 Kant, *Perpetual Peace and Other Essays*, 114.

just policing, especially with regard to human security, because this con-federation is more likely to secure both the rights of their own citizenry and the laws governing international sovereignty.[52] Like most maximalist thinkers, Orend's principal concern is for human security rather than the international balance of power considerations that have been identified in some of the minimalist thinkers' concerns, especially within realist circles. In a nutshell, most maximalist thinkers, including Orend, advocate a more cosmopolitan view of sovereignty and privilege order in the lives of people over order within the international system.[53]

Orend emphasizes human security while Patterson and Elshtain are more concerned with preserving and promoting state sovereignty as the first and foremost task needed to build an order to secure people's safety. This priority listing of either state security or human security may be best viewed in terms of degrees along a spectrum of plausible choices.

Further, it is worth noting that both of these positions have significant limitations in dealing with the issue of just policing. The research scope of the current literature within the minimalist position is limited to functions and does not feature a comprehensive set of objectives, capacities, con-straints, and relationships to other actors. For example, in Patterson's priority listing of security, order, and reconciliation, he overlooks that the function of security in postwar society cannot always be guaranteed in order to pro-ceed with just order or reconciliation. Human security matters, but it is not grounded in a chronological sequence or the order of importance. Social analysis of cause and effect should be multidimensional, that is, there is no one linear way to arrive at or achieve an objective of moral and social order; the channels are diverse and dynamic. For example, even ensuring safety involves other social functions. Safety cannot be completely achieved by the armed forces without the cooperation of public education, legislative assis-tance, truth commissions, international tribunals, and a judiciary. To be clear, this is not an argument that the functionalist perspective is ineffective but rather that a one-sided functionalist view risks the absence of an integrated and comprehensive picture of a just society after war. This practical matter will be further illustrated with practical examples in the last three chapters.

---

52 Kant, 112.

53 For a similar yet less densely concentrated Kantian cosmopolitan theory of the just war, see Cécile Fabre, *Cosmopolitan War* (Oxford: Oxford University Press, 2012). Compared to Orend's, her stance rather adopts a relatively minimalist account of cosmopolitan justice, especially when it comes to dealing with asymmetrical wars.

The maximalist position also has limits. Unlike its seemingly acute emphasis on establishing a human rights system prior to one based on state sovereignty, the existing *jpb* literature within the maximalist position lacks research into humanitarian norms. The maximalist position has failed to fully examine the essential features of human reality in postwar societies: What are the most difficult challenges that people in postwar societies face? Who are the most vulnerable populations with these problems? The literature developed in international law and politics pays too much attention to the legal obligation of certain actors, mainly the intervening armed forces, legal courts, and the local governments. The focus becomes the dilemma or dysfunction of each actor involved in *jpb* and how to resolve the institutional dilemma. Therefore, despite its emphasis on human security, the maximalist position too often overlooks who should benefit most from the practices of the social institutions. This inconsistency gives rise to more practical questions. Does justice exist for the sake of justice itself or for the sake of those who are most vulnerable to war and violence? Should not justice shape developing humanitarian norms within the *jpb* framework beyond security? It has been noted that "strong emotional dynamics produced in the traumatized society after severe human rights violations may in fact lead to new human rights violations."[54] Thus, humanitarian norms and values must not become just another compartmentalized aspect of peacebuilding work. Rather, they must be infused throughout all the activities of *jpb*. At stake is human rights on the ground, rights understood as both universal human rights and the particularity of their application to local societies (i.e., finding local terms with which to define that universality). This is why humanitarian norms have to be carefully developed and further applied to *jpb*, especially with regard to the reconstruction of just policing.

Lastly, the biggest challenge of *jpb* in terms of the establishment of just policing is that the discourse still focuses on nation-states or sovereign political entities, not on people who suffer from war or violence. It seems that national security comes before human security. For example, Walzer, Elshtain, and other just war thinkers, especially minimalist thinkers, include human rights in their arguments, but only within the protection of a sovereign state, or the third party (e.g., humanitarian intervention). However, while sovereign states attempt to protect human rights, the rights of human

---

54 Inger Agger and S. B. Jensen, *Trauma and Healing under State Terrorism* (New York: Zed Books, 1996), 202.

beings (especially vulnerable populations) are often violated during war in the name of national security. Humanitarian norms should be developed more clearly and applied in the JWT, at least in the context of *jpb*.[55]

Reconstruction of Just Punishment

In general, when we discuss the issues of just punishment, the underlying question is what the victorious states or just actors may do to their former enemies or war criminals. There are many repercussions associated with issues of just punishment, such as war crimes tribunals, potential financial reparations, and legal and political practices of postwar punishment. While I will touch on them more extensively in chapter six, this section will present one of these common controversial issues found in both the minimalist and maximalist *jpb* literature. It is the question of reparations, namely, the question of whether victorious states have a right to reparations or remuneration from the losing states, and if so, how. An underlying issue is that the vanquished are indebted to the winners or just actors, thus resulting in the owing of something, typically money, that the vanquished are under an obligation to pay. The question of punishment and reparations arises as soon as war is over, and thereby, it becomes a central dilemma in the *jpb* discourse. Attention to this issue is a good start as it enables an overview of the fundamental moral and political issues of just punishment.

May, Philpott, and Walzer point to the overwhelming reparations and remuneration placed upon Kaiser Wilhelm II's German Empire in the aftermath of WWI as a genuine cause of the emergence of Adolf Hitler's Nazi regime, and subsequently, the carnage of WWII. Introduced as a way to consider a necessary moderation through the concept of *meionexia*, May points to the demands that were made of German citizens in the wake of WWI. Through the lens of *meionexia*, this demand was too heavy to endure for the citizens, and subsequently, it sowed the seeds of further hostilities. He compares this case with the end of WWII, when the victorious Allies

---

55 In this short introduction of the reconstruction of just policing, my provisional conclusion is made by stating "humanitarian norms should be developed more clearly," but this still leaves open the question of whether these norms are truly going to be implemented. This question is exactly the same as Orend's question (and that of some human-rights-based *jpb* thinkers such as Robert Williams Jr. and Dan Caldwell). In particular, this shared inquiry will be further examined in the following chapters in two different domains: (i) chapter three will present a proposal of theological reconstruction on human security, seeking what works in a moral and theological sense; and (ii) chapter five will discuss *jpb* practices of just policing for human security, looking into what really works on the ground.

paid most of the costs of reparation and restitution for the victims of the losing Axis Powers, resulting in a long-term peace for both those victims and occupied nations.[56]

Philpott also thinks the punitive treatment of Germany after WWI sowed the seeds of further hostilities. He explains that the biggest problem facing reparations in cases of large-scale political injustice as shown by the example of WWI is the unavailability of resources, by which he means not only the scarcity of material goods but also the premature manner in which the resources are delivered to the victims.[57] In response, Philpott attempts to examine how reparations bring restorations. Assuming that reparations intend to heal the wound of social ignorance, he argues that reparations should function in publicly identifying victims as objects of injustices as they defend the legitimacy of human rights, both those of the individual victim and those of the entire society. When victims receive reparations in this way, "they are more likely to view a new regime or peace settlement as legitimate, to place trust in it, and to forge bonds of trust and commitment with their fellow citizens—all secondary restorations."[58]

For Walzer, reparations are broadly understood as the processes of making amends for wrongs one has done. For example, this would be carried out by paying money to or otherwise helping those who have been wronged. The question of reparations is not merely about the compensation for war damage paid by defeated states, but also, it is inherently about achieving justice by punishing the state guilty of initial aggression.

Moving from this general idea of the ethic of punishment and reparations, another central topic to discuss is who ought to be responsible for reparations. Walzer points out the collective aspect of reparations. He believes that reparation is a legitimate case of "collective punishment," because "citizenship is a common destiny, and no one, not even its opponents, can escape the effects of a bad regime."[59] In other words, Walzer, as a communitarian thinker, understands that reparation is a principle of law referring to the obligation of one community, a wrongdoing state, to redress the damage caused to another community, a wronged state. As a result, there comes an idea of common responsibility within a state community that the

56 May, *After War Ends*, 9.

57 Philpott, *Just and Unjust Peace*, 196.

58 Philpott, 197.

59 Walzer, *Just and Unjust Wars*, 297.

guilty state is responsible for war. This idea remains with all citizens of the aggressor state (usually with financial responsibility such as paying higher taxes in order to provide for monetary compensation).

However, there seems a major flaw in this argument. It is not clear whether Walzer's argument for legitimizing collective punishment is intended as a moral justification built on an idea of common responsibility or merely a factual claim about inevitability in postwar politics. Can we say it is a fair judgment that the hardship of reparations will be incurred on those citizens who did not have responsibility for the war, or those who were even against the war? Further, Walzer argues that American voters who supported the Vietnam War should be responsible for compensation; however, should they also be responsible for war crimes by combatants, especially in *jus in bello*? In the same vein, Orend points out the flaw of Walzer's argument. He argues that there are some ways that responsibility for reparations should be imposed on only those who were fully responsible for war crimes in light of both *jus ad bellum* and *jus in bello*. In order to do this, Orend believes that the JWT principles of discrimination and proportionality should apply in determining reparations and financial compensation for the victims of war during war crimes tribunals. These criteria determine who ought to be held responsible for war crimes. He argues that reparations will be given by those citizens, especially "those political and military elites" who must have profited considerably and knowingly from the waging of the war or matters directly associated with it.[60]

Patterson agrees with Orend's idea that the punishment of elites is critical to postwar justice.[61] Elshtain never explicitly defines who ought to be responsible for reparations and remuneration, but she also agrees with both Walzer and Orend that reparations are an allowable form of punishment as long as not taken too far. In particular, she makes a point that punishment too often becomes "gratuitous" in the wake of postwar settlement, as she is concerned about the danger of "victor's justice."[62] She believes that fair trials should not overlook the war crimes of victors or stronger nations. Little literature explicitly states that *jpb* should not be the victor's peace or justice, but also, and more importantly, Elshtain's concern appears to justify an observation that current literature on *jpb* tends

---

60 Orend, "Justice after War," (2002), 48.
61 For details, see Patterson, *Ending Wars Well*, 80.
62 Elsthain, "The Ethics of Fleeing," 166.

to overemphasize mercy and political reconciliation rather than the moral responsibility of justice.

Lastly, I must include Orend's idea of rehabilitation within the discourse of just punishment; in his view, all the *jpb* praxis of postwar punishment, as well as potential financial reparations, should not be done in the spirit of vengeance but with the idea of rehabilitation. For Orend, there are two competing *ideal* models of postwar justice: revenge and rehabilitation. He argues that *jpb* as a moral end to war should focus on rehabilitation rather than revenge.

According to the revenge model, there need to be public peace treaties, an apology from the aggressor, war crimes trials for those who are responsible, an exchange for Prisoners of War (POWs), and demilitarization of the aggressor. Also, it requires the aggressors to give up any gains that they have earned during the course of the war. For Orend, what then differentiates the revenge model is that the aggressor has to suffer *further losses* beyond due renunciation *as a punishment*. What Orend means by *further losses* is "[hefty] reparations payment to the victims of the aggressor, plus [long-lasting] sanctions slapped on the aggressor as a whole."[63] Both the reparations and sanctions victimize the vanquished society, hamper the economic growth of that society moving forward, and punish them economically. After levying these rules upon the defeated state, there remains no further responsibility but withdrawing. There is no responsibility for reconstruction; the proponents of the revenge model believe that it is too costly and risky, thus encouraging a "leave it to the locals" attitude. In Orend's view, this line of reasoning affirms that justice demands this kind of punishment in revenge. Orend opposes the revenge model for the following reasons: (i) historically it seems to create future wars; (ii) it yields new generations of enemies; (iii) there is a lot of evidence that vengeful policies, especially sweeping sanctions, hurt innocent civilians; (iv) justice does not demand revenge; and (v) the revenge policy does not deal with the continuing structural problems of bad regimes still in power.[64]

Orend points out there is no strict dichotomy between the revenge model and the rehabilitation model. There is an overlapping consensus, which consists of public peace treaties, apologies, exchanges for POWs, trials

---

63 For details, see Orend, "Justice after War," (2012), 179–81. According to Orend, two recent examples of the revenge model are the Treaty of Versailles of 1919 and the ending of the first Iraq war of 1991.

64 Orend, 181–82.

for war criminals, the giving up of the aggressor's gains from the war, and demilitarization (though permitting the means to ensure a state's security). However, unlike the revenge model, Orend's model of postwar rehabilitation rejects sanctions and reparation payments not only because they harm innocent civilians in the defeated state, but also because they prevent reconstruction by removing money and resources. Instead, he urges the international community to invest in a defeated aggressor in order to help it reconstruct the war-torn society and smooth over the wounds of war. Further, Orend's model of postwar rehabilitation supports a long-term strategy for regime change if necessary. In some cases, regime change can lead to "the creation of a new, better, nonaggressive, and even progressive member of the international community," as occurred in Germany and Japan following WWII.[65]

For Orend, it is important to distinguish between the goal of *jpb* and the means. As shown in chapter one, for Orend, the goal is the reconstruction or rehabilitation of "minimally just society" by the means of an international treaty, namely, a new Geneva Convention. By codifying the rehabilitation model in an international treaty, Orend hopes to set minimal guidelines for *jpb* and ensure that rehabilitation, not revenge, is the goal of postwar operations.

All of these authors, whether they be minimalist or maximalist *jpb* scholars, consider the need of some form of postwar justice as part of their expectation for just punishment. As shown above, reparations are one possible means to this end. However, interestingly, when it comes to the consideration of monetary reparations, minimalists and maximalists agree that this practice is not always a good way to enact justice. In response, most of our authors suggest the adoption of war crimes tribunals as a means of punishing the guilty without placing too large a burden on the society as a whole, and, more importantly, they caution that there must be some system to ensure discrimination and proportionality in the quest for just punishment, such as Orend's rehabilitation model-based proposal of the new Geneva Convention.

Reconstruction of Just Political Participation

With respect to just political participation, my third foundational *jpb* theme, this book aims to address how peacebuilding practices endorsed by local communities (including the Church and other faith-based organizations)

---

work in relation to the decision-making process of postwar interim governments. The ultimate concern is not merely the local communities and their practices, but the broader implications for public administration, which necessitates knowledge of how to collaborate with, and even within, the local communities with respect to their peacebuilding assets. All in all, the first and foremost task of just political participation is to prevent future violence in the immediate aftermath of war. Without a doubt, there are a lot of pressures on the victor's shoulders after war to rebuild society in the vanquished state, and just actors are usually expected to promote just political participation, ultimately leading them to implement the common good in postwar society. Rebuilding a fairly just society necessitates just political participation for success in human security, political reconciliation, or other *jpb* missions. This concern to rebuild just political participation will be revisited with a more careful analysis in chapter seven; in this closing subsection I will take up the discussion of defining how those just actors are relevant to the work of just political participation.

Most *jpb* thinkers agree that the victorious state(s) and the international community are two actors to be examined whether they are involved in the implementation of just political participation or not. There is some consensus among the minimalist and maximalist *jpb* scholars on this question. However, while there are numerous works on the obligations of the victor to the defeated state and its citizens, there is little work on the topic of the obligations of the international community toward the vanquished state and its citizens in the aftermath of war.

As introduced earlier, Evans argues that the victorious state has incurred an obligation to reconstruct the war-torn societies, drawing on both Augustine's conception of war and Kant's idea of atonement. He points out further that this moral obligation has been legitimized by the United Nations General Assembly's ratification of the R2P document (2005) calling for the victor's responsibility to rebuild war-torn societies, especially in cases of intervention. Like Evans, Walzer argues for the victorious state's obligation for reconstruction, but only when it is involved in wars against a nation-state that has committed crimes against humanity, genocide, or ethnic cleansing. In fact, these crimes are included under the four grave crimes (of genocide, war crimes, crimes against humanity, and ethnic cleansing) that are defined as humanitarian crises by the R2P. Based on this discrete responsibility, Walzer believes that once the victorious state exercises its rights to occupy, it then incurs obligations on the basis of that decision; and once this decision is made, its obligation is to reconstruct the vanquished state for an improved situation than that which existed prior to the conflict. As shown by Walzer's proposal for "restoration plus," he argues that this obligation marks the final objective of *jpb* as a more stable and secure situation than that which existed prior to the war, thereby boosting the odds for just political participation. In particular, Walzer's democratic vision for *jpb* maintains that (re)building a democratic regime, or at least its political culture, is the best—or close to best—way to ensure that a state of affairs for realizing just political participation is achieved.

Elshtain takes a slightly different approach than Walzer's. She believes that neither a return to the status quo *ante bellum* (including "the restoration plus") nor an attempt at major transformation (e.g., regime change for democratic government) will always attain peace. Rather, she suggests that the victorious state should assess its degree of responsibility for the postwar situation, corresponding to the status of its role in the war. Hence, if the victor has committed to major military operations, then they should bear a major burden in reconstructing the society. However, to be clear, Elshtain is a minimalist in that she does not place the burdens of reconstruction in every case. Her argument for reconstruction is limited to repairing the infrastructural harm that is "a *direct* result of [the victor's military] operations."[66]

Orend is distinguished from the aforementioned thinkers in that he does not consider the idea of the obligations of the victor as much as they do. Instead, his major concern is to see whether, and if so, how, the international community can undertake forcible regime change and thus remake the vanquished state into a functioning member of the international community. Orend argues for the minimally just society as an ideal model of *jpb*. As was shown in chapter one, minimal justice is achieved when the vanquished state is recognized as a legitimate government by its own citizens and the international community while it makes a reasonable effort to avoid violating the rights of other nation-states and to ensure the basic human rights of its own citizens. In attempting to achieve this justice, there will be an opening for the vanquished state to have a greater chance of facilitating just political participation. In particular, returning to his Kantian philosophical underpinnings, Orend's model of a minimally just society is more global in nature. In other words, he is interested in the international system, as a whole, for *jpb*, not just the actions and reactions of the

---

66 Elshtain, "Just War and an Ethics of Responsibility," 127.

more-involved states in war. Furthermore, this Kantian vision of *jpb* leads him ultimately to recognize the end of war as an opportunity to promote "perpetual peace" through the creation of a federation of republican states. For Orend, the greater the international stability, the greater the chance of reconstructing just political participation.

However, what is missing from all these authors' understanding of just political participation is the question of the roles of local actors—including the Church or a faith-based organization—in *post bellum* areas. The discussion of who is *actually* involved in just political participation remains to be developed with further and more universalized interactions in social, economic, and political life. This entails including more inclusive interactions beyond that of only top-down actors such as the victorious states and the international community. No doubt there are obligations of the victor and the international community to the defeated state and its citizens. However, their obligations usually appear to be bound to the top-down implementation that starts with the big picture of rebuilding a just society but often ends with policy implementation narrowed down to certain focused-interest groups unlikely to be reflective of the entire community's interests. In chapter seven, we will take a closer look at these challenges, and further reflect upon the roles for bottom-up and mid-out actors—and how they can help implement the common good in postwar society by reconstructing just political participation in a fuller sense.

Chapter 3

Moral Theology of *Jus Post Bellum*: Human Security

INTRODUCTION: MOVEMENT TOWARD THEOLOGICAL REFLECTION FROM PHILOSOPHICAL ANALYSIS

In the previous chapter, I attempted to thread philosophical concepts and issues throughout the recent *jpb* literature to understand the key divide in *jpb* philosophers: minimalist versus maximalist positions. This attempt intended to strike the right balance between the two positions but may leave more theologically oriented or religious readers wondering at times if I could not have presented a more rigorous defense of some of the moral investigations I made in relation to theological questions. For example, Mark Allman and Tobias Winright, who offered one of the first book-length engagements with *jpb* from a Christian theological perspective, pointed out the lack of theological material on the topic of *jpb*, noting, "mostly philosophers, political theorists, international law scholars, and military scientists have treated this neglected dimension of just war, while bishops and theologians have largely been silent on the issue."[1] Therefore, one must ask: *why does (moral) theology matter to jpb?*

Chapters three and four will attend to this question.[2] Keeping this question in mind, these chapters must begin with two main theses of the *jpb* discourse found in the previous chapter:

(1) The norm of *responsibility*, as a liberal foundation of *jpb*, is added to the established norm of *right* in the JWT. In particular, the norm of R2P has framed a new way to discuss *jpb*. It applies to *post bellum* situations, especially when the vanquished people are left to suffer under oppression and turmoil. This norm raises the question of how each

---

1 Allman and Winright, *After the Smoke Clears*, 12.

2 A revised version of chapter three was published as "Human Security: Revisiting Michael Schuck's Augustinian and Kenneth Himes's Thomistic Approaches to Jus Post Bellum," *Journal for Peace and Justice Studies* 29, no. 2 (2020): 3–24.

position implements it: the minimalist position, by arguing that moral principles must constrain what just actors are entitled to do after war, and the maximalist position, by viewing the *post bellum* principles as imposing duties upon just actors rather than granting them permissions. This split is not an absolute rule for discernment but a critical touchstone to guide just actors in attaining a balanced view, since the distinction is best viewed in terms of degree rather than type.

(2) Defining minimalist and maximalist positions helps shed light on the three foundational themes of *jpb*: first, with respect to the reconstruction of just policing, humanitarian norms have to be carefully developed and clearly applied to the overall *jpb* practice, of which the fundamental characteristic must be human security; second, there must be some legal system to ensure the principles of discrimination and proportionality are observed in the quest for just punishment, the ultimate goal of which must be rehabilitation; and third, just political participation must emphasize forging a local consensus to prevent further violence in the aftermath of war. Both top-down actors, such as the victorious states and the international community, and bottom-up (and midlevel-out) actors, such as local actors—including the Church and other faith-based organizations—must work together toward a just peace. This local consensus should be a primary concern when answering the question of how humanitarian norms and rehabilitation models are truly going to be implemented.

Based on these two propositions distilled from the philosophical *jpb* discourse, chapters three and four aim to develop a theological discourse on *jpb*.

First, unlike moral philosophers who are divided between minimalism and maximalism, most moral theologians who support the idea of *jpb*—at least those major contemporary writers to whom I am referring in this book—advocate a maximalist version of *jpb*.[3] At the same time, depending on the situation, some of their arguments partially embrace the minimalist idea as they present some of the *jpb* principles, which constrain what just actors are entitled to do after war. In this regard, the first proposition found in the moral philosophy of *jpb* also applies to moral theologians' studies on *jpb*, that is, the distinction between minimalist and maximalist positions is

---

3 Despite the possibility of disagreement regarding *ad bellum*, most theologians agree about postwar moral obligation. For example, both Gerard F. Powers, an opponent of the Second Gulf War, and Jean Bethke Elshtain, a sponsor of that war, share a common sense of postwar obligations owed the Iraqis. See Gerard F. Powers, "Our Moral Duty in Iraq," *America* 198, no. 5 (February 18, 2008): 13–17; and Elshtain, "The Ethics of Fleeing."

viewed in terms of degree rather than type. In other words, although moral theologians are generally viewed as *jpb* maximalists, they do not absolutely neglect minimalist positions, but attempt to guide just actors in attaining balanced views. Hence, this book primarily intends to explore and articulate the distinct discourse of moral theology on *jpb* rather than merely extend the discourse of minimalist versus maximalist views to moral theology.

The second proposition illuminates the ultimate aim of human security-oriented *jpb* practices, the fundamental characteristics of which must be built on humanitarian norms, a rehabilitation model, and local consensus. Considering these two propositions together, we will examine how *jpb* theologians understand the norm of *responsibility* after war. More importantly, we will learn that these theologians' projects defend the maximalist position primarily because their findings commonly contribute to the *jpb* discourse of human security, even as we look to the "political reconciliation" movements within the Church and society as a visionary long-term project. From this stance, we will anticipate a very distinct discourse in the moral theology of *jpb* in chapters three and four: human security and political reconciliation. The theme of human security, guaranteeing that basic human needs are met, has been widely discussed across disciplines, while the theme of reconciliation, especially in the form of mercy or forgiveness, has mainly been discussed outside of politics. Yet things began to change in the twentieth century, when horrible violence started to break out in postwar societies. Some *jpb* theologians such as Mark Allman and Tobias Winright, as well as political and legal scholars such as Daniel Philpott and Larry May, started to reconsider the place of mercy and forgiveness in debates about justice, especially in the form of political reconciliation. My argument begins with a statement that dealing with these two moral visions together in a wise manner is key to finding the moral compass for reconstructing just policing, just punishment, and just political participation. However, a question of *how* remains, which we will discuss in these two chapters.

My approach to the moral theology of *jpb* has two central tasks: identifying the distinct discourse of moral theology on (i) human security and (ii) political reconciliation. Chapter three reviews the studies of moral theologians such as Michael Schuck, Kenneth Himes, Tobias Winright and Mark Allman, examining not just how their findings are related to the *jpb* discourse of human security, but also reframing their work in terms of Augustinian, Thomistic, and Neibuhrian *jpb* thought respectively. Chapter four then moves on to the discourse of political reconciliation. In particular, it reviews the work of theological ethicist Anna Floerke Scheid, as well as that of political ethicist Daniel Philpott, whose ethic has been widely cited by moral theologians concerned with political reconciliation. After this critical review, the remainder of the chapter proposes what I call a "maxim(um) of ethical minimalism" responding to a practical dilemma or tension between the two poles of human security and political reconciliation.

There are two points that I must address before we begin the discourse of moral theology on *jpb*. They will recur throughout the rest of this book, so it is worth clarifying them. First, there are other moral theologians who oppose the idea of *jpb* for a variety of reasons. Some of them are pacifists who are against the JWT, thus opposing *jpb*. Others propose a theory and practice of "just peace" as an alternative to the *jpb* discourse (e.g., Maryann Cusimano Love, Eli McCarthy, and Glen Stassen). For example, the April conference of 2016 in Rome, sponsored by the Pontifical Council for Justice and Peace and Pax Christi International, submitted a proposal that the Church should renounce just war theory and replace it with a theory and practice of just peace. Moral theologian Lisa Sowle Cahill summarizes this ethical vision and its central debate clearly: "The just peace ethic insists that peacemaking practices, virtues, and criteria are constitutive of Christian discipleship. More controversially, however, the conference document demands that Catholics 'no longer teach or use just war theory,' ... [as] 'just war theory' is used more to endorse war than to prevent or limit it."[4] Although this approach has certain merits that further the discourse on ethics of war and peacebuilding, for the sake of clarity, these (counter-) arguments will not be part of the main discourse in the rest of this book.

Second, as noted in the introduction, the central tenet of my proposal remains that postwar justice is distinguished from transitional justice in terms of its aim (i.e., oriented to the establishment of a just peace but not slanted toward building democracy) and scope (i.e., limited to postwar contexts, but not extended to post-repression contexts). In this book, the question of transitional justice is not part of the central *jpb* discourse, and therefore, no discussion of this kind of division needs to be included. Keeping that in mind, chapters three and four, in particular, aim to illuminate the distinct discourse of moral theology on *jpb* as I approach the

---

4 Lisa Sowle Cahill, "A Church for Peace? Why Just War Theory Isn't Enough," *Commonweal*, July 11, 2016. cf. Mark Allman and Tobias Winright, "Protect Thy Neighbor: Why Just-War Tradition Is Still Indispensable," *Commonweal*, June 2, 2016.

ethic of war and peace, specifically that of postwar justice, through the lens of the JWT.

HUMAN SECURITY:
WHY AND HOW DOES THEOLOGY MATTER?
The Church's Response to the Norm of R2P

Seeking the Church's Mission for the Postwar Community

Chapter two presented that *jpb* measures are important to actors who are responsible not only for ending war well but also for completing the R2P's vision, namely, "preventing (future violence and injustices), reacting (to human rights violations), and rebuilding (postwar societies)" in light of catastrophes, with prevention being the primary concern. For heuristic purposes, these praxes may be roughly divided into economic recovery and advancement on the one hand, and social and political reforms on the other, with both tasks aimed at restoration of peace, security, and prosperity among the common people of postwar societies. The Christian community, as a member of a global society, needs to ask the question of how best to (re)establish a just peace following violent conflict.[5] For this reason, this chapter is committed to the Christian tradition's emphasis on restoring peace following warfare, and it aims to develop *jpb* categories, which have thus far been considered more by moral theologians than by scholars in moral philosophy, security studies, and international law.

Moral theologians Tobias Winright and Mark Allman argue that since two recent wars— the US-led wars in Afghanistan in 2001 and in Iraq in 2003—many challenges have faced both the Roman Catholic and Protestant churches, as well as the US government and the international community, in these postwar societies.[6] Every day newspapers report that armed violence continues to wreak havoc on communities across postwar societies, while war and hate drive millions of people from their homes in both war-torn areas and open-conflict zones. Further, these two vanquished nations, Afghanistan and Iraq, like most postwar communities, are facing humanitarian crises and public health issues. Therefore, it is imperative that the

---

5 Allman and Winright, *After the Smoke Clears*, 1–6. Some *jpb* theologians also raise a similar question. In particular, Winright and Allman introduce their theological inquiry: "why should Christians care (about *jpb*)?"

6 Allman and Winright, 1–12.

Church and its faith-based communities ask how their ministries of compassion, peace, and justice should advocate for positive change through their missions—not just proclaiming the Good News of God's Peace, but also sharing the love of Jesus Christ with neighbors, thereby contributing to rebuilding a safe and livable society in war-torn areas.

At the same time, the Church's mission requires political prudence, especially when the Church is engaged in warfare issues, including *jpb* practices, primarily led by the state and the international community. This social mission does not mean simply a ministry of compassion but the Church's overall response to the overwhelming culture of violence in postwar societies. Working toward a just peace, by transforming cultures of violence into communities of peace, is an essential mission of the Church: "Peace at all times in all ways" (2 Thes 3:16). Hence, there is no doubt that the Church should work with all residents in the postwar community to inspire approaches to active peacebuilding, to equip God's people to be compassionate and prophetic peacemakers, and to connect communities of peace to learn from each other in shared solidarity leading to action for the transformation of the postwar society. However, as a member of society, the Church needs to be discreet. The Church is an institution that also supports the JWT in some cases, usually when waged for humanitarian intervention or self-defense. At the same time, the Church pursues reconciliation in order to promote a just peace. Yet, the fundamental orientation of promoting that peace is human security, primarily led by the state or the international community. The Church needs *jpb* practices to work fairly and effectively with the state and the international community, while the Church develops its praxis grounded in moral discernment.

The first question to ask is how the Church ought to respond to these challenges of *post bellum* issues. In response, I will first review how the Church has responded to the norm of R2P. The R2P centers around three prongs: the responsibility to prevent, the responsibility to react, and the responsibility to rebuild. The third prong particularly falls into the category of *jpb*, while the first prong broadly falls under the umbrella of *jpb*, since the failure of *jpb* work of prevention sows the seeds of further hostilities. Although the norm of R2P can be argued in various aspects, there is one major concern of R2P that is found in the foreword of the R2P document: "This report [R2P] is about the so-called 'right of humanitarian intervention': the question of when, if ever, it is appropriate for states to take coercive—and in particular military—action, against another state for the purpose of protecting people at risk in that other state."[7] In other words, the norm of R2P is understood as a legal and political attempt to justify an initial use of armed force, with a primary concern for the well-being of the "people at risk"—including people in postwar societies. On no account, therefore, should the situation after the intervention be equal to or worse than it was prior to the intervention.

The Catholic Church's Response

The Church, like the UN, has been amenable to the norm of R2P. In particular, the Catholic Church has been supportive of the norm in a larger context, since the Holy See understands peace not only as the end product of armed conflict but also as a political movement toward actively remaking structures in both postwar and open-conflict societies and reestablishing relationships among people that will help ensure peace. In his 2003 World Day of Peace message, Pope John Paul II urged the international community to take responsibility for "[building] a world of peace on earth" and "[nurturing] peace by spreading a spirituality and a culture of peace" amidst the divisions that plagued the world of his time.[8] He was particularly concerned about the Iraqi crisis of 2003 even before the invasion of Iraq by a US-led coalition launched on March 20, 2003.[9] The Holy See conducted various diplomatic campaigns to prevent war in the early months of 2003, including the last-minute visit of papal envoy Pio Laghi to the White House on March 5, 2003.[10] However, despite these desperate efforts to prevent the Second Gulf War, the pope generally maintained his position that the international community must disarm the aggressor, "when a civilian population risks being overcome by the attacks of an unjust aggressor and political efforts and nonviolent defense prove to be of no avail."[11] Archbishop Silvano Tomasi, Vatican representative to UN agencies in Geneva, affirmed that these papal messages offer "a clear orientation and precise guidelines" for

---

7 ICISS, *The Responsibility to Protect*, vii.

8 John Paul II, "*Pacem in Terris*: A Permanent Commitment," *Origins* 32, no. 29 (January 2, 2003): 9–10.

9 See John Paul II, "Address to the Diplomatic Corps Accredited to the Holy See," January 20, 1993, 13.

10 For details, see "Papal Envoy Meets Bush," *America*, March 17, 2003, 4.

11 John Paul II, "Peace on Earth to Those Whom God Loves," Message for the World Day of Peace," January 1, 2000, 11.

humanitarian intervention.[12] Plainly, John Paul II's teaching demonstrates the Church's concern with R2P, especially with protecting people whose own government fails to protect them.

Pope Benedict XVI has, on occasion, more explicitly discussed and sought to enact R2P. Tobias Winright clearly confirms the pope's ethical vision on R2P.

> The Roman Catholic Church has also begun to refer to R2P, with Pope Benedict XVI mentioning it in his address to the General Assembly of the UN on 18 April 2008 and, more recently, in his major social encyclical *Caritas in Veritate*, which was issued on 29 June 2009, calling for R2P's implementation.[13]

In particular, in his 2008 address to the UN, the pope emphasized the grounds of R2P that the international community must intervene when a state is unable to protect its own people. In this speech, he called the norm of R2P the "foundation of every action taken by those in government with regard to the governed" and "an aspect of natural reason shared by all nations."[14] Further, he included theological guidance for R2P: "This principle [of R2P] has to invoke the idea of the person as image of the Creator, the desire of the absolute and the essence of freedom." With that theological mindset, the pope urged the UN to remember its mission and that "the universality, indivisibility and interdependence of human rights all serve as guarantees safeguarding human dignity" as "this reference to human dignity . . . is the foundation and goal of the responsibility to protect." He referred to human dignity as an "objective foundation of the values inspiring and governing the international order," including human rights.[15] This is because he believes that human rights are grounded in the dignity of the human person, which is itself a universal idea.

> [Human rights] are based on the natural law inscribed on human hearts and present in different cultures and civilizations. . . . This great variety of

---

12 Silvano Tomasi, "Time to Act: Church Teaches Duty to Intervene to Prevent Genocide," *Catholic News Service*, August 12, 2014.

13 Tobias Winright, "Just Policing and the Responsibility to Protect," *The Ecumenical Review* 63, no. 1 (2011): 85.

14 Pope Benedict XVI, "Address of His Holiness Benedict XVI," Meeting with the Members of the General Assembly of the United Nations Organization, April 18, 2008.

15 Pope Benedict XVI, "Address of His Holiness Benedict XVI."

viewpoints must not be allowed to obscure the fact that not only rights are universal, but so too is the human person, the subject of those rights.[16]

For Benedict XVI, therefore, it is evident that human rights are derived from the idea of human dignity. The protection of human dignity as the norm of R2P is "the first and last of the fundamental rights" and should be "the criterion that inspires and directs all . . . efforts."[17] The pope urged that the Church must work with the UN in order to "increase the protection given to the rights of the person . . . [which] are grounded and shaped by the transcendent nature of the person, which permits men and women to pursue their journey of faith and their search for God in the world." Therefore, Christians have a responsibility to create the conditions for peace and goodwill throughout the earth. This responsibility accompanies the task, which is essentially "motivated by the hope drawn from the saving work of Jesus Christ."[18]

More recently, Pope Francis called upon the UN to consider the norm of R2P, especially with regard to the US-led airstrikes in Northern Iraq against the terrorist group known as ISIS, or the Islamic State. In August 2014, the pope wrote to the then UN Secretary-General Ban Ki-moon, calling for the UN to take action to stop the humanitarian tragedy and prevent systematic violence against ethnic and religious minorities underway in Northern Iraq. Pope Francis elucidated this request in a press conference.

> In these cases where there is unjust aggression, I can only say that it is licit to stop the unjust aggressor. I underscore the verb "stop"; I don't say bomb, make war—stop him. The means by which he may be stopped should be evaluated. To stop the unjust aggressor is licit, but we nevertheless need to remember how many times, using this excuse of stopping an unjust aggressor, the powerful nations have dominated other people, made a real war of conquest. A single nation cannot judge how to stop this, how to stop an unjust aggressor. After the Second World War, there arose the idea of the United Nations. That is where we should discuss: "Is there an unjust aggressor? It seems there is. How do we stop him?" But only that, nothing more.[19]

---

16 Pope Benedict XVI.

17 Originally delivered as a message to Director General of FAO on the Occasion of World Food Day 2005, October 12, 2005, quoted in David G. Kirchhoffer, "Benedict XVI, Human Dignity, and Absolute Moral Norms," *New Blackfriars* 91, no. 1035 (September 2010): 589.

18 Pope Benedict XVI, "Address of His Holiness Benedict XVI."

19 Francis Rocca, "Pope Talks Airstrikes in Iraq, His Health, Possible US Visit," *Catholic News Service*, August 18, 2014, http://ncronline.org/new/global/pope-talks-airstrikes-iraq-his-health-possible-us-visit.

According to moral theologian Kenneth Himes, four points from this statement are worth noting: (i) Francis drew a critical distinction between "stop[ping]" the aggressor, as opposed to "mak[ing] war" on the aggressor. The humanitarian crisis being induced by the Islamic State must be stopped. (ii) Just actors must "evaluate" the means of intervention. (iii) In reality, alleged humanitarian interventions have rather served as cover for "making a real war of conquest." (iv) The determination to intervene ought not to be done by "a single nation." It must be carried out multilaterally or through the mediation of the UN. With these four points, Himes concludes that on the one hand, Francis affirms the idea of a moral duty to protect vulnerable innocents victimized by aggressor actors, but on the other, he is reluctant to endorse "armed intervention as the most appropriate response." With these teachings, Francis entreats the UN to evaluate "the proposed means of intervention." Himes believes that Francis's hesitancy begins with his concern about "the risk that under the guise of humanitarian motives more self-interested ambitions may be at work." He continues: "this is why [Francis believes that] unilateral action ought to be avoided for it can too easily slide into [narrow] national interest[s] and away from authentic humanitarian intervention."[20]

The Protestant Church's Response

Protestant churches have generally been positive—but ambivalent, depending on the denomination—to the norm of R2P. In January 2001, the Central Committee of the World Council of Churches (WCC) received a request to examine issues on the humanitarian crises in the world, which resulted in the document titled, "The Protection of Endangered Populations in Situations of Armed Violence: Toward an Ecumenical Ethical Approach." In this document, the committee did not explicitly employ the term R2P, but appealed to the Christian community about the responsibility to protect vulnerable populations in both open-conflict areas and postwar societies. This document also presented humanitarian norms such as the goal of human security, which "should be undertaken for police and military forces at both national and international levels. This should include training in nonviolent intervention techniques that

---

20 Kenneth Himes, "Humanitarian Intervention and the JWT," in *Can War Be Just in the 21st Century?*, ed. Tobias Winright and Laurie Johnston (Maryknoll, NY: Orbis Books, 2015): 60–61.

take full advantage of the organizational, logistical and command skills of the military."[21] Further, the WCC led research seminars on R2P. They started in April 2005, when twenty-one experts from around the world gathered and published their report, titled "The Responsibility to Protect: Ethical and Theological Reflections."[22] In the following year, the WCC, representing 345 member churches across nations, sent a letter to the then UN Secretary-General Kofi Annan on March 16, 2006, at the conclusion of the WCC 9th Assembly in Porto Alegre. In the letter, they supported the norm of R2P: "[The WCC] is not prepared to say that it is never appropriate or never necessary to resort to the use of force for the protection of the vulnerable."[23]

However, some of the historic peace churches, such as the Mennonite Church, have not reacted positively to this movement led by the WCC. Rather, they have criticized the WCC's work on the R2P and have clear reservations concerning the acceptance of the norm. They have agreed to act in solidarity with those in need of protection but have made crystal clear that this protection must be provided without the use of weapons. For example, James Fehr, director of the German Mennonite Peace Committee, offers legal and pragmatic critiques. As a legal critique, he challenges the original R2P document's redefining of the sovereignty tenet: The moral duty to endangered peoples is more important than the moral duty of respecting territorial sovereignty."[24] He argues that this statement is not legitimately justified simply because it violates the fundamental notion of territorial sovereignty legally defined and internationally agreed on by the Peace of Westphalia in 1648. In addition to this normative challenge, Fehr points out three issues with respect to pragmatic challenges to the R2P.

---

21 The Central Committee of the World Council of Churches (WCC), "The Protection of Endangered Populations in Situations of Armed Violence: Toward an Ecumenical Ethical Approach," §2.4.3, http://www.oikoumene.org/en/resources/documents/central-committee/2001/the-protection-of-endangered-populations-in-situations-of-armed-violence.

22 For reference, see Semegnish Asfaw, Guillermo Kerber, and Peter Weiderud, *The Responsibility to Protect: Ethical and Theological Reflections: Geneva, 21–23 April 2005* (Geneva: World Council of Churches, 2005).

23 WCC, "The Responsibility to Protect: Letter to H. E. Kofi Annan, UN Secretary-General, 16 March, 2006," https://www.oikoumene.org/en/resources/documents/commissions/international-affairs/responsibility-to-protect/the-responsibility-to-protect.

24 James Fehr, "The Responsibility to Confront Evil: A Pacifist Critique of R2P from the Historic Peace Churches," unpublished manuscript, 2, http://www.dmfk.de/fileadmin/downloads/Responsibility%20to%20Confront%20Evil.pdf.

There are issues of assessing crises (e.g., rules for determining when griev-
ous mistreatment of a people has become genuine genocide or the like),
issues of implementation (e.g., rules for determining when the stage of
"responsibility to prevent" has to be abandoned for the "responsibility to
react"), . . . [and] issues of enforcement (e.g., rules for designating which
states are to be asked to intervene).[25]

With these three issues, Fehr intends to express his wider practical concerns
in two central ways. First, timing matters. Just actors must track and detect
when the elements of social risk become feasible social threats, further turning into humanitarian crises. Likewise, finding an appropriate time to transition from one phase of an R2P-driven intervention (e.g., the phase when
just actors prevent war) to the next phase (e.g., the phase when just actors
react to unjust aggression), is an important task.[26] Second, authorized agents
matter. Just actors must discern which persons or political institutions are
to be assigned as authorized agents to enforce the norm of R2P in response
to particular situations of unjust aggression. However, Fehr argues that the
R2P document does not specify these practical concerns of when and who.
Without considering them, R2P cannot validate the use of weapons. No discussion of such practical concerns includes any account of how a war—even
a just war—substantially helps build a peace. On the one hand, therefore, it
is reasonable to discuss further when R2P will be enforced in particular situations and who will be allowed to perform corresponding action for the
purpose of building a just peace. In addition, Fehr's practical concerns have
merit for future investigation, as I will include two of his concerns—
discerning timing and authorized agents—in the last three chapters.

On the other hand, Fehr's argument opposing the whole R2P initiative
for these practical concerns alone is inadequate. This is because the R2P
document is primarily expected to present a norm, not to be a practical
manual. The norm of R2P definitely serves as a moral imperative expressed
in the three prongs of R2P (prevention, reaction, and rebuilding). However,
the R2P initiative is not a consequentialist approach arguing that an R2P-
based action is right if it is in the interests of the just actors who perform it,

---

25 Fehr, 3.

26 R2P has a broader scope of intervention than humanitarian intervention. R2P adopts armed
intervention as one of the ways to intervene, whereas humanitarian intervention employs armed
forces alone to intervene. Thus "humanitarian armed intervention" might be the best term to
describe the nature of that intervention. Therefore, a R2P-driven intervention includes humanitarian intervention but is not reducible to that.

if the consequences of the just actors' action are the ultimate basis for any judgement about the rightness or wrongness of that action, or if the net intrinsic value that the R2P-based action brings into the world is at least as great as that which any other possible action in the situation (e.g., pacifism) would bring into the world.

Further, Fehr does not fully realize that just actors' obligations, expressed in the R2P initiative and its corresponding intervention, are understood in a *prima facie* way, not in an actual way. Borrowing from Himes's definition, "*prima facie*' is a Latin expression meaning 'at first sight' or 'at first glance.' So a *prima facie* duty is one that appears to be real upon first consideration or at first sight." He continues, "it must be asked if [R2P] is to be understood in an actual or *prima facie* way." In line with this distinction, Himes argues, "the theory of humanitarian intervention establishes a presumptive (*prima facie*) moral duty that other nations ought to intervene on behalf of the victimized population."[27]

In a nutshell, Fehr criticizes R2P because it provides no principle for determining what our actual moral obligations are in particular situations. However, this does not mean that just actors should not consider their duties in a *prima facie* way. In other words, there is no cause to assume that the basic reasons why just actors have the moral obligations that they do are the same in every situation. In recognizing their responsibility as a *prima facie* duty, they are apprehending what is self-evident—that certain kinds of actions, such as protecting innocents, are morally significant. In fact, the only practical concerns that are available to just actors are the moral convictions these actors arrive at via serious thought and reflection. In this regard, Himes also affirms, "translating that [*prima facie* moral duty] into the actual practice of intervention, however, requires further steps. In other words, the movement from moral principle to action is neither automatic nor straightforward."[28]

Conclusion

Although there are degrees of difference in understanding the norm of R2P, we have learned that the imperative to protect innocents is universal, encouraging the entire Christian community to respect the concept of human dignity, which requires human security. Further, the Christian

---

27 Himes, "Humanitarian Intervention and the Just War Tradition," 61.
28 Himes, 61.

notion of sovereignty, captured in R2P, means that the principle of non-interference in the domestic affairs of a sovereign state—a principle at the heart of the UN charter—cannot be used as a shield that enables tyrants to slaughter their political subordinates, rivals, and citizens.[29]

Michael Schuck's Augustinian *Jus Post Bellum*: Pursuing Right Intention

A Survey of Schuck's *Jus Post Bellum* Principles

Within this historical context of how the Church has responded to the R2P, it is worth noting that Catholic ethicist Michael Schuck develops his *jpb* principles from a theological viewpoint, reflected in humanitarian norms, with the use of Augustine's just war principle of right intention. We will first briefly discuss Schuck's *jpb* principles, and then explore how they are related to Augustine's right intention. Schuck is known as the first theologian who employed the terminology "*jus post bellum*" and built a Christian brand of *jpb* with three principles rooted in humanitarian norms: repentance, honorable surrender, and restoration.[30] Failure to comply with any of these requirements means that the victors undermine both the prior *jus ad bellum* motives and *jus in bello* rationales. Schuck proposed the principle of repentance as the central foundation of a *jpb* moral framework in the aftermath of the First Gulf War, after expressing his dismay concerning the "scandalous trivialization of war" displayed by General Norman Schwarzkopf's victory march, which paraded down the streets of Disney World with Donald Duck and Mickey Mouse.[31] He argues that everyone involved in warfare needs to have a sense of Augustinian remorse if they are Christians who are humbly aware that the suffering endured on both sides of the war must be given due respect. Repentance is a moral posture of humility for victors.[32]

---

29 As noted earlier, there is an exception: some historic peace churches have different understandings of sovereignty.

30 Michael Schuck, "When the Shooting Stops," 982–84. Although a short article in *Christian Century* in 1994 is the only piece that he has written on the topic of *jpb,* it marked a significant turning point concerning theological reflection on *jpb* concerns.

31 Schuck, 982.

32 Schuck, 982. Schuck understands the need of remorse and repentance from his reading Augustine, who said, "a just war . . . is justified by the injustice of an aggressor, and that injustice ought to be a source of grief to any good man, because it is human injustice." Augustine, *The City of God*, 19.17. For a recent review of Augustine's work on remorse and repentance, see Lisa Sowle Cahill, *Blessed Are the Peacemakers* (Minneapolis: Fortress Press, 2019), 128–32.

The principle of repentance not only rules out any chauvinistic celebrations of victory but also expresses the victor's respect for human life and dignity lost on the tragic battlefield. This humanitarian norm contributes to postwar healing for both victorious and defeated societies, as it draws upon a posture of humility and moral sensitivity to all parties involved in the war.

The second principle is that of honorable surrender, the attempt of *jpb* to "protect [. . .] the fundamental human rights of the vanquished."[33] This proposal presents two humanitarian visions regarding terms of honorable surrender: (i) terms of surrender must seek to foster hope for a peaceful and harmonious future, because demeaning and unjust terms of surrender have a greater chance of fostering feelings of humiliation on the part of the vanquished; and (ii) measures meant to humiliate the defeated should be prohibited by ruling out excessively punitive terms in peace treaties.

Schuck's third principle is the principle of restoration, which seeks a way to assist in rebuilding the basic social infrastructure of marginalized and life-threatening areas. In particular, the vanquished, many of them innocent noncombatants, are left to contend with the aftermath of a war-torn landscape. Given the severity of these threats, Schuck finds that there is a fairly broad consensus in the literature that one must mitigate these postwar environmental threats. He provides the example of unexploded ordinances and landmines remaining throughout the countryside in post-Iraqi society. Schuck argues that "victors must return to the fields of battle and *help* remove the instruments of war" to spare lives of those who are least able to fend for themselves who are affected the greatest in the *immediate* aftermath of war such as the children, the elderly, the sick, the poor and other socially vulnerable populations.[34]

Therefore, when just actors oversee reconstruction operations or enact postwar reforms without the moral considerations found in these three principles, the risk of future violence is heightened. Each of these principles

---

However, one may disagree with Schuck in that there is no direct connection between grief and repentance. For example, Doug McCready argues: "repentance is an inappropriate criterion if the decision to go to war met *jus ad bellum* criteria and if the fighting itself complied with *jus in bello* criteria. The victor might regret war had become necessary, but the victor should not feel a need to repent of doing the right thing." Doug McCready, "Ending the War Right," *Journal of Military Ethics* 8, no. 1 (2009): 71. Also see, Darrell Cole, "Just War, Penance, and the Church," *Pro Ecclesia* 11, no. 3 (2002): 313–28.

33 Schuck, "When the Shooting Stops," 982.
34 Schuck, 983.

serves to achieve humanitarian goals in postwar societies: (i) repentance, fostering moral sensitivity to all human individuals involved in the war, (ii) honorable surrender, protecting the human rights of the defeated, and (iii) restoration, removing the implements of war as far as human security is concerned in the vanquished nation.

Schuck's Augustinian Approach to *Jus Post Bellum*

It is important to note that Schuck's humanitarian vision of *jpb* is Augustinian. Schuck is clear that he is drawing on and developing Augustine's central piece of just war reasoning: right intention. As widely acknowledged, one of Augustine's main goals when explicating just war teaching was "to reconcile the Christian vocation with the goods of the temporal sphere; thus, to provide a justification for Christian participation in warfare."[35] In order to achieve this goal, Augustine draws attention to right intention. Likewise, Schuck begins with right intention, but exclusively within the context of *jpb*. This notion of right intention is ultimately love (*caritas*) for one's neighbor which, unlike in the pacifist tradition, is not in contradiction to the use of military force and the "desire for more authentic peace."[36] Considering how difficult it is to evaluate true motivations of the human heart and the fact that human behavior consists of mixed, complex motives, it is not surprising that Schuck does not put strong emphasis on this principle in his writings.

Nonetheless, I make two points to address how Augustine's right intention can be understood within the context of Schuck's *jpb* principles, which are rooted in humanitarian norms. First, I must discuss a holistic approach to *jpb* commonly observed in both Augustine and Schuck in order to fully grasp the relationship between right intention and the end of a just war. Augustine takes a holistic approach to warfare, which begins and ends with an emphasis on peace. In a letter to Boniface, Augustine notes, "war is waged in order to obtain peace. Be a peacemaker, therefore, even in war, so that by conquering them you bring the benefit of peace even to those you defeat."[37]

35 Serena Sharma, "Reconsidering the *Jus Ad Bellum / Jus In Bello* Distinction," in *Jus Post Bellum: Towards a Law of Transition from Conflict to Peace*, ed. Carsten Stahn and Jann K. Kleffner (The Hague: T.M.C. Asser, 2008), 11.

36 Jean Bethke Elshtain, "Why Augustine? Why Now?," in *Augustine and Postmodernism: Confessions and Circumfession*, ed. John D. Caputo and Michael J. Scanlon (Bloomington: Indiana University Press, 2005), 254.

37 Augustine, "Letter 189: Augustine to Boniface," in *Augustine: Political Writings*, ed. E. M. Atkins and R. J. Dodaro (New York: Cambridge University Press, 2001), 217.

Although Augustine does not explicitly enumerate lists of just war criteria, he concerns himself with *jpb* ("bring the benefit of peace even to those you defeat") in addition to *jus ad bellum* ("war is waged in order to attain peace") and *jus in bello* ("be a peacemaker, then, even by fighting"). Peace provides the first and the last word in warfare. The fundamental characteristic of peacebuilding can be seen as *jpb* since Augustine looks at the pursuit of a just peace as the right intention of a just war. Schuck also adopts this Augustinian version of a holistic approach to war.

Further, Schuck employs an analogy to justify his holistic *jpb* approach. He argues that his *jpb* principles could "serve as a litmus test for the sincerity of the just war claims made before and during the conflict."[38] In particular, he draws attention to how *jpb* can serve as a discipline for claims made before and after conflict and therefore how his three *jpb* principles— repentance, honorable surrender, and restoration—serve as a litmus test for the sincerity of *ad bellum* claims. As a result, these *jpb* principles can serve to limit overreach by just actors once the conflict has ended. In other words, echoing Augustine's right intention, Schuck believes that *jpb* principles serve to test *ad bellum* claims about the originally stated intention. In particular, his argument is developed at two levels, the national and the individual. At the national level, Schuck focuses on the relationship between the various phases of war.[39] The moral justifications presented for having entered into a war may become tainted or diminished if one utilizes disproportionate and indiscriminate armed force in the prosecution of the war. One's actions in the war may speak loudly concerning one's true motives for entering the war. The moral conduct in one phase affects the conduct in other phases. Thus, how one understands the relationship between the various phases of war (*jus ad bellum, jus in bello,* and *jpb*) is important, as it can influence one's understanding of the *telos* of just war thinking.

The litmus test for the individual soldier centers around the just war principle of right intention. Schuck notes, "the critical factor [for Augustine] in determining the possibility of a person's involvement in a war *as a Christian* is attitude. . . . As a result, Augustinian thought may well accommodate the *jpb* principles as a test for discerning the warrior's true attitudes before and during war."[40] In other words, Schuck contends that the principle of

38 Schuck, "When the Shooting Stops," 983.

39 Schuck, 983.

40 Schuck, 983–84.

right intention, drawn from Augustine's understanding of just war reasoning, must be understood in *jpb* contexts. For Schuck, the principle of right intention, as it relates to both *jus ad bellum* and *jus in bello*, implies the existence of norms applicable to the end, and the aftermath, of war. This viewpoint echoes Augustine's just war reasoning that wars might be authorized and with cause, and yet still not be peaceful if they lack right intention.

Second and most importantly, for Schuck, *Christian* actors' right intention toward the establishment of a just peace begins with the protection of human life. His three *jpb* principles "could expand—like the already existing *jus ad bellum* and *jus in bello* principles—the moral sensibilities of people who believe that war, while evil, is sometimes necessary for the protection of human life."[41] Schuck is clearly aware of the importance of right intention, which leads to rebuilding a just political order that promotes a just peace in postwar societies. In order to achieve this postwar justice and peace, he allows some degree of evil violence for the protection of human life. Like Augustine, Schuck contends that what matters are not the person's deeds (even killing some to save others) but the state of mind (intent) in which the person acts.

However, Schuck, as an Augustinian *jpb* theologian, is also fully aware of human sinfulness and the consequences of sin; humans are tempted to deny themselves or others, to deny their finitude on account of pride, and to deny their transcendence on account of nature in sensuality and sloth. Schuck himself witnessed this aspect of human nature in General Schwarzkopf's victory march. In the parade, as noted earlier, Schuck began to contemplate the Augustinian repentance that just actors need to consider; even if they do their best according to their right Intent in war, there is always limited moral discernment from the human side. As such, although peace is a universal good, not all forms of peace are good, and sinful human beings embrace a corrupt earthly peace. On these grounds, Schuck builds on Augustine to develop his theological anthropology of *jpb* as he attends to human nature, drawn from the theological discourse of sin and *imago dei*. While human beings are created in the *imago dei*, they are also tainted by original sin and as such do not emerge into the world in a *tabula rasa* condition.

Therefore, Schuck believes that the human world has been broken by human violence (i.e., human freedom and the free will to choose sinful acts). As such, the human world is not morally acceptable, and humans are

---

41 Schuck, 983.

part of the problem. But at the same time, rather than this brokenness of the world heading toward despair, Schuck contends that God's grace calls humans to repentance; their basic posture in the world and with their neighbors is to be one of confession and humility. Humans confess that they have done wrong, that they have not loved, and that they live in a tragically unacceptable condition. But humans also live in hope. Rather than allowing the moral unacceptability of their world to lead them to the desperate attempt to remake the world (which always results in more violence) or denial of their real condition, they respond to the promise that God is able to justify the world and that God will resurrect human lives, which gives them grace to continue embracing the world, loving their neighbors, and pursuing justice in the mediocre, minimally decent ways they are able to—while constantly repenting and seeking forgiveness when they fail. For Schuck, this repentance is the central moral and theological foundation for human actors involved in warfare to recover *imago dei* after war, as they continuously respect themselves and other fellow human beings, including enemies.

Kenneth Himes's Thomistic *Jus Post Bellum*: From Discerning Just Cause to (Re)Building Legitimate Authority

Beyond Right Intention

Unlike Schuck's *jpb* approach, Himes's *jpb* thinking is not limited to the *jus ad bellum* discourse of right intention. Instead, he takes on the agenda that is the establishment of a just social order—or more precisely, what he calls "rebuilding a civil society." Drawn from Aquinas's just war principles (right intention, just cause, and legitimate authority), this proposal entails the positive aim of securing peace. Himes understands peace as a positive concept, as the establishment of a just social order, or a result of a rightly ordered political community, directed toward the common good.[42] In what follows, calling upon Aquinas's just war principles, I will discuss Himes's work on just cause: how he understands just cause in association with his notion of right intention; what these just causes would be, especially in light of contemporary warfare issues; and how he discerns these causes in response to rising concerns of humanitarian norms. This discussion will include his

---

42 Kenneth Himes, "Ethics of Exit: The Morality of Withdrawal from Iraq," excerpted, *The Jesuit Conference*, Fordham University, March 21, Fordham University, March 21, 2005; reprinted, "A Job Half Done," *Foreign Policy* (May–June 2005): 65–66

idea of the establishment of a civil society, especially regarding building legitimate authority.

Like Schuck, Himes takes a holistic approach that war must begin and end with a pacific intentionality. Both thinkers highlight that the principle of right intention prohibits the pursuit of unjust ends because it aims to fight for a just peace and to establish this peace at war's end. However, Himes relies on Aquinas's notion of right intention, whereas Schuck relies on Augustine's. As shown in chapter one, Aquinas's notion of right intention is more practically illustrated than Augustine's, especially with regard to defending the common good.[43] Further, Himes affirms that for Aquinas, "an intention is the will focusing on its *telos* so that the desired end is not just a wish, but a practical goal."[44] This common good establishes human laws in *jpb* contexts that determine the responsibilities of the legitimate sovereign to provide for the people.[45]

More importantly, while Schuck focuses on Augustine's attention to right intention as the first and foremost criterion to consider in *jpb*, Himes adopts that of Aquinas, who ultimately affirms the equal importance of all of his just war principles: legitimate authority, just cause, and right intention.[46] Keeping this in mind, Himes asserts that because the main purpose of *jpb* is establishing a just peace—or a peace ordered to the common good—the deeds of just actors during all three phases of war (*ad bellum, in bello,* and *post bellum*) must be legitimately authorized with just causes, as well as having a pacific intention.[47] Just like Aquinas proposes these principles to protect the common good, Himes develops his *jpb* ethic with them—in order to recover the just order of *post bellum* society for the common good. This means that just actors need an intent to establish a peace ordered to the common good, but also must discern just causes and (re)build legitimate authority to make the *jpb* work complete.

---

43 Recall that Allman and Winright make this point. See their book *After the Smoke Clears*, 32. For more detailed theological accounts, see Cahill, *Blessed Are the Peacemakers*, 147–68.

44 Kenneth Himes, "Humanitarian Intervention and Catholic Political Thought: Moral and Legal Perspectives," *Journal of Catholic Social Thought* 15, no. 1 (2018): 164.

45 For Aquinas's discourse on legitimate authority, see Cahill, *Blessed Are the Peacemakers*, 149–51.

46 *ST*, II-II, q.40, a.1. For Aquinas, just war is one that must be waged with these three necessary conditions.

47 Kenneth Himes, "The Case of Iraq and the Just War Tradition," The National Institute for the Renewal of the Priesthood, accessed September 25, 2020, http://www.jknirparchive.com/himes2.htm.

Himes's Thomistic Approach to *Jus Post Bellum*

Himes observes that an academic consensus is emerging in the recent discussion of *jpb*, stressing the importance of just cause for war termination.[48] This highlights an insightful *jpb* thought—how just actors define *jpb* for a certain context is closely tied to their reasons for going to war. In other words, just actors must discern just cause *ad bellum* for the usefulness of *jpb* moral considerations. For example, just actors going to war to stop an aggressor will have narrower *jpb* concerns than states going to war to implement democracy. In this mode of *jpb* thinking, Himes does not merely assert that the aim of *jpb* is the establishment of just peace, but he is keen on presenting how just cause for termination leads to this peace.

Having stressed the importance of just cause for war termination, Himes's *jpb* projects discuss major modern warfare issues of just cause such as self-defense and humanitarian intervention.[49] In particular, Himes expresses his wider concerns in two primary areas, with regard to his *jpb* thinking: discerning regime change as a just cause and proposing a principle of establishing a civil society.

These two areas are interwoven in his writings. First, Himes critically reviews the issues of regime change as part of the discussion of both self-defense and humanitarian intervention. Himes finds that the armed interventionists, whether they are strong states or the international community, have shifted their rationale behind supporting regime change from the notion of humanitarian intervention (or defending citizens from the targeted oppressive regime) to that of self-defense (or protecting the interventionists themselves from the targeted harsh regime). Himes argues that war with the intention of regime change is not an entirely novel policy for the US. The US military removed Manuel Noriega from power in Panama (December 20, 1989–January 31, 1990), as it did for the change of the leadership of Haiti, known as Operation Uphold Democracy (September 19, 1994–March 31, 1995). "What is new," Himes continues, "is the rationale . . . that unless we act a country will obtain

---

48 Himes.

49 Church leaders such as Pius XII and Paul VI asserted that the principle of just cause for war should be conceived as self-defense. Himes expands this discussion of self-defense to issues of humanitarian intervention, which he defines as the use of armed force by one state in the sovereign territory of another to prevent the target government from harming its citizens. See especially, Himes, "Humanitarian Intervention and Catholic Political Thought."

weapons of mass destruction that will embolden a tyrant. The cause for war is a future danger."[50]

However, Himes clarifies that regime change with this new rationale of preventing some attack in an unspecified future is not necessarily a just cause for war "as the situation prior to the war is to be avoided not restored [nor merely replaced with another political regime]."[51] There is always a possibility that a *post bellum* society remains unstable even after actors remove risky factors that threaten their own citizens or the aggressor state's citizens. For example, Himes is concerned with the unstable postwar Iraqi society even after the US-led forces' successful mission to overthrow the Hussein regimes: "The very purpose of such a war will be to alter the internal situation of the Iraqi nation, so as to increase stability and the chances for peace in the region. But what kind of Iraq will emerge from the war?"[52] Likewise, waging a war for prevention, humanitarian intervention, or other *jus ad bellum* objectives *per se* might not be sufficient to make the *jpb* work complete, especially when the vanquished have no, or less, capability of establishing a just social order or when external actors fail to build a peace ordered to the common good due to domestic political concern. In other words, Himes proposes intervening actors need not only discern just causes but also must be practically engaged in the postwar society by establishing a civil society, of which the foundation must be a just order. It is this order that will prevent potential future threats.

Simultaneously and with regard to Himes's second concern, I will pay attention to Himes's proposal for establishing a civil society. Himes begins to discuss this principle when he introduces humanitarian intervention as a just cause that has prompted *jpb* concerns: "One result of the debates over humanitarian intervention has been greater attention to the aftermath of war. The question of what was achieved by humanitarian intervention is important, especially since the purpose was to enhance the well-being of people rather than punish or vanquish them."[53]

Himes finds that just actors have growing *jpb* concerns, especially in light of the heightened frequency of humanitarian crises *post bellum* over

---

50 Himes, "The Case of Iraq and the Just War Tradition."

51 Himes.

52 Kenneth Himes, "Intervention, Just War, and U.S. National Security," *Theological Studies* 65, no. 1 (2004): 156.

53 Himes, 156.

the past decades. In his findings, just actors have increasingly considered the norm of R2P, especially with its corresponding humanitarian intervention endeavors. Himes understands that "there is an obligation from an occupying army to guarantee that the occupied people are safe and secure."[54] Further, this R2P expands the purview of international relations to include prevention and rebuilding.[55] Thus, just actors must be responsible to prevent, react, and rebuild in light of catastrophes, with all of these responsibilities aiming to prevent future violence and lead to peace. In other words, Himes's *jpb* thinking does not solely focus on restoring a postwar society. It must further encompass preventing future threats after war. Himes distinguishes this kind of rebuilding work from that of Schuck's third principle of restoration. Himes's argument for rebuilding looks similar to Schuck's principle of restoration because they share the similar vision of endorsing human security in *post bellum* societies as they incorporate humanitarian norms to the *jpb* discourse. However, with emphasis on the *jus ad bellum* just cause principle, Himes adds more insights into the discourse of restoration as he presents how it relates to the norm of R2P. In particular, he argues that in the aftermath of war, the establishment of "civil society" is necessary to foster the repair and (re)growth of the societal infrastructure that ultimately prevents future threats. He calls this proposal a "moderate form of institutional therapy," which constitutes the three-fold obligation of just actors: "to restore basic material infrastructure, create space for civil society, and assist with the establishment of the essential institutions of public life." Himes continues: "once this [therapy] is done, that ought to end [the *jpb* work]."[56]

For example, Himes applies his "institutional therapy" to the Second Gulf War. His proposal affirms that as an initial step for the establishment of civil society, the US-led forces in a postwar society ought to assist with restoring normal life in the defeated area. In addition to disposing of explosives, they must help with delivering humanitarian aid and restoring utilities. This military operation is a part of the whole *jpb* practice; the entire military police unit is deployed to a postwar society in order to both pre-

---

54 Himes, "A Job Half Done," 65–66. He also refers to The Hague Convention: "The Hague Convention stipulate[s] at least one thing [just actors] must do, and that is, protect innocent life and preserve public order (*Hague IV*); *October 18, 1907, Annex, Section III*."

55 ICISS, *The Responsibility to Protect*, viii.

56 Himes, "A Job Half Done," 65–66.

serve order and prevent possible abuses, contributing to the vanquished state in repairing the basic infrastructure of society. Himes argues that with such an infrastructure in place, citizens of that vanquished state are then able to begin to restore life *post bellum* and thus to create a space for civil society. Himes continues, "the principle of establishing civil society complements the principle of restoration by extending 'basic infrastructure' to include not just the material infrastructure of roads, electricity, and communication but the human infrastructure for peaceful communal life."[57] Therefore, for Himes, postwar reconstruction programs without this principle of rebuilding a civil society would fail not only to repair the destruction of wars but also would unsuccessfully restore the structural components whose absence created the initial need for hostilities.

Plainly, Himes's Thomistic vision of the establishment of a civil society, especially with regard to building legitimate authority, calls upon Aquinas's just war rationale of defending the common good. This emphasis on the common good would further set up human laws in *jpb* contexts that determine the responsibilities of the legitimate sovereign—we call them the responsibilities of the government today—to provide for citizens.

With this preliminary proposition in mind, Himes argues that restoring the legitimate public order is the first and foremost task in the aftermath of war. Himes focuses on building the organization of "police and judicial institutions" for the purpose of creating "the necessary social space . . . for men and women to begin the work of restoring public life."[58] For Himes, restoring public life constitutes restoring a secure and true peace. This peace "requires the establishment of public order that ratifies basic human rights."[59] In other words, creating the necessary social space means building a just social order that fulfills basic human rights. This proposal not only signifies his *jpb* thinking as reflected by humanitarian norms, but it also guides legitimate authority for the benefit of common people, not for the business of a private individual. With the example of the Second Gulf War, Himes clarifies the importance of local consensus: "It is not American pride or interests or arrogance, but Iraqi well-being that ought to be the main focus of the conversation. That is the moral imperative to be served. The United States should do all it can to see that a political

---

57 Himes, "The Case of Iraq and the Just War Tradition."
58 Himes, "Intervention, Just War, and U.S. National Security," 156.
59 Himes, 155.

regime legitimated by the approval of a majority of Iraqis assumes sovereign authority promptly."[60]

What is at stake here is that Himes develops his principle of establishing civil society that aims "to enhance the well-being of [local] people rather than punish[ing] or vanquish[ing] [the vanquished]."[61] This is his forward-looking humanitarian *jpb* vision for *post bellum* actors whose responsibility is to promote rehabilitation for the vanquished, not to foster or allow revenge against them.

The Strength of Himes's Thomistic Approach to *Jus Post Bellum*

Similar to Schuck's understanding of Augustinian right intention, Himes's Thomistic right intention must be considered within the framework of Christian thought that God is "the ultimate good," which just actors seek as an end since human beings seek to mirror God's goodness.[62] In *jpb* practices, then, like Aquinas, Himes demands of just actors that they reflect on the object of their good will when they respond to a threat in order to secure a peace ordered to the common good.[63] As discussed earlier, Aquinas places justice, as one of the cardinal virtues, within the realm of the will (action).[64] This Thomistic justice is directed toward one's relation with other human

---

60 Himes, "A Job Half Done," 65–66.

61 Himes, "Intervention, Just War, and U.S. National Security," 156.

62 See Davies, *Thomas Aquinas on God and Evil*, chaps. 6 and 8. I cited Davies's work in relation to Himes's Thomistic approach to *jpb*. However, one may argue that Davies's approach cannot fully represent Himes's Thomistic right intention. For example, contemporary Thomistic CST would not explicitly say that actors have to intend (Christian) God to be just. Still, Davies's approach is effective at a narrow level since all good wills are originated from God's goodness, at least in the Christian tradition where Himes and Aquinas belong. Yet, Himes's approach must also be understood at a broad level. Since Vatican II, the Church has taken a position on theology and ethics similar to or inspired by that of Karl Rahner's famous dictum: "love of neighbor is love of God." Plainly, all those who strive to love their neighbor and act justly are indirectly testifying to the presence of God in their lives, even if they are not believers. The magisterial anchors for this are *Nostra Aetate* and *Dominus Iesus*. But also note how John XXIII appeals to "all men of good will" for his vision of justice; and contemporary Catholic political thought or its related social teaching discusses the universal common good, dignity of the person, and mutual rights and duties—referring to all peoples and societies, not just Christians. Justice and adherence to justice (or even love for that matter) are not assumed to require a religious basis or intention. Therefore, it is necessary for people of good will to forge an overall concept of *jpb* to protect human dignity and life. Vatican Council II, *Gaudium et Spes*, December 7, 1965.

63 For Himes's understanding of right intention in Catholic political theory, see Himes, "Humanitarian Intervention and Catholic Political Thought," 166–69.

64 *ST*, I-II, q.60, a. 2–3.

beings, and signifies an idea of the common good in light of *communal* humanitarian norms such as *equally granted* human dignity, *equally seeking* human happiness, and *equally guaranteed* human security.[65] As the Thomistic tradition emphasizes, there is an intrinsic relationship between justice and the common good. Himes also sees this integral tie between justice and the common good that is a common thread of his *jpb* thinking; his reflection on justice and its object, the common good, has something to teach about the moral legitimacy of political authority and the conditions for fulfilling *jpb*. This is different from Schuck's Augustinian right intention, which primarily focuses on each individual just actor's *internal* intention in war.

More distinctively, Himes understands this peace as a political peace "that is within the grasp of human possibility."[66] This peace is distinct from an eschatological peace, or "a distant goal for the end time." It is also not like the internal peace, which is "achieved by knowing one's self to be in right relationship with one's Creator." Rather, as Himes emphasizes, "political peace is the construction of an exterior space through institutions and practices that permit men and women to live together, if not as a community of faith, then at least as a properly human community."[67] In this respect, Himes concludes that the postwar society should rest on a *just political* order, whereby everyone should have *basic security*—to be equally free, equally protected against violence and morbidity, and have equally good opportunity to develop their competencies and capabilities. For him, establishing this just political order means achieving a political peace *post bellum*. It secures the vanquished people's civilization and their civility, and is the basis for healing their broken, divided, and unstable society, as reflected in his argument for institutional therapy. In this civil society, as he emphasizes, humans are equally free. This freedom is characterized as the opportunity and capacity to function rationally and purposefully and to develop human capabilities and institutional capacities for the common good.

A major strength of Himes' understanding of just cause in *jpb* thinking is his clarity. First, unlike Schuck whose *jpb* concern is limited to the just war discourse of right intention, Himes takes a more comprehensive approach to *jpb*. He develops his *jpb* thinking from Aquinas's just war principles in order to recover the just order of society for the common good.

65 *ST*, II-II, q.57, a.1.
66 Himes, "A Job Half Done," 65–66.
67 Himes.

This approach illuminates the *jus ad bellum* objectives that must secure the common good in postwar societies. Second, unlike Schuck, whose *jpb* concern is sought in a postwar context when just actors ask how to morally govern their actions after war, Himes's concern is sought in a prewar context, thus looking for the usefulness of *jpb* moral considerations. For him, because *jpb* precedes peace, it is worth noting that implementing *jpb* affects the quality of peace. Emphasizing that bad peace agreements sow the seeds for future war, Himes believes futile peace agreements that reaffirm the status quo only bring us back to the precarious position we were in before war and that unclear postwar situations deter combatants from standing down.[68] Third, in the course of explicating his account of a *jpb* ethic, Himes elucidates some of the nascent elements of *jpb* ethics that are present in the JWT: humanitarian intervention and rebuilding postwar societies, with prevention being the primary concern. Finally, Himes clarifies what constitutes the just cause, and which causes ought to be just causes in light of contemporary warfare issues. Like Aquinas, he sees that war is just as long as it is carried out by a legitimate authority for the common good, whether it be for self-defense or humanitarian intervention. Other *jpb* theologians and philosophers do not clarify what these just causes are. Despite his clarification of right intention defined as seeking a just peace, Schuck does not clarify the difference between right intention and just cause. Likewise, Brian Orend conflates just cause with right intention, claiming, "a state may go to war only with the intention of upholding its just cause."[69] Although Allman and Winright emphasize the importance of the just cause principle, their discourse is limited to the question of how this just cause, especially with regard to its *post bellum* context, works all the way through the entire phase of warfare.[70] However, unlike Himes, they do not clearly define what these just causes are, especially in light of the contemporary warfare issues.

All in all, Himes argues that while just actors—the armed forces in particular—focus on the period immediately after war has ended (usually addressed as part of the exit strategy) and bear some responsibility for this

---

68 Himes, "Humanitarian Intervention and Catholic Political Thought," 154–55.

69 Brian Orend, "Kant's Ethics of War and Peace," *Journal of Military Ethics* 3, no. 2 (2004): 161–77.

70 In particular, Allman and Winright argue for three requirements to make this just cause principle effective from the *ad bellum* to the *post bellum* phase: accountability, a means of restraint, and proportionality. See Allman and Winright, *After the Smoke Clears*, 85–89.

period, *post bellum* responsibilities further fall on the larger civil society, that of both the vanquished and vanquishing states. Himes, however, also offers a cautionary word. Just actors involved in armed intervention have *post bellum* moral responsibilities toward vulnerable people but must be aware that there are always limits to what they can do for the vanquished. For example, Himes points out these limits, as found in the Second Gulf War: "Stability, democracy, and prosperity—such hopes and goals are estimable. But how realistic? Iraq is rife with ethnic leaders who would see the end of Hussein as an opportunity to promote their particular faction's agenda not build a nation."[71] This astute recognition of the limit of *jpb* practices not only signifies the incongruity between political ideals and realities, but it also implies that just actors' intervention contains the possibility of its own destruction in the illusions they hold, whether for humanitarian or other purposes. Therefore, just actors should be equipped with the ability to see through such illusions as a condition for avoiding the worst pitfalls they face. Himes does not develop this concern in depth, but as we will see in the next section, Allman and Winright revisit this issue as they discuss their just cause principle in relation to Reinhold Niebuhr's Christian realism.

Mark Allman and Tobias Winright's Niebuhrian *Jus Post Bellum*: Imperfectly Just War

A Holistic Approach and Imperfect Justice

Mark Allman and Tobias Winright wrote one of the few relatively recent theological book-length treatments of *jpb*, titled *After The Smoke Clears*. A major strength of this *jpb* work is its comprehensiveness. In surveying the current *jpb* literature, the authors analyze various thinkers in philosophy, political science, and international relations. In particular, these two coauthors uncover nascent elements of *jpb* throughout the JWT, while extending the *jpb* discourse with diverse contemporary interlocutors including contemporary *jpb* philosophers such as Brian Orend, as well as just peacemaking theologians such as Glen Stassen. The authors then make a claim that they understand this *jpb* ethic from a broader perspective of the Christian JWT, sympathetic toward both just peacekeeping and just policing, as well as the US Catholic Bishops' pastoral letter *The Challenge of Peace*.[72] With

71 Himes, "The Case of Iraq and the Just War Tradition."
72 For details, see Allman and Winright, *After the Smoke Clears*, 9–11.

this *jpb* project, they intend to focus their wider research concerns into two primary areas: a holistic approach and imperfect justice. In this section, I will first discuss what their holistic *jpb* approach constitutes and how it guides their four *jpb* criteria. These criteria are: the just cause principle, the reconciliation phase, the punishment phase, and the restoration phase. For the second part of this section, out of these four criteria, I will pay particular attention to the just cause principle to see the two authors' central argument for Niebuhrian *jpb*, or that which signifies an idea of imperfect justice.

A Holistic Approach to *Jus Post Bellum*: Just Peacemaking Praxes

Similar to Schuck, Allman and Winright see a relationship between right intention and the end of a just war and adopt a holistic approach to *jpb*, that warfare begins and ends with an emphasis on actors' intent of peace. However, the authors distinguish themselves from Schuck. Schuck's holistic approach to *jpb* pursues a just peace as the right intention of a just war. For Schuck, *jpb* is understood within the just war principle of the right intention alone. Whereas Allman and Winright extend their holistic *jpb* approach from the just war discourse of the right intention to a more comprehensive discourse of just peacemaking within both the JWT and Christian pacifism. In particular, they argue that Christian pacifists with just war tendencies are often sympathetic with the norm of R2P, whose primary direction is prevention. They see this shared concern with the responsibility to prevent, in both Christian just war proponents and pacifists. Further, they believe this shared concern has led to just peacemaking practices, which focus on "addressing the root causes of conflict."[73] Despite the fact that the JWT and pacifism disagree about the justifiable use of force, Allman and Winright highlight a point of convergence between the JWT and pacifism, in that both agree that just peacemaking is their primary mission.

More importantly, Allman and Winright see themselves as extending the work of Baptist theologian Glen Stassen, one of the most distinguished just peacemaking theorists. They believe *jpb* is fundamental in order to "propose a more comprehensive and honest just war theory" by emphasizing "that expanding the JWT to encompass *jus post bellum* will actually 'close the loop,' and make for a more honest just war theory by bringing us back to the practices of just peacemaking."[74] In this holistic approach to *jpb*,

73 Allman and Winright, 55.
74 Allman and Wright, 55–56.

Allman and Winright attempt to integrate *jpb* into just peacemaking theories and practices, even as they look to a subtle divergence between *jpb* and just peacemaking praxes in terms of their different theologically rooted criteria. While the overall just peacemaking vision sheds light on theologically rooted criteria for *jus ante bellum* (i.e., the responsibility to prevent), Allman and Winright intend to ultimately root *jpb* in theology. However, despite their awareness of this different orientation, these two authors assert that *jus ante bellum* as a fourth phase must be added to the three phases of just war (*ad*, *in*, and *post bellum*). They propose combining all four phases together as a comprehensive just war theory, or what is further "exemplified by the just peacemaking approach."[75]

Admittedly, however, Allman and Winright's understanding of their *jpb* work as part of a just peacemaking project is controversial. As noted in the beginning of this chapter, just peacemaking theory is not part of the JWT. Despite their argument that Christian actors must be alert peacemakers *ante bellum* and observant adherents to the norms of *jus ad bellum*, *jus in bello*, and *jpb*, these authors also do not provide a clear distinction between *jus ante bellum* and *jus ad bellum*. *Jus ante bellum*, or the responsibility to prevent, is not equal to *jus ad bellum*. Therefore, I think that the authors misunderstand *jpb* in this regard; *jpb* is still part of the JWT, not that of just peacemaking theories.[76]

Further, similar to *jpb*, just peacemaking theories also embrace humanitarian norms. As Eli McCarthy notes, however, these humanitarian norms are not equal to those norms championed by *jpb* due to their counter-potential to use violent direct action. For example, despite its irrelevance to *jpb*, McCarthy's just peace approach provides a vision of human flourishing with emphasis on nonviolent actions to *transform conflict, break cycles of violence, and build more sustainable peace.*[77] Whereas, *jpb* as part of the JWT *discreetly defends its potential to use violent means for peace.* Therefore, it is somewhat inconsistent that Allman and Winright provide a historical review of the JWT in the course of explicating their account of a

---

75 For details, see Allman and Winright, 3–13.

76 This debate is not my main point in this book, and therefore I will not discuss it in detail. However, for details, see Eli S. McCarthy, *Becoming Nonviolent Peacemakers: A Virtue Ethic for Catholic Social Teaching and U.S. Policy* (Eugene: Wipf and Stock, 2012); Maryann Cusimano Love, "What Kind of Peace Do We Seek?" in *Peacebuilding: Catholic Theology, Ethics, and Praxis*, ed. Robert J. Schreiter, R. Scott Appleby, and Gerard F. Powers (Maryknoll, NY: Orbis Books, 2010).

77 For details, see McCarthy, *Becoming Nonviolent Peacemakers*.

jpb ethic, while exploring some of the nascent elements of *jpb* ethics that are present in a just peacemaking theory.[78]

A Holistic Approach to *Jus Post Bellum*: Four Phases of *Jus Post Bellum*

With this holistic approach—despite its inconsistent and puzzling attitude toward making *jpb* a part of a just peacemaking project—Allman and Winright intend to focus their wider research concerns into four areas that they call "the four phases of *jpb*." These are the just cause principle, the reconciliation phase, the punishment phase, and the restoration phase. They posit these four phases, which they often interchangeably call "categories" and argue they are "consistent with the Christian JWT" and necessary for a just peace after war.[79] Under the heading of just cause, Allman and Winright include three distinct requirements: "accountability," "a means of restraint," and "proportionality." In other words, they are holding just actors accountable for the accomplishment of the initial goals of the war, restraining the actors from expanding these goals, and preventing "overly zealous *post bellum* responses," such as vengeance in postwar societies. Allman and Winright find that in these three requirements "the logic is simple and clear: the end of a just war must be accomplishing the objectives that served the grounds for going to war in the first place."[80]

As to reconciliation, the authors argue for restorative justice from the Christian perspective, that a just and lasting peace cannot be realized without transforming the relationships of the belligerents from animosity, fear, and hatred to tolerance. They emphasize that "this phrase [of reconciliation] is not about cheap grace or taking a forgive-and-forget approach." Rather, the goal of reconciliation is "justice tempered by mercy."[81] They believe that this notion of justice is rooted in the Christian tradition, and thus that the *jpb* work of the reconciliation phase would benefit from the theological discourse of reconciliation and restorative justice championed by Christian humanists such as John de Gruchy, as well as theologians such as Robert Schreiter and Charles Villa-Vicencio.

Regarding the third *jpb* phase, Allman and Winright explore the value of punishment in establishing justice, accountability, and restitution as they

---

78 For details, see Allman and Winright, *After the Smoke Clears*, 21–66.
79 Allman and Winright, 85.
80 Allman and Winright, 100.
81 Allman and Winright, 14.

focus their wider concerns on two practices: compensation and war crimes tribunals. With regard to compensation, they pay particular attention to the symbolic importance of reparations. They emphasize that "reparations require a reversal of power. Those who once were dominant are now in a submissive/vulnerable position" in relation to those who were once power-less.[82] They view reparations as part of the power dynamics in postwar societies. The authors adopt a generic approach to understand war crimes tribunals. The just actors, whether they are victors or the international com-munity, need the tribunals in order to bring war criminals to justice through trials for belligerents on both sides suspected of having violated the law of armed conflict.

Finally, Allman and Winright propose a restoration phase in the *post bellum* context. Under the phase of restoration, they assert that there must be restoration of all "political, economic, social and ecological conditions that will allow all citizens to flourish."[83] To satisfy these conditions, basic security must be (re)established, and secondly, just actors will help secure political reforms enacted to preclude any return to the status quo *ante bellum*. For Allman and Winright, these political reforms must accompany economic, social, and ecological reforms. This means that all actors involved in the phase of restoration, such as the victors, the international community, and the local government, must ensure the economic recovery of the vanquished, provide for the needs of the war's most socially vulnerable victims (e.g., war orphans and widows), and clean up military sites, environmental dangers, and poten-tial hazards that resulted from the battlefield and warfare operations.

Just Cause Principle: Imperfect Justice

Having introduced Allman and Winright's own *jpb* proposal, especially with regard to their four *jpb* criteria, I now treat at greater length their just cause principle as it is the most pertinent principle for the project at hand. For Allman and Winright, the other three criteria "are the natural consequences of the just cause principle and are best characterized by phases."[84] More importantly, this just cause principle is central to the authors' understanding of justice, further demonstrating their key *jpb* concept of "imperfect justice." In their argument, this principle is contrasted with Orend's heavy emphasis

---

82 Allman and Winright, 13.

83 Allman and Winright, 15.

84 Allman and Winright, 101.

on just cause and his ethical purism principle. For the rest of this section, I will present these two authors' just cause principle. I will then examine how the just cause principle is rooted in the authors' Niebuhrian thought as I introduce their critique of Orend's just cause, which is distinct from their own version of the just cause principle.

A central merit of positing a *post bellum* just cause principle—together with its closely related *ad bellum* just cause principle—is that it contributes to highlighting the importance of the relationship of the phases of war (*ad bellum, in bello,* and *post bellum*). This matter was first brought up by Orend and Walzer, and later Allman and Winright compared their approaches. They see Orend's work as representative of a rigid association of the phases of war; whereas, for Walzer, it is a loose association.[85] To put it differently, Orend argues that if there is an unfair behavior in any of the three stages, the outcome will be an unjust war; whereas, for Walzer, an unjust war may lead to a just outcome.

On the one hand, Allman and Winright affirm that Orend offers a more nuanced approach than Walzer, primarily because the three phases of war (*ad bellum, in bello,* and *post bellum*) cannot be treated in isolation of one another—they are generally interrelated. In other words, Allman and Winright accept a rigid association between each of the three phases: they assert that to fail in one area generally leads to a moral failure of the entire just cause principle. In this regard, Orend's approach specifically reminds them of how their *jpb* just cause principle is closely related to the *jus ad bellum* just cause principle. Further, Allman and Winright illustrate what they discern throughout all three phases of just cause principles as they offer a practical illustration of how the just cause principle might work. In *post bellum* practice, they note, "having a publicly declared *post bellum* plan in place before the shooting starts is essential to create an environment in which the nearly vanquished will see surrender as a viable option."[86] In other words, in accord with Orend's approach, Allman and Winright encourage just actors to set out *post bellum* schemes in advance. This initiative at least begins the process of thinking about *post bellum* issues before the war begins.

On the other hand, Allman and Winright find the practical implications of the just cause principle problematic because no one can accurately predict war. Emphasizing that "war is a Pandora's box," they affirm that warfare is

---

85 For details, see Allman and Winright, 90–91.
86 Allman and Winright, 89–91.

dynamic as it changes in response to other political circumstances and legal constraints, such as the entrance of other nations in the middle of war, the challenges of natural disasters during war, and the change of public support for war.[87] These unexpected conditions may change the efficacy of just actors' practices, their corresponding interests—including just causes—and strategies, and ultimately, the entire war. For example, one may wonder if just actors are still morally and legally accountable to their *post bellum* claims made prior to the war when other nations join the fight during the course of the war. This inquiry is not just about a practical implication of the just cause principle but highlights the dynamic, flexible, and realistic nature of war. Allman and Winright find that Orend's way of thinking is limited because his approach of associating the phases of war is *too* rigid. This excessive rigidity ignores practical concerns.

Allman and Winright are critically aware not only of these practical concerns, but also their root causes. In fact, exploring these root causes is Allman and Winright's ultimate concern in their entire *jpb* work, as well as their first criterion of the just cause principle. As we will see in the following section, this task deeply relates to their understanding of justice in their *jpb* ethic. In particular, they express these root causes in two primary areas, as shown in their critique of Orend, including his (i) heavy emphasis on the *jus ad bellum* criterion of just cause and (ii) ethical purism.[88] Despite their partial agreement with Orend that the three phases of war must be interrelated, these two critical departures serve as a cornerstone for the foundation of Allman and Winright's account of a *post bellum* just cause principle.

First, Orend does not merely seek to link the three phases of war, but he prioritizes the *jus ad bellum* criterion of just cause by making all the other just war criteria categorically contingent upon it. Orend uses analogies of a virus and "the crucial opening notes [of a musical performance] that set the tone for all that follows" in order to illustrate the polluting effects of a faulty just cause.[89] Therefore, for him, the *jus ad bellum* criterion of just cause is the overarching criterion for the whole warfare ethic. As discussed in chapter one, Allman and Winright also see that this way of thinking is rooted in Kantian thought: "[just actors] must declare how they intend to prosecute a war from start to finish before the first shot is fired. Orend's insistence (and, for that

---

87 Allman and Winright, 93.
88 Allman and Winright, 94–96.
89 For details, see Orend, *The Morality of War*, 49, 162–65.

matter, Kant's) that *jus post bellum* be fully considered in the *ad bellum* phase makes for a more honest just war theory."[90] Allman and Winright see this one absolute criterion as problematic because it "reduces the other criteria to sub-servient roles, which only supports the all-too-common abuse of just war thinking [. . .] wherein the totality of just war theory is reduced to [the *jus ad bellum*] just cause."[91] Simply put, Orend's heavy emphasis on the *jus ad bellum* criterion of just cause does not allow for any exceptional cases. In contrast, Allman and Winright argue that the criteria of all the phases of just cause are equally important and relevant. More precisely, despite the fact that they argue for the just cause principle as the first criterion to consider, they ultimately affirm the equal importance of all the criteria to make the *jpb* complete. This is different from Orend's Kantian deontological idea that the *jus ad bellum* just cause is virtually the sole criterion.

Second, as a practical concern, Allman and Winright emphasize that Orend's approach to *jpb* as representative of a rigid association of the phases of war is inadequate. They regard Orend as an ethical purist. His ethical purism is a direct consequence of his understanding of justice in *post bellum* circumstances. This justice is achieved only when actors first fulfill the *ad bellum* criteria, and then the *in bello* and *post bellum* ones. However, Allman and Winright argue that this moral execution of war would be impossible in practice: "Concerning Orend's assertion that 'if a war fails to meet the *ad bellum* criteria (especially just cause), then it cannot be *jus in bello* or *post bellum*,' . . . we respond that while this position may make sense in a purely academic setting or in a theoretical discussion, it is nonetheless too rigid to hold in practice and it has the potential for disastrous results."[92]

In fact, Orend's intellectual forefather, Kant, is often regarded as an eth-ical purist who was never seriously tempted by empiricism. According to Kant, moral agents should perform the right act from duty; that is, they should recognize that the moral law demands a certain act, and thus they should perform that act because of that recognition. However, when they perform the right action, if they are motivated by other practical concerns such as self-interest, then their act must have no moral worth. In other words, Kant is concerned with encouraging moral agents to foster the right intentions, as well as performing the right act.

---

90 Allman and Winright, *After the Smoke Clears*, 93.
91 Allman and Winright, 95.
92 Allman and Winright, 95.

It seems to Allman and Winright that Orend adopts an ethical framework similar to Kant's. For example, Orend does not believe that an actor's decision to fulfill the *jus ad bellum* criterion of just cause for practical reasons is a genuine moral action because this act, however right it might be, lacks the right motivation. What ethical purists like Orend might be overlooking is that individuals also have duties to others, in addition to the duties they have to themselves. I am not simply arguing against Orend by claiming that just actors must be consequentialists, who primarily focus on the outcome of actions and policies rather than the intentions of the actors. Rather, I argue that his ethical purism has a tendency to pay too much attention to an actor's own right intention, while overlooking the practical reality of war that just actors must deal with. In the actual reality of war, just actors must strive for justice while facing other moral and political agents such as their enemies, allied forces, domestic supporters and contenders, as well as the international community and the target population to be protected from violence. Likewise, Allman and Winright conclude that while Orend's ethical purism may be theoretically satisfying in a way, it does not correspond well with practical reality.

Allman and Winright's Niebuhrian Approach to *Jus Post Bellum*

This failure to comport with practical reality is the most critical problem that Allman and Winright find with Orend's ethical purism. They suggest an alternative, drawing upon the Christian realist Reinhold Niebuhr's notion of imperfect justice. They argue, "a dose of [Niebuhr's Christian] realism takes just war theory out of the ivory tower and brings it down into the mud and blood of human existence."[93] Niebuhr believed that humankind lives in a complicated and fallen world, so we often do not get to choose between good and evil but rather between evil and still greater evil. He adds, "human happiness in ordinary intercourse is determined by the difference between a little more and a little less justice, . . . between varying degrees of imaginative insight with which the self enters the life and understands the interests of the neighbor."[94] Niebuhr's attitude relates to his description of human nature as finite, and he extends his idea that the politics people create are also bound to be characterized by finitude. Hence, people cannot make decisions on the basis of the pursuit of complete and absolute justice.

---

93 Allman and Winright, 95.
94 Reinhold Niebuhr, *An Interpretation of Christian Ethics* (New York: Seabury Press, 1979), 62.

However, for Allman and Winright, this Christian realist account is neither as apologetic nor as pessimistic as it sounds. Rather, Allman and Winright assert that Niebuhrian realism's emphasis on the need for humility is welcome and much needed, a similar point to one Schuck and Himes highlighted in their *jpb* discussions. Recognizing humility helps just actors evaluate the deliberative processes they use and the limitations of their moral deliberations. This holistic approach is well summarized by ethicist John D. Carlson:"[Just war thought] needs to concern itself with not only the deliberation and conduct of war but also with war's aftermath, an observation picked up by some just war thinkers in their discussion of *jus post bellum*. What Christian realism lacks in its deliberative precision, it regains in a comprehensive approach to the morality of war."[95]

In addition to emulating Niebuhr's imperfect justice, Allman and Winright draw upon the phrases of John Dilulio (e.g., "tolerably just"), John Langan (e.g., "imperfectly just"), and Mark Evans (e.g., "suboptimal acceptable peace") in order to bolster their notion of imperfect justice.[96] Despite a slightly different nuance, all these notions imply a "sliding scale" of just war. According to Allman and Winright, on the high end of the scale would be a perfectly just war, one that satisfies all the just war criteria in all phases of war. On the low end of the scale would be the perfectly unjust war, one that fails all just war criteria in every phase of the war. In between these two extremes are imperfectly just and unjust wars. The imperfectly just war fulfils "*jus ad bellum* with only minor isolated violations of *jus in bello* and *jus post bellum*." In contrast, the unjust war is a war "that fails to meet all *jus ad bellum* criteria" or "that satisfies jus ad bellum, but systematically violates jus in bello and/or ignores *jus post bellum*."[97] Thus, the authors aim for imperfectly just wars.

With emphasis on this notion of imperfect justice, Allman and Winright criticize Orend's ethical purism and subsequently, his excessively rigid just cause principle. They confirm their own Christian realist brand of just cause principle for *jpb*: "A war that fails to meet the *jus ad bellum* requirements, but observes the *in bello* restraints and fulfills the *post bellum* responsibilities does not turn an unjust war into a just war, but it does make it less

---

95 John D. Carlson, "Is There a Christian Realist Theory of War and Peace? Reinhold Niebuhr and Just War Thought," *Journal of the Society of Christian Ethics* 28, no. 1 (2008): 154.

96 For details, see Allman and Winright, *After the Smoke Clears*, 96–97.

97 Allman and Winright, 98.

unjust than it would have been if the *in bello* and *post bellum* obligations had been ignored."[98] Like Orend, Allman and Winright emphasize a close relationship between the various phases of war. Unlike Orend, they recognize that perfect justice is not possible on this side of the eschaton. Orend's pursuit of perfect justice is understood as an attempt to bring a completely idealistic justice and peace to the earthly world. As Niebuhrian just war thinkers, Allman and Winright argue that complete justice and perfect peace can be reached in heaven, but not on earth. In other words, for Allman and Winright, it is impossible to authentically immanentize or fully bring about the eschaton in the temporal world. However, as their sliding scale indicates, there are better and worse instances of "imperfect justice." On that account, "'imperfect justice' is not synonymous with 'unjust,'" for it is still a form of justice.[99]

Further, similar to Schuck, Allman and Winright are fully aware of the limit of *jpb* practice, mainly due to their understanding of human finitude. This notion is shared with Schuck's Augustinian notion of sin in one's pride: "[We] do not live in the City of God. Ours is a world mired in sin, suffering, and violence."[100] But also, they argue that *jpb* is best understood within the frame of Niebuhr's Christian realism. In other words, there is no perfect justice, and therefore, achieving justice in a complete and idealistic sense is unattainable by humans due to human finitude. Consequently, there are no perfectly just wars, no perfect *jpb*, only striving for relative justice, the attainable approximation of perfect justice in an imperfect world: "While [our world] is also home to the growing reign of God, a world of perfect justice and love has not yet been firmly established. It is what we hope for. In the meantime, our ethics must balance the ideal with the real."[101]

In this understanding, therefore, the intent behind *jpb* is to limit what virtually all agree is evil, or that which represents the greater of two evils. In other words, Allman and Winright are not rigid *jpb* maximalists. Rather, they are loose maximalists as they note the minimalist structure of much of this *post bellum* work and seek to offer a more theologically and morally robust account of postwar ethics. As a result, they base their *jpb* studies on the grounds that "the goal of a war must be to establish social, political and

---

98 Allman and Winright, 98.

99 Allman and Winright.

100 Allman and Winright, 100–101.

101 Allman and Winright, 101.

economic conditions that are more stable, more just and less prone to chaos than existed prior to the fighting."[102] Therefore, on the one hand, Allman and Winright are clearly *jpb* maximalists who argue that just actors will inherit substantial obligations to the citizens of the defeated state. On the other hand, they are loose maximalists, or what I call "Niebuhrian maximalists," who assert that just actors will recognize the limit of their human conditions and *jpb* practices, and thus that they will discreetly manage their *post bellum* work to comport with practical reality.

Finally, moral theologians such as Allman and Winright are generally viewed as being *jpb* maximalists while not absolutely neglecting minimalist positions, but attempting to guide just actors in attaining balanced views. For example, Allman and Winright's belief that an account of imperfect justice serves to temper sycophantic and overzealous postwar expectations and allows for degrees of *jpb*. In fact, this argument for seeking balanced views is not novel in the Christian just war discourse. Like Allman and Winright, many Church leaders as well as Christian realists attempt to guide just actors in holding such a balanced view, while recognizing the limit of just war measures. For example, Pope John Paul II argues that while just actors have a responsibility "to take concrete measures to disarm the aggressor," these measures "must be limited in time and precise in their aims."[103] Pope Francis notices that the decision for armed intervention is fraught with difficult judgments; it is always questionable whether (and if so, how) a presumptive (*prima facie*) moral responsibility—that just actors must intervene for the sake of the victimized population—is translated into the actual practice of intervention.[104] However, Allman and Winright are distinct from these Church leaders—and other *jpb* theologians whom I have examined in this chapter—since the two authors illuminate the limits of these measures, particularly in *jpb* practices, not just overall just war practices.

CONCLUSION

In this chapter, we discussed four major approaches to the study of human security that emerge from the theological development of *jpb* ethics. They are (i) the Church's response to the norm of R2P; (ii) Schuck's Augustinian *jpb* approach, with emphasis on pursuing right intention; (iii) Himes's Tho-

---

102 For details, see Allman and Winright, 12–14.
103 John Paul II, "Peace on Earth to Those Whom God Loves," 11.
104 Francis Rocca, "Pope Talks Airstrikes in Iraq."

mistic *jpb* approach thoroughly developed within the JWT, especially right intention, just cause, and legitimate authority; and (iv) Allman and Winright's Niebuhrian *jpb* approach reflected in a just cause principle signifying imperfect justice.

By analyzing these approaches, I intended to express their wider research concerns in four common areas. First, they find that just actors have growing *jpb* concerns, especially in light of the heightened frequency of humanitarian crises *post bellum* over the past decades. In response, just actors have increasingly brought attention to R2P, especially its corresponding humanitarian intervention endeavors. Second, they highlight the relationship among the phases of war (*ad bellum*, *in bello*, and *post bellum*) to see how *jpb* concerns may inform just actors' understanding of a proper relationship among the phases of war. This holistic approach to *jpb* expands just actors' moral sensibilities concerning the ethical use of force. Third and most importantly, all these approaches emphasize the importance of human security, as shown by their arguments for building humanitarian norms, a rehabilitation model, and local consensus. In particular, Himes's Thomistic approach clearly proposes that the establishment of a just peace must be directed toward human security. Himes argues that while just actors, and the armed forces in particular, tend to focus on the period immediately after war's end and bear some responsibility for this period, *post bellum* responsibilities further fall on the larger civil society of both the vanquished and vanquishing states. This approach forefronts a political peace ordered to the common good, aiming to protect the lives of every individual, especially those most vulnerable. Finally, at the same time, these thinkers recognize the limit of *jpb*, as found in their attempts to guide just actors in holding such a balanced view while recognizing the insufficiency of just war measures. Schuck, Himes, and Allman and Winright are all loose maximalists of *jpb* who argue that just actors should recognize the limit of their human conditions and *jpb* practices, and thus that they should discreetly manage their *post bellum* work to comport with practical reality.

Chapter 4

Moral Theology of *Jus Post Bellum*: Political Reconciliation

INTRODUCTION
Political Reconciliation:
Distinguishing Transitional Justice and Postwar Justice

The previous chapter discussed the central theme of human security that emerges from the theological development of *jpb* ethics. In addition to this theme, the discourse of postwar justice includes the theme of reconciliation. Do just actors need to make a commitment to embrace the vanquished enemies as well as keep them safe? Plainly, a basic question should be whether postwar societies can have human security *without* any reconciliation. UN Security Council Resolution 1325 on gender-based crimes after peace accords have been signed specifically addresses the fact that lower-level conflict will continue if the adversaries continue to view each other in the same terms. Hence, there is no true human security. Fifty percent of conflict resolutions break into violence again for precisely this reason.[1] Therefore, political reconciliation has to coexist with human security at least a basic level. In fact, as we have learned so far, the moral theologians examined here often agree on political reconciliation as part of the *post bellum* duty, generally because such reconciliation, being often tempered by mercy, helps the vanquished people mend the brokenness in their lives. However, a question remains as to whether political reconciliation is *primarily* necessary for *jpb*. If actors fail to achieve political reconciliation in the aftermath of a war, then does that failure constitute an injustice?

Few theologians provide a clear answer to this question in light of just war ethics. Yet, several recent attempts explore the notion of political reconciliation within the JWT, including moral theologian Anna Floerke Scheid's restorative justice project, as well as Allman and Winright's second

---

1 For details, see Radhika Coomaraswamy, *Preventing Conflict, Transforming Justice, Securing the Peace: A Global Study on the Implementation of UNSCR 1325* (New York: UN Women, 2015).

principle of *jpb*. To be fair, some major theologians, such as the former South African TRC research director Charles Villa-Vicencio, explore what political reconciliation means to post-conflict societies. Other Christian leaders and theologians, such as Alan Torrance, Miroslav Volf, Robert Schreiter, and Pope John Paul II, attempt to delineate what theological elements constitute reconciliation in political realms. However, most of these theologians' discussions are primarily bound to the discourse of transitional justice, not postwar justice, and address issues of political reconciliation outside the JWT. As emphasized consistently throughout this book, some *jpb* discussions involve a wider set of postwar issues but have not addressed them in depth. Therefore, the rest of this book maintains to delineate the boundary, from a theological perspective, between transitional justice and *jpb*.

In relation to this task, I must address two points for clarification. First, one may argue that sometimes it is hard to distinguish *jpb* from transitional justice, since they coincide in certain areas, as in the case of Argentina after the Falklands War (1982) or other dictatorships that first repressed their own citizens and then started wars.[2] Even these complex case examples should be carefully examined by defining how to set the stage for each *jpb* and transitional justice in the practice of peacebuilding—as well as when to transition from *jpb* to transitional justice, or vice versa. *Jpb* is not antithetical to transitional justice, but they are placed on a different stage or phase in practice that will be further discussed in the last three chapters.

Second, one may ask why this book relies on Daniel Philpott's notion of political reconciliation. In other words, one may wonder if there is a significant difference between how Philpott uses political reconciliation and how the aforementioned theologians use it. For example, like Philpott, Villa-Vicencio explicitly uses the term political reconciliation to promote transitional justice. For him, transitional justice intends political reconciliation, of which the prime purpose is "co-existence" per se, but not necessarily the

---

2 Like the case of the Falklands War, the distinction between *jpb* and transitional justice is not always clear. Part of the problem is that transitional justice means different concepts across disciplines. It could concern the broad question of what justice is in contexts like the aftermath of a transition from war, autocracy, or both. It could also mean an approach to past injustices that focuses on trials. This is what it meant when the field (esp. international law) first developed in the late 1980s and 1990s. For details, see Paige Arthur, "How 'Transitions' Reshaped Human Rights: A Conceptual History of Transitional Justice," *Human Rights Quarterly* 31 (2009): 321–67; and Ruti G. Teitel, "Transitional Justice Genealogy," *Harvard Human Rights Journal* 16 (2003): 69–94.

restoration of relationships. The latter for Villa-Vicencio is a desideratum but not a necessary condition of political reconciliation.[3] For example, he criticizes his friend Archbishop Desmond Tutu in South Africa's TRC for conceiving of political reconciliation as large-scale interpersonal reconciliation in which there was an acknowledgment of the victims' harms/feelings with a combination of the offenders taking responsibility and attempting to right their wrongs. In contrast, Philpott's understanding of political reconciliation endorses the importance of the restoration of relationships, as similarly emphasized in Tutu's TRC approach. However, this distinction will not be further investigated in this chapter. Instead, three points should be noted: (i) the notion of political reconciliation used in this book relies on Philpott's understanding of political reconciliation. This is not only because his work is acknowledged across disciplines, but also because some theologians like Anna Scheid use his ethic of political reconciliation in order to build a theological work for *jpb*. Further, Villa-Vicencio's work is solely built upon a particular local context for transitional justice. Moreover, no theologians have employed his work for *jpb*. (ii) I see the difference between Philpott and Villa-Vicencio as not based on a type, but a degree. Philpott also admits that the restoration of relationships is not always necessary for political reconciliation. And (iii), like Philpott's work, and even more so, Villa-Vicencio's research is conducted for the argument of transitional justice. However, unlike Villa-Vicencio, Philpott expands his discussion to include *post bellum* cases and concerns. For the sake of focus in this book, I aim to distinguish postwar justice from transitional justice but not to distinguish among the different branches of transitional justice.

Therefore, this chapter excludes theologians who explicitly address political reconciliation for transitional justice *alone*—regardless of their approach to defining and working on transitional justice. Rather, it pays attention to *jpb* theologians, such as Scheid and Allman and Winright, who attempt to discuss issues of political reconciliation within the JWT. In particular, they are interested in the question of political reconciliation, as they attempt to bring a theological idea of reconciliation to the discourse of postwar justice.

This chapter has three main sections. The first section revisits and more carefully reviews Daniel Philpott's discussion of political reconciliation. As

---

3 For details, see Charles Villa-Vicencio, *Walk with Us and Listen* (Washington, DC: Georgetown University Press, 2009).

outlined in the previous chapter, the logic of Philpott's ethic of political reconciliation, even though he is a political scientist, often relies on theological
concepts and helps enrich the *jpb* discourse across disciplines. The second
section discusses *jpb* theologians and their claims about political reconciliation in *post bellum* contexts. In particular, it attends to Scheid and her
approach to *jpb*, called "a consistent ethic of reconciliation." While examining her theological reflection on the role of reconciliation for *jpb*, it compares her work with Philpott's and reviews them to address the reason most
of their arguments are not adequate for *jpb* discourse *within the JWT*. At
the same time, this section includes potential areas where their theological
ideas and resources on the theme of political reconciliation can be developed and incorporated into the discourse of human security, thereby constructing a more balanced *jpb* framework. To resolve these different
approaches, this section suggests an alternative *jpb* approach, namely, a
"maxim(um) of ethical minimalism," balancing concerns for human security with the need for political reconciliation.

DOES POLITICAL RECONCILIATION MATTER TO *JUS POST BELLUM*?

Daniel Philpott's Ethic of Political Reconciliation

A Theological Foundation

Philpott's central question explores the concept of justice in the immediate
wake of mass despoliation, characterized as systematic violations of human
rights. Addressing that question, he first challenges mainstream thought
within political liberalism that is overwhelmingly embedded in current peacebuilding practices endorsed by the UN, the majority of developed countries,
and most of the human rights community. Philpott labels these mainstream
peacebuilding practices as "liberal peace," which urges actors to prioritize the
establishment of liberal institutions and the prosecution of war criminals. In
place of this ideology, he introduces an ethic of political reconciliation rooted
in the three Abrahamic religious traditions (Judaism, Christianity, and Islam);
his central argument is that justice demands political reconciliation.

Philpott addresses two points regarding this ethic of political reconciliation in terms of its relations to liberal peace. First, challenging the advocates of liberal peace, whose interests are in recognizing past wrongs with
an emphasis on punishment for perpetrators and reparations for victims,
he proposes political reconciliation, which means the restoration of right

relationships. This reconciliation encompasses some of the core commitments of liberal peace—such as human rights and restoration of right relationships—yet, it is far more holistic, both in its recognition of the damages that human rights violations and war crimes inflict as well as in the set of restorative practices it proposes. Reconciliation is broader than a liberal peace with respect to restorative justice in three ways: it is "wider in the range of wounds that it redresses, wider in the practices through which it redresses these wounds, and wider in the participants that it involves."[4]

Second, by providing a religion-based account of political reconciliation for discerning justice as right order and for equating right order with right relationships, Philpott ensures that his proposal is not entirely antithetical to liberal peace. Rather, he attempts to reach a moral consensus concerning fundamental human values by rethinking the meaning of justice and its relationship with other moral values, especially a form of political reconciliation rooted in a religious grounding.

At the foundation of his understanding of justice and reconciliation drawn from the three Abrahamic faiths, Philpott's justice is not merely a political creed but a religious aspiration and a moral attitude as it "holds great promise for restoring political orders with disastrous pasts."[5] In *Just and Unjust Peace*, he points out that a theological understanding of reconciliation offers a robust proposal: the core concepts of justice drawn from the Abrahamic rationales are "remarkably deep, broad, and old in religious texts and traditions."[6] He demonstrates how these core concepts of justice are about maintaining right relationships, responding in an appropriate manner to wrong conduct, and restoring a condition of right political relationships to those involved in political injustice. After surveying scriptures of each Abrahamic tradition, Philpott argues that justice commonly means righteousness, defined comprehensively as right relationships between all members of a post-conflict community in all of their affairs. In other words, in the Abrahamic rationales, justice is best understood in relationship to righteousness in a manner, "including but far exceeding judicial norms." Because of this, the concept of righteousness "is often expressed conjointly with the pairing of kindness and mercy as well as with salvation."[7] This

---

4 Philpott, *Just and Unjust Peace*, 72.
5 Philpott, 8.
6 Philpott, 288.
7 Philpott, 124.

understanding demonstrates that reconciliation not only refers to either a
state of right relationship or a process of restoring right relationship but can
be understood as a broad and profound concept of justice. Plainly, it is a
saving justice, an active transformative process that calls for the restoration
of right relationships in the political realm. The Abrahamic traditions highlight that political reconciliation is a component of justice that involves a
restoration of right relationships animated by mercy and peace, which characterizes the resulting state of social harmony.

Abrahamic concepts of peace converge closely with Abrahamic concepts of justice, heightening political reconciliation's status as an element of
peacebuilding as well as of justice. Like justice and righteousness, the Abrahamic tradition's peace must be broadly understood. The Hebrew scripture's
notion of peace, *shalom*, which means "health and prosperity, economic
and political justice, as well as honesty and moral integrity in relations
between persons," corresponds to reconciliation as a state of justice. Here,
Philpott distinguishes this peace from negative peace: "The peace expressed
in *shalom* encompasses far more than the absence of war. *Shalom* means
wholeness . . . ; thus all ethical values are found within *shalom*."[8] It is therefore a quality of God's covenantal right relationship with his people.

Mercy is another concept in the Abrahamic scriptures that resonates
closely with reconciliation. It is reconciliation's revivifying, uplifting, and
vital virtue, as it corresponds to reconciliation as a regenerating process of
justice. This notion of mercy is translated in two ways: *hesed* and *rahamim*.
Hesed, meaning "steady love," entails God's faithfulness to the requirements
of relationships set forth in the covenant; as a broader concept of mercy,
hesed signifies "God's willingness to restore his people after they have been
diminished by the consequences of their sin." *Rahamim*, meaning "a
mother's love for her children," encompasses a willingness to forgive. Philpott uses these terms to construct a more comprehensive concept of mercy
in relation to justice: "Mercy restores justice and realizes it, and, if justice is
much like mercy, then it is a matter of restoring people, relationships, and
communities, just like the restorative dimension of reconciliation."[9]

Philpott pays attention to the Abrahamic scriptures not only in terms
of their linguistic concepts, which bolster an ethic of political reconciliation,
but also in light of their broad narrative account of God's response to evil,

8 Philpott, 126.

9 Philpott, 127.

which is understood as political injustice or wrongdoing.[10] He refers to this evil not only as the Augustinian notion of evil, which is a privation of good, but also as one that breaks "the right relationships that the covenant and its laws sustain," which are especially emphasized in Jewish scripture. God restores his people after they have turned away from him; for example, in Genesis, God restores the world after the great flood and promises Noah that he will never again destroy the earth. In this sense, for Philpott, God's response to evil is, by and large, a restorative response. Further, this restorative justice is God's *active* response to evil, which results in the actual transformation of individuals, relationships, and communities. As an active response, God enacts restorative justice "not in a singular way but through an array of actions, corresponding to the multiple respects in which evil wounds persons, relationships, and communities—much like the practices of political reconciliation."[11]

At the same time, like many aforementioned *jpb* theologians, Philpott is aware of the limit of this divine justice when it is presented to us as political justice. However, unlike theologians who believe that the limit stems from human finitude, Philpott emphasizes that his notion of justice, political reconciliation, often suffers shortcomings and inadequacies because the nature of reconciliation itself is too comprehensive to apply to political realms alone. This critical reflection addresses two key points. First, Philpott acknowledges the limited nature of political reconciliation in practice. Like applications of other political vehicles in the reality of post-conflict societies, especially vanquished ones, practices of political reconciliation are "weakened by political institutions that have been destroyed and then repaired partially."[12] However, recognizing this limit does not mean that Philpott holds a pessimistic outlook, sometimes presented as realism, which is never associated with positive social change; yet he also denies naïve optimism, sometimes presented as idealism, which is more dangerous than it might seem at first.[13] Rather, Philpott calls for an in-between approach, which can

---

10 Philpott uses the term "evil" primarily drawn from the three Abrahamic faiths, but he also attempts to link it to nonreligious thought and discourse by demonstrating that the "problem of evil has been the guiding force of modern thought." For details, see Philpott, *Just and Unjust Peace*, 126–30.

11 Philpott, 130.

12 Daniel Philpott, "Reconciliation: A Catholic Ethic for Peacebuilding in the Political Order," in *Peacebuilding: Catholic Theology, Ethics, and Praxis*, ed. Robert J. Schreiter, R. Scott Appleby, and Gerard F. Powers (Maryknoll, NY: Orbis Books, 2010), 106.

13 For details, see Philpott, *Just and Unjust Peace*, 61.

be termed either realistic idealism or idealistic realism; he recognizes limits, and at the same time, is capable of dreaming.[14] His ethic of political reconciliation is hopeful and energizes others in the struggle for the common good. This ethic recognizes certain complex and painful conditions that follow the end of conflict and serves to diffuse the criticisms of those political institutions or actors *post bellum* who would use it as an excuse to avoid taking less than perfect steps forward.

Second, recognizing these limits clarifies why Philpott is critical of political liberalism for political reconciliation; it is because of liberal peace's overly restrictive distinction between public and private matters that does not allow for religious discourse. His ethic of political reconciliation demands more than bare political coexistence based upon the reciprocal recognition of common political rights. Part of this recognition is the renouncement of violence as a means of resolving disputes. At the same time, because of the expanding, holistic nature of political reconciliation, Philpott is cautious about this comprehensive dimension of the restoration of right relationships with regard to the political order. For Philpott, political reconciliation is essentially different from the fullness of religious reconciliation that will take place in the kingdom of God. Political reconciliation primarily applies to the political realm, which is relevant to citizens, unlike comprehensive reconciliation, which is relevant to all of human life. It is more circumscribed and less ambitious than religious reconciliation. Therefore, although his ethic of political reconciliation has its roots in the three Abrahamic religious traditions, Philpott proposes the possibility of formulating the goals of political reconciliation without having to embrace a theologically substantive account of reconciliation.

Applying to *Jus Post Bellum*

Philpott moves from this theological foundation to articulate his ethic of political reconciliation—how his Abrahamic concepts of justice are enacted in the political order both within states and in relations between states. Through a wide range of practices whose *telos* is to restore right relationships, this justice redounds to building a just peace, which resonates not only as transitional justice in light of post-conflict circumstances, but also

---

14 Some philosophers call this approach "realistic idealism" or "idealistic realism." For example, see Inis L. Claude, Jr., "Toward a Definition of Liberalism," *The Humanist* XVII, no. 5 (1957): 259–68. For more recent work, see Pedro Alexis Tabensky, "Realistic Idealism: An Aristotelian Alternative to Machiavellian International Relations," *Theoria* 113 (August 2007): 97–111.

as *jpb* in *post bellum* contexts. Although he does not explicitly frame *jpb* within the JWT as Walzer, Orend, and the other authors reviewed do, his approach to *jpb* serves to build a deeper understanding of the expanding, holistic nature of political reconciliation in *post bellum* contexts. For example, he notes that some practices of political reconciliation, such as forgiveness and acknowledgment, best take place after a war has ended.[15] In these contexts, he is concerned with understanding how political injustice or wrongdoing harms "individuals" (both individual victims and perpetrators), "relationships" (political relationships among citizens), and "social orders" (political orders with calamitous pasts), as well as how this harm might be repaired. In particular, Philpott characterizes the harm from such wrongdoing as "wounds" that have a negative impact on individual flourishing, political relationships, and political orders.

Philpott posits two kinds of wounds: "primary wounds" and "secondary wounds."[16] Primary wounds stem directly from the wrongdoing itself, as they include the six levels of woundedness that sever right relationships: violation of the victim's human rights, harms to the victim's person, the victim's ignorance of the source and circumstances of political injustices, the lack of acknowledgement of the suffering, the standing victory of the wrongdoer's political injustices, and harm to the person of the wrongdoer. Secondary wounds arise out of these primary wounds. When primary wounds are conducive to further acts of injustice, they result in secondary wounds. For example, secondary wounds encompass a chain of painful memories of cruelty suffered by oneself or those with whom one is close, or the resulting negative emotions such as resentment, hatred, and fear. These memories and emotions may engender judgments about the illegitimacy of a particular political order; they may cause many victims to determine that wrongdoing ought to be avenged; and they may be transformed into the victims taking a collective action that may result in further armed conflicts.[17]

Philpott is especially concerned with postwar societies, where "the acts that create secondary wounds may also take place years after the primary wounds, sometimes through memories and emotions that are passed down over generations."[18] Political reconciliation, which signifies processes of *jpb*,

---

15 For details, see Philpott, *Just and Unjust Peace*, 181.

16 Philpott, 32–41.

17 Philpott, 42.

18 Philpott, 42.

must repair primary and secondary wounds in response to these postwar societies. Philpott defines such processes as forms of restoration. With respect to potential primary restorations, Philpott's ethic of political reconciliation recognizes the array of primary wounds and proposes corresponding practices that seek to restore persons who have suffered them and, more broadly, to restore right relationship in or between political orders. Secondary restorations follow first restorations because they are justified consequently in terms of how they change emotions and judgments. Although memories cannot be erased, these restorations can remove the impediments, such as painful emotions and negative judgments that arise from secondary wounds.

Considering the dynamics of wounds and restorations, Philpott identifies the six *jpb* elements that are jointly necessary to restore relationships *post bellum* and thereby fulfill the demands of justice: building socially just institutions, acknowledgement of suffering caused, reparations, punishment, apology, and forgiveness. Philpott defines them together as a set of practices for acting out political reconciliation. First, with respect to building socially just institutions, he is especially concerned with just actors' *post bellum* involvement in regime changes that replace dictatorships with democracies. He argues that building democratic institutions helps provide a social space for a politics of reconciliation, further fostering human rights. Second, acknowledgement means a practice of political acknowledgement of wrongs. The third is similar to Orend's concept of reparations, with particular attention to the ongoing effects of historical injustices for descendants. Fourth, punishment refers to a judicial practice of punishment, insisting that unjust aggressor states redress the violation of human rights insofar as they express, reaffirm, and restore human rights as legitimized values. The fifth is apology, which must be performed in a political context. Finally, forgiveness is "a constructive act," which comes after apology. This sixth *jpb* element "re-empowers the victim as an agent, as something other than the recipient of an assault."[19] This re-empowerment leads to the victim's liberation from anger and resentment, the perpetrator's recognition of the victim's suffering, and the surrounding community's mutual respect for human rights.[20] Philpott argues that these six *jpb* elements are touchstones to guide ethical reflection

---

19 Philpott, 267.

20 For details, see Philpott, 236–68. For a theological reading of this reempowerment, see Gustavo Gutierrez, *On Job: God-Talk and the Suffering of the Innocent* (Maryknoll, NY: Orbis Books, 1985).

on political reconciliation in diverse post-conflict contexts. To be clear, this ethic of political reconciliation does not aim to prescribe specific courses of action. Rather, it intends to guide moral discernment.

In a nutshell, I find that three central themes of Philpott's ethic of political reconciliation relate to *jpb*. They are: (i) political reconciliation is a practical postwar duty found in religious traditions, including Christianity; (ii) political reconciliation is a political movement to restore a right relationship between the warring parties, including unjust aggressors, victims, and just actors; and (iii) despite his primary attention to transitional justice, developing this political vehicle in relation to the protection of human life must be an ultimate direction for *jpb* practices. In particular, Philpott is interested in the morality of responding to a wider range of past wrongs to overcome the limits of liberal peace. Hence, his theory aims at restoring right relationships in a holistic sense. He makes a compelling case for placing reconciliation at the core of one's *jpb* thinking about justice and for theorizing justice in a more comprehensive manner.

The Limits of the Ethic of Political Reconciliation

However, I must clarify that Philpott's ethic of political reconciliation would be insufficient to comprehensively engage in *jpb* discourse if one attempts to apply Philpott's ethic directly to the issues of *jpb*. In fact, despite the importance of reconciliation for *jpb*, his main concern is not *jpb*. Recall that his ethic of political reconciliation deals primarily with transitional justice and makes some rather limited claims about *jpb*. His brand of transitional justice aims to create restoration-oriented projects, not to prevent possible injustices in the *immediate aftermath* of interstate war, which rather belongs to a contemporary warfare mission for *jpb*. Such restoration projects often encompass a long-term peacebuilding agenda. This divergence of the transitional justice and *jpb* lineages demonstrates that even the best comprehensive work for transitional justice will not yield ethical reasoning that is strong enough to tame the vastly situational judgment that just actors must bring to their choices for *jpb*.

In this book, I have proposed that the *jpb* discourse includes three foundational themes: just policing, just punishment, and just political participation. However, setting aside the issue of political participation for regime change, Philpott almost exclusively touches on issues of just punishment, especially when discussing two of the *jpb* elements: punishment and forgiveness.

For example, Philpott offers ethical guidance for just action by showing how the logic of political reconciliation responds to issues of just punishment, such as a debate over retribution versus reconciliation. He adopts a holistic, restorative logic of justice and peace, highlighting that retribution and reconciliation cannot be viewed as antithetical to each other, but are compatible in principle. Opposing the dominant retributivist view, he proposes "restorative punishment," which arises from the Abrahamic rationales of reconciliation, pointing to forms of accountability that aim to reintegrate perpetrators into communities. For this restorative purpose, punishment can be compatible with a forgiveness that is defined as involving not only a waiver of resentment and of entitlements owed, but also as a constructive act that seeks to build right relationships. Such punishment and forgiveness are interdependent and complementary. Each redresses a different array of wounds of political injustice in a unique way and, in turn, restores a dimension of human flourishing and just political order. On a restorative justification, Philpott also notes a political implication of *jpb*.

> All of the practices find application in various institutional contexts, including . . . between states that have fought war, or in the wake of armed intervention, though how the practices find application in each context differs and requires further exploration. The fundamental contention of the ethic is that addressing the range of wounds of injustice, both for their own sake and because they may lead to further injustices, is a matter of justice, the justice of right relationship. So, too, it is a matter of peace and a matter of mercy.[21]

Furthermore, this *jpb* implication also signifies Philpott's strategy, which is to demonstrate that this conception of justice, restorative punishment, could be the subject of an overlapping consensus among religious and nonreligious moral traditions alike.

Despite the merits of Philpott's restorative justice, which serves as a clear alternative to the dominant thought of retributivism in the *jpb* discourse, I find difficulty in fully applying it to the *jpb* discourse. I doubt the degree to which his ethic seeking restorative punishment could become the main subject of an overlapping consensus as he believes it can. As Allman

---

21 Daniel Philpott, "An Ethic of Political Reconciliation," lecture given at *Key Issues in Religion and World Affairs*, Institute on Culture, Religion & World Affairs, Boston University, Boston, MA, January 30, 2015, 4, https://www.bu.edu/cura/files/2013/10/Philpott-Summary-of-CURA-Talk1.pdf.

and Winright rightly note, restorative justice, together with corrective and distributive justices, is one of the crucial ways that *jpb* theologians understand postwar justice, whereas it is rarely how nonreligious *jpb* scholars understand justice. Notably, Colleen Murphy and Leslie Vinjamuri criticize Philpott's work on the grounds that his ethic of political reconciliation is inadequate because his conception of restorative justice—rooted in the Abrahamic religious rationale itself—falls short of demonstrating that it could garner support from secular traditions more generally.[22] Philpott is aware of their critiques and responds that "it is difficult to say *ex ante*, prior to the hard work of searching for mutual resonance, how much convergence between the ethic and any given tradition will be possible. No tradition will converge fully."[23]

My contention is that Philpott's understanding of restoration remains questionable on strictly theological grounds. His analysis of religious terms, such as justice, peace, and mercy—each integral to the constitution of restorative justice for political reconciliation—is insufficient. His analysis is understood from a surface-level linguistic perspective, not a comprehensively theological one.[24] As a result, his work sometimes appears as if it is falling into disciplinary and methodological niches with little awareness outside of those niches. Although he includes a theological account of God's response to political evil, a more consistent lack of an overarching theological perspective on understanding these religious terms weakens his argument.

My concern is not that he simply denies the challenge and the likelihood of partial results in finding resonance for the ethic among traditions. Nor is my concern that each tradition itself contains internally conflicting schools for understanding justice, peace, and mercy. Instead, I expect that, at least in Christianity, these notions of justice, peace, and mercy are understood in various, dynamic dimensions. However, Philpott's proposal overlooks this aspect

---

22 See Colleen Murphy, "Justice and Reconciliation," *The Immanent Frame*, November 29, 2012, http://blogs.ssrc.org/tif/2012/11/29/justice-and-reconciliation/; Leslie Vinjamuri, "Recasting an Agenda for Peace," *The Immanent Frame*, January 31, 2013, http://blogs.ssrc.org/tif/2013/01/31/recasting-an-agenda-for-peace.

23 See Daniel Philpott, "Reconciliation in The Real World," *The Immanent Frame*, March 1, 2013, http://blogs.ssrc.org/tif/2013/03/01/reconciliation-in-the-real-world/.

24 Once again, recall that Philpott is a political scientist, not a theologian. Hence, it would be somewhat unfair to criticize his weaknesses, from a theological perspective, regarding his generalizations about the Abrahamic faiths and scripture. Admittedly, I have to point out that he does not acknowledge the diversity of biblical views of justice and peace. For details, see the next paragraph and footnote.

of understanding the notions. Rather, it follows a simple linear direction that war is always a political evil whereas political reconciliation, specifically restorative punishment, is the right response to it.[25] Thus, a proposition arises. If intervening actors—whether they are victorious states or the international community—fail to achieve political reconciliation in the aftermath of a war, then that failure itself must constitute an injustice regardless of their successful campaign of human security. Hence, for Philpott, these actors must *not* be called just actors. However, I hold that *jpb* cannot be primarily determined by an approach to seeing whether a certain phase of war fulfills political reconciliation or not. It is not simply about whether every (would-be) just actor should always take up restorative punishment. Instead, the question is how reconciliation is built after war. In addition, scripture deals with issues of war and reconciliation, as well as of punishment and forgiveness, in a diverse, dynamic, and perhaps self-contradictory and mysterious, way. In scripture, God brings justice to the world through both war and reconciliation; it is not always that war is injustice whereas reconciliation, specifically political reconciliation, is justice.[26] Without deepening his theological reflection on war and reconciliation, Philpott's work cannot address what justice, peace, and mercy truly mean to each tradition, particularly to the Christian tradition, and the Catholic tradition within it.

Unlike the issue of just punishment, however, Philpott does not clearly delineate the topics of just policing and just political participation in light of his ethic of political reconciliation. He addresses certain issues of political

---

25 The notion of "right relationships" is one among other notions within the Bible, along with obeying the command of God, fulfilling one's promises, personal righteousness, and fidelity to the Law. In fact, one can find from the Hebrew Bible that particularism (i.e., God loves Israel, to hell with the nations) alternates with a more minor note of universalism. At various points, right relations are considered perfectly consistent with genocide. In addition, even in the New Testament, Jesus' passages are not always reconciliatory (especially in Johannine literature, but also in passages of woes [Luke's beatitudes] and judgment [Mt 25:31–46]). Philpott clearly understands that *hesed* is God's steadfast love seeking to reconcile the people. However, the Psalms and other biblical literature witness this as perfectly compatible with the judgment of sinners who refuse to be faithful to God (e.g., Ps 53:5 and Jer 8:1–2). Therefore, it does not seem to be the case that biblical justice is always right relationship striving for reconciliation—sometimes, yes, but at other times quite the opposite. This does present a challenge to Philpott's view of God's justice as an overall restorative one.

26 For example, Dt 20:10–20 presents the rules of warfare, dealing with the justice of war (more precisely speaking, justness of war)—whether and how the Israelites engage in wars with/for God since they believe that they are the people of God and thus follow God's way. In the narrative, there are two kinds of ban depending on the opposite nations: a mitigated ban against distant or external foes (20:12–15) and a total ban against the proscribed nations of Canaan (20:16–18)—so no discretion on their part for political reconciliation purposes or so.

participation, such as building a democratic regime in post-conflict societies. Yet, his cases mostly concern historical accounts of successful involvement in regime change replacing dictatorships with democracies, not how his ethic of political reconciliation can deliver guidance for action for just political participation. He does not elucidate how regime change helps restore the injured relationship *post bellum*.

With respect to just policing, Philpott's ethic of political reconciliation does not present any useful thoughts and examples. The discourse of just policing, as we have discussed throughout this book, highlights the importance of human security and its corresponding means of developing humanitarian norms. Therefore, it is a distinct matter from political reconciliation. Its primary concern is to protect people in the *immediate* aftermath of the war; there is little or no time for just actors to engage in political reconciliation with the enemy, especially when policing the vanquished area where violence—oftentimes intensive—still abounds.

In addition to these primary reasons, there is another reason why Philpott's ethic of political reconciliation is not suitable for the *jpb* discourse within the JWT, or at least why one should not apply his ethic of political reconciliation directly to the context of *jpb*: the apparent absence of, or at least lack of focus on, *jpb* and its defining roles in practice. As emphasized throughout this book, I am cautious about approaches in which both the terms postwar justice and transitional justice are interchangeably used without denoting any particular direction to distinguish them. I included Philpott's approach to *jpb* as one such case. In his *jpb* thinking, both types of justice represent two distinct but compatible theories, meant to address the postwar challenges.[27] However, he fails to—or does not intend to—clarify the compatibility of the two views on justice and integrate them into his account of such challenges in a consistent manner. Examples that he provides include postwar states such as Germany, Japan, and Iraq. With these examples, he asserts that building a democratic regime is necessary for postwar justice.[28] As highlighted in the previous chapter, however, many *jpb* theologians argue that building a democratic regime is not necessary for postwar justice. In particular, Himes clarifies that the just cause of war excludes regime change (to a democratic regime). He asserts that just actors

27 To be clear, Philpott is aware that looking into *jpb* issues deserves more treatment than he offers in his discourse on transitional justice. For details, see Philpott, *Just and Unjust Peace*, 181.

28 For details, see Philpott, 6.

ought to adopt whatever route best takes them to the safe space for securing the vanquished people's civilization and their civility. In contrast, the idea of transitional justice is implicit in an assumption that a post-conflict community is transitioning to democracy, or at least toward the political culture of democratic government. On that account, it is clear that postwar justice is not identical with transitional justice; yet, Philpott interchangeably uses these two ideas of justice to conclude that a democratic regime is necessary for postwar societies.

Further, in his attempt to affirm the necessity of justice in political reconciliation, Philpott is often vague not only about which justice he has in mind but also through which particular institutions that justice is to be pursued. For example, he explicitly puts forward that his approach to political reconciliation strongly overlaps with the concept of restorative justice. This justice demands restorative practice, particularly through preventing and reacting to the violation of human rights, as well as rebuilding just institutions to protect human rights. In defining this restorative practice, Philpott proposes a very wide comprehensive approach.

> What does the guarantee of human rights involve? It entails laws, institutions, and enforcement measures that protect against the most egregious political crimes: war crimes, crimes against humanity, genocide. . . . It also involves protections against other crimes that are characteristic of dictatorships: surveillance, illegal detention, and the restriction of expression, assembly, religion, and movement. As articulated in international law . . . , human rights include and are themselves sustained by features of democracy such as elections, legislative institutions, the right to vote, participation, and representation. Guaranteeing human rights also requires the rule of law: judicial institutions that provide fair trials and criminal procedures, humane and proportionate punishments for valid crimes, equal protection under the law, and other related values. Essential, too, are basic economic provisions such as the right to form unions, to own property, and to enjoy the means of subsistence, a fair wage, and safe working conditions. In sites of civil war and genocide, providing and guaranteeing rights requires not only sound institutions but also the range of activities that U.N. peace operations have come to undertake.[29]

While primarily seeking justice for protecting human rights, Philpott associates the demand of justice with almost all of the vital moral values within the

---

29 Philpott, 176–77.

jpb discourse, such as human security, responsibility to protect (R2P), equality, mercy, criminal justice, and economic justice. Further, he links the demand of justice with central practices of *jpb*, such as rebuilding socially just institutions in which liberal peace and the ethic of political reconciliation converge most clearly. For Philpott, the reestablishment of these socially just institutions happens by way of promoting democracy, establishing the rule of law, respecting certain constraints in economic interaction, and endorsing international actors and institutions like the UN. In this approach, justice demands that each of these moral values and practices be respected. However, despite his attempt to give a comprehensive account of justice, Philpott's approach is too broad and nebulous to determine which justice is prioritized and how that works.[30] Although the inclusion of each condition of all the moral values and their corresponding practices is intuitively plausible, there is no clear account of details given for why achieving all these moral values and practices must be sufficient for protecting human rights institutionally.

However, my comment about this lack of awareness of *jpb* concerns does not mean that Philpott should be accountable for doing *jpb* work framed within the JWT that he has not intended to undertake. Therefore, I must note that it can be unfair to criticize his work in regard to *jpb*, as it is not his main concern. Of more concern is that some theologians, like Anna Floerke Scheid, overemphasize Philpott's work in the *jpb* arena. Scheid's work is a welcome contribution to refining our theology for *jpb*.

Anna Scheid's Consistent Ethic of Reconciliation

A Theological Foundation and Application to *Jus Post Bellum*

Considering the aforementioned limits, I attest that Philpott's theory of political reconciliation needs to be carefully reviewed in terms of its aptness

---

30 Some major scholars, both social scientists and ethicists, share a similar critique. Mark Freeman addresses a critical question as to whether Philpott stretches the terms of the argument too widely in attempting to accommodate multiple perspectives at once. He does not simply criticize Philpott's work on the ethic's aspiration to holism, but points out Philpott's failure to make that holistic approach effective. Also, Bronwyn Leebaw, Colleen Murphy, and Leslie Vinjamuri are concerned that Philpott's ethic of political reconciliation is unable to provide guidance, resolve dilemmas, or handle backlash, adverse effects, and political manipulation. See Mark Freeman, "A New Theory on Political Wounds," *The Immanent Frame*, November 27, 2012, http://blogs.ssrc.org/tif/2012/11/27/a-new-theory-on-political-wounds/; Bronwyn Leebaw, "Janus-Faced Justice," *The Immanent Frame*, January 29, 2013, http://blogs.ssrc.org/tif/2013/01/29/janus-faced-justice; Colleen Murphy, "Justice and Reconciliation"; and Leslie Vinjamuri, "Recasting an Agenda for Peace."

for *jpb* discourse. This is also partially because his ethic better fits the topic of transitional justice than that of postwar justice in light of the JWT. Scheid, along with several other theologians, is concerned about these limits of Philpott's work.[31] Scheid develops her own theological argument for an ethic of political reconciliation and its implication for *jpb*. She attempts to resolve some of these limits, especially responding to the criticism that Philpott's framework for an ethic of political reconciliation is vague, abstract, and removed from political reality in light of *jpb* practices.

However, this does not mean that Scheid attempts to reduce the gap between theory and practice by providing significant guidance for just action as most social scientists and policy analysts often do. She agrees with Philpott that an ethic of political reconciliation cannot and should not supplant the zone of choice in which intervening actors *post bellum* must apply prudential judgment, but her ethic does point the way to some approaches rather than others. Unlike Philpott, Scheid provides an ethic that treats the justice of dealing with past wrongs or political injustice in a clear and consistent manner.

As noted earlier, Allman and Winright categorize reconciliation as one of the four *jpb* phases, which function as restorative justice—transforming the relationships of the belligerents from hostility to tolerance, leading to postwar justice tempered by mercy.[32] Likewise, Scheid understands reconciliation as restorative justice in the postwar society. She proposes that the "just" aspect of a "just war" must be defined as restorative justice, not retributive justice. She defines political reconciliation *post bellum* by incorporating aspects of both the minimalist and maximalist positions. She first understands political reconciliation "to signify minimally a commitment by formerly warring parties to refrain from future acts of retaliation."[33] In addition to this necessary condition for political reconciliation, she urges just actors to consider a maximalist view that aims to include a wide range of *jpb* practices "from reparations for war's victims, to measures that hold accountable war's aggressors, to religious and indigenous rituals of acknowledgment, forgiveness, and apology between and among former enemies . . . that align well with the ideals of restorative justice."[34] Similar to Allman and

---

31 Some of the theologians that I will examine here are Allman and Winright, and Louis Iasiello.

32 Allman and Winright, *After the Smoke Clears*, 14.

33 Anna Floerke Scheid, "Just War Theory and Restorative Justice: Weaving a Consistent Ethic of Reconciliation," *Journal of Moral Theology* 5, no. 2 (2016): 100.

34 Scheid, 100–101.

Winright's loose maximalist position, Scheid argues that just actors inherit substantial obligations to pursue political reconciliation. But her argument simultaneously recognizes the limit of just war measures in meeting the ideals of restorative justice, therefore attempting to guide just actors in attaining balanced views between the maximalist and minimalist positions.

Further, Scheid is similar to Allman and Winright in that they all adopt a holistic approach to *jpb*. In particular, with respect to reconciliation, she states, "reconciliation ought to be integral to *jus ante bellum*, *jus ad bellum* and *jus in bello* as well as its more common designation *jus post bellum*." Taking this holistic approach, combined with her loose maximalist position, she concludes that "weaving reconciliation throughout the various phases of a just war ethic strengthens both its capacity to restrain the most detrimental harms wrought by contemporary warfare and its capacity to restore a just and sustainable peace."[35]

However, Scheid's argument for political reconciliation is critically distinct from Allman and Winright's work on reconciliation. Scheid criticizes them, as well as other *jpb* theologians who treat reconciliation merely as one of the critical components of *jpb*.[36] Instead, she proposes an approach called "a consistent ethic of reconciliation" in which she emphasizes reconciliation through all phases of war. She believes that this approach has an edge, in that it can help develop each phase of the JWT in order to restore a just peace in a comprehensive manner. In particular, she believes this restoration of a just peace means "peace with reconciliation," quoting from Philpott. She summarizes her own view.

> A consistent ethic of reconciliation begins *jus ad bellum*, with the development of attitudes and inclinations toward truth-telling, forgiveness, apology. It runs through *jus ad bellum*, demanding that the intention toward peace includes an understanding of the kind of peace that is aimed for; . . . missions in war ought to be designed with reconciliation in mind. *Jus in bello*, a consistent ethic of reconciliation shapes the concept of micro-proportionality: the means in war must not thwart the overarching goal of reconciliation. Instead they should invite de-escalation and negotiation. Finally, *jus post bellum*, former enemies bring the consistent ethic

---

35 Scheid, 101.

36 For details, see Scheid, 101–4. Also, as discussed earlier, Allman and Winright see reconciliation as one of the four *jpb* principles, along with the just cause principle, punishment, and restoration.

of reconciliation to fruition, using truth commissions, restorative punishment, vetting, and other *post bellum* practices to forge a sustainable reconciled just peace.[37]

The Limits of the Consistent Ethic of Reconciliation

Scheid's assertion that reconciliation, mainly political reconciliation, should be the first and foremost ambition of *jpb* is unsurprising. As discussed in chapter two, many *jpb* scholars, such as Walzer, Orend, and Elshtain, point out that current literature on *jpb* tends to overemphasize mercy and political reconciliation rather than the moral responsibility of justice. With this concern in mind, we are led to ask whether, and if so, to what extent, Scheid's approach lacks a balanced view of *jpb*. Overlooking the importance of justice and its corresponding *jpb* practices, such as civil and nonpartisan policing and fair and impartial punishment, her argument for a consistent ethic of reconciliation is a clear yet not comprehensive approach to *jpb*. As Allman and Winright argue, *jpb* cannot be determined by a single, dichotomist approach to see whether a certain phase of war fulfills reconciliation or not. Rather, since the nature of warfare is always changeable, dynamic, and multidimensional, *jpb* must be examined from various perspectives.

Most importantly, Scheid's notion of "just peace" as "peace with reconciliation" is not sufficient to characterize postwar justice. Rather, it is *de facto* transitional justice. As she draws from Philpott's account of political reconciliation, Scheid adopts a concept of justice that involves one's will to respond to another's wounds of political injustice that sever right relationships. For Scheid, the primary definition of justice in this context of wounds is political reconciliation, that is, the restoration of right relationships. This notion serves Philpott's transitional justice. As noted earlier, Philpott puts forth the aim of political reconciliation as the *telos* of transitional justice. Like Philpott, Scheid proposes an ethic of reconciliation along with an array of matching practices that seek to restore the right relationship. Likewise, her ethic encompasses some of the core commitments of the liberal tradition, such as the establishment of an environment characterized by respect for the basic human rights of all members of society, as well as the restoration of political rights and the rule of law. Simply put, Scheid's claim is that justice demands political reconciliation, the restoration of right relationships. Her only difference from Philpott in this regard is that she incorporates

---

37 Scheid, 115.

this notion of transitional justice not only into *jpb* practices but also the entire body of just war practices throughout all the phases of war.

However, in my view, it is problematic that Scheid builds her *jpb* theory by borrowing a notion of justice from the discourse of transitional justice, not that of the JWT. Her project is not confined to the JWT discourse. Recall that postwar justice is different from transitional justice in light of its scope and purpose. She does not provide a clear direction that would guide how these two justices coherently work together in practice. Nor does she explain why postwar justice demands political reconciliation prior to other *jpb* concerns, such as human security. As a result, Scheid fails to convince that this priority works best to achieve the ultimate end of a just war, a peace ordered to the common good. Scheid does not clearly grasp or agree that the JWT's fundamental aim is to prevent injustice (*jus ad bellum*), halt ongoing injustice (*jus in bello*), and preclude future injustice (*jpb*), not to focus on political reconciliation. The primary purpose of building peace within the just tradition is to protect people, whether for self-defense or humanitarian intervention. In contrast, transitional justice serves broader purposes with its aim of political reconciliation, specifically the restoration of right relationships. Scheid's approach, just like Philpott's, is more interested in building restoration-oriented practices than preventing injustices through the development of a clear frame of moral principles. Therefore, she has fallen into the constraints imposed by peacebuilding practices rather than the *jpb* discourse within the JWT.

Additionally, as shown earlier by *jpb* theologians' practical concerns, in the immediate aftermath of war there is little or no policing, punishment, or political participation to protect the lives of individuals, especially those most vulnerable. This notion of human security is a neglected theme in Scheid's *jpb* discourse. Instead, whether just war measures meet the *jpb* criterion of political reconciliation is the overarching and supreme standard for her whole warfare ethic. Alternatively, I suggest that a more balanced understanding of *jpb* must pay direct attention to the elements comprising human security in a postwar context, as well as to the quest for political reconciliation, not the norm of reconciliation alone, as Scheid proposes.

Conclusion: Rethinking Philpott's Ethic of Reconciliation through Scheid's *Jus Post Bellum* Approach

As Scheid relies heavily on Philpott's notion of political reconciliation, it is worth recalling Philpott's argument that just actors should pay attention to restorative justice, which aligns more directly with the idea of transitional justice than with postwar justice. However, his theological adherence to rec-onciliation prevents the deepening of a holistic theological reflection of *jpb*, which is concerned with both war and reconciliation. These limits prevent it from applying directly to the *jpb* dialogue.

Nonetheless, Philpott's understanding of restorative justice remains helpful for developing some theological elements in light of *jpb* practices. As discussed earlier, he does not effectively address the third theme of *jpb*, just political participation, since his discussion mostly focuses on one's *post bellum* involvement in regime change. Other than this proposal for regime change, Philpott does not explicitly address how his ethic of political rec-onciliation contributes to just political participation. However, there is one potential area of *jpb* that can be extensively developed on the theme of just political participation, which I intend to discuss in the final chapter of this book: Philpott's appreciation of religion and reconciliation for peacebuild-ing practices. He challenges liberal peace movements, especially those led by liberal skeptics. These skeptics fear that rigid religious dogma is likely to sow division and to play such a destabilizing role that even violent means will be used in the rebuilding of already-fragile relationships in post-conflict areas. In place of this skeptical view, Philpott demonstrates that faith-based peacebuilding activists and scholars, by drawing on their the-ology, have directly participated in the widening and deepening of liber-alism's goals. At its most rudimentary level, these faith-based practices associated with political reconciliation share the liberal aim of establishing an environment characterized by respect for the basic human rights of all members of a society.[38]

At the broadest level, Philpott shows how to promote reasonable dia-logue within the Abrahamic tradition that could provide guidance for the *jpb* discourse of just political participation. First, his Abrahamic rationales invite the three religious traditions to speak from each of their depths.[39] Then, he extends this interreligious dialogue into the public discourse. In doing so, he offers a place for religion in *jpb* as he sets the stage for further interdisciplinary research on that matter. What Philpott proposes is "a graft-ing in which . . . concepts from ancient scripture merge with ideas drawn

---

38 For details, see Daniel Philpott, "An Ethic of Political Reconciliation," *Ethics and International Affairs* 23, no. 4 (December 2009): 389–407.

39 For comment and discussion, see Glen Stassen, review of *Just and Unjust Peace: An Ethic of Political Reconciliation*, by Daniel Philpott, *Journal of the Society of Christian Ethics* 33, no. 2 (Fall/Winter 2013): 211–12.

from the modern liberal tradition."[40] For example, he argues that such an overarching concept of human rights, characterized as justice, has been built upon the theological idea of *imago dei*, although it can also be articulated in secular language.[41] Plainly, human rights language for political reconciliation, as the subject of an overlapping consensus among the religious and the nonreligious, does not preclude religion.

This advocacy for an inclusion of religion in Philpott's ethic of political reconciliation has the potential to develop the *jpb* discourse, especially regarding just political participation. Yet, it is also vital to recall that Philpott is neither a philosopher nor a theologian but, rather, a political scientist. Despite his noble efforts at building an interdisciplinary ethic of political reconciliation, every discipline has certain strengths and certain limitations. As examined earlier, for example, Philpott's discussion of Christianity, Islam, and Judaism are at times bogged down in linguistic questions of translation, giving the impression that Philpott's analysis needs to be complemented by those who work with theological expertise. This is, in part, Scheid's likely goal for her consistent ethic of reconciliation, although she overemphasizes Philpott's work, which is primarily designated for transitional justice, in the *jpb* arena.

A WAY FORWARD FOR CHRISTIAN *JUS POST BELLUM*: THE MAXIM(UM) OF ETHICAL MINIMALISM
A Recap of Two Moral Visions: Human Security and Political Reconciliation

Moral theologians of *jpb* have reached a near-universal consensus that just actors will inherit substantial obligations to the citizens of the defeated state, whether their *jpb* position emphasizes human security or political reconciliation. At this point, one may simply conclude that dealing with these two moral visions—human security and political reconciliation—together in a wise manner is key to finding the moral compass for reconstructing just policing, just punishment, and just political participation.

However, this statement does not fully represent my viewpoint. As reviewed, some moral theologians, such as Scheid, hold that political rec-

---

40 Philpott, *Just and Unjust Peace*, 9.

41 For an overview (including skeptical view) of Philpott's interreligious dialogue method, see Colleen Murphy, review of *Just and Unjust Peace: An Ethic of Political Reconciliation*, by Daniel Philpott, *Ethics* 123, no. 3 (April 2013): 579.

onciliation is necessary, as peaceful means of ending war are always available, if both warring parties have the will to look for them. Others believe the central Christian mission is reconciliation at all levels after war, since this mission will be the antidote to war. War is evil because it essentially involves hatred of the enemy and carelessness toward human life. I do not utterly oppose these moral tendencies to promote reconciliation. However, at the same time, I have challenged the view of those who argue that political reconciliation is the first and foremost ambition of *jpb*. I have paid particular attention to Scheid's consistent ethic of reconciliation for *jpb* and her theoretical benefactor Philpott's ethic of political reconciliation. To be clear, despite the limits I find in Philpott's work, my main criticism is not directly against Philpott, as it would be unfair to criticize his work in regard to *jpb* as it is not his main concern.

Of more concern is Scheid's overemphasis on Philpott's work in the *jpb* arena. In particular, the way Scheid's theology strongly adheres to political reconciliation prevents direct application to a broader range of *jpb* issues (e.g., just policing, punishment, and political participation) and thus hinders *post bellum* movements toward human security and peacebuilding efforts in the immediate aftermath of war.[42] Overall, there are three critical points regarding political reconciliation. First, political reconciliation is appropriate for rebuilding postwar societies in the long run, but not as a focus during the immediate aftermath of war, which is primarily regarded as the *post bellum* phase of the JWT. Second, the Christian reconciliation that Scheid emphasizes does not always need to be executed in the form of political reconciliation as the two are distinct: the former belonging to the Church and the latter belonging to the state or other legitimate actors such as the international community and local government. Finally, the overemphasis on political reconciliation overlooks another central theological aspect of *jpb*, namely, human security.

At the same time, I have concluded that in comparison to the political reconciliation promotion view, the human security promotion view is more appropriate for guiding postwar conduct, mainly due to its theological sig-

---

42 I take a different approach to political reconciliation than Scheid: (i) Reconciliation may not be achievable, but security is, and immediate postwar response is directed to maintaining human security, especially for protecting women, minority genders and ethnic groups and their families, and other socially vulnerable populations. (ii) I suggest how reconciliation might occur later on. (iii) We need to take Philpott's recommendations to the concrete level and give more emphasis to just policing and ongoing political participation, in addition to just or restorative punishment. And, to repeat, human security is fundamental.

nificance in the JWT. I have contoured this guidance by demonstrating the Church's reaction to *jpb* (especially with its concerns arising from R2P) and distinguishing three theological approaches to *jpb*: Schuck's Augustinian, Himes's Thomistic, and Allman and Winright's Niebuhrian *jpb* views. In so doing, I have attempted to defend the proposition that achieving just policing (through advancing humanitarian norms), just punishment (through developing rehabilitation models), and just political participation (through building local consensus) are key to building a just peace. By defending this proposition, I have affirmed that the establishment of a just peace must be primarily directed toward human security, not political reconciliation. This conclusion also affirmed that political reconciliation is perhaps best promoted for transitional justice, but not for postwar justice.

However, despite that limit, I have also made clear that the discourse of *jpb* must not completely exclude political reconciliation. As noted earlier, Philpott's ethic of political reconciliation has the potential to develop the *jpb* discourse, especially with regard to just political participation. Just political participation is distinguished from just policing and just punishment in that, despite its urgency during the immediate aftermath of war, its practical implication relates to long-term postwar reconstruction. In contrast, *jpb* practices of both just policing and just punishment must happen during the immediate aftermath of war.[43] Simply put, just political participation takes place in a threshold period between the end of war and the beginning of peacebuilding. I must note that because of the complex nature of this timeline, a variety of just actors are involved in the practice of just political participation. I envision the scope of just actors as corresponding to each *jpb* theme, although a strict algorithm is impossible (see Figure 1, next page).

There are two types of just actors: "classical" just actors and "nonclassical" just actors. "Classical just actors" refers to armed forces run by victorious states and/or the international community. I label these just actors as "classical," indicating that they are generally defined within the classical JWT, as in the cases of *jus ad bellum* and *jus in bello*. "Nonclassical" just actors are outside of the domain of those considered classical just actors. They include local communities, NGOs, the Church, and other civil organizations. Both classical just actors and nonclassical just actors are proactive in the entire body of *jpb* practices. With respect to the first theme of just policing, just actors are narrowly defined as the classical ones. These classi-

---

43 I will revisit each of these timeline issues in the next chapters.

Just Policing
"Classical" just actors: armed forces of victorious states and/or the international community

Just Punishment
Classical just actors, but potentially open for "nonclassical" just actors as auxiliary ones

Just Political Participation
Classical just actors and "nonclassical" just actors

Figure 1. The Scope of Just Actors for Each *jpb* Theme

cal just actors are also the main *jpb* agents that carry out postwar conduct for actualizing the second theme of just punishment. However, unlike the *jpb* practice of just policing, the work of just punishment does not limit the scope of just actors to these classical just actors alone. There are some potential areas that are open for a broader range of just actors, including nonclassical just actors. Nonetheless, these nonclassical actors are still limited in implementing just punishment, as they are subject to the demand of the classical just actors. For example, the Truth Commission works as a nonclassical just actor for post-conflict justice in a broad sense, but it cannot and must not be a primary legal and political institution for postwar justice. Rather, it is an auxiliary one, cooperating with the classical just actors in their *jpb* work of implementing just punishment in a balanced and fair manner. In other words, nonclassical actors serve classical just actors, not vice versa. Finally, both the classical and the nonclassical actors are equally involved in the work of just political participation. While the classical just actors remain significant *jpb* agents for assuring human security *post bellum*, the nonclassical actors have their own distinct roles in rebuilding a civil society. With respect to the *jpb* theme of just political participation, all these just actors work independently but also interdependently, and their work requires integration.

Extending the scope of just actors means that some nonclassical just actors contribute to just political participation differently than classical just actors. This contribution could include political reconciliation, as long as it serves human security first. More precisely, if practices for political reconciliation help prevent future violence and foster the common good, they will be considered *jpb* practices. While a theology of *jpb* must serve human security, it must also incorporate a moral vision of political reconciliation when its ultimate intention is to restore a dimension of human flourishing and of just political order. This political reconciliation can be affected by just political participation. A carefully balanced position is required, on the one hand constraining what classical just actors are entitled to do for human security, and on the other hand actively encouraging nonclassical just actors' practice of political reconciliation, as long as it promotes human security. I call this position a "maxim(um) of ethical minimalism." The practical groundwork of this position and its corresponding theological reflection will be discussed in the next three chapters, as each of these chapters will address distinctive tensions between the two poles of human security and political reconciliation in practice.

The Maxim(um) of Ethical Minimalism: The Norm of the Common Good

Before discussing such practical concerns, I first define the position I call the maxim(um) of ethical minimalism for *jpb—the principle of achieving, to the highest extent, possible human security, which is the necessary and essential outcome for jpb.* In other words, it is the norm for *jpb* of achieving the common good to the highest extent possible, with the priority of human security and using nonviolent means as much as possible and violent means only when necessary. Next, I will engage in a theological reflection on the position, demonstrating why the maxim(um) of ethical minimalism is a way forward for Christian *jpb*, which must be constantly implicit within the Christian JWT.

A major theme in both philosophical and theological *jpb* literature is that humanitarian norms ought to be applied to the overall *jpb* practice, of which the fundamental characteristic must be human security. Likewise, with respect to just policing, most *jpb* thinkers argue that just actors must guarantee the security of the occupied people in the immediate aftermath of war by committing to the equal protection of all citizens.

Despite this common interest in human security, *jpb* theologians are distinguished from *jpb* philosophers by the means they suggest for just policing. Most *jpb* philosophers are divided between two camps: minimalists, who advocate a restorative viewpoint of *jpb* and believe that it is not possible to escape from the cycle of conflict without the use of armed force, and maximalists, who adhere to a transformative view of *jpb* and see *the potential of* nonviolent resolution for solving postwar conflicts.[44] In contrast, most *jpb* theologians—at least the Christian ethicists to whom I have referred in this book, such as Schuck, Himes, and Allman and Winright—attend to the use of both armed force and nonviolent means. They hold a transformative scheme of just policing through just and peaceful means. This transformative scheme aims to improve the overall human condition in the postwar society while still valuing military means as a last resort to restore state sovereignty and secure people's safety.

The aforesaid transformative *jpb* corresponds to my "Maxim(um) of Ethical Minimalism: the Norm of the Common Good" approach, which attends to the use of both armed force and nonviolent means. Further, this approach prioritizes armed force over nonviolent means for just policing, as its primary aim is to protect people in the postwar society from *imminent* threats. This protection enables just actors to provide *basic* needs for vulnerable people before moving into a more comprehensive *jpb* scheme.

As proposed, this approach in practice necessitates further reflection on just actors' obligations, first with respect to putting an end to *post bellum* violence *appropriately*, which I call "ethical minimalism," and then with respect to holding *potential* aggressors of armed conflicts accountable for political unrest, economic destabilization, and loss of human life, which I call "maxim(um) of [that] ethical minimalism."

The ethical minimalism I define, like the *jpb* philosophers' minimalism, aims to restrict what just actors ought to do. This view limits the rights of victors to actions that protect people in the postwar society. The idea of putting an end to postwar violence *appropriately* is a reaction to historical instances of the victor's violence, such as "raping and pillaging" their defeated foes.[45] The maxim(um) of [that] ethical minimalism aims to take *full* advantage of this minimalist belief that just actors must secure the just war principles of just cause and proportionality within the *jpb* criteria.[46]

---

44 As noted in chapter two, there are other exceptional philosophers such as Walzer, whom I consider a "loose minimalist," namely, attending to both minimalist and maximalist means of just policing. More importantly, unlike most *jpb* thinkers argue, I clarified that this distinction in practice is viewed in terms of degree rather than type.

45 Orend states that both ancient (the Greeks and Romans) and modern nations (the Nazis) often demanded that their enemies surrender unconditionally, effectively granting the victors the right to take whatever they like from the defeated country. cf. Orend, "*Jus Post Bellum:* The Perspective of a Just War Theorist," 579.

46 This book primarily attempts to justify *jpb* as part of the JWT. This means that my argument cannot overlook the minimalist view of *jpb*; rather, it must acknowledge the minimalist rules of

Notwithstanding, this view also contends that *jpb* is different than *jus ad bellum* and *jus in bello* in that the idea of just cause *post bellum* is drawn from rebuilding the common good as opposed to merely defending the common good. As proposed, rebuilding the common good requires a transformative idea of *jpb*, typically drawn from maximalism, which imposes moral obligations upon just actors rather than seeking justification. In effect, just actors begin to secure the just cause *post bellum* by deterring *potential* aggression through both violent and nonviolent means. They thus assume responsibility for preventing the abandonment of a dysfunctional state leading to a chaos that cannot meet its citizens' basic needs and safety and ultimately bring about the conditions under which these citizens can lead minimally decent and just lives. Therefore, this maxim(um) of ethical minimalism intends to use both violent and nonviolent means to achieve the common good, as these means are seen as integral elements of a transformative *jpb* scheme.[47]

This maxim(um) of ethical minimalism has three tasks: (i) identifying fundamental theological elements within each of the three *jpb* themes; (ii) broadening the topic of human security to the discourse of political reconciliation; and (iii) theologically affirming the ultimate intention of political reconciliation as the same as that of human security, namely, the (re)establishment of the common good.[48] The first task addresses the overarching purpose of *jpb* across the three themes, which is to achieve human security prior to political reconciliation. The second task must be actualized not simply by making political reconciliation the ultimate end of *jpb* work but also by defining it as a virtuous means to achieve human security. The third

---

jpb as the foundation of *jpb* work. This is the main reason I emphasize "ethical minimalism" while taking advantage of the maximalist rules of *jpb* to enforce that minimalist approach. As noted by Bellamy, the minimalist rules of *jpb* find their roots in the JWT, invoking familiar ideas of just cause and proportionality; whereas, the maximalist rules are grounded in more general liberal theory and international law. See Bellamy, "The Responsibilities of Victory," 615.

47 As shown in chapter two, this "ethical minimalism" intends to constrain what just actors are entitled to do for security, just as in the orthodox minimalism endorsed by the *jpb* philosophers. Yet, this minimalism is different from the philosophers' minimalism; while the former intends to use both violent and nonviolent means to achieve the common good (*jpb*), the latter attends to violent means in order to terminate war itself (*jus terminare bellum*).

48 This notion of "maxim(um) of ethical minimalism" will be more concretely discussed with a *jpb* scheme of comprehensive human security in the next chapters. Also, Christian theologians are often better prophets than peacemakers on the ground, but they need clarity on praxis that actually can bring peace. Furthermore, if the Church or a Christian wants to think about it in a concrete manner, it is imperative to attend to practical implementation of *jpb*.

task highlights that the ultimate intention of incorporating political reconciliation into human security ought to be the (re)establishment of the
common good. In other words, it aims not just to redress a different set of
wounds of political injustice in a distinct way but also to restore a dimension
of human flourishing and of just political order. In so doing, the first task
signifies ethical minimalism, the second suggests the maxim(um) of that
ethical minimalism, and finally, the third integrates the first two as the
(re)establishment of the common good, the ultimate end of *jpb*. In a nutshell, there are three theological elements that constitute the maxim(um)
of ethical minimalism: the norm of human security, requiring classical just
actors to do their due *jpb* duty; the norm of political reconciliation, suggesting both classical and nonclassical actors do their virtuous acts to assist
the norm of human security; and the norm of the common good, calling
for these two norms to complete the ultimate *jpb* mission, that is, the establishment of a just peace. For the rest of this section, I will discuss how both
the norm of human security and the norm of political reconciliation relate
to the norm of the common good in light of *jpb* practice.

All in all, the fundamental theological characteristic of *jpb* must be
human security; the central task of *jpb* for just actors is to protect people in
a vanquished society after war. This human-security-centered *jpb* vision
highlights that achieving the common good secures a just postwar society
where the fulfillment of basic needs and respect are forthcoming for all persons no matter whether they were on "our" side or "their" side of the war.
The common good is fully realized when all individuals share in the political, social, and cultural life of the postwar communities whose activities
affect their well-being.[49] Seen in this light, the ultimate purpose of *jpb* is to
ensure that the common good is truly common, that is, shared in by all. In
this way, just actors—whether classical or nonclassical—must accomplish
the core mission of human security through the establishment of a just
peace, ordered to the common good.

In particular, I have emphasized the Thomistic tradition reflected in
Himes's *jpb* thinking because it signifies an intrinsic relationship between
postwar justice and the common good. For Himes, establishing that justice,
ordered to the common good, means achieving a political peace. This particularly means restoring the vanquished people's civilization and their

---

49 David Hollenbach, *The Common Good and Christian Ethics* (Cambridge: Cambridge University
Press, 2002), 69.

social civility, which is the basis of healing their ruined society. In this restored civil society, people enjoy reasonably equal freedom that facilitates the development of each of their human capabilities for the common good. As a result, they will have a growing sense of civic responsibility to that post-war society, the extent of their concern being for the welfare of others as well as themselves. With this proposition, I have affirmed that the issue of *jpb* is not the problem of the Christian community alone but of the entire human family. Hence, a more publicly oriented and comprehensively measured theological approach to the *jpb* discourse must be developed. This approach should continuously focus on the (re)establishment of political peace that begins with the protection of human life. This discourse must be distinguished from traditional theological approaches to eschatological peace or internal peace, which are mainly discussed as the theological basis for political reconciliation in *jpb* practices.

At the same time, as Allman and Winright state, just actors must recognize the limit of their human conditions and *jpb* practices, and they must discreetly manage their *post bellum* work to comport with practical reality. It is not difficult to say that *Christian* just actors must work toward the establishment of the common good beginning with the protection of human life. However, this statement is accompanied by certain practical questions. How do just actors treat all these individuals and groups *post bellum*, especially the poorest and most vulnerable? How do such various just actors—both classical and nonclassical—take care of not only themselves but also one another, especially the hostile? How do all these just actors move beyond their particular or their shared interests (oftentimes justified or propagandized in the name of the common good) and become accountable to a higher good? In chapter one, I argued that solving the postwar society's problem requires a commitment to a very ancient idea whose time has suddenly come: Aristotle's argument for the common good. More importantly, I distinguished his understanding of the common good from that of Aquinas. I emphasized that only by inspiring a spiritual and practical commitment to the common good can just actors make the personal and public lives of the members of the postwar society better and more virtuous. Hence, I will extend this distinctive theological stance in answering the aforementioned questions that will be practically examined in the next three chapters. At this point, I note that the public discussion about the common good, which is necessary for just actors in postwar societies, concerns not only politics but also all the decisions about personal, communal, and public lives. It is those individual and communal choices that will ultimately create the cultural shifts and social movements that truly change postwar politics in the long run.

Unlike those ancient secular ideas of the common good, in Christianity the central idea of the common good derives from Jesus' commandment to love our neighbor, including "the least of these" (Mt 25:40). This means that Christian faith traditions agree that loving our neighbor is required if we say we love God. Using how we treat the most vulnerable among us as the moral test of any society's "righteousness" or integrity is ultimately the best way to make absolutely sure that we are protecting human life and the dignity of all God's children. In postwar societies, this common good means that just actors must care for people in a vanquished society after war.

This understanding of righteousness is not radically different from Philpott's view of righteousness, which is defined as restoring right relationships in a holistic sense. This Christianity-informed, common-good-seeking justice also takes restorative justice as a fundamental direction, especially when it helps achieve human security for *jpb*.[50] This justice is similar, in part, to Philpott's justice, as it begins with a call to a relationship that changes all our other relationships. Although Philpott acknowledges this stance, he proposes the possibility of formulating the goals of political reconciliation without having to embrace a theologically substantive account of reconciliation. Therefore, in my view, his analysis can be well complemented by further theological reflection. The common-good-seeking justice I propose emphasizes not only that building a new relationship with God brings us into a new relationship with our neighbors but also that such a renewed relationship transforms us into people who care for our neighbors, especially the most vulnerable of this world, and even our enemies. This call to love our neighbor is the foundation for reestablishing and reclaiming the common good, which has fallen into cultural, political, and even religious neglect, especially in postwar societies.

Like Philpott's ethic of political reconciliation, this common-good-seeking justice also sees our relationship with God and our neighbors through the lens of the entire Abrahamic tradition. However, my approach focuses on God's love for us and our response to his love that is shown in our transformation by his love.[51] Judaism, of course, agrees that our

---

50 And, to repeat, it is "a" fundamental direction, not "the" one as Scheid proposes.
51 One may wonder whether Philpott also takes this stance. He would agree that righteousness involves compassion. However, first, he does not explicitly address that a renewed relationship

relationship with God is supposed to change all our other relationships, and Jesus' recitation of the Law's great commandments to love God and your neighbor flows right out of the books of Deuteronomy and Leviticus (Dt 6:5; and Lv 19:18). Likewise, Islam connects the love of Allah with love and responsibility to our neighbors. In fact, nearly all the world's major religions highlight that we cannot separate our love for God from our love for our neighbor. Even the nonreligious will affirm the secular equivalent of "the Golden Rule," which can be compared to the Christian moral teaching: "do to others as you would have them do to you" (Lk 6:31).

That transformation of all our relationships, especially the clear connection between loving God and loving our neighbor, has always been the best catalyst for movements aimed at improving the human community. However, the common good is quite *un*common in postwar societies, where this unifying vision seems to have been lost in the postwar community and public life, especially in politics. In short, the common good is virtually ignored in the immediate aftermath of war; therefore, just actors ought to attend to the (re)establishment of the common good, which is the first step for human security, and later to political reconciliation if possible. The common good welcomes all people into God's beloved community, and our social behavior and public policies must demonstrate that. It is a central vision of *jpb* drawn from the heart of our Christian tradition that allows us to make our faith public but not narrowly partisan, and to join with others of different faiths, or even no faith, who share common moral sensibilities, especially toward protecting human life after war. Christian just actors need to discern and transcend the distorted power of state politics by holding themselves accountable to the common good. Therefore, the common-good-seeking justice *post bellum* requires not only restoration of our relationships but also the transformation of ourselves. Christians' compassion for all of God's creatures, especially vulnerable fellow humans, transforms us to act when evil threatens them.

---

transforms us into ones who care for our neighbors, *especially the most vulnerable ones*. Second, regardless of whether he agrees with this position or not, he does not explain how this call to love relates to the common good. This distinction exists perhaps because Philpott's primary aim is to find a way of building a common ground among the Abrahamic traditions that leads him to attend to a linguistic analysis rather than a theological exposition. In contrast, my common-good-seeking justice is grounded in the Christian moral tradition, especially Himes's understanding of the common good.

The Common-Good-Seeking Justice:
Social Charity and Political Prudence

In Christian faith, this task of seeking the common good begins with the notion of God's care; God has a particular care for everyone, especially for those who have gone astray (Lk 15:1–7; Is 53:6).[52] This is a comfort to everyone involved in warfare but especially to those defeated people who have suffered immensely through war. They have lost their loved ones as well as their own ways of life in the vanquished economy, state, and civil society. The loss of their community culture, social infrastructure, and even religious and moral ethos leaves them with a lifetime of pain. Jesus primarily cared about these people.

> What do you think? If a shepherd has a hundred sheep, and one of them has gone astray, does he not leave the ninety-nine on the mountains and go in search for the one that went astray? And if he finds it, truly I tell you, he rejoices over it more than over the ninety-nine that never went astray. So it is not the will of your Father in heaven that one of these little ones should be lost (Mt 18:12–14).

Likewise, just actors, Christian ones in particular, need to care for the "little ones," those who are vulnerable and cannot cope with life's demands. In this regard, the Church also must speak more prophetically—and react more responsibly—to our world where violence still abounds, especially in post-war societies. Drawing upon Pope Francis's teaching on the parable of the Good Samaritan, I must set out my theological argument for *jpb* based in charity, more precisely, social charity. On July 10, 2016, the pope emphasized that the Good Samaritan is not just a nice passage to reflect on but signifies a concrete choice that everyone must make in deciding how to live a life with compassion. He notes, "the Good Samaritan indicates a lifestyle, the center of which is not ourselves, but others, with their difficulties, who we meet on our path and who challenge us."[53]

This message on being the Good Samaritan, or social charity, is nothing novel and is consistently found—though with slightly different nuance and context—in the Catholic Social Teaching (CST), such as Leo XIII's "friendship,"

---

52 For further discussion, see Peter Phan, "Catholic Social Thought," *Message of the Fathers of the Church* 20 (Wilmington, NC: Glazier, 1984), 153.

53 For Pope Francis's message on the parable, see Elise Harris, "The Good Samaritan Isn't Just a Parable, It's a Way of Life, Pope Says." *Catholic News Agency*, July 10, 2016, http://www. catholicnewsagency.com/news/the-good-samaritan-isnt-just-a-parable-its-a-way-of-life-pope-says-85517.

Pius XI's "social charity," Paul VI's "civilization of love," and John Paul II's "solidarity."[54] These similar notions commonly share two aspects: (i) the sacredness of human life and the dignity of the human person and (ii) the notion of solidarity. For the former, humans are created in the image and likeness of God, redeemed by Jesus Christ, and destined for Beatitude.[55] It is the foundation of a moral vision for society, including the postwar society, as discussed regarding *jpb*'s concern of human security. For the latter, drawing upon the notion of solidarity, all human beings are one human family despite national, religious, political, and ideological differences—and thus are interdependent on and responsible for each other. More precisely, as John Paul II notes, "[Solidarity] is not a feeling of a vague compassion, . . . [but] it is a firm and persevering determination to commit oneself to the common good; that is to say, to the good of all and of each individual, because we are all really responsible for all."[56] In other words, solidarity is not simply about a feeling toward people in a vanquished society but about "a moral virtue," or a commitment to act out of compassion and thereby achieve the common good in the society.[57] In this way, the virtue of solidarity is also more judiciously understood as that of social charity, especially in *jpb* contexts.

However, this social charity does not simply mean that just actors rule out some courses of human security action *post bellum*, like just policing, and offer other courses of action for political reconciliation, like a Truth Commission. Even these actions, especially the latter ones, leave substantial room for judgment as to whether they are fully accomplished; furthermore, no clear criterion can substitute for the likely effects of choosing one course of action over another. Likewise, this social charity does not always mean that just actors— even nonclassical ones—perform political reconciliation for a just peace. Plainly, political reconciliation sometimes disturbs human security and undermines other kinds of justice, such as fairness. How then does this human security *jpb* scheme lead to a true just peace? No ethic can answer such questions.

Like Philpott and Scheid, the Franciscan priest and Navy chaplain Louis Iasiello argues that the obligations of *jpb* extend far beyond the restoration of

---

54 For comment and discussion, see Pontifical Council for Justice and Peace, *Compendium of the Social Doctrine of the Church* (Washington, DC: USCCB Publishing, 2004), chap. 4, 421.

55 For further discussion, see John XXIII, Encyclical Letter *Mater et Magistra* (1961), 219; and John Paul II, Encyclical Letter *Centesimus Annus* (1991), 11.

56 John Paul II, Encyclical Letter *Sollicitudo rei Socialis* (1987), 38.

57 Pontifical Council for Justice and Peace, *Compendium of the Social Doctrine of the Church*, chap. 4, 193.

order and include reconciliation among the warring parties. However, as shown earlier by the challenges of political reconciliation in light of both normative and practical concerns (e.g., its inappropriateness for a short-term-based postwar justice project), the possibility of applying this theme directly to the *jpb* framework is questionable. In fact, Iasiello himself admits the limitations of this political reconciliation approach. He founds his conception of obligations of the victor on a mixture of pragmatic self-interest, international law, and morality. In this regard, he concludes that some of the political praxes of reconciliation (such as the prosecution of post-conflict justice) "are better left to an international group or organization, not to the victors themselves."[58]

In response to these challenges, my *jpb* moral theology, bolstered by the maxim(um) minimalism, needs another key element of social virtue, that is, political prudence. I adopt Aquinas's notion of the virtue of prudence, along with the ethic of maxim(um) minimalism that provides criteria to rule out some choices and narrow down others. Moreover, this ethic certainly provides more developed criteria than Allman and Winright's Niebuhrian view grounded in political realism's open-ended notion of national interest. Aquinas cites prudence as the central virtue since it is "right reason in action" by giving concrete "shape" to the moral aspirations of a person.[59] Moral norms seldom dictate one clear action in concrete situations; given the constraints of politics and the power of others in the *jpb* context, most outcomes comport only partially with one's moral aspirations. On the other hand, prudence actively seeks to accomplish good, and political prudence pursues common good.[60] Hence, a prudent just actor's intelligence looks for opportunities that permit action to be taken practically consonant with goals and power in postwar societies.

Political prudence disposes of the practical reason to discern, in every circumstance of *jpb*, our true good and to choose the appropriate means for achieving the common good. Indeed, political prudence's intellectual content arises from the full dimensions of excellence in political achievement. However, political prudence does not cover all morality, nor does it guarantee success. Paradoxically, even prudent just actors can fail, just like reckless actors can succeed by accident or by luck. In this regard, the Niebuhrian *jpb* on imperfect justice due to the human Fall and finitude is convincing.

---

58 Louis Iasiello, "*Jus Post Bellum*: The Moral Responsibilities of Victors in War," *Naval War College Review* 57, no. 3/4 (Summer/Autumn 2004): 47.

59 *ST*, II-II, q.47, a.2, 5, 7.

60 *ST*, II-II, q.52, a.2.

However, the Thomistic *jpb* does not end with the pessimistic attitude or realism heightened in the Niebuhrian view. Unlike the Niebuhrian view, the Thomistic view of the human person is that, in a nutshell, regardless of the wounds from the Fall that remain in humans, including sins of violence, the goodness of God's creation still reigns over the evil disobedience of Adam and Eve.[61] Recognizing the goodness of each human person not only opens wide the doors to the positive peace of healthy relationships and merciful hearts but also encourages them to practice the virtue of prudence, thereby cooperating to ensure that justice reigns in a *post bellum* society. Therefore, the virtue of prudence is not only the art of taking principles and applying them to concrete situations, but also allowing us with an honest examination of reality—yet with trust—to divine providence.

CONCLUSION

In the period immediately following war, human security is key and fundamental. However, it is also interdependent with political reconciliation in that it is not fully prior to political reconciliation chronologically. This human security paves the way for long-term social restoration, participatory government, and cooperative institutions going forward, all of which are integral to achieving political reconciliation. Furthermore, these characteristics of political reconciliation are also seen as *jpb* elements among some theologians such as Allman and Winright.[62] However, *jpb*, as part of the JWT, must be distinguished from transitional justice in terms of its purpose and scope. While these distinctions will be more concretely discussed in the next three chapters, this chapter focused on answering the question as to whether political reconciliation is always necessary for *jpb*.

This chapter argued that human security must be prioritized over political reconciliation, not vice versa. My understanding of *jpb* is different from some major theologians, such as Allman and Winright, who see *jpb* as stretching into the long term and would, in fact, see it as part of a longer

---

61 *ST*, I, q.81, a.2–3.

62 Gerald Schlabach is another theologian who shares this perspective. See Gerald Schlabach, ed., *Just Policing, Not War: An Alternative Response to World Violence* (Collegeville, MN: Liturgical Press, 2007), chap. 5. Further, one may argue that because Scheid and Philpott are "theological" their ethic of political reconciliation cannot be applied to just policing, punishment, and political participation. To be clear, however, this is not true, as many theologians like Allman, Winright, and Schlabach discuss exactly these topics. See Gerald Schlabach and Duane K. Friesen, eds., *At Peace and Unafraid: Public Order, Security, and the Wisdom of the Cross* (Kitchener, ON: Herald Press, 2005).

peacebuilding trajectory. Instead, my guidance for *jpb* is based on the classical JWT, which is an ethic of war that primarily deals with armed forces
whose mission is to end war in the vanquished nation. Certainly, there are
other nonclassical just actors that are involved in this phase of *jpb*, but they
should be protected by classical actors from on-going and potential violence. If the postwar society fulfills human security at least at a basic level,
then the society requires a larger, longer-term-based agenda than what *jpb*
proposes. This agenda calls upon transitional justice, moving from the phase
in which armed forces are in charge of just policing to the phase in which
a nonmilitary civilian force, namely police, is in charge of just policing.

In particular, this chapter discussed why Philpott's ethic of political reconciliation is not effectively suitable for postwar justice, or at least why one
should not apply his ethic of political reconciliation directly to the context of
jpb. Philpott sheds light on "wounds" and what is necessary to overcome
them. He usefully recognizes that the process and outcome are always partial
and imperfect. Even though he works with religious sources and backing, his
call for political reconciliation is not exclusive to the churches and theologians.
His ethic of political reconciliation should be understood as a direction for
jpb, but not *the direction,* as in the case of Scheid's consistent ethic of reconciliation. In addition, despite the limits in Philpott's ethic of political reconciliation, it must be kept in mind that *jpb* is not his main concern. Of more
concern is the fact that some theologians like Scheid overemphasize Philpott's
work in the *jpb* arena. Finally, I reiterate that human security is fundamental.
The argument that human security is the primary concern prevails throughout the book. When we, as children of God, choose to ignore the cries of our
most vulnerable, we are failing to secure the common good. However, I do
not say that security does not include coexistence with political reconciliation.
Rather, my common good approach demands social charity and political prudence. In particular, the *jpb* vision of political reconciliation needs to be
clearly, concretely, and comprehensively manifested throughout two stages
of *jpb*: just punishment and just political participation. For example, political
participation involves forming political parties, open public policy debates,
fundraising, lobbying, vote-getting, and public advocacy, all of which require
the extensive buildup of civil society as well as strong public institutions.
However, all these practices are also dependent on time commitment and
cost *post bellum*, giving a reason why (relatively) short-term-based *jpb* needs
to be distinguished from transitional justice. This argument will be discussed
in depth throughout the last three chapters.

Part II

Policy-Oriented and Practical Concerns in *Jus Post Bellum*

Chapter 5

Reconstruction of Just Policing

INTRODUCTION
From Theory to Practice

The ethic of *jpb* as part of the JWT is a moral instrument for assessing the justness of the resolution of conflict. The previous two chapters have clarified that the moral and theological rationale of *jpb* must be the establishment of a just peace that serves the common good. Additionally, this *jpb* rationale carries with it an insistence that justice persists even in the fallen condition of humankind. Finally, the development of this *jpb* ethic, from a theological view, is closely tied to the two morally and politically pressing norms of human security and political reconciliation.

Therefore, my ultimate concern is with how *Christian* actors should think about the problem of war in the *post bellum* phase. I want to ask whether, and how, these just actors should think differently about the ethic of *jpb* once they have established a range of practical frames of reference for *jpb*. These practical frames of reference, which I will present in the following chapters, are just policing, just punishment, and just political participation. In particular, this chapter begins by setting the parameters of the field of security studies, especially with regard to two practices for just policing: peacekeeping and nation building.

Just Policing: Refreshing and Refining the Theoretical Ground for Practice

As proposed in the previous chapter, my "Maxim(um) of Ethical Minimalism: the Norm of the Common Good" approach responds to a practical dilemma or tension between the two poles of human security and political reconciliation. This approach attends to the use of both armed force and nonviolent means to achieve the common good, as they correspondingly and comprehensively contribute to a transformative *jpb* scheme. In particular, utilizing these means for just policing must be the first task of the entire continuum of *jpb* practice toward the "maxim(um)" of *jpb*, or the ultimate end of *jpb*, namely, the attainment of the common good.

My common-good-seeking approach affirms that just actors must consider utilizing both means of just policing in a wise manner to achieve a *comprehensive* version of human security. This approach is drawn from Himes's understanding of the establishment of a just peace that must be directed toward a political peace ordered to the common good, aiming to protect the lives of every individual, especially those who are most vulnerable. The comprehensive version of human security required by my approach—understood as a vehicle for the "maxim(um)" of the "ethical minimalism"—needs to incorporate aspects of both traditional notions of human security and national security, which are integral to a transformative scheme of just policing.[1] These aspects include the protection and welfare of the individual citizen or human being, as in the definition of the traditional notion of human security, along with the necessary aspects of national security, such as the protection of state sovereignty through rebuilding a social order, securing the safety of people through international authority, and promoting external autonomy and national independence. Moreover, these aspects must be primarily subject to the transformative just policing agenda, not the restorative one.[2] Therefore, some aspects of traditional national security adherent to a restorative scheme of *jpb* must *not* be prioritized, such as the *restoration* of territorial integrity and domestic order. In other words, this extended notion of human security has evolved from a rudimentary sense of human security—such as protecting people from imminent threats and providing basic needs for them—to a transformative idea of just policing, even incorporating the necessary aspects of national security, insofar as these

---

1 There are two popular ways of defining "comprehensive security" in security studies. First, the notion of comprehensive security, more often known as "comprehensive human security" is employed by security studies scholars to recognize the interdependent natures of the natural environment and humanity's collective social security related to that environment. Second, it is referred to as "comprehensive defense." It means a set of government integrated policies—foreign, defense, economic, technological and sociocultural—that articulate the ways and means by which a state's national interests can be preserved. While my approach to a comprehensive version of human security in this book is closer to the latter, since the latter also touches on a transformative idea of security through a continuum of government practices, the latter is different from my approach since it lacks an idea of human security, as it prioritizes national interests over human life. For details of the former concept, see Arthur Westing, *Arthur H. Westing: Pioneer on the Environmental Impact of War*, ed. Hans Günter Brach (New York: Springer, 2013), 15–16; and for the latter, see United States Department of Defense, *US Army Counterinsurgency Handbook* (New York: Skyhorse Publishing, 2007), chap. 6.

2 Informed by Walzer's *jpb* work, I defined the restorative agenda as drawn from the idea of restoring the status quo *ante bellum*.

aspects serve the priority of ensuring people's safety over restoring the status quo *ante bellum*.

This chapter proposes a comprehensive version of human security for just policing, returning to the central agenda of the "Maxim(um) of Ethical Minimalism: the Norm of the Common Good" approach. Keeping that in mind, I will analyze *jpb* from the perspective of security studies, emphasizing just policing practices for dealing with "the present injustice."[3] I define the present injustice *post bellum* as the ongoing violent threats with which the vanquished state is confronted, such as internal insurgency, sizable communal violence or persistent low-level violence, as well as other politically and economically life-threatening challenges. In response to *post bellum* challenges from this present injustice, we will discuss two major practices for just policing: arms control and peacekeeping, drawn from ethical minimalism, along with nation building, an implicit vehicle for the maxim(um) of ethical minimalism.

JUST POLICING FOR DEALING WITH PRESENT INJUSTICE
Classical Just Actors: Peacekeeping and Nation Building
Classical Just Actors and Just Policing

With respect to just policing, some actors are characterized as classical, namely the armed forces run by victorious states and the international community.[4] Although the army is the main agent conducting policing practices, as in *jus ad bellum* and *jus in bello*, it is important to distinguish between the army in *jus ad bellum* and *jus in bello* and the army in *jpb*. In *jus ad bellum* and *jus in bello*, the army wages war through violent means. In *post bellum*, the army is involved in all of the just policing areas working toward comprehensive human security, not just arms control and peacekeeping, but also humanitarian assistance, disaster relief, reconstructing public goods, training local security forces, and supporting civilian/business organizations. This dual referent of the armed forces *post bellum* means that just policing requires

---

3 Here I draw on Thomas Weiss's understanding of the present injustice as "perceived present and potential threats to physical and psychological welfare," from all manner of agents and forces "affecting lives, values, and property." Thomas Weiss and David P. Forsythe, eds., *The United Nations and Changing World Politics* (Boulder, CO: Westview Press, 1997), 260.

4 As defined in the previous chapter, there are two types of just actors: "classical" and "nonclassical" just actors. While "classical just actors" refer to armed forces run by victorious states and/or the international community, "nonclassical" ones refer to unarmed forces, such as NGOs, the Church, and other civil organizations. And with respect to the theme of just policing, I made a proposition: just actors are principally the classical ones.

nation building as much as it requires arms control and peacekeeping. The JWT defends the use of armed force in situations when "the fundamental rights to life and liberty cannot be secured in any other way."[5] Likewise, justified violence in the *post bellum* phase may secure these rights, but it does not automatically protect them; the cessation of hostilities is not the beginning of peace but simply the end of the armed conflict. Peace does not come until stability and tolerance have been established so the threat of future conflict is greatly diminished.[6] Therefore, the two major tasks for just policing must be considered in order to remove the present impediments to peace. Those tasks are peacekeeping, protecting individuals from constant volatility even after the ceasefire is declared, and nation building, providing comprehensive rebuilding efforts that will tackle the root cause of the conflict and hostilities.

Arms Control and Peacekeeping Operations

One of the major just policing practices required for an occupied nation *post bellum* is the establishment of peacekeeping and arms control operations. Unstable and unassisted wartorn nations are politically and economically vulnerable. As shown by most postwar literature across disciplines, this vulnerability creates an increased chance for an escalation of domestic crime, violence, and hostility, all of which exacerbate the instability. This instability, accompanied by repeated unlawful and unjustified aggression, is what the just policing agenda primarily seeks to address. Protecting individuals, especially the innocent and vulnerable, from constant volatility is a moral good of justified armed force, nullifying those conditions of instability in the vanquished nation that may result in future wars. This goal of just policing intersects with both the common-good-seeking *jpb* and the Church's teaching—drawn from Vatican documents such as *Gaudium et Spes*, *Compendium of the Social Doctrine of the Church*, and *Sollicitudo rei Socialis*, as well as the US Bishops' letter "Forming Consciences for Faithful Citizenship"—in that the common good "can be understood as the social and community dimension of the moral good" and that "direct attacks on innocent persons are never morally acceptable . . . in any condition."[7]

---

5 Williams and Caldwell, *"Jus Post Bellum,"* 316.

6 For a similar argument from security studies scholar Alan Collins, see Alan Collins, *Contemporary Security Studies* (Oxford: Oxford University Press, 2013).

7 Catholic News Service, "Human Dignity, the Common Good, and Solidarity Are 'More than Mere Words,' Bishops say," *America*, November 23, 2016.

Figure 2. Conflict Continuum

Applying this elementary sense of human security, we will review two scholars whose ideas are in broad accord with the just policing agenda of arms control and peacekeeping practice. James Ayers and Ivar Scheers are both human security advocates who emphasize individual human rights to life and liberty and consider the military as the primary agency of that security. However, they are distinguished from each other when it comes to the question of whether to privilege the victor or the international community as responsible for just policing in the postwar society.

James Ayers: The US Mission of MOOTW

In his article "Military Operations Other Than War (MOOTW) in the New World Order," James Ayers attends to the duty of the victor, in particular US forces, in the postwar society. He argues that MOOTW should focus on deterring war, resolving conflict, promoting peace, and supporting civil authorities in response to Low Intensity Conflict (LIC) in post-conflict areas. The term LIC was first introduced by the Reagan administration to define MOOTW, viewed as a continuum of conflict intensity. Ayers defines MOOTW as any military activity that falls short of war (see Figure 2, above).[8]

However, Ayers argues that this broad definition poses another question: "how does MOOTW differ from war?"[9] He acknowledges that it can be hard for a nation involved in humanitarian intervention to grasp the differences between war and operations short of war. This is mainly because the nature of LIC cannot be clearly defined between the phase of conflict and peacetime. The phase of LIC is a threshold between war and peace, which intends to return to full peacetime, while also remaining a time of conflict in a unique environment in which the military works closely with

---

8 Adapted from John B. Hunt, "Emerging Doctrine for LIC," *Military Review* (June 1991): 23–24, quoted in James Ayers, *Military Operations Other Than War in the New World Order: An Analysis of Joint Doctrine for the Coming Era* (Wright-Patterson Air Force Base, OH: Air Force Institute of Technology, May 1996), 10.

9 Ayers, *Military Operations Other Than War*, 44.

other political means to control hostilities. Despite these challenges, Ayers maintains that MOOTW become more vital where the options for traditional application of military instruments are growing more limited and suggests six principles.

(1) The aim of MOOTW is not as clear as that of wartime activities. Despite that, the US leadership must at least avoid any ill-defined end that can lead to Mission Creep, which could endanger the lives of the US forces and civilians.

(2) US forces committed to MOOTW are not always designated as the primary agency in attaining US policy objectives. Therefore, deployed commanders must emphasize a common understanding and vision among the entire body of postwar agencies involved in arms control and peacekeeping operations.

(3) MOOTW are often conducted in the absence of a direct threat to US forces. Despite that fact, the military must remain conscious of security issues.

(4) Restrictive rules of engagement are the norm in MOOTW. Rules governing the use of armed force must be appropriate without unnecessarily endangering the lives of US forces and the local citizens in conflict-ridden societies.

(5) MOOTW projects take years to attain their desired goals, as they may involve more than military efforts alone. The US leadership must balance the desire for prompt, decisive action with a sensitivity for long-term mission goals.

(6) The entire practice of MOOTW must support the legitimacy of host local governments. In other words, occupying forces must cede power to that local community when seen as a legitimate and independent government.[10]

These principles of MOOTW largely intersect with the mission of just policing, from protecting individuals from constant volatility even after the ceasefire is declared to providing comprehensive rebuilding efforts. As Ayers emphasizes, without careful plans to properly occupy and reconstruct a postwar society, victorious states will risk conflating political progress and a decrease in violence with sustainable stability.

---

10 For details, see Ayers, 31–41.

Ivar Scheers: The UN's Peacekeeping Operations

Like Ayers, Scheers's proposal includes deterring potential aggressors and protecting national interests, but his work is distinguished from Ayers in that his proposal focuses on UN objectives, not just those of a single nation. Also, while Ayers does not specify his practical inquiries for *jpb*, Scheers explicitly comments that postwar peacekeeping should be seen as valuable for further developing *jpb*: "Theoretical and empirical perspectives regarding *jus post bellum* and intra-state conflict [within the postwar society] can be derived from peacekeeping, since the UN is, internationally, the main actor in post-conflict situations."[11] Further, he defines peacekeeping as the catalyst for a "modern [*jpb*] approach" since (i) peacekeeping missions' mandates have changed to such an extent that contemporary peacekeeping operations have actually become *peacebuilding missions*; and (ii) that changed nature of peacekeeping highlights the importance of peacebuilding for modern *jpb*, especially shown by recent peacekeeping missions, which established *ad hoc* transitional administrations that "involve UN-(authorized) governments focusing on nation building and provide for the broadest available practice."[12]

After defining the prevalence of peacekeeping missions for the *jpb* concept, Scheers articulates practical reasons why UN peacekeeping must play a major role for *jpb*. First, he confirms the validity of war under the UN chapter seven enforcement; hence, UN peacekeeping under that condition maintains a legal resort to war in JWT.[13] Second, he emphasizes that UN peacekeeping conveys a spirit of consent because "a coalition of states . . . will enjoy more international support than in the case of unilateral action."[14] Third, a peacekeeping force consisting of a broad international coalition

---

11 Ivar Scheers, "Peacekeeping and *Jus Post Bellum*," *The Central European Journal of International and Security Studies* 5, no. 3 (March 2011): 81.

12 Scheers, 77. This discourse of peacekeeping and peacebuilding originally took off from 1992 when the former UN Secretary-General Boutros Boutros-Ghali issued the report, "An Agenda for Peace." See Boutros Boutros-Ghali, *An Agenda for Peace*, 2nd ed. (New York: United Nations, 1995). This report was updated in 2001; from this revision, the former UN Secretary-General Kofi Annan used a mnemonic device to address peacebuilding related issues: the 4 Ps, which consist of "preventive diplomacy," "peacemaking," "peacekeeping," and "peacebuilding." In the 4Ps, while peacekeeping is the idea of deploying people on the ground to keep disputants apart from one another and to establish no-fly zones to protect refugees or other human beings, peacebuilding is a concept that follows upon successful peacekeeping as it is understood to address postwar situations that attempt to strengthen and solidify a peaceful order.

13 Scheers, "Peacekeeping and *Jus Post Bellum*," 87.

14 Scheers, 88.

will be seen as ethnically neutral toward the combative ethnic groups within the occupied population. Finally, both peacekeeping and *jpb* aim to create sustainable peace, while peacekeeping forms a hybrid system combining different legal paradigms within *jpb*. This system represents a holistic view of *jpb* by indicating some recent successes of peacekeeping missions across human rights, war criminal prosecutions, and nation-building practices, all of which are fused into a hybrid framework.[15]

In particular, Scheers presents the so-called "comprehensive *jpb* proposal" based on the lessons learned from earlier peacekeeping operations in Kosovo, East Timor, and Afghanistan, all of which show "the broad set of duties and responsibilities post-conflict peacekeeping missions are endowed with, including a strong focus on nation building."[16] For example, he attends to the fact that the UNSC Resolution established the Peacebuilding Commission in 2005, which aimed to assist these three vanquished states not merely through peacekeeping but also peacebuilding, working toward the sustainable development of nation building.[17] He concludes that in his comprehensive *jpb* proposal, peacekeeping must be accompanied by nation building.

Further, Scheers attends to human rights issues as a major element of his comprehensive *jpb* proposal. This emphasis on human rights in his proposal not only demonstrates why peacekeeping should play a large role in defining *jpb* but also clarifies that the ultimate characteristic of UN peacekeeping must be a *relatively* longer-term process of peacebuilding. He highlights a point of convergence in that peacekeeping and peacebuilding share human security as their primary mission. His understanding of peacekeeping is as a positive notion of peace, including "freedom, justice, liberty, and equity," all of which are integral to "the *attainability* of peace" in postwar societies.[18] Therefore, UN peacekeeping aims to protect the human rights of life and liberty. He suggests four distinct peacekeeping practices in order to secure human rights.

(1) Supporting, protecting, and monitoring human rights—A broad focus on human rights must be established, which focuses on supporting,

---

15 Scheers, 89. The recent successful cases which he notes are Kosovo and East Timor.

16 Scheers, 95. Also, for details of Scheers's *jpb* proposal, see Scheers, 95–109.

17 Cf. UN Security Council, Resolution 1645, S/RES/1645 (December 20, 2005), https://digital-library.un.org/record/563509.

18 Scheers, "Peacekeeping and *Jus Post Bellum*," 80.

protecting, and monitoring human rights by post-conflict peacekeeping forces. Legal support for the extraterritorial application of human rights law can be seen as a basis for this.

(2) Investigating and sanctioning violations—[The presence of] investigational units and a judicial system sanctioning the discovered violations is a requirement for the just vindication of human rights in post-conflict situations, as they send strong signals to the community regarding the creation of a stable human rights situation and a deterring message to violators.

(3) Accountability for human rights violations by proxy—Members of international peacekeeping forces and UN personnel should be accountable for human rights violations in a way any other person will be held accountable. The international community must equally apply the rights it endeavors to promote to all sides involved in the conflict.

(4) Restitution of sovereignty—One of the objectives of jpb is the return of a government with full domestic sovereignty and thereby the recognition of self-determination. The restitution of this domestic sovereignty by the peacekeeping mission is therefore required and will pave the way for full reintegration into the international community.[19]

This comprehensive *jpb* proposal for peacekeeping corresponds to my "Maxim(um) of Ethical Minimalism: the Norm of the Common Good" approach, at least in terms of its orientation toward a comprehensive version of human security. As shown by the four peacekeeping practices, Scheers attempts to incorporate aspects of both traditional notions of human security (the first three peacekeeping practices) and national security (restitution of domestic sovereignty). While he sees how this recognition of the dual referent for security is critical to the development and implementation of the UN's peacekeeping operations,

Scheers also clarifies that the restitution of sovereignty through the promotion of external autonomy and national independence must be part of a transformative just policing agenda. Ultimately, the purpose is human security, not merely national security.

Therefore, Scheers's suggested means for just policing, namely, UN's peacekeeping forces, constitute a transformative *jpb* scheme more than a traditional sense of peacekeeping, which usually refers to securing the postwar

19 Scheers, 99–100.

area following a ceasefire or respite from fighting. Rather, this wider brand of peacekeeping opens the possibility of a longer-term process of peacebuilding, which is concerned with transforming relations with outlying states to increase the chance of enduring stability, especially when it is accompanied by nation-building efforts. However, Scheers's comprehensive *jpb* proposal does not clearly identify what constitutes nation building, nor does his proposal specify how such nation building is presented in practice.

Nation-Building Practices

It is vital for classical just actors, whether they are run by the victor or the international community, not only to undertake the mission of arms control in order to put an end to violence, but also to carry out peacekeeping missions that hold potential aggressors of armed conflicts accountable for political unrest, economic destabilization, and loss of human life. As Scheers emphasizes, these missions must be understood as the actors' primary duty for the establishment of social order on the ground, which in turn helps to ensure human security in the process of postwar nation building. This distinction affirms my comprehensive human security proposal, as it endorses military involvement for nation building. Expanding upon Scheers's work, this section will discuss what constitutes nation building and how it is articulated in practice.

In particular, we will review three *jpb* scholars who hold both a normative and practical approach to just policing that broadly intersects with the nation-building agenda. Dan Caldwell, James Dobbins, and Noah Feldman are all human security advocates who emphasize individual human rights yet recognize that the connection between state sovereignty and human rights is essential to ensuring a comprehensive and realistic version of human security for just policing. This perspective is commonly found in their work on postwar nation building, but they are distinguished from one another by different emphases in practice.

Dan Caldwell:
The Victor's Obligation to Political and Economic Transformation

Dan Caldwell's major question asks how to protect human rights in postwar societies. In "*Jus Post Bellum*: Just War Theory and the Principles of Just Peace," an article coauthored with Robert E. Williams, Caldwell argues that nation building obligates victorious states to ensure human rights in the defeated nations. In other words, victorious states are the indispensable actors necessary to actualize just policing achieved through fully committed and all-encompassing *jpb* missions. In particular, he makes three recommendations: restoration of order, economic reconstruction, and self-determination.[20] He argues that these are nonnegotiable duties of the victor in any conception of *jpb* predicated on the vindication of human rights. Despite his emphasis on these essential duties of the victor, Caldwell acknowledges that, in reality, there are limits to the implementation of nation building.

In 2011, Caldwell published a book, *The Vortex of Conflict: US Policy towards Afghanistan, Pakistan, and Iraq*, which details the experiences of the US as a victor in both Afghanistan and Iraq. Drawn from a study by the RAND Corporation, Caldwell makes several policy proposals that entail political transformation and reconstruction. He begins his work with the proposition that "postwar operations are vital to the execution of a successful campaign."[21] Caldwell's two practical concerns are: human security at what cost and human security during what time period. He believes that just actors must expect war to be extremely costly in both human and material terms. For example, he says that in both the Afghan and Iraqi wars "as of November 2010, the US and its coalition partners have lost 2,220 in Afghanistan and 4,745 in Iraq. . . . 35,000 Americans have been . . . injured." In addition, he argues that the economic cost of these wars is massive.[22] Nevertheless, for the sake of human security, he believes that once the war is over, victorious states must not immediately leave the defeated society. Based on RAND's 2010 report, he argues that "successful occupations require . . . enormous investments of resources for a period of five years at a minimum."[23]

Finally, Caldwell's emphasis on nation building in practice requires two major rules: (i) "develop plans for postwar reconstruction and development before the war begins and make adjustments as the war develops"; and (ii)

---

20 For details, see Williams and Caldwell, *"Jus Post Bellum,"* 317–18.

21 Dan Caldwell, *Vortex of Conflict: U.S. Policy toward Afghanistan, Pakistan, and Iraq* (Stanford, CA: Stanford University Press, 2011), 171.

22 Caldwell, 171. According to the Watson Institute at Brown University, as of November 2019, total costs of post-9/11 wars since 2001 is approaching $6.4 trillion. Neta C. Crawford, "US Budgetary Costs and Obligations of Post-9/11 Wars through FY2020: $6.4 Trillion," *Costs of War*, Watson Institute, Brown University (November 2019).

23 Caldwell, 172.

"sustain economic development programs over the long term."[24] The first rule insists that just actors should not only deal with postwar issues after the end of war but also make postwar planning an initial requirement of war fighting. This rule is essential because just actors can fight wars in a manner that is conducive to a positive postwar environment. The second rule signifies that economic programs must be developed and sustained over the long term in order for the postwar society to fully emerge from a *post bellum* phase. Further, this economic reconstruction secures the local postwar community's capability of self-determination.

James Dobbins:
Involving the International Community in Political Transformation

James Dobbins's view is similar to Caldwell's in that he is concerned with postwar nation building for human security. However, unlike Caldwell, who attends to the obligation of the victor to secure human rights, Dobbins pays attention to the duty of both the victor and the international community. Additionally, unlike Caldwell's focus on a wide range of security concerns across both political and economic domains, Dobbins focuses primarily on the subject of political transformation.

Dobbins uses the same RAND database of nation building intervention cases as Caldwell, but he uses it mainly in relation to political transformation in seven nations: Germany, Japan, Somalia, Haiti, Bosnia, Kosovo, and Afghanistan. Based on a comparative analysis of the seven intervention cases, the RAND report seeks to establish the factors associated with success or failure for just policing. One factor linked to success was the use of armed force to underpin a process of democratization. Akin to Caldwell, Dobbins believes that the use of armed force ensures "the ability to promote an enduring transfer of democratic institutions," which demonstrates his interest in a transformational *jpb*.[25] In particular, his book *America's Role in Nation Building* presents a policy analysis of US military-led enforced democratization. However, unlike Caldwell, Dobbins emphasizes that nation building is more about successful political transformation to a democratic form of government than economic reconstruction.

---

24 The two rules are originally drawn from Caldwell's twenty-six rules regarding postwar operations in general. For details, see Dan Caldwell, 255–62.

25 James Dobbins, *America's Role in Nation Building: From Germany to Iraq* (Santa Monica, CA: Rand Corporation Publishing, 2003), 2.

Dobbins is most distinguished from Caldwell in that he attends to the obligation of the international community toward the vanquished society. Although multilateral nation building is more complex and consumes more time and resources than unilateral nation building, he emphasizes that "it can produce a more thorough-going transformation and greater regional reconciliation than can unilateral efforts."[26] Dobbins also points out that this multilateral strategy helps relieve the US and other superpower nations from pressures on both human and material resources. For example, when the US took the lead in transforming Germany and Japan after WWII, the US economy was strong enough to support these two states. At that time the US produced almost fifty percent of the world's GDP, while today that percentage is below twenty-five percent.[27] Hence, facing the current reality, he recommends greater multilateralism in future nation-building efforts, as burden sharing has become necessary for the US and more affordable for other economically strong nations.

Despite these different emphases of their nation-building projects, Dobbins shares the same practical concerns with Caldwell: security at what cost and security over what time period. For Dobbins, the level of effort in terms of time, manpower, and money is the largest predictor of success. For example, he believes that while staying long does not ensure success, leaving early ensures failure. No forced democratization effort to date has taken hold in less than five years, which demonstrates the costliness of transformational *jpb*. For him, state rebuilding will require at least five years in order to succeed and will require political transformation in addition to maintenance of human security and a degree of economic reconstruction.[28]

Noah Feldman:
Just Policing toward Self-Determination and Self-Governance

Both Caldwell and Dobbins argue for the substantial possibility of successful political transformation and democratization. Their shared conclusion is that successful nation building is time and resource intensive. Noah Feldman's approach to just policing is slightly different than theirs. While he, like Caldwell and Dobbins, is aware that the level of just actors' efforts in terms of both time and money is one of the largest indicators of success for

26 Dobbins, xxv.
27 Dobbins, xxii.
28 Dobbins, xxv.

nation building, another major concern of his work is ensuring the liberties of all citizens in a postwar society.

Feldman's work *What We Owe Iraq: War and the Ethics of Nation Building* relates his own practical experiences working on the development of the rule of law in Iraq. He sees postwar occupation and nation building in terms of the development of a state that is capable of independent governance and providing liberties to all of its citizens. For Feldman, ensuring this outcome constitutes an ethical obligation on the part of the occupying state or states as well as a requirement for the security of the occupied state, and potentially, the international system as a whole. Therefore, Feldman's referent for security is both the state and the individual, which corresponds to my comprehensive security scheme.

In order to ensure the liberties of all the citizens in the occupied society at the level of both the state and the individual, Feldman argues that nation building should first employ democratic means to secure that postwar society. These democratic means should proceed on the basis of UN trusteeship with a priority of providing *order*. This UN-led occupying power should hold the government in trust and facilitate the development of a political system in the occupied area that will allow for eventual self-determination and self-governance by the occupied people. However, Feldman considers it vital that the occupying power remain engaged even after elections have been conducted as he states, "elections are not the end point of nation building."[29] This demonstrates his cautious attitude in regard to working toward nation building.

Feldman extends his practical concerns to the political domains of the occupying state, which is also part of the postwar society. He discusses how to treat the citizens of the defeated state with the same care an occupying state would devote to its own citizens. For him, "self-interest is not inherently unethical" as he constructs his ethics of nation building upon the dual requirements of increasing security for the nation builder's own citizens while avoiding the violation of the defeated state's citizens' interests.[30] The occupiers must govern in their interests.

---

29 Noah Feldman, *What We Owe Iraq: War and the Ethics of Nation Building* (Princeton: Princeton University Press, 2006), 97.

30 For further discussion, see Feldman, 25–27.

Challenges of Just Policing

Common Practical Challenges for Just Policing

Each of the aforementioned scholars' views on just policing aligns with my comprehensive human security scheme. Their views differ, however, when it comes to the selection of a primary agency for undertaking the scheme. With respect to arms control and peacekeeping, Ayers attends to the duty of the victor, while Scheers sees the UN as the most important agency. Likewise, regarding nation building, Caldwell primarily focuses on the duty of victorious states to ensure the prospect of human security in defeated nations, while Dobbins and Feldman see the international community as important agents for attaining just policing.

Additionally, the policy recommendations of Dobbins and Feldman for keeping the postwar society safe illustrate that they favor policies consonant with a transformative vision of just policing. At the same time, the limited five year timeline for nation building demonstrates that their idea of just policing is not based on a rigid maximalist version of *jpb*. Despite their aspirations for human security from a long-term policy perspective, they believe that, in reality, the issues of cost and time commitment are the variables that need to be considered first when determining appropriate postwar operations for just policing. This view demonstrates that *post bellum* military means are necessarily balanced with political objectives.[31] Hence, it is critical to consider just actors' practical concerns in just policing, such as the issues of cost and time commitment, when examining the relationship between military means and political ends.[32]

In practice, classical just actors should not only be understood as military actors but also as state actors who are drawn from both victorious states and the international community.[33] This means that their just policing work must be within the realm of *state practice*, whether individually

---

31 As Ayers notes, during the LIC phase, the military works closely with other political means to control hostilities.

32 Carl von Clausewitz, *On War*, 1832, ed. and trans. Michael Howard and Peter Paret (Princeton: Princeton University Press, 1984), 75. Remember Clausewitz's famous dictum that "war is a mere continuation of policy by other means." Also see Fred Charles Iké, *Every War Must End* (New York: Columbia University Press, 2005), chap. 1. Fred Charles Iké conducts a historical survey, positing that the disconnection between armed means and political ends led to a failure to attain security policy objectives, and by extension, made the achievement of *jpb* a practical impossibility.

33 This book defined the international community as a league or cluster of nations, such as the UN. See chapter four.

or collectively. Given this, it is essential that these actors consider the current expectations of what constitutes just policing while seeking to shape the *common good*. Nonetheless, considering just policing from the perspective of state practice requires a realistic understanding of the complex interplay between war and politics. As discussed earlier, there is a near consensus among security studies experts about the importance of this connection. The remaining chapter will focus on their unanimous conclusion that successful nation building is time and resource intensive and often determined by diverse political actors who act not just for moral reasons.

I will conclude this chapter by first examining the characteristics of these time and cost concerns as I see their origin in an ethos of utility and accomplishment commonly found in the military ethos. I define this as a utilitarian perspective that deters just actors' full efforts toward building the common good. Second, I will revisit one exemplary proposal commonly initiated by both Dobbins and Feldman that addresses a way to promote the common good while overcoming time and cost problems through multilateral operations for just policing. Finally, I will wrap up this discussion of just policing by addressing these practical concerns as integral to theological reflection on just policing.

Cost and Time Commitment

Caldwell, Dobbins, and Feldman affirm that classical actors, whether victorious states or the international community, are still key agents for just policing. Moreover, as these scholars' practical concerns for just policing have emphasized, success is determined by two factors: security at what *cost* and over what *time* commitment. Therefore, the important theme that has emerged from this review is the disconnection between the political ends of war and the methods used to implement policing in the phase of *post bellum*. This disconnect affects the two central means of just policing—peacekeeping and nation building—especially the latter, as it is always conditioned by the concern for the extraordinarily high costs of successful postwar reconstruction and political transformation projects.

In the reality of postwar societies, both political and military leaders from victorious states and the international community have often overlooked their original mission of achieving the common good in favor of catering to their own good or survival while finding a way to end the mission earlier than optimal due to the pressures of time and finances.[34] For example, Richard Hass suggests four tests that any proposed armed intervention should pass: (i) that it be worth doing, (ii) that it be doable, (iii) that likely benefits exceed likely costs, and (iv) that the ratio of benefits to costs be better than that provided by another policy.[35] The last two tests on cost-benefit analysis were originally intended to criticize US armed interventions that turned into unrestricted wars. However, as explicit comparisons of costs and benefits are essential in the more limited confrontations that just actors need to attend to, this cost-benefit analysis test cannot alone be the measure of something worth doing *post bellum*. Although it is vital for classical just actors to adhere to responsible expenditures of both fiscal resources and timeframes to actualize their agenda of policing in the reality of the postwar society, this utilitarian emphasis prevents the actors from considering other moral and practical dimensions in just policing.

In the hierarchical structure of a military society, two objectives need to be maximized: utility and accomplishment.[36] Utility is understood as the ability to set off a cause-effect process that will produce the result the military authority wants. Accomplishment refers to a mastery of cause-effect achievement balanced with cost-effective execution. I am not simply arguing that this logic of utility and accomplishment justifies the use of armed force for just policing, nor am I arguing that Christians should disregard these practical concerns. Rather, I see that this utilitarian view reflects Caldwell's and Dobbins's critical observation that the just policing efforts of classical just actors are limited in terms of time and resources. Although I see these practical concerns as part of the reality grounded in postwar military decision-making, I am concerned that the actors may overlook other important moral values in practice, such as securing the liberty of a vanquished nation's citizens, as Feldman notes. A situation such as this could happen if the actors are obsessed with time and cost factors within the boundary of their own utilitarian ethos, especially during the transitional

---

34 Gideon Rose addresses this concern in his study on *jpb*, stating, "time and again, throughout history, political and military leaders have ignored either the need for careful postwar planning or approached the task with sugar plums dancing in their heads and been caught up short as a result." See his *How Wars End: Why We Always Fight the Last Battle* (New York: Simon & Schuster, 2010), 5.

35 For details, see Richard Hass, *Intervention: The Use of American Military Force in the Post-Cold War World* (Washington, DC: Brookings Institution Press, 1999), 69–70.

36 For details, see William H. Shaw, *Utilitarianism and the Ethics of War* (New York: Routledge, 2016).

period immediately after the end of war when the armed forces are in control of the political and economic systems of the defeated nation. For example, the United States tacitly allowed military-based authoritarian regimes in South Korea after the Korean War in the name of political stability and economic development. This decision was made for armed stability in the Far East in fiscal and resource terms; the regimes were notorious for the violation of human rights and individual liberty.[37]

In particular, just actors who focus solely on fiscal and timeframe-related concerns overlook other essential aspects of the common good. For example, classical actors who have mainly considered *jpb* through the lens of money and time, but have not been able to creatively and constructively allot those assets to others, have failed to achieve the common good that the JWT pursues. Success, in this sense, should *not* be "accomplishment," a profit margin or the ability to harness instruments for one's advantage. Rather, it ought to be about the capacity to enact something that is vaster than "mine," namely, to *give and empower*. In other words, success must be about forging a form of the common good that enables other goods to prosper in the postwar society, such as human life and flourishing, hospitality, and hope.

Exploring Just Policing Efforts for the Common Good: Multinational Operations

How can just actors achieve the common good while overcoming such a utilitarian ethos? The works of Dobbins and Feldman are worth revisiting. Although they do not employ the term "the common good," their proposals intersect with my notion of the common good.

For example, Feldman argues that just actors' first job is to build a basic order to make the postwar society safe; until then, they must hold off other policing obligations and turn away from large-scale and long-term *post bellum* stability and rebuilding projects. For Feldman, calculations of the total costs and time required must factor in the phase of rehabilitation, not just policing. This distinction demonstrates his practical concern that establishing public order is required to build the political and economic institutions that will ultimately allow long-term stability to return in a postwar society. However, Feldman's distinction also indicates the primary duty in just actors' policing: "the first duty of nation-building power is to produce order in the very literal sense of monopolizing

---

37 Cf. Bruce Comings, *The Korean War: A History* (New York: Modern Library, 2010).

violence."[38] In a nutshell, to have any chance of achieving just policing, the first requirement for just actors is to ensure that *basic* order is returned within the vanquished society. Although Feldman does not clarify how this order contributes to the common good, his argument can be understood as similar to what we find from Himes' common-good-oriented approach to *jpb*. They both agree that the (re)establishment of a social order is the first step toward achieving a comprehensive version of human security.

Dobbins builds upon Feldman's emphasis on establishing order by suggesting that the international community is best situated to administer this initial attempt at social order. In Dobbins's vision, international cooperation is essential to establishing that order. Although just actors are required to first determine whether they will take a restorative or transformative version of just policing, Dobbins believes it is always better for them to find multinational solutions. This is not only because multilateral operations allow the US to relieve its fiscal burdens and timeframe pressures but also because there is a higher chance of achieving the common good with the help of other nations. Despite the fact that multilateral nation-building projects are more costly to execute at the outset, Dobbins finds that such operations have a higher success rate overall than projects undertaken by an individual state.[39] Multinational participation is also the best way to hold legitimate authorities accountable *post bellum*, as it provides more capable checks and balances for governance and controls. Further, multilateral nation-building projects are more likely to receive adequate levels of funding and achieve success when the fiscal burden is shared among a larger number of states. As a result, these projects command a greater degree of legitimacy than those initiated and carried out by a single state. One of the central characteristics of a just peace ordered to the common good is the just actors' legitimized authority to exercise their missions.

Furthermore, the RAND report suggests a number of prerequisites, including military presence over time by the occupying country, international police presence over time, reduction of postwar combat-related deaths, the timing of elections, effective dealing with refugees and IDPs, initial external assistance measured by adequate external per capita assistance, and external assistance as a meaningful percentage of GDP.[40] These

---

38 Feldman, *What We Owe Iraq*, 79.

39 For more information, see Dobbins, *America's Role in Nation Building*, xxv.

40 Dobbins, 149–66.

prerequisites particularly entail a multilateral commitment to provide substantial resources to the redevelopment effort, invest considerable time to
nation building, and ensure that appropriate security arrangements are
made for the common good. Further, this international cooperation is
imperative to ensure the transition from war to peace. In particular, these
multinational solutions should not only focus on member states as potential
contributors to the UN and other top-down efforts for just policing but also
on nonclassical just actors, such as private and nonprofit actors, as critical
to the entire continuum of *jpb* practice toward the "maxim(um)" of *jpb*—
the achievement of the common good—through just punishment and just
political participation.

However, although I believe it is often vital to the ultimate success
of any nation-building projects, I do not see international cooperation
as mandatory for just policing in all postwar cases. Unlike peacekeeping
and nation-building practices endorsed by classical just actors—who are
limited by time and resources—even when large military forces are
involved, long-term rehabilitation of civil societies must be further sustained by nonclassical just actors, who are more freely and independently
committed to peacebuilding efforts across time and space. As Caldwell
and Dobbins argue, the classical actors' work is conditioned by the
requirements of their host agency, whether they are victorious states or
the international community. Their obligation to the defeated state needs
to be balanced with other missions or interests of the states involved.
Hence, the importance of Feldman's belief that self-interest must be balanced with an acknowledgment of duties to the occupied population. His
construction of an ethic of nation building that consciously balances
duties to the victorious states' citizens with those to the defeated state's
citizens, along with the interests of the international community writ
large, is a necessary caution in debates over multinational projects in just
policing.

Still, one must ask: is balancing self-interest and the common good possible? I argue that, at least from a strict policy-oriented perspective, this *jpb*
vision of an occupying state treating the citizens of the defeated state with
the same care as it would treat its own citizens is unlikely to occur in practice. Self-interest may not be inherently unethical, but it guides the priori-
tization of resources over other *jpb* concerns. Ensuring the well-being of
the average citizen of an occupied state is certainly an admirable goal, but
history has shown that in practice, it is a goal that is prioritized below the

security of the classical actors' own citizens.[41] Therefore, Feldman's conclusion must be more carefully examined.

Why Human Security? Who Is Really Vulnerable?

The title of this subsection poses the questions that I addressed in relation to Feldman's practical dilemma of the "balancing" act. Given these questions, we return to the theological element of the common good to complement security studies literature. When one cannot satisfy both the citizens of the occupied and the occupying states, the question from a theological perspective is rather simple: who is the most vulnerable in a life-threatening crisis *post bellum, or* who were those murdered in the war and whose lives are in danger *post bellum*? In answering these questions, the priority must be given to those communities who suffered mass death and life-threatening events. This approach corresponds to the Christian version of the common good drawn from Jesus' commandments to love our neighbors, especially *the least* among us.[42] In times of crisis, especially in the immediate aftermath of wars in the vanquished states, it is important for Christian actors, or people of good will, to return to basic questions of human life and safety and, together, seek renewed moral clarity and conviction. Consider those postwar communities where people continue to murder each other because of squalor, revenge, or other unjust reasons, all of which lead to dysfunctional societies. As murdered bodies still lie in the streets and people fear increasing violence, just actors concerned with human security first must ask: how should we protect the innocent people at risk?

As discussed with Himes's approach to the common good in chapter three, the common good must be understood in the postwar community as a dimension of the moral good that states life-threatening attacks on innocent persons are never morally acceptable, at any stage or under any condition. In other words, just actors ought to attend to the (re)establishment of the common good, which is the first step for human security. In the phase of just policing, my "Maxim(um) of Ethical Minimalism: The Norm of the Common Good" approach must first develop a discourse on policing present

---

41 For example, as illustrated in chapter two, the overwhelming reparations and remuneration placed upon Kaiser Wilhelm II's German Empire in the aftermath of WWI was a genuine cause of WWII.

42 See chapters three and four for details on the theological discourse regarding the Christian version of the common good. Also see chapter one, especially with regard to Aquinas's understanding of the common good.

injustices after war. This discourse includes my central question: whether, and if so, how, just actors can balance both means for just policing—peacekeeping and nation building—to contribute to human security.

The Duty of "Christian" Just Actors: Repentance and Reconciliation with God

Just actors, including Christian ones, must consider my comprehensive human security scheme of just policing. However, I suggest that Christian actors must further reflect on the necessary violence of just policing, especially the violent means often required of just actors. Although its goal is to protect innocent and vulnerable people of a vanquished nation, it inevitably results in human communities being damaged on personal, social, and political levels. For this reason, as discussed in chapter four, some moral theologians attend to political reconciliation as an alternative to recovering damaged relationships in the postwar community. One cannot simply argue that security is the only concern because security does not include coexistence with political reconciliation. Indeed, the entire *jpb* project does not completely exclude political reconciliation, as it is true that political reconciliation contributes to human security in some areas, especially in the two phases of *jpb*: just punishment and just political participation. As I illustrate in the upcoming chapters, it is equally important to embrace the enemy through these phases. Admittedly, however, just policing is distinguished from the other two phases since it is the phase of *jpb* practice more directly and urgently treating an unstable and unsafe postwar society. Due to limited time and resources, just actors need to balance addressing immediate human security concerns with silencing threats from the present enemy, such as violent insurgents or other politically and economically life-threatening challenges, rather than reconciling with the past or the wartime enemy. This is because long-term security agendas require the *extensive* buildup of civil society and strong public institutions, which is even beyond the foundational *jpb* scope of just policing for both peacekeeping and nation building.[43]

However, this lack of focus on political reconciliation in the phase of just policing does not mean just actors, especially Christian classical just

---

43 This *extensive* buildup of civil society and strong public institutions is distinguished from nation building, which requires a five-year plan or a relatively short-term strategy, most security scholars argue. It is more directly related to the topic of transitional justice, grounded in a comprehensive range of peacebuilding studies, than postwar justice, *grounded in the JWT*, as this distinction is defined throughout the book.

actors, are free from all duties of reconciliation. While they are motivated by their faith and convictions to act as agents of political reconciliation in the public sphere through the phases of just punishment and just political participation, they must seek another level of reconciliation through the phase of just policing. Namely, through reflection, they must reconcile their use of violent means when involved in arms control and peacekeeping operations, often resulting in the killing of others. These classical actors are the armed forces used to achieve the common good *post bellum* but also wounded creatures who have taken the life of another divine image-bearing creature. From a strictly theological perspective, these wounded actors need grace, which is the divine assistance toward achieving the common good, as it heals wounds in their nature and perfects what is basically good.[44] Grace is necessary for Christian actors, who are also members of the human community. God wants us to reconcile with God himself (i.e., vertical reconciliation) as well as with our enemies/neighbors (i.e., horizontal reconciliation)—as through this process of war and reconciliation we are losing ourselves, being born again, and becoming one in love that is God himself: "God is the source of human good."[45] After war, especially in regard to Christian actors, reconciliation must be achieved both horizontally and vertically. This is because reconciliation with God also leads to reconciliation with fellow humans, including political reconciliation.[46] It is impossible to fully reconcile with others without first being reconciled to God; that is, reconciliation with God enables reconciliation with humans. It is not right to be reconciled to God yet remain in enmity with other human beings, nor vice versa. The struggle of achieving this full reconciliation is inevitable

---

44 *ST*, I-II, q.111.

45 James Gustafson, *Moral Discernment in the Christian Life* (Louisville: Westminster John Knox Press, 2007), 97. James Gustafson further develops this line of thought: "God is the source, but not the guarantor of the human good."

46 As an example, throughout Is 40–54, the following descriptions of Israel appear. First, Israel was exiled because of her sin, which is a form of God's alienation from Israel. Second, God restored the relationship with Israel, not only as a new creation, but also not to forsake its people again. Israel was "reunited" with God, as they came to "know" and "believe" God. God forfeited his "anger" and "reestablished" peace with Israel. This vertical aspect of peace resulted in and characterized the new creation, which resembles the original paradise. For Isaiah, this original paradise also means a horizontal peace. This is because he understands the original peace in the same sense as the Hebrew word *shalom*. Unlike the Greek word *eirene*, which is defined as peace in the absence of war and prosperity after the war, the Hebrew word *shalom* means a state of well-being, peace, friendship, fulfilment, and salvation to the whole society and nature, further to political reconciliation and eschatological peace.

because of the effect of sin. However, because God is gracious enough to reconcile with us, Christian just actors must continually strive to replicate that reconciliation.[47]

Therefore, as we have learned from Schuck's theological anthropology of *jpb*, even if just actors do their best according to their right intent in (post)war, there is always limited moral discernment from the human side, primarily because all humans are tainted by original sin—their freedom and free will to choose sinful acts. I agree with Schuck that God's grace calls even just actors to repentance.[48] This is not just because they have taken away the lives of others created in the *imago dei* but also because there is always a chance that as *imperfect* just actors, they would have failed to love their enemies on the road to the fullest reconciliation and peace.[49] Just actors who inevitably use lethal force in war ought to sustain the common-good-seeking justice, which they also must do to mend their relationship with God as well as their neighbors *post bellum* for the responsibility of their *imperfect* (loving) acts of just killing.

With respect to discussing whether killing is compatible with love, some Augustinian scholars such as Elshtain and Nigel Biggar argue that just war defends killing in love. However, their brand of Augustinian ethics on "killing in love" appears to contradict itself or at best allows just actors, especially Christian ones, a challenging question that remains to be answered from a theological perspective. Schuck regards Augustine as thinking that repentance and remorse are proper responses to war, while Elshtain follows Augustine on understanding love and war as compatible. Elshtain believes that love is an interior attitude or disposition compatible with various actions, including self-defense.[50] However, unlike many other Augustinian thinkers, especially Nigel Biggar, who believe that Augustine's theology of love in just war should be based on punishing injustice, which can be regarded as correcting the enemy in love, Elshtain argues for love built on

---

47 In Christianity, this theological reconciliation is conventionally understood in the view of the gift that God Himself first reconciled with us, along with all of our neighbors. The gift is Jesus Christ (cf. Jn 3:16).

48 For details, see chapter three. Also, supra note 176.

49 The "imperfect" characteristic of just war is more substantially and widely reflected in practice in the modern era than in earlier periods of human history (e.g., collateral damage, residual responsibilities). For details on this viewpoint with historical examples, see Jeff McMahan, *Killing in War* (New York: Oxford University Press, 2009).

50 Elshtain, "Why Augustine? Why Now?," 254

a paradigm of self-defense.[51] She embraces Augustine's theology of sin and emphasizes *imago dei* as a lens for looking at all of human life and appreciating human dignity and equal regard.[52] She seeks Christian hope and responsibility in the context of tragic war and the finitude of human nature.[53] Acknowledgment of this tragic context accompanies a sense of remorse that she finds in Augustine's work, as does Schuck.

Given these divergent views among Augustinian just war thinkers, we return to the work of Aquinas to complement the discussion of whether killing is compatible with love. Unlike Augustine's broad and somewhat arbitrary understanding of the meaning of just (loving) act, Aquinas's point is straightforward and systematically comprehensive, as the heart of Aquinas's position is captured in this statement: "Hatred of a person's evil is equivalent to love of his good. Hence also this perfect hatred belongs to love."[54] No one would love for a friend to have vices. To love the person is to hate their vices and thus to desire their virtues and flourishing, even if it requires a violent intervention. Likewise, to truly love the aggressor, just actors ought to hate the enemy's abuse with "perfect hatred" and thus try to defeat it for the other's ultimate well-being and the common good. To be clear, Aquinas makes it explicitly clear that private persons' defense of themselves (e.g., self-defense against crime) is different from the public officials' legitimate defense of the common good (e.g., just war). While the former is permissible only if it includes no intent to kill, the latter is permissible with, if need be, intent to kill the aggressor.[55]

Aquinas gives two practical rationales in defense of his position. First, Aquinas contends that forcefully opposing the aggressors prevents them from further harming others, and thus it promotes the common good.[56] When just actors stop the enemy's abusive behavior such as harming

---

51 Nigel Biggar, *In Defence of War* (Oxford: Oxford University Press, 2013), 10–13, 190–99, 212. Also see Lisa Sowle Cahill, "How Should War Be Related to Christian Love?," *Soundings* 97, no. 2 (2014): 187. Lisa Sowle Cahill criticizes Nigel Biggar's approach that is not founded in Christian tradition. She presents three points: (i) "violence and killing are not works of Christian love properly speaking;" (ii) "Christians should not characterize war as loving punishment, but as just defense of the common good;" and (iii) "a Christian evaluation of war should always pay attention to the priority of peace and peacebuilding, for both theological and practical reasons."

52 For details, see Elshtain, "International Justice as Equal Regard for the Use of Force," 63–75.

53 Elshtain, *Just War against Terror*, 70.

54 *ST*, II-II, q.25, a.6.

55 *ST*, II-II, q.64, a.7.

56 *ST*, II-II, q.40, a.1.

innocent children, they love the neighbors that the abusers would harm. For Aquinas, the common good justifies and requires forceful intervention against injustice as an act of love. Second, Aquinas asserts that the act of punishment can motivate the abuser to repent and be saved, despite temporary pain.[57] For example, if the aggressors know that abusing the innocent children could lead to prison, Aquinas thinks there is a better chance that they will not do it, which is good for them and good for everyone involved in war and postwar, including the innocent and vulnerable individuals. But if they have already committed injustice, proportionate punishment can force them to face the seriousness of their vicious actions and lead them to repent, which is ultimately saving. Thus, for Aquinas, there is not ultimately a tension between loving the enemies and condemning their violence. Aquinas insists that just actors can *love* their enemies precisely by hating their evil and preventing them from committing it—even to the death if necessary. These rationales certainly provide the foundation for just war theory and principled resistance to evil, whether that be *jus ad bellum, jus in bello,* or *jpb.*

The command to love our neighbors as ourselves is a cornerstone of the Christian tradition and the essence of what it means for a human being to bear the *imago dei* and imitate God. Further, human beings summoned into life at their very origin of creation (i.e., ensoulment) means that God has prepared for them a place in God's kingdom and a sharing in God's divine life. Hence, human life is given a sacred and inviolable character that necessarily justifies the sole and absolute lordship of God over human life and death.[58] Therefore, taking a human life (i.e., intentional killing) is fundamentally wrong as an object of one's action; however, lethal force in war and postwar can be justified when the intention is to stop an unjust attack.[59]

---

57 A further point is that forcefully stopping the aggressors would prevent them from sinning further and thus from increasing their guilt before God in the afterlife. For example, the Taliban surged back to power two decades after the US-led forces toppled its regime in what led to the United States' longest war. However, one may argue that mishandling of the rushed withdrawal from Afghanistan while not forcefully stopping the abusive Taliban extremists has left thousands of people stranded and local communities exposed to chaos and violence. For Aquinas, stopping abusers from doing this, even if it requires fatal intervention, is loving them in light of the afterlife. In other words, letting people get away with their abusive actions is not loving them and leads to their eternal death.

58 *ST*, I-II, q.100, a.8. See John Paul II, *Catechism of the Catholic Church*, 2nd ed., (Washington, DC: United States Catholic Conference, 2011), 2258, 2318–19.

59 A good defense of the similar position is Gerard V. Bradley, "No Intentional Killing Whatsoever: The Case of Capital Punishment," in *Natural Law and Moral Inquiry*, ed. Robert P. George

In other words, private intentions to kill (even defensively) are intrinsically immoral, but it is morally permissible for just actors to act on such an intention while defending the common good.

Admittedly, one may argue that even Aquinas's "altruistic" just killing is an *imperfect* act violating the greatest love command (specifically, Jesus' groundbreaking command to love the present enemy).[60] In whatever way the just killing of an enemy may be considered an act of love, it can only be considered an imperfect act of love. Nevertheless, this imperfect act intends for the common good. Sustaining the common-good-seeking justice in the *jpb* context is more than securing a tranquil order; it goes beyond punitive justice in love (Biggar) or love built on a paradigm of self-defense (Elshtain). This justice or *jpb* is a result of concord (*concordia*) and love (*caritas*), which are manifested in the process of recovery, reconstruction, reconciliation, and amelioration of the cause of harm the imperfect just intervention is designed to prevent.[61]

CONCLUSION

Drawn from my "Maxim(um) of Ethical Minimalism: the Norm of the Common Good" approach, this chapter considers a transformative view of *jpb*. This approach must immediately attend to armed force for just policing before providing basic needs through nonviolent means shortly thereafter. These two means are articulated in just actors' peacekeeping operations and nation-building practices. However, unlike this priority for order from a theoretical and normative perspective, it is questionable whether just actors utilize both means in practice mainly because just actors not only engage in *post bellum* as military actors but also as state actors whose practical decisions are determined by various political considerations. Nonetheless, drawn from my understanding of Himes, the establishment of just peace

---

(Washington, DC: Georgetown University Press, 1998). This is a volume written in tribute to Germain Grisez, who argues that killing is always wrong but that armed force in war can be justified when it intends to stop an abusive injustice or unjust war. Cf. From a biblical perspective, the correct translation of the fifth (the Protestant sixth) commandment is "thou shalt not murder." In other words, the restriction is against murder, not against all killing. Cf. See *CCC*, 2263–65, 2307.

60 A challenging question remains; at least from a Christian pacifist view, Aquinas's defense of violent love is not what Jesus taught (Lk. 6:27–29). The point of turning your other cheek is to make a defiant but nonviolent statement of agency in the face of one's abuser; yet this nonviolent protest is different from Aquinas's "altruistic" violence.

61 *ST*, II-II, q.29, a.1.

must be directed toward a political peace ordered to the common good. Moreover, just actors must aim to protect the lives of every individual— especially the most vulnerable—by balancing violent with nonviolent means of just policing to achieve a comprehensive version of human security.

Further, my aim in this chapter is to explore moral and theological visions manifested in the two major practices of just policing, peacekeeping and nation building, in the search for a deeper meaning than matters such as time and cost. Identifying, codifying, and integrating the lessons of moral and practical implications for just policing in security studies are necessary steps toward developing a comprehensive version of human security. It is equally crucial for lessons learned and best practices developed to be integrated into military doctrine and political practice. At the same time, it is also imperative for Christian just actors to understand the practical matters of just policing within the JWT, a tradition that has been developed through both secular and Christian political thought. Forging this understanding will strengthen the entire body of *jpb* thinking and practice as it helps to explain how members of specific postwar communities might cultivate a more comprehensive and constructive version of just policing. This version of just policing encourages just actors to use available resources to save human lives *post bellum*.

Chapter 6

Reconstruction of Just Punishment

INTRODUCTION

From Just Policing to Just Punishment

In the previous chapter, we defined that just policing must be directed toward a political peace ordered to the common good, aiming to protect the lives of innocent and vulnerable people. From this perspective, just actors must assume moral responsibility for engaging in reconstruction and thus achieve a *comprehensive* version of human security through both armed force (i.e., peacekeeping) and nonviolent means (i.e., nation build-ing). In this chapter, I make a similar suggestion in the context of just pun-ishment, which will be articulated by addressing two questions. The first question asks: how do armed forces carry out their peacekeeping operations in legal terms? The second question asks: how do nonviolent means, such as international tribunals, contribute to rebuilding the common good? Viewed in this way, one could argue that just punishment is understood within the larger context of just policing. Securing the public's safety in a postwar society must be achieved prior to amending the past wrongdoing. If the legal authority to judge the past wrongdoing is threatened by the defeated warring parties, or if the court decision is influenced by the victor's justice, then the justice of the punishment will not appear impartial, which may cause public rage or even future violence.

Just Punishment:
Refreshing and Refining the Theoretical Ground for Practice

With respect to the ethic of just punishment, international law has played an integral role. As emphasized throughout the book, major contemporary *jpb* thinkers, such as Walzer, Orend, Allman and Winright, view the tradi-tional just war principles of *jus ad bellum* and *jus in bello* primarily as prin-ciples of international law, emphasizing the laws of war along with their ethics. In particular, Orend clarifies that many of the principles that come out of the JWT have been instantiated in bodies of law, the Geneva

Conventions of 1949 being one such example. Likewise, most scholars believe that the international law of *jpb* primarily attends to *international criminal law* for amending the past wrongdoings, namely, treating violations of the *jus ad bellum* and *jus in bello* principles according to just war theory. Simply put, one must pose a question: what is the proper way to deal with violations of the rule of war?

However, this question needs to be reconstructed, as it should be enshrined in a *comprehensive* human security scheme that fundamentally embraces just policing in legal terms. This scheme means treating violations of the rule of war in a way that requires both the security of individuals and accountability for crimes committed against them. Therefore, another area of *jpb* law, *occupation law*, which primarily aims to establish a safe and secure environment *post bellum*, must be included in the agenda of just punishment.[1] Viewed in this way, the question must be rephrased: what is the proper way to deal with violations of the rules of war *and postwar*? In other words, how should the law of war and postwar achieve the common good, or at least make a decently just and safe postwar society? Therefore, I define just punishment not only as a fair trial practice of amending violations of the rule of law in wartime but also as a legitimate act of imposing just policing that secures a proper way of treating violations of the rule of law *post bellum*. In this book, while the former version of just punishment corresponds to international criminal law, the latter corresponds to occupation law.

The next two sections attend to two practical concerns. First, I will address the issue of occupation law, including whether, and how, it should apply to an emerging concept of *jpb*. Recognizing this issue will in turn serve to illuminate the second concern, the practical issue of war crimes tribunals covered in the *jpb* literature, especially with regard to the question of human security and political reconciliation. Hence, in order to articulate these two concerns, one must first define the fundamental sources of international law, which are the basis for just punishment in practice. These sources include the Hague Conventions, the Geneva Conventions (especially the 4th), the Charter of the United Nations (the UN Charter), and the

---

1 Gregory Fox, *Humanitarian Occupation* (Cambridge: Cambridge University Press, 2008), 222. Drawn from the notion of occupation stated in the Hague Conventions, occupation law regulates the conduct of states taking control over foreign territory during or after war: "With a foreign power in residence, the state's government will generally cease to function. During this time . . . the occupying power becomes the temporary de facto power in the territory."

United Nations Security Council (UNSC).² I will briefly define these sources, positing a preliminary set of propositions about aspects of the current *jpb* context of occupation law and international criminal law.

JUST PUNISHMENT FOR AMENDING PAST WRONGDOINGS AND SECURING THE RULE OF LAW

The Fundamental Sources of International Law for Just Punishment

International Humanitarian Law

The UN Charter's appendix, Article 38 of The Statute of the International Court of Justice (ICJ), identifies the fundamental sources of international law as follows.

(1) International conventions, establishing rules recognized by the contesting states;
(2) International custom as evidence of a practice generally accepted as law;
(3) The general principles of law recognized by civilized states;
(4) The judicial decisions of the most highly qualified publicists of states.³

For the sake of determining the status of *jpb* practice from a legal perspective, especially with regard to occupation law and international criminal law, this chapter primarily attends to the first source.⁴ Specifically, it deals with the UN Charter and the relevant conventions and treaties that essentially comprise the body of international humanitarian law.

International humanitarian law is prominent in the legal scholarship concerning *jpb*, as it proposes how to treat violations of law, both in wartime and *post bellum*. The International Committee of the Red Cross (ICRC) Advisory Service defines international humanitarian law as "a set of rules which seek, for humanitarian reasons, to limit the effects of armed force. It

---

2 For details, see Joel Westra, *International Law and the Use of Armed Force: The UN Charter and the Major Powers* (New York: Routledge, 2007); and Lung-Chu Chen, *An Introduction to Contemporary International Law: A Policy Oriented Perspective* (New Haven: Yale University Press, 2015).

3 United Nations Charter, "Chapter XIV: The International Court of Justice," June 26, 1945, https://www.un.org/en/about-us/un-charter/chapter-14.

4 International law scholar Lung-Chu Chen also emphasizes the first source in relation to occupation law and international criminal law. For details, see Chen, *An Introduction to Contemporary International Law.*

protects [both civilians and military personnel] . . . who are no longer participating in the hostilities and restricts the means and methods of warfare."[5]
This law contains a variety of international treaties and conventions. The
most distinguished among them are the Geneva Convention and the Hague
Convention.[6] Their primary concern is the protection of civilians during
and after war, concerning the issue of belligerent occupation. Therefore,
they are also major determinants of the rules of law for shaping the status
of *jpb* practice from an international legal perspective, especially with regard
to both occupation law and international criminal law.

In particular, the 4th Geneva Convention and the Hague Conventions
are more directly concerned with violations of *jus in bello*, both during the
war and the time of occupation *post bellum*.[7] When it comes to international criminal law treating wartime violations, the conventions are
employed in conjunction with a variety of other international agreements.
They seek to prohibit the use of certain armed forces (corresponding to
"the principle of proportionality") or protect certain people (corresponding
to "the principle of discrimination").[8] With respect to occupation law treating violations *post bellum*, they are the first and foremost sources to consult.
The importance of these sources is particularly illustrated by two sections
contained within them. First, Article 42 of the Hague Convention of 1907
defines the notion of occupation: "Territory is considered occupied when
it is actually placed under the authority of a hostile army. The occupation
extends only to the territory where such authority has been established
and can be exercised."[9] Second, Section III of the 4th Geneva Convention
instructs how to treat people—both civilians and former military personnel—in occupied territories.[10]

5 International Committee of the Red Cross (ICRC), "What Is International Humanitarian Law?,"
Advisory Service on International Humanitarian Law, https://www.icrc.org/en/doc/assets/
files/other/what_is_ihl.pdf.

6 More specifically, they are the Geneva Convention of 1949 (and its two additions of 1977) and
the Hague Conventions of 1899 and 1907. See Geneva Convention (IV) Relative to the Protection
of Civilian Persons in Time of War, Geneva, August 12, 1949, *United Nations Treaty Series*,
vol. 75, no. 973, available from https://treaties.un.org/Pages/showDetails.aspx?objid=
0800000280158b1a&clang=_en.

7 See Gregory Fox, *Humanitarian Occupation*, chap. 7.

8 Fox, 225–30. For original reference, see ICRC, "What Is International Humanitarian Law?"

9 The Hague Conventions of 1907 (IV) Respecting the Laws and Customs of War on Land, the
Hague, October 18, 1907, art. 42, available from https://ihl-databases.icrc.org/ihl/INTRO/195.

10 See Geneva Convention of 1949, *United Nations Treaty Series*, vol. 75, no. 973.

The UN Charter is the most acknowledged multilateral treaty, as it is considered substantial international law, relating to the legitimacy of the use of force. In particular, Article 2.4 of Chapter I of the UN Charter features within the legal scholarship regarding violations of *jus ad bellum* and is relevant to the practice of international criminal law. The UN Charter establishes this article to proscribe both the use of armed force and the threat to use it. However, the Charter also allows three exceptions to Article 2.4 of Chapter I: a nation-state's self-defense, the UNSC's intervention for preventing any threat to peace, and the UNSC's intervention for restoring peace.[11] This article, in tandem with these exceptions, aims to serve as a standard or rule of legitimacy for assessing the use of armed force within the international system.[12] In order to discuss the legal concerns of *jpb*, I must begin with international humanitarian law.

International Humanitarian Law in Conjunction with International Human Rights Law

There are three major groups of international law scholars who discuss international human rights law as part of the *jpb* law discourse. Anthony Clark Arend and Robert Beck are in the first group, and they assert that the current paradigm of *jpb* law—namely, international humanitarian law—has been challenged over the last few decades by both changes in the nature of war from interstate to intrastate and the strategic failure of the international community to enforce international humanitarian law.[13] They find that these challenges have been accompanied by the emergence of international human rights law, especially regarding the issue of state-centric norms of national and international security versus a norm of human security. However, they do not clarify what constitutes international human rights law. Additionally, no specific proposals are made for building a new treaty for international human rights law.

---

11 The first exception is Article 51, which secures the right of self-defense for all nation-states (United Nations Charter, Chapter VII, Article 51). The second is Chapter VII of the charter, which permits the use of force to be authorized by the UNSC in cases where there is "any threat to the peace, breach of the peace, or act of aggression" (United Nations Charter, Chapter VII, Article 39). Finally, this chapter beckons the UNSC to "make recommendations . . . to maintain or restore international peace and security" (United Nations Charter, Chapter VII, Article 39).

12 Anthony Clark Arend and Robert Beck, *International Law and the Use of Force* (London: Routledge, 1993), 31.

13 Arend and Beck, 4.

The second group is composed of *jpb* law scholars concerned with a void in the current internal legal framework in regard to a law of transition from war to peace, specifically from international humanitarian law to international human rights law.[14] In particular, Charles Garraway is careful to differentiate between international humanitarian law and international human rights law in the context of *jpb*.[15] He cites the distinction made by the ICRC Advisory Service that recognizes that international human rights law "applies in peacetime, and many of the provisions may be suspended during armed conflict."[16] In contrast, international humanitarian law primarily applies in the case of armed conflict. Proposing that the transition from war to peace encompasses matters associated with both laws, he sees a void in the international legal paradigm since the two types of law cannot and must not apply simultaneously. As a result, it is difficult to determine exactly which, if either type of law, applies to a specific instance in the immediate aftermath of war. This difficulty is especially acute in the phase of Low Intensity Conflict (LIC), a threshold between war and peace in which the military works closely with other political means to control hostilities.[17] Furthermore, Garraway argues for the potential to incorporate international human rights law into international humanitarian law since they share the same purpose, which is human security in the face of events that threaten human dignity and life in the world.[18] Therefore, he believes

---

14 For an overview of the second group, see Inger Osterdahl, "What Will *Jus Post Bellum* Mean? Of New Wine and Old Bottles," *Journal of Conflict and Security Law* (June 1, 2009); Charles Garraway, "The Relevance of *Jus Post Bellum*: A Practitioner's Perspective," in *Jus Post Bellum,* ed. Carsten Stahn and Jann K. Kleffner (The Hague: T.M.C. Asser Press, 2008); and Gary Solis, *The Law of Armed Conflict: International Humanitarian Law in War* (Cambridge: Cambridge University Press, 2010).

15 Garraway, "The Relevance of *Jus Post Bellum*," 218. More precisely, international humanitarian law consists of the body of international law formerly referred to as "the law of war" or "the law of armed conflict." Gary Solis's analysis is helpful for further reflection on the change in terminology. He argues that "the laws of war and the law of armed conflict have become deemed as passé by some legal scholars and are now being referred to as international humanitarian law." Gary Solis, *The Law of Armed Conflict*, 22.

16 ICRC, "What Is International Humanitarian Law?"

17 Garraway, "The Relevance of *Jus Post Bellum*," 162. Garraway sees that it is almost impossible to distinguish these two laws in the reality of *jpb* practice not just because these two types of law do not apply simultaneously, but also because the *post bellum* phase itself is regarded as neither war nor peace. As shown by Ayers's study in the previous chapter, this phase is regarded as the stage of LIC, which implies a law of transition applicable from the state of war to the state of peace.

18 Gary Solis takes a similar stance, as he explains that "the purpose of international humanitarian law is not to prevent war, . . . [but] to preserve an oasis of humanity in battle." Solis, *The Law of Armed Conflict*, 23.

just actors must create a new treaty that adheres to these two laws. This integrated law would establish clear transition points from the law of war to the law of peace in a consistent manner.

The final group, which aligns most closely with my approach for this chapter, features scholars who embrace the principle of the protection of human rights drawn from international human rights law but oppose the second group's desire to build a new treaty that would be excluded from *jpb* discourse. Rather, this group sustains the existing international humanitarian law. They argue that humanitarian norms and the relevant principles of the protection of human rights that essentially comprise the agenda of human security for *jpb* are already embedded in international humanitarian law. Therefore, this humanitarian law is enough to bring a human security perspective that adds value to the postwar community. Patrick Hayden advocates this form of international humanitarian law, noting that "the traditional realist claims to sovereignty and nonintervention on the part of states are being supplanted in international relations by a norm of humanitarian assistance driven by human rights and the security interests of individuals."[19] Richard Falk takes a similar stance as he affirms that no international human rights law needs to be instantiated or incorporated into the body of international humanitarian law. He criticizes those who argue that the Universal Declaration of Human Rights (UDHR) has a legitimate authority to enforce human rights law in the postwar society. Rather, he clarifies that the mission of the UDHR is not and does not mean to be obligatory but encourages actors to voluntarily address human rights issues.[20] Further, he confirms that the UDHR is not a treaty law or set of conventions, which are the common sources of international law. Therefore, the declaration should not be part of the *jpb* paradigm established by the UN Charter.[21]

These three groups present different understandings of human rights law in relation to humanitarian law, as they are concerned with the tension created by the competing demands of state sovereignty and human rights

---

19 Patrick Hayden, "Security beyond the State: Cosmopolitanism, Peace and the Role of Just War Theory," in *Just War Theory: A Reappraisal*, ed. Mark Evans (Edinburgh: Edinburgh University Press, 2005), 157.

20 Richard Falk, *Achieving Human Rights* (New York: Routledge, 2008), 3.

21 Although the UDHR is not treaty law, the International Covenant on Civil and Political Rights is a treaty that does codify much of the language of the original declaration. International Covenant on Civil and Political Rights, New York, December 16, 1966, https://treaties.un.org/Pages/ViewDetails.aspx?chapter=4&clang=_en&mtdsg_no=IV-4&src=IND.

at the center of the debate over a legal codification of *jpb*. Therefore, the third group's argument most closely adheres to my own. I will further detail this position later in this chapter with regard to humanitarian occupation law, which is one of the integral features incorporated into my common-good-seeking approach to justice.

Classical and Nonclassical Just Actors

With this preliminary knowledge of the fundamental sources of international law and its major issues when applied to the *post bellum* context, this chapter sets the basic parameters of the field of international law studies, especially instantiated in two codified bodies of law for just punishment, namely, occupation law and international criminal law. However, the UNSC is another source of international law that must be considered. The UNSC is technically not a treaty nor any documented statute of law. In contrast, the UNSC itself works as a legal authority for treating violations of the rule of law *post bellum*, and we will discuss the role of the council throughout the remainder of this chapter. Further, the UNSC is the most important classical just actor, as it is an authorized representative member of the international community, in addition to being composed of strong nations that have often engaged in wars as victors.[22] In particular, the UNSC is authorized to make enforceable decisions under international humanitarian law.[23] This empowerment signifies who is allowed to practice law and conduct punishments in the *jpb* context and how this justice system leads to the establishment of a just peace. Therefore, the role of a classical actor like the UNSC is key to rebuilding the common good, as the Security Council is involved in the practice of both occupation law and international criminal law.

However, as outlined in chapter four, unlike the *jpb* practice of just policing, the work of just punishment does not limit the scope of actors to these classical actors alone. There are some potential areas in criminal law that are open for a broader range of just actors including nonclassical actors. Nonetheless, these nonclassical actors are still limited in implementing just punishment, as they are subject to the commands of the classical actors. For

---

22 The permanent members of the UNSC are the United States, the United Kingdom, France, Russia, and China, which are the five with veto power.

23 United Nations Charter, Chapter V, Articles 24 and 25. For example, both Articles 24 and 25 of the UN Charter allow the UNSC to authorize military operations under international humanitarian law.

example, local community-based initiatives, such as the Truth Commission and the Gacaca trials, work as nonclassical actors for post-conflict justice in a broad sense. Their efforts working toward political reconciliation are widely acknowledged in the literature of *transitional justice*. Thus, as defined in chapter four, these courts are not the primary legal and political institutions for *postwar justice*. Rather, they are auxiliary ones, cooperating with the classical actors in their *jpb* work of implementing just punishment in a balanced and fair manner. These needed nonclassical actors will be discussed in the next chapter since their practices can be further understood in a larger *jpb* frame of reference for just political participation.

Occupation Law:
Just Punishment for Securing the Rule of Law

The subject of occupation law has been studied primarily by scholars who ask a question about the problems of military occupation. However, the practical issues found in occupation law should also attract wider attention from *jpb* thinkers and practitioners, especially those interested in the evolution and effectiveness of norms for acceptable conduct regarding just policing. The primary concern regarding the legal implications of occupation law must be how just policing practice—whether articulated in peacekeeping or nation building—ought to be enforced by law. The previous chapter may have left a question of whether such just policing that works toward the comprehensive human security scheme aims too high and cannot be achieved if the rule of law is not secured. What guarantee is there that the rule of law will be honored in a postwar society emerging from the rubble of war?

Traditional Occupation Law: The Principle of Conservation

Occupation law is a well-established section of international humanitarian law. Practicing this law is a response to certain situations *post bellum*, specifically in the aftermath of ensuing hostilities where mass atrocities and other human rights gross violations occur. Therefore, the practice of occupation law is and should be a main theme of *jpb* ethic when it comes to the establishment of just punishment. However, the 4th Geneva Convention and the Hague Conventions are insufficient to respond to ensuing conflicts *post bellum* due to the anachronistic qualities of their conservationist principles, along with their state-oriented occupation agenda. Given that these Conventions represent a paradigm for occupation law, occupation law is traditionally viewed as statist in its orientation. This conventional version of occupation law is basically believed to address the obligations of the victor to the defeated state and its citizens in the postwar society where the victorious nation-state temporarily occupies the territory of another state in the immediate aftermath of a war.[24] In particular, Section III of the Hague Convention of 1907 defines occupation law as a treaty to preserve the laws and governmental structure of the state being occupied, as well as to secure public safety in the occupied territory.[25] This definition is known as the "principle of conservation."[26]

In addition to Section III of the Hague Convention, Article 38 of the 4th Geneva Convention supports the principle of conservation related to armed occupation.[27] This article provides a Bill of Rights for protected personnel living in occupied postwar areas. These rights include but are not limited to: (i) right to receive relief, (ii) right to receive health care services, (iii) right to receive spiritual assistance from religious organizations, and (iv) right to move away from areas exposed to the dangers of violent threats.[28]

However, according to Adam Roberts, the principle of conservation encompasses a short duration of military occupation, the end of which is to return the territory to the government of the state once the hostilities are concluded.[29] This traditional version of occupation law provides no basis for the transformation of the postwar society, nor does it require infrastructure reconstruction.[30] Instead, this version of occupation law is based solely on a traditional conception of a war as a state of armed conflict between

---

24 Geneva Convention Relative to the Protection of Civilian Persons in Time of War; and the Hague Conventions of 1907 (IV).

25 The Hague Conventions of 1907 (IV), Section III.

26 See two articles of the Hague Conventions of 1907 (IV), Articles 43 and 55. They are the most acknowledged ones relevant to the principle of conservation. Article 43 states, "The authority . . . passed into the hands of the occupant [who] shall take all the measures in his power to restore . . . public order and safety, while respecting, unless absolutely prevented, the laws in force in the country." Article 55 notes, "The occupying state shall be regarded only as administrator and usufructuary of public buildings, real estate and agricultural estates belonging to the hostile state." It must safeguard the capital of these properties, and administer them in accordance with the rules of usufruct."

27 For details, see Simon Chesterman, "Occupation as Liberation: International Humanitarian Law and Regime Change," Ethics and International Affairs 18, no. 3 (December 2004): 51–64.

28 Geneva Convention Relative to the Protection of Civilian Persons in Time of War, Article 38. For more details, see Chesterman, "Occupation as Liberation," 51–64.

29 Adam Roberts, "Transformative Military Occupation: Applying the Laws of War and Human Rights," American Journal of International Law 100, no. 3 (2006): 580.

30 Fox, Humanitarian Occupation, 263–69.

two or more sovereign states, the conclusion of which is thus determined among the warring parties themselves. Be that as it may, the conservationist principle is nothing but a return to the status quo *ante bellum* that is not equal to *jpb*. Further, this traditional occupation law, with its statist orientation, is "anachronistic" in that many of the de facto occupations that have occurred in the post-Cold War era have been multilateral in nature.[31] Moreover, the current occupations have been sanctioned either initially or retroactively by the UN, specifically the UNSC. In this regard, Roberts clarified that the UN has become the de facto occupier of war-torn societies, and that many of the recent cases drawn from the UNSC Resolutions (UNSCRs) that have been instantiated in bodies of law, UNSCR 1244, UNSCR 1272, and UNSCR 1483, serve as examples of this assertion.[32]

Humanitarian Occupation Law

The UNSC Chapter VII Resolutions: A Transformative *Jus Post Bellum* Scheme

Most contemporary *jpb* law scholars agree with Roberts that traditional occupation law, along with its statist orientation and conservationist principle, is insufficient for dealing with current postwar situations. Instead, they propose so-called "humanitarian occupations law" under UN mandates that have been implemented since the end of the Cold War. They consider this occupation law to exist for humanitarian reasons, which aligns well with the stated legality of the UNSC Chapter VII resolutions. The UNSCRs advocate a transformative *jpb* scheme rather than sticking to the conservationist principle approach of a military occupation agenda. The postwar administrations created by the UNSCRs, such as Kosovo, East Timor, and Iraq, were designed to take a transformational action for the sake of the local citizens *post bellum*, such as the establishment of the postwar institutions of governance and law for securing human life.[33]

---

31 Fox, 249–55.

32 Adam Roberts, "The End of Occupation: Iraq 2004," *The International and Comparative Law Quarterly* 54, no.1 (2005): 36

33 Chapter VII resolutions established UN administrations in Kosovo (UNSCR 1244), East Timor (UNSCR 1272), and Iraq (UNSCR 1483). See: UN Security Council, Resolution 1244, S/RES/1244, (June 10, 1999), https://digitallibrary.un.org/record/274488; UN Security Council, Resolution 1271, S/RES/1272, (October 25, 1999), https://digitallibrary.un.org/record/291410; and UN Security Council, Resolution 1483, S/RES/1483, (May 22, 2003), https://digitallibrary.un.org/record/495555.

Gregory Fox: Social Engineering Project

One of the first major scholars to propose humanitarian occupation is Gregory Fox. He argues that "creating a liberal, democratic order" authorized under the auspices of the UNSC Chapter VII resolutions is the first and foremost mission of humanitarian occupation. He calls this mission a "social engineering project," which must adopt "international standards of human rights and governance as [its] blueprints."[34] He recognizes a link between stability and liberal democracy with high positive correlations between them. This belief requires the UNSC's technical support for assistance in building democratic institutions, as well as the need to assist in infrastructure projects.[35] For example, he argues that Iraqi society is too vulnerable to consider the conservationist principle alone, largely because of its longstanding history of repressive political violence that has been perpetuated to benefit a few at the expense of many, and thus that the UNSC must adopt his social engineering project in order to support the transformation of deficient national structures and capabilities. However, the emphasis he gives to the creation of liberal democracies as set forth in Chapter VII UNSCRs must be more carefully examined since the nature of postwar situations and the relevant political transformative scheme is always changeable, dynamic, and multidimensional. As the ensuing discussion of other humanitarian occupation law authors will show, an overly prescriptive approach to constitution-making—whether it be a liberal democratic regime or not—is unlikely to be functional.

Eyal Benvenisti: Transformative Scheme for Human Sovereignty

In his book *The International Law of Occupation*, Eyal Benvenisti writes about the issue of occupation law in order to shed light on the traditional international legal norms regarding the protection of people in a postwar society (or "an occupied area" in his terms). In addition, he introduces the changes that have occurred to these rules in the late twentieth and the early twenty-first centuries, as well as the possible emergence of new rules having their origin in the legal field of human rights that have arisen from

---

[34] Fox, *Humanitarian Occupation*, 3–4.

[35] Fox's argument for the deliberate linkage between stability and liberal democracy is drawn from the former United Nations Secretary General Boutros Boutros-Ghali's *An Agenda for Peace*. For more details, see Boutros Boutros- Ghali, *An Agenda for Peace*, 2nd ed. (New York: United Nations, 1995), 12.

the law of peace rather than the law of war. In other words, he contends that occupation is not always an indispensable effect of "actual fighting," so it should "not necessarily be linked to war."[36] Rather, he confirms that recent occupations have been practiced primarily for humanitarian reasons, while being concerned with international human rights laws—along with the expression of human rights norms and the principle of self-determination—over the preservation of the preexisting government. He asserts that this change has occurred fundamentally because of a shift of norm focus on sovereignty in the post-Cold War era. Since then, sovereignty has been determined by the population in the postwar society, not the prewar governmental structure.[37] For this reason, Benvenisti believes that occupation law should not be based on a status quo *ante bellum* restorative scheme. Instead, it should be a transformative *jpb* scheme of occupation.

Further, Benvenisti not only presents the aforementioned reason to believe that many of the occupations have occurred in the wake of massive human rights violations, but he also finds a practical legal means to signify just actors' duty to humanitarian occupation. This legal vehicle features UNSCR 1483, which not only recognizes the United States' de facto occupation of Iraq, but also signifies the practical implications of Operation Iraqi Freedom for the law of occupation. Benvenisti refers to UNSCR 1483 as the latest and most authoritative restatement of rudimentary principles of the contemporary law of occupation. He regards UNSCR 1483 as a humanitarian occupation expressed in threefold manner.

(1) UNSCR 1483 allows for sovereignty to "inhere in the people [of the postwar society]," rather than in the government, the traditional sense of sovereignty.

(2) UNSCR 1483 does not purport that occupation is necessarily linked to war. Instead, it states that occupation ought to be primarily advanced for humanitarian reasons. In other words, it "grants a mandate" for governmental transformation as it "recognizes in principle the continued applicability of international human rights law [or the law of peace] . . . in tandem with the law of occupation."

36 Eyal Benvenisti, *The International Law of Occupation* (Princeton: Princeton University Press, 2004), 2–4.

37 Benvenisti, viii–xi.

(3) UNSCR 1483 requires the classical just actors (or "the occupiers" in his terms) to become "heavily involved regulators," which is a substantial departure from the Hague Convention.[38]

These three principles correspond well to my comprehensive version of human security, which includes sovereignty determined by the population, a transformative vision of *jpb*, and a maxim(um) of judicial enforcement of the minimalist rules of *jpb* as fundamental characteristics incorporated into my common good approach.

However, despite the advance of occupation law affected by UNSCR 1483 in order to express its humanitarian concerns, Benvenisti also recognizes the limit of its legal implication in practice. There are two areas in which the law remains inexplicit and vague, and hence, it needs to develop in a practical manner. The first area he finds problematic is the lack of legitimate and real accountability within the resolution, especially with regard to whether the occupiers—whether they are victorious states or the international community—are not only legitimately eligible but practically permitted to conduct diplomacy and foreign affairs on behalf of the occupied population. Second, if the occupiers are allowed to undertake such public affairs, how should they be practiced in legal terms? Plainly, Benvenisti highlights a substantial absence of logistic guidance regarding the occupier's responsibilities for the sake of the occupied. Notwithstanding this concern, he maintains his affirmative position that "[the law] prevents the occupant from hiding behind the limits imposed upon its powers as a pretext for inaction."[39]

Nehal Bhuta and Carsten Stahn:
Ad Hoc Process of Chapter VII UNSC Resolutions

Nehal Bhuta shares Benvenisti's concern with humanitarian occupation, especially with regard to the question of sovereignty and the practical nature of contemporary occupation. He is particularly concerned with the practical challenge of including constitutional transformation under the aegis of the UNSC as a legitimate standard of *jpb*. He believes that outside powers like the UNSC have a tendency to adopt "an overly prescriptive approach to constitution making," in which these powers have been incapable of utilizing

---

38 Benvenisti, xi.

39 Benvenisti, 11.

the local political and legal resources to fulfill the substantial demand of the postwar society's projects to rebuild a constitutional order.[40] As an alternative to these difficulties in practice, Bhuta argues for an *ad hoc* approach toward creating constitutions for postwar societies, which he believes is closely tied to the idea of transformative occupation.[41]

Further, Bhuta criticizes that "UN missions are not belligerent occupation within the meaning of the laws of war."[42] This criticism is more clearly developed by Carsten Stahn, who sees that there is a void in the internal legal framework to deal with situations of *jpb*, especially with regard to a law of transition from war to peace, specifically from international humanitarian law to international human rights.[43] In particular, Stahn argues, "the law of occupation, as the only branch of *jus in bello* which deals explicitly with post-conflict relations, is ill-suited to serve as a framework of [UN] administration."[44] He sees the void in the international legal paradigm from a historical viewpoint, arguing that "since Grotius's *De Jure Belli ac Pacis*, the architecture of the international law has been founded upon a distinction between war and peace," which he believes is no longer valid in the current international legal paradigm.[45] He posits that three changes in the international system during the post-Cold War era—or to some extent over the past century—have led to this condition. First, the criminalization of war in the mid-twentieth century, especially after World War II, has led war to become "regulated by law." Second, the dividing line between war and peace is no longer clear due to changes in the nature of conflict, namely, the shrinking number of interstate wars and the increasing number of civil wars and internal armed violence. Third, these new types of conflict have defied management under existing international legal regimes. Considering all these situations, Stahn concludes that "some of the problems arising in the period of transition from conflict to peace cannot be addressed by a simple

40 Nehal Bhuta, "New Modes and Orders: The Difficulties of a *Jus Post Bellum* Constitutional Transformation," *University of Toronto Law Journal* 60 (2010): 850.

41 For comment and discussion, see Roberts, "The End of Occupation," 36.

42 Bhuta, "New Modes and Orders," 826.

43 As noted earlier, this void, hole, gap, or lacuna (the *jpb* authors examined here use them interchangeably) is the concern of the second group who discuss international human rights law as part of the *jpb* law discourse.

44 Carsten Stahn, "'Jus ad bellum', 'jus in bello'. . . 'jus post bellum'?—Rethinking the Conception of the Law of Armed Force," *European Journal of International Law* 17, no. 5 (November 2006): 921–22.

45 Stahn, 935.

application of the 'law of peace' or the 'law of war', but require 'situation-specific' adjustments," as shown in the case of the *ad hoc* process of Chapter VII UNSCRs that he believes have worked fairly well.[46] As a result, Stahn agrees with Bhuta's *ad hoc* approach toward creating constitutions under the aegis of the UNSC.

Inger Osterdahl: Building a New Treaty

Given these practical issues to consider, there is a divide among *jpb* law scholars as to whether there should be a call for a new international treaty governing the laws of occupation or whether the current system of UNSCR Chapter VII authorizations will suffice. Inger Osterdahl advocates for the drafting and adoption of a new treaty to deal with the gaps in the law. Outlining the fundamental sources of her approach to building a new treaty for humanitarian occupation law must be completed by refining a foremost practical issue of international law and its relationship to occupation law. The issue to address is that there is a void in the current internal legal framework with regard to a law of transition from war to peace, specifically from international humanitarian law to international human rights law. Many *jpb* scholars, including Osterdahl herself, agree that the legal literature concerning *jpb* revolves around this issue and the question of what constitutes the proper response under occupation law.

Osterdahl begins her argument by indicating that there is a near universal consensus regarding the void in the legal framework with regard to a law of transition from war to peace; the disagreements ensue regarding whether something should be done about this gap or whether the current system of *ad hoc* solutions remains functional in practice. As opposed to the latter, specifically contrary to Bhuta's argument for situation-specific adjustments, Osterdahl sees that *ad hoc* approaches overlook a recurring issue in the present-day international system: human rights violations. As an alternative, she asserts that the establishment of a new treaty helps fill the legal void to address such issues in a clear and timely manner.[47]

Osterdahl's argument for the establishment of a new treaty is similar to some transformative *jpb* schemes such as Orend's proposal for the establishment of an entirely new Geneva Convention, which I have opposed

---

46 Stahn, 924.
47 Osterdahl, "What Will *Jus Post Bellum* Mean?," 4.

throughout the book.[48] Despite the dispute regarding the establishment of a new treaty, Osterdhal's *jpb* ethic of law largely aligns with my comprehensive human security scheme, as she posits that humanitarian norms ought to be applied to the practice of establishing the new treaty, that just actors must guarantee the security of the occupied people in the immediate aftermath of war by coming to the equal protection of all citizens, and that her transformative scheme clearly advocates including the requirements of the R2P doctrine into a treaty for *jpb*.[49] In particular, Osterdahl believes that the establishment of a new treaty will secure the establishment of the common good. The treaty will primarily aim to secure the public's safety in the occupied areas in legal terms through both international humanitarian law and international human rights law and thus contribute to rebuilding the common good in the vanquished society. Additionally, this newly enforced treaty rationale carries with it an insistence that justice persists even with the practical obstacles that just actors will encounter, as shown in the previous chapter.

Like international security studies scholars Caldwell, Dobbins, and Feldman, Osterdahl recognizes the practical concerns of cost and time commitment. If such a treaty were to be ratified, it is likely that classical actors would become even more reluctant to intervene in humanitarian crises as a result of the additional costs and time commitments they would incur. Nonetheless, Osterdahl advocates for the creation of this treaty and for the obligation of the international community writ large to cover the costs and time commitments of *jpb*.[50] As indicated in the previous chapter, this vision of obligation imposed on the international community—rather than on one single victorious state or a small number of victorious allied states—will allow a greater chance for the postwar society to rebuild the common good.[51]

While Osterdahl's approach has many merits that align with my common good approach, this chapter does not advocate her proposal for building a new treaty for practical reasons. Rather, this chapter advocates Bhuta's *ad hoc* approach toward constitution creation authorized under the

---

48 Orend, "Justice After War," (2012), 211–14. Osterdahl agrees with Orend's proposal to building toward a new Geneva Convention. See Osterdahl, "What Will *Jus Post Bellum* Mean?," 4.

49 Osterdahl, "What Will *Jus Post Bellum* Mean?," 8.

50 Osterdahl, 5.

51 This multilateral feature of just actors has been discussed throughout the book, especially with the role of the UN. This feature of just actors works reasonably well with my common-good-seeking approach to justice, as shown in chapter five.

auspices of the UNSC Chapter VII resolutions, as well as Benvenisti's humanitarian approach toward transformative occupation through the use of UNSCRs in general. Further, there are other *jpb* law scholars who agree that Benvenisti's humanitarian approach is working well enough to ensure *jpb* on a case-by-case basis. Bhuta argues, "the current practice of *ad hoc* regulation of post-conflict political transformation under the aegis of the UNSC should continue."[52] For Stahn, requiring "situation-specific" adjustments means that there is no need for the establishment of a new treaty to regulate postwar situations when it comes to facing the issue of the void in the current internal legal framework of transition from war to peace. This rationale is drawn from his beliefs that (i) the *ad hoc* process of the Chapter VII UNSC resolution has worked fairly well, (ii) the possibility of actually drafting and ratifying a new treaty is low at the moment, and (iii) any new treaty law could cause the law to become self-contradictory with the concern that too many fundamental questions regarding the idea of *jpb* remain unanswered, as does its practice.[53] He argues, "the notion [of *jpb*] is unsatisfactorily narrow and overly broad at the same time."[54] Therefore, Stahn cautions that moving from an *ad hoc* approach to a codified framework could provoke contradictions within the current international legal system. For Stahn, as well as Bhuta and Benvenisti, it is hard to imagine that a new treaty—whether it is radically revised or even totally reconstructed with a goal of creating a whole different system for *jpb*—could foresee and encompass all of the potential variations of military occupations that might occur in the coming decades and beyond.

International Criminal Law: Just Punishment for Amending Past Wrongdoings

International Criminal Law as International Humanitarian Law

As shown in the preceding section, the legal literature concerning *jpb* largely revolves around three practical issues. First, several scholars of international

---

52 Bhuta, "New Modes and Orders," 853. Fox has written extensively on this issue and echoes Bhuta's *ad hoc* approach, especially with respect to the role of the UNSC. He cites the uniqueness of the UNSC in its ability to regulate postwar situations. For details, see Fox, *Humanitarian Occupation*, 2–10.

53 Carsten Stahn, "The Future of *Jus Post Bellum*," in *Jus Post Bellum: Towards a Law of Transition from Conflict to Peace*, ed. Carsten Stahn and Jann K. Kleffner (The Hague: T.M.C. Asser Press, 2008), 233.

54 Stahn, 234.

humanitarian law have been concerned with the legal status of the subjects of *jpb* practices encompassed within humanitarian occupation law, such as governmental transformation, economic reconstruction, education, and infrastructure repair. Second, other writers have argued that the transition from conflict to peace includes matters that are normally associated with both the laws of war and the laws of peace, but that these two types of law could not be applied simultaneously. Third and most crucially, these writers subsequently have addressed the question whether a new treaty should be devised or whether the current system of *ad hoc* solutions remains functional in practice. I am convinced that *ad hoc* approaches will continue to be the only ones available, and that is acceptable in my mind, as long as they are concerned with rebuilding the common good.

With these three concerns in mind, the second part of this chapter will turn the attention to authors who write about the *jpb* issue of international tribunals. It should be noted that most authors writing on international criminal law take such tribunals as a given at this point in history. For this reason, the scholarly writing on international tribunals is generally oriented to the details of how they ought to be managed rather than whether they belong among the criteria for *jpb*. Nonetheless, for the sake of the focus of this book, the rest of this chapter will narrow the scope of the legal regimes of international criminal law as it is concerned with war crimes tribunals, so that they fall within the parameters of *jpb*. In other words, the international criminal law of *jpb* must be understood from the perspective of international humanitarian law, treating just punishment as a larger project of just policing.

We first will discuss who ought to be responsible for violations of international humanitarian law in the *jpb* context: states or individuals. We will then discuss how this justice system leads to the establishment of a just peace. Furthermore, the core dilemma of *jpb* in international criminal law studies is: how can we balance security and reconciliation? This analysis revisits my common-good-seeking approach to justice, which will be a guide for developing a discourse on punishing the past wrongdoer and embracing the past enemy.

International Criminal Law: State Responsibility and Individual Criminal Responsibility

Given the significant developments of international criminal justice in the last few decades due to the creation of several international criminal tribunals, such as the International Criminal Court (ICC), the prosecution of war crimes is often considered to be the most effective judicial means of enforcing international humanitarian law and sanctioning its violations.[55] In particular, the emphasis is put on the responsibility of individuals for violations of international humanitarian law that amount to war crimes. However, the traditional way of enforcing international obligations between states, through state responsibility, should not be forgotten. Hence, the two types of responsibility, state responsibility and individual criminal responsibility, must be clearly distinguished, even though they are interconnected. Two major concerns highlight the difference.

First, individual criminal responsibility deals with the responsibility of individual persons, and the consequences of this responsibility are criminal sanctions, which generally consist of the privation of liberty. Individual criminal responsibility is established by criminal courts, including, at the international level, the ICC. However, not all violations of law may give rise to individual criminal responsibility, but only those that amount to serious international humanitarian law violations are considered crimes under the ICC.[56] The ICC has limited jurisdiction and can only intervene when national courts are unable or unwilling to bring criminals to justice. The ICC then can take action as the last legal resort. Further, although a projected offender's state is not a member party to the Rome Statute, the ICC under its laws and regulations can still prosecute citizens of nonmember states, especially when nonmember states commit illegal acts in member states.[57]

55 The ICC, governed by the Rome Statute, is the first permanent, treaty-based international court established to help end impunity for the most serious criminals of concern to the international community. For more details, see David Luban, Julie R. O'Sullivan, and David P. Stewart, *International and Transnational Criminal Law* (New York: Wolters Kluwer, 2010), chap. 21.

56 As discussed in chapter two in relation to R2P, the Rome Statute stipulates four types of international offenses as follows: genocide, crimes against humanity, war crimes and atrocities, and crime of aggression. To be precise, as shared in chapter two, while humanitarian interventions have in the past been justified in the context of varying situations, the R2P focuses only on the four mass atrocity crimes: genocide, war crimes, ethnic cleansing, and crimes against humanity. The first three crimes are clearly defined in international law and codified in the Rome Statute that established the International Criminal Court. Ethnic cleansing is not a crime defined under international law but has been defined by the UN as "a purposeful policy designed by one ethnic or religious group to remove by violent and terror-inspiring means the civilian population of another ethnic or religious group from certain geographic areas." For details, see Boutros Boutros-Ghali, *Letter Dated 24 May 1994 from the Secretary General to the President of the Security Council*, http://www.un.org/ga/search/view_doc.asp?symbol=S/1994/674.

57 As of August 2020, there are 123 member states. Nonmember states do not have to abide by the ICC laws and regulations. Yet, citizens of nonmember states in member states have to obey the rules authorized under the ICC.

State responsibility, by contrast, concerns the responsibility of states and resembles civil or tort responsibility in national law, which signifies that the main consequence is cessation of the unlawful conduct and reparations for the injury suffered. Hence, the notion of international criminal responsibility of states does not exist.[58] State responsibility is not established by criminal courts but by institutions such as the International Court of Justice. In addition, state responsibility is not limited to only serious international humanitarian law violations but can cover any violation of international humanitarian law norms.[59]

Second, state responsibility and individual criminal responsibility are regulated by two different legal regimes, each composed of different rules. The result is that the two types of responsibility are independent of each other; one does not imply the other. Just because an individual who is acting on behalf of a state is guilty of war crimes does not automatically entail the responsibility of that state for violations of international humanitarian law under the law of state responsibility. The reverse is also true. It is perfectly possible that a state may be held internationally responsible for a serious violation of international humanitarian law without the concrete perpetrator of that violation being considered as criminally responsible for such violation, even if that author is acting on behalf of the state.[60] That being said, one type of responsibility may have effects on the other type of responsibility.[61]

---

58 Bartram S. Brown, "US Objections to the Statute of the International Criminal Court: A Brief Response," *New York University Journal of International Law and Politics* 31 (1999): 890.

59 Marco Sassoli, "State Responsibility for Violations of International Humanitarian Law," *International Review of the Red Cross* 84, no. 846 (June 2002): 404, 421–34.

60 For details, see Thomas Rauter, *Judicial Practice, Customary International Criminal Law and Nullum Crimen Sine Lege* (New York: Springer, 2017), chap. 1.

61 One of the most important areas of overlap concerns the establishment of "facts." Roger O'Keefe, *International Criminal Law*, (Oxford: Oxford University Press, 2015), 504. The facts established by the criminal court may be crucial for the court ruling on state responsibility, especially since that court is often deprived of the effective means to collect evidence. For example, in the case regarding the application of the Genocide convention to the war in the former Yugoslavia, the ICJ ruled that it could rely on evidence established by the International Criminal Tribunal for Yugoslavia (ICTY). As emphasized by the court itself, this case de facto had "an unusual feature. Many of the allegations before [it had] already been the subject of the processes and decisions of the ICTY." The court concluded in that regard that, "it should in principle accept as highly persuasive relevant findings of facts made by the Tribunal at trial, unless of course they have been upset on appeal. For the same reasons, any evaluation by the Tribunal based on the facts as so found for instance about the existence of the required intent, is also entitled to due weight." cf. ICJ Reports, *Application of the Convention on the Prevention and Punishment of the Crime of Genocide (Bosnia and Herzegovina v Serbia and Montenegro)*, February 26, 2007), paragraph 223.

Defining the Scope of *Jus Post Bellum* for Just Punishment Practices

With emphasis on the dynamics of both state and individual criminal responsibilities, international criminal law treats violations of the rules of law in wartime and *post bellum*.

Treating Violations of *Jus Ad Bellum*, *Jus In Bello*, and *Jus Post Bellum*

International criminal law recognizes postwar conflicts principally as a political phenomenon occurring between two or more sovereign states that is resolved by the same parties or third parties. In particular, international humanitarian law as a legal paradigm for treating violations of *jus ad bellum* (e.g., Article 2.4 of Chapter I of the UN Charter) and *jus in bello* (e.g., the 4th Geneva Convention and the Hague Conventions) is a basis for the practice within international criminal law to make an argument for the obligations of actors to the citizens in the defeated state. In addition, international criminal law is concerned with yet another legal paradigm for treating violations of *jpb*, namely, violations of humanitarian occupation law (e.g., the UNSCRs) by a postwar administration operated by the victor or the international community. Recall that this law includes the creation of an elected representative government, the establishment of the postwar institutions of governance and law, and the respect for human rights of all citizens living within the occupied territory, all of which aim to secure the public safety of postwar societies. Therefore, treating violations of law *post bellum*, specifically that of occupation law, must also be understood as part of just punishment.

However, treating violations of occupation law *in practice* is hard to define in a single, unitary, codified legal framework, much in the same way that occupation law seems best determined by an *ad hoc* approach. This is so primarily because treating violations of *jpb* in occupied states is determined by various legal agreements, as well as the UNSC Chapter VII resolutions, including military agreements, such as Status of Forces Agreements (SOFA), which are agreements between a host country and a foreign nation stationing military forces in that host country. For example, treating violations *post bellum* means not only for the time of occupation but also for the time when SOFA is effective, namely, when US military personnel are legitimately present and stationed for intervention in occupied states. Therefore, the affirmation, codification, and practice of such military agreements

have been determined by diverse political influences and diplomatic over-
tures besides the legal regimes.[62]

Further, these military agreements retain their legal status and political
influence after the occupation, as their policy implications often apply
beyond the theoretical range of postwar justice. I define this as a threshold
between the two phases of war and peace, specifically a phase of Low Intensity Conflict, falling short of war. However, as opposed to this theoretical
guidance, occupiers hold the same legal status and privilege even after the
time of occupation. For example, SOFA has been present in Japan, South
Korea, and other nations in which the United States has staged interventions
for over a half century, not just during the time of occupation. Given these
historical contexts, the issue of criminal jurisdiction has caused major and
prolonged legal and diplomatic disputes between the United States and
these nations, especially the question of whether the US Department of
Defense can claim legal immunity on foreign soils. One prominent example
is the postwar Japanese society. Dale Sonnenberg, the former Chief of International Law of US Forces in Japan, examines a confidential agreement of
1953 concluded by both Japanese and US policymakers, which has committed Japanese authorities to waive primary jurisdiction over most criminal offences committed by off-duty US military personnel, the civilian
component, and their dependents. This agreement was developed into the
US-Japan SOFA on January 19, 1961. He argues that with the signing of this
agreement, "Japan did enter into an informal agreement that it would waive
its primary right to exercise jurisdiction."[63] Plainly, it means that Japan is
not completely free from the intervention of postwar occupation even after
the end of the occupation period. Further, a significant number of US military personnel-related criminal cases have been continuously reported even
in recent years.[64] In addition, at least ten US SOFAs, including the one

62 For further discussion, see Alexander Cooley, *Base Politics* (Ithaca, NY: Cornell University Press, 2008).

63 Dale Sonnenberg, "The Agreements Regarding Status of Foreign Forces in Japan," In *The Handbook of the Law of Visiting Forces*. ed. Dieter Fleck (Oxford: Oxford University Press, 2001), 387.

64 During the occupation (1945–1952), specifically from the date of effect of the US-led postwar Administrative Agreement on August 15th, 1945 to April 28th, 1952, US military personnel-related criminal cases reached 1,612. Meanwhile, the total number of cases that were caused by on-and-off-duty US servicemen in Japan between 1952 and 2013 is 209,577. For details, see Takeuchi Makoto, "Beigun Jiko Nitsuite Nendo Betsu, Koumujyou-gai Betsu Kensuu, Shibousha, Baishoukin, Showa 27-heisei 25 Nendo." *Department of Defense Report* (Japan, 2014). For an overview of SOFA in Japan, see Dayna Barnes, *Architects of Occupation* (Ithaca, NY: Cornell University Press, 2017).

created in 1961, are kept classified, and this has caused more contentions attached to the conflict over criminal jurisdiction.[65] One could argue that these complex issues seem to be in large part the result of a number of questions, still unresolved, regarding the scope of *jpb*. Although a consensus exists that legal requirements for treating violations of law *post bellum* should be one of the central pillars of any codification of *jpb*, the consensus stops there. Instead, treating violations of law *post bellum* requires further investigation, specifically a careful and thorough case study analysis. However, despite its significance, this investigation will not be further included in this chapter for the sake of clarity in discussion.[66] Therefore, the remainder of the chapter will attend only to the question of treating violations of law in wartime, not *post bellum*.

Criminal Justice and Political Reconciliation

When it comes to treating the violations of law in wartime, a central question of *jpb* is whether criminal justice requires political reconciliation. As outlined in chapter four, during the phase of just punishment this inquiry essentially relates to the normative value of attaining two objectives, that of criminal justice and that of political reconciliation. On the one hand, criminal justice poses the problem of law and moral obligation, such as penal sanctions against the guilty. On the other hand, political reconciliation poses the problem of finding a legitimate and acceptable outcome to the conflict for all involved, leading to political reconstruction and stability. However, criminal justice (demanding correction and requests for reparation in the wake of mass crimes committed during war) and political reconciliation (efforts at democratization and political equilibrium) are not always mutually exclusive. The question is whether the law of criminal justice is needed for determining justice leading to political reconciliation, and if so, how? As suggested in chapter four, while a legal practice of just punishment must serve human security, it must incorporate a moral and legal vision of

---

65 For further discussion, see Jonathan Flynn, "No Need to Maximize: Reforming Foreign Criminal Jurisdiction Practice under the U.S.-Japan Status of Forces Agreement," *Military Law Review* 212 (2012): 1–69.

66 For examples of such case study analysis, however, see Benedict DeDominicis and Jaemyung Kim, "Nationalism and Postwar Japanese Society," *Korean Political Science Review* 48, no. 3 (2014); and William Wetherall, "The Girad and Kupski Cases: Extraterritoriality and Jurisdiction in Post-occupation Japan," *Yosha Bunko*, August 20, 2016, Accessed October 15, 2020, http://www.yoshabunko.com/anthropology/Girard_and_Kupsik_cases.html.

political reconciliation when its ultimate intention is to restore human flourishing and a just order. This guidance has three components in light of the *jpb* praxis of state responsibility and individual criminal responsibility.

First, the underlying agenda for rebuilding the common good suggests that any finding of state responsibility must reject or minimize reparations and sanctions imposed upon innocent and vulnerable people in the defeated state. The questions surrounding reparations were specifically discussed in chapter two (e.g., just punishment by developing Orend's rehabilitation model), so they will not be replayed in detail here.

Second, other state responsibilities for postwar justice issues are associated with transitional justice, such as efforts at democratization and political equilibrium in the time of transition. These belong to the *jpb* phase of just political participation that will be discussed in the final chapter. This is an area of *jpb* that pursues both political reconciliation and human security aimed at rebuilding the common good.

Third, as opposed to these two state responsibility matters, I suggest that just actors must *not* consider political reconciliation as their primary mission, especially when addressing individual criminal responsibility by conducting war crimes tribunals. Court decisions too often result in nothing but a plea bargain in order to secure the interests of the offender or the victors for the sake of political reconciliation. Furthermore, as defined by the ICC, most cases of individual criminal responsibility entail *grave* crimes, and such past wrongdoings ought to be treated similarly to other serious criminal acts.[67]

The Protection of Fair Trials to All:
Neither for Vengeance nor Utilitarian Justice

With respect to the third proposition regarding individual criminal responsibility, one scholar, Davida Kellogg, excludes political reconciliation in

---

67 Guided by the jurisprudence of Nuremberg and Tokyo tribunals, the Special Working Group on the Crime of Aggression (SWGCA) reaffirmed in its earliest legal instruments that the crime of aggression is "reserved" only for high-ranking state officials. People who are unable to "influence the policy of carrying out the crime" could be excluded from criminal responsibility. In addition, by the virtue of their position, lower-ranking state agents cannot be aware of aggressive plans. Since they do not possess the cognitive segment of mental element of *mens rea*—or the awareness—they could not be liable for the crime of aggression. cf. Report of the Informal Intersessional Meeting of the SWGCA, Liechtenstein Institute for Self Determination, Woodrow Wilson School, Princeton University, Princeton, June 13–15, 2005, ICC-ASP/4/SWGCA/INF.1, paragraph 19.

order to bring justice to war criminals. She argues that war crimes tribunals must become a central pillar of any codification of *jpb*: meting out punishment for serious war crimes is nothing but "the end-stage of just war." Kellogg reasons that "stopping short of trying and punishing" those most responsible for war crimes for *any reason* makes "no strategic sense since the purpose for which war was undertaken is never achieved, . . . no legal sense since the criminal activities the war was undertaken to . . . curtail are allowed to continue unchecked" and "no moral sense since justice is not done for the victims of atrocities in such an outcome to war."[68] She continues, "in the case of the victims of atrocities, sweeping these injustices under a thick dusty rug of history, whether to keep a fragile peace or in a foredoomed effort at reconciliation, only continues their abusive treatment as non-persons who do not even register on the radar screen of international justice."[69]

Others like Orend would argue that despite her deep concern for the victims of atrocities, Kellogg's criminal justice is nothing else but retributive justice, which is vengeance based. Recall that Orend understood retribution as vengeance, yet what he overlooked was that there are a wide range of variations of retributive justice.[70] For example, retributive justice has social functions.[71] H. L. A. Hart argues that the modern view of retributive justice has shifted its focus from the inherent good of avenging the evil act by inflicting pain on its actor to the value of authoritative expression, in the

---

68 Davida E. Kellogg, "*Jus Post Bellum*: The Importance of War Crimes Trials," *Parameters* 32, no. 3 (Autumn 2002): 88.

69 Kellogg, 89.

70 To recap, Orend's understanding of retribution is limited to vengeance. His analysis does not rest entirely on the contemporary criminal law paradigm of retributivism, which identifies three broad streams of retributivism: assaultive retribution, protective retribution, and victim vindication. First, assaultive retribution, called public vengeance or societal retaliation, argues that punishment is justified without any consideration of the criminal's rights or best interests; it deters private vengeance. Drawn from James Fitzjames Stephen's famous quote that "[it is] morally right to hate criminals," this stance posits that it is right for society to hurt them back because the criminals have hurt society. Second, protective retribution emphasizes keeping a moral balance in society that is shared as a benefit and burden to all members; a just society has the right to punish wrongdoers, under an analysis of benefits and burdens, restoring the balance of order in society. Third, victim vindication, called vengeance retribution (*lex talionis*— "an eye for an eye"), insists that the wrongdoer should be mastered in much the same way that they mastered the victim. For details, see Joshua Dressler, *Understanding Criminal Law* (Durham, NC: Carolina Academic Press, 2022); and Sanford H. Kadish, Stephen J. Schulhofer, and Rachel E. Barkow, *Criminal*, 9th ed. (New York: Wolters Kluwer, 2012).

71 Kadish, Schulhofer, and Steiker, 79–80.

form of punishment, of moral condemnation for offense.[72] James Fitzjames Stephen reasons that punishments give society a public means for expressing the healthy and natural sentiment of hating criminals.[73] In addition to these law thinkers, sociologist Emile Durkheim also points out that punishment's real function in retributive justice is to maintain the cohesion of society by reassurance that shared values and beliefs are still intact.[74] Hence, retribution cannot always be reduced to vengeance simply because it creates an *obligation* to punish past wrongdoings.[75] Rather, retributive justice is understood as punishment primarily because people deserve it, especially those in top-level political and military leadership who are prosecuted and tried for their grave responsibility for individual criminal activity.[76]

To be clear, the emphasis on retributive justice does not mean that just actors should not consider any form of political reconciliation or rebuilding the common good in the postwar society. Orend's rehabilitation model for state responsibility, such as reparations, matters because his model not only prevents developing a spirit of vengeance, but it also refrains from imposing any unbearable burdens in a form of collective punishment on the defeated citizens. However, although this model works well with state responsibility, it does not work for the case of individual criminal responsibility.

It is not clear how seeking political reconciliation when weighing individual criminal responsibility actually contributes to the common good. Max Pensky raises this question of *how* to examine individual criminal matters,

---

72 Kadish, Schulhofer, and Steiker, 79–80. Hart's approach to retributive justice is distinguished from a pure retributivist model, or vengeance-centered justice. For him, moral blameworthiness validates punishment, but whether we should punish depends on the likely effect on the offender or on the fabric of law/morality in general. Michael Moore has written extensively on this issue and echoes Hart's approach, which he calls a mixed retributivist model, and is distinct from a pure retributivist one. cf. H. L. A. Hart, "Prolegomenon to the Principles of Punishment," *Punishment and Responsibility* 1, no. 8 (1982): 8–12, 22.

73 Joel Samaha, *Criminal Law* (Belmont, CA: Wadsworth, 2011), 23.

74 Mary Stohr and Anthony Walsh, *Corrections: The Essentials* (London: Sage Publications, 2012), 7–8.

75 George Fletcher notes, "retributivism is not to be identified with vengeance or revenge, any more than love is to be identified with lust." George Fletcher, *Rethinking Criminal Law* (Oxford: Oxford University Press, 2000), 417.

76 For example, three major thinkers define retribution in different ways. Kant regards it as a principle of equality (e.g., eye for an eye). Moore understands it as a moral culpability sufficient for punishment. Hart has a more concrete understanding of retribution. He has three retributive criteria, saying that a person can only be punished if the person (i) has voluntarily done something wrong, (ii) punishment is equivalent to harm of offense, and (iii) punishment is justified as morally good in itself. They all believe that society has a duty to punish.

especially with regard to an amnesty aimed at "big fish" (his term, referring to those leaders in high-level prosecutions). His concern is that several *jpb* thinkers who are particularly influenced by the idea of transitional justice "began to see reconciliation as an overall social and political goal in which amnesties might not be just tolerable but in many cases even desirable."[77] Drawn from May's *jpb* concept of *meionexia*, which means asking less than one's due, these thinkers seek a way of "offering to waive prosecution to specific persons in return for omissions or predetermined acts on their part."[78] Pensky's criticism is about the heavy reliance on utilitarian justice when highlighting the role of political reconciliation. Further, he argues that it is often hard to calculate and determine the cases of desirable amnesty "where they generate more favorable outcomes than their measurable costs" for the sake of common good in the complex *jpb* context.[79]

In addition to this inquiry on *how*, Pensky poses another question: political reconciliation for *whom*? He answers the inquiry himself by illustrating that political reconciliation in relation to individual criminal responsibility matters not for the good of citizens in the postwar society; it rather hurts the society, as it weakens its justice system and causes postwar conflicts. He believes that political reconciliation—especially in a form of amnesty waiving individual criminal responsibility—"facially deprive[s] victims or their survivors their rights to legal remedy, effectively reinjuring them by making their legitimate legal complaint null and void."[80] Hence, these amnesty programs may have the indirect and unintended effect of undermining—or even failing—rule of law institutions by publicly staging the elasticity of rule of law institutions for the sake of political expediency, but not, or less, with legality.[81]

---

77 Max Pensky, *"Jus Post Bellum and Amnesties,"* in *Jus Post Bellum*, ed. Larry May (Cambridge: Cambridge University Press, 2016), 16. As discussed in chapter four, major transitional justice advocates, such as Philpott, understand political reconciliation as a primary objective of just punishment. And, to repeat yet again, I found difficulty in directly applying this approach to the *jpb* discourse mainly because the transitional justice approach is more suitable for treating past wrongdoings in a larger context of transitional justice, not in the postwar context. Pensky also shares this viewpoint. For details, see Pensky, 21–23.

78 Pensky, 5.

79 Pensky, 5.

80 Pensky, 21–22.

81 Pensky, 22. Pensky explains, "Both individualized amnesties and larger and more complex amnesty programs can presumably have the indirect effect of weakening rule of law institutions by publicly staging the plasticity of rule of law institutions for the sake of political expediency."

Finally, the political reconciliation argument for individual criminal responsibility speaks to a utilitarian justice but not to my common-good-seeking justice. My approach aims to contemplate natural law's implications for the promotion of the common good in the postwar society through a theory of punishment. Various explanations are given for what right anybody has to punish somebody for crime. Among the explanations frequently given are public safety and retribution, as well as deterrence, yet deterrence is not a natural law justification.[82] The deterrence argument, in which just actors punish criminals harshly as an example so other people will not commit crimes, is a *rigid* utilitarian argument that claims a better long-term result.[83] I argue that this deterrence argument is not a natural law justification for punishment because it does not speak to the question of whether a prospective war criminal deserves it but rather just focuses on how other people react to it. On the other hand, justifications for punishment that are founded in public safety and retribution are natural law justifications. Part of natural law is that the government must be responsible for the safety of its citizens, especially the safety of the innocent, the vulnerable, and the weak. In order to secure that common good, the government has a duty to punish those who are convicted of a crime in a given situation. The natural law argument for punishing them exists precisely because of the duty that the government has in justice to protect the safety of citizens.[84] Likewise, the debt of punishment for a criminal comes as retribution, namely, that this is in fact what is due.[85]

The Protection of Fair Trials for All: The Victorious and Defeated Sides

I have discussed why just actors must not prioritize political reconciliation over individual criminality responsibility. Then how can international tribunals contribute to rebuilding the common good? Mark Freeman and

---

82 Sandie Taylor, *Crime and Criminality: A Multidisciplinary Approach* (New York: Routledge, 2015), chap. 16.

83 One may argue that natural law uses deterrence as one goal of just punishment. However, even from that viewpoint, deterrence should not be a formative or primary goal of natural law justification. For further discussion, see James Fieser, *Capital Punishment: From Moral Issues that Divide Us*, September 1, 2017, accessed October 15, 2020, http://www.utm.edu/staff/jfieser/class/160/7-cap-pun.htm.

84 For a similar argument, see E. Christian Brugger, *Capital Punishment and Roman Catholic Moral Tradition* (South Bend, IN: University of Notre Dame Press, 2014).

85 Jeffrie Murphy, "Legal Moralism and Retribution Revisited," *Criminal Law and Philosophy* 1, no. 1 (2007): 11.

Drazan Djukuc suggest *ad hoc* approaches. While "big fish" or grave past wrongdoers must be treated the same as other serious criminals, each case must be individually examined in order to prevent more victims in the cases where the prospective defendants have been inappropriately accused either for legal or political reasons. Freeman and Djukuc do not champion Kellogg's assertion on the requirement for tribunals because the form of conducting a fair trial should not be prescribed, as the need for fair criminal justice in individual matters often exceeds the capabilities of the institutions charged with providing it.[86] As a result, Freeman and Djukuc conclude that there are too many unknowns regarding the content of *jpb* to make any concrete proposals for international criminal law beyond *ad hoc* approaches to fair criminal justice.

However, a court's decision shaped by these *ad hoc* approaches may not always result in justice. My argument is that *ad hoc* approaches ought to first conduct a careful and thorough investigation. Thus, these approaches must dismiss any option for political reconciliation which acts solely on behalf of the interests of the perpetrators who were directly involved in serious war crimes. This option should not be considered, especially if the court finds clear and sufficient evidence to bring them to justice. Admittedly, an option for political reconciliation should also be considered as a substantial and extensive alternative if it prevents punishing the victims of atrocities or innocent and vulnerable citizens in the defeated state. At the same time, in accordance with *jpb* principles, *ad hoc* approaches must deal with the criminal responsibility of individuals by targeting and prosecuting all parties who were involved in war crimes, including victors that were also responsible for war crimes. Therefore, I argue that just actors must ensure prevention of victors' justice in order to rebuild the common good in a comprehensive manner.

The foundational *jpb* thinkers—Aristotle, Aquinas, Walzer, and Orend—noted that court decisions often have concluded in accordance with victors' justice. As discussed in chapter one, the views of the four foundational thinkers were limited in that there were no detailed comments about the war crimes of victorious states. To fill this void, the remainder of the chapter will examine three practical matters surrounding "victors' justice."

---

86 They argue "there are no universal answers" and that each court should be allowed "to choose its own path." Mark Freeman and Drazan Djukuc, "*Jus Post Bellum* and Transitional Justice," in *Jus Post Bellum: Towards a Law of Transition from Conflict to Peace*, ed. Carsten Stahn and Jann Kleffner (The Hague: T.M.C. Asser Press, 2008), 215–18.

The first practical matter to consider is that international criminal trials do not premise their decisions on fair criteria to bring justice to leaders of defeated states. In particular, when these trials deal with top military and political leaders for their violations of *jus ad bellum*, the legal and political resources are often weighted in favor of the international community, which tactically cloaks a victor's justice.[87] In the twentieth century, there were four national leaders who stood before an international tribunal as war criminals. They were former Prime Minister of Japan, Hideki Tojo; former Rwandan Prime Minister, Jean Kambanda; former President of Yugoslavia, Slobodan Milosevic; and former Iraqi President, Saddam Hussein. Hussein's trial was the most controversial of these tribunals for both its process and the execution of the death penalty. Noah Feldman posed this question in his *New York Times* post of 2007: "That the Iraqi dictator deserved to be punished was never in question. But from what source did the tribunal, which was established under US occupation and then affirmed by the sovereign Iraqi government, derive the right to do so?"[88] A fair trial was not carried out for the accused Hussein, as it was held behind closed doors by Iraqi judges trained by the United States. Moreover, the hasty execution of Hussein eliminated the opportunity to reveal the truth about the controversial Kurdish genocide as well as what relationship existed between the US Reagan Administration and the Iraqi Hussein regime during the Iran-Iraq War in the 1980s. Hence, it would have been better if Hussein had been tried fairly for his crimes against humanity at a recognized court such as the ICC.

As pointed out by Feldman, the court must be able to explain the legal basis for giving the death sentence in order to satisfy the rule of law and avoid the criticism of being a case of victor's justice. However, the Iraqi judges did seek the legal basis for Hussein's case in international law. Instead of applying the general murder charge, they applied "crimes against humanity" as stated in the international law.[89] The Rome Statute of the ICC stipulates that crimes against humanity should receive severe punishment. Hussein's trial followed the example of the Nuremberg Trials. The problem here is whether the Iraqi Special Tribunal formed to try Hussein had the same legitimate authority as the Nuremberg Military Tribunal. Nazi Germany had provoked war and

87 James Meernik, "Victor's Justice or the Law?" *The Journal of Conflict Resolution* 47, no. 2 (April 2003): 140–62.

88 Noah Feldman, "Not the Case," *New York Times Magazine*, January 2, 2007, http://www.nytimes.com/2007/01/02/magazine/07wwln_lede.html.

89 Feldman.

committed flagrant war crimes including the massacre of Jews and the abuse of prisoners of war. There was hardly anyone willing to object to prosecuting the war leaders of Germany as war criminals and executing them. However, the war in Iraq, caused by the US invasion in 2003, was different from WWII. The dominant perception of the international community was that the Iraq War was far from just because the United States used the logic of preventive war as a cover for invasion.[90] Therefore, the Iraqi Special Tribunal formed by the United States, the victor, had difficulty in establishing its legitimate authority before the international community.

Secondly, when superpowers are the aggressor nations, or when superpowers commit *jus ad bellum* war crimes even if they were the invaded nations in the first place, the people of the superpowers involved in the violations of *jus in bello* are rarely punished. For example, the United States has remained an exception in war crimes trials. In light of the principles of *jus in bello*, both the Allied Powers and the Axis Powers during WWII committed war crimes. The German Air Force randomly bombed London, and the Japanese Army indiscriminately raided cities in China. The UK-US Alliance was no different.[91] The bombing of Dresden, Germany, by the US fighter-bombers in February 1945, carried out even when Germany was most likely to lose the war, was criticized as a war crime committed by the Allied Forces.[92] At that time, 130,000 citizens were sacrificed. However, there was no punishment for those responsible for this raid. Critics accused the United States of committing a war crime because the Dresden raids were indiscriminate, had no strategic significance in the war, and were nothing more than an air raid of psychological terror aimed at spreading the atmosphere of defeat to German society. All nations used unjust air-raid

---

90 For further discussion, see John Hammond, "The Bush Doctrine, Preventive War, and International Law," *The Philosophical Forum* 36, no. 1 (2005).

91 Of course, each case is not exactly identical. One may want to distinguish aerial bombardment practiced by both sides from how US and UK troops treated the civilians of occupied countries. Meanwhile, a good source on Japanese war crimes is the US National Archives at http://www.archives.gov/iwg/japanese-war-crimes. For the sake of focus on victor's justice, this subsection does not distinguish between war crimes and crimes against humanity in legal practice that requires further case studies. For example, US soldiers and marines took no prisoners in the Pacific Theatre. See: Niall Ferguson, "Prisoner Taking and Prisoner Killing in the Age of Total War," in *The Barbarization of Warfare*, ed. George Kassimeris (New York: New York University, 2006), 126–58.

92 Walzer emphasizes that attention should be paid to minimizing the casualty of unarmed civilians. The act of causing civilian casualties by ignoring this on purpose is nothing other than war crime.

terror tactics, but the side that was punished for them was the leaders of Germany and Japan, not the leaders of the Allied Command. Further, many civilians were victimized by the US military airstrikes in the two recent wars (the Afghanistan and Iraq Wars) that the United States has waged in the twenty-first century in apparent violation of the 1949 Geneva Convention defining war crimes.[93]

Finally, international law scholars consider that the legitimacy and the legality of war are two separate matters. When war has been declared, it is only proper to try the people who have committed war crimes even if they are members of a nation that maintains the legitimacy of war. Article 51 of the Charter of the United Nations stipulates that the UNSC is the principal agent for making an objective judgment as to which country has violated international law and illegally waged war. However, this function of the UNSC is hindered when there is a conflict of interest in making that judgement, such as when a permanent member of the UNSC with veto rights or an ally nation to a member of the UNSC is directly involved in the war. If the permanent member vetoes a declaration, the UNSC ceases to function effectively in the dispute. This is not to say that there are no international organizations that will objectively determine which country has violated the rules of just war or which country is responsible for waging a war. As discussed earlier, the ICJ and the ICC have, at least in theory, the right to fairly screen war crimes that threaten human security. However, given the international order dominated by power politics, it is difficult to have sanctions if the superpowers or their allies wage war. In reality, there are no principal bodies that can put the leaders of these nations in the stand before the ICC for war crimes. That being the case, war crimes trials should not be a procedure in accordance with victors' justice. War crimes must be subject to legal proceedings through fair and proper investigation procedures. This is the true way of following *jpb* principles.

The most reasonable way of realizing the course of justice is to punish the war crimes committed by the victorious states in international war crimes tribunals. Currently, the ICC is the only court that deals with war crimes at all times. Revitalizing the ICC is a crucial task given to most *jpb*

---

93 In the First Protocol Additional to the Geneva Conventions of 1949 amended in 1977, Article 52 stipulates that "attacks shall be limited strictly to military objectives" and that attacking areas where civilian populations reside, and thus causing the death or injury of civilians is defined as a war crime. However, it is a problem that there is scarcely a case where the acts of killing and injuring civilians by air raids committed by the victor are properly punished.

law scholars, and the cooperation of the superpowers is indispensable. However, it has been staunchly opposed that the United States participate in the ICC. In June 2002, right before the official inauguration of the ICC, the US Senate passed the American Service Members Protection Act, protecting US forces from being prosecuted by the ICC with an overwhelming majority of seventy-one to twenty-two.[94] The law even permits the use of US forces in order to free US military personnel and US government officers detained in a court of a third-party nation. This theoretically means that if foreign states seize US soldiers as war criminals in their own country, these states can be attacked by the United States. Strengthening the legal system and the institutions that hold substantial authority to punish war crimes by the superpowers remains a challenge in the study of international criminal responsibility in light of *jpb*.

CONCLUSION

This chapter discussed two *jpb* issues in international law. First was how just actors ought to carry out their peacekeeping operations legally, specifically occupation law. Second was how tribunals should contribute to rebuilding the common good in the *jpb* context of international criminal law. Considering these two issues together, just punishment must be understood within the larger context of just policing. Securing the public's safety in the present day must be achieved prior to amending the past wrongdoings. If the legal authority to judge the past wrongdoing is threatened by the defeated warring parties, or if the court decision is influenced by the victor's justice, the justice of punishment may not be impartial, which can be a source of future conflict.

There is a substantial disconnect between what is codified in the system of international humanitarian law (e.g., treaty law) and what has actually been approved by the UNSC in the post-Cold War world of occupation law. In contrast with the 4th Geneva Convention and the Hague Convention of 1907, which affirmed and codified a principle of conservation in the law of occupation, the UNSC endorsed UNSCRs 1244, 1272, and 1483 in order to create postwar administrations in Kosovo, East Timor, and Iraq, all of which, at least principally, intended to obligate the occupiers to a series of transformational actions on behalf of the citizens. The promotion of this

---

94 American Service Members' Protection Act of 2002, 22 U.S.C. §7421.

UNSC-led practice, known as humanitarian occupation law, is central to a comprehensive human security scheme and, in particular, aligns with Ben-venisti's human occupation law agenda requiring human sovereignty, transformative schemes, and maximalist obligation for human security, all of which contribute to rebuilding the common good.

Moreover, humanitarian occupation law proposals must be developed in the future for practical reasons, focused on the *ad hoc* approach affected by Chapter VII UNSCRs rather than a new treaty development approach. One reason for this is that during the post-Cold War occupation, the UNSC, which de facto exists outside of the normal scope of international law, holds the unique position of having been able to create obligatory—substantially binding and effective—*jpb* law on a case-by-case basis. Although *ad hoc* approaches are not perfectly satisfactory in treating what have become recurring issues in the postwar society, such as human rights violations, they have the legal and political capabilities of being tailored to each specific case.

International criminal law addresses violations of law during the war and *post bellum*. From the Nuremberg and Tokyo multinational military tribunals after WWII, through the more recent *ad hoc* international or internationalized tribunals, to the establishment of the ICC, international criminal law has evolved into a complex and sophisticated system of norms, institutions, and ideas. However, there is a recurring controversy over when circumstances make tribunals appropriate in light of the need for political reconciliation: whether it is allowed for state responsibility and/or individual criminal responsibility and how it ought to work and for whom. Addressing these questions requires investigating the details of how international tribunals ought to be managed rather than simply determining whether they belong among the criteria for *jpb*. Until these root questions are resolved, it seems that *ad hoc* approaches to *jpb* will continue to be the only ones available. Nevertheless, a policy that just actors should prevent victors' justice is essential. Among military and political leaders who have influenced the conduct of war, those involved in war crimes should rightly be punished as war criminals. The emphasis is that such punishment must be treated fairly for both the victorious and defeated sides for the sake of the common good.

Finally, although I have not discussed specific criteria of court decisions for just punishment in this chapter, just actors must develop norms for how far punishment should go in terms of length and severity. One thing I note is that a natural law approach rules out certain types of punishment as unreasonable and arbitrary. This is the reason why the Catholic JWT argues that just actors must not torture prisoners or employ capital punishment. That kind of punishment is an offense against the prisoners' human dignity even though they have gravely offended the human community. Just actors must ask the question of whether or not a punishment is fair as they pursue the common good.

Chapter 7

Reconstruction of
Just Political Participation

INTRODUCTION
Just Political Participation:
Refreshing the Theoretical Ground for Practice

The previous chapter suggested that while just punishment must serve human security, it must also incorporate a moral and legal vision of political reconciliation in which the intention is to restore human flourishing and a just political order. One of my three tenets for defending this stance argues that just punishment can be understood in a larger context of just political participation. This is especially so when addressing state responsibility for *jpb* issues, such as peacebuilding and reconciliation efforts achieved through local consensus and political equilibrium in the time of transition. Just political participation aims to prevent future violence in the immediate aftermath of war while working toward rebuilding the common good through such peacebuilding practices.

However, I distinguished just political participation from the other two *jpb* elements—just policing and just punishment—in that it attends to peacebuilding practices endorsed by both classical and nonclassical just actors. This leads to a question: how should these actors work together while participating in the decision-making process of postwar interim government? I emphasized that the ultimate concern of just political participation has broader implications for public administration, which require knowledge of how both classical and nonclassical just actors collaborate with each other in order to employ their peacebuilding assets in a comprehensive manner. In chapter two, I found that many *jpb* thinkers do not pay the same attention to nonclassical actors that they do to classical actors. I introduced classical actor approaches of just political participation, whether they are victors (e.g., Evans, Walzer, and Elshtain) or international community based (e.g., Orend). However, as also emphasized, these approaches overlook the question of the peacebuilding roles of local actors, largely composed of both secular NGOs and churches/faith-based organizations (FBOs). This finding led to a conclusion, which I developed into the norm of a comprehensive human security scheme, especially with the need for broad social "buy-in" in order to get "elite" peace agreements observed in practice. In other words, there needs to be both top-down and bottom-up (and midlevel-out) action in order to fully achieve human security and rebuild the common good.

Just Political Participation: Refining the Theoretical Ground for Practice

With respect to the ethic of just political participation, this chapter will pay particular attention to the peacebuilding roles of local actors. This form of just political participation is not an entirely new or separate area of *jpb* practice, but it supports peacebuilding in the postwar society, which must create an enabling environment and improve interactions with classical just actors (as a reminder, see figure one and chapter four). In particular, local actors must not merely assist but also proactively mediate the classical (top-down) actors in undertaking their policing and punishment practices to engage in reconstruction and achieve comprehensive human security through both peacekeeping and nation building. In other words, ensuring just political participation as part of *jpb* will illustrate my argument that *jpb* and peacebuilding are two distinct, but related, topics that compose just war reflection. This chapter suggests that *jpb* with locally based peacebuilding must be understood as an integrated approach for just political participation.

My suggestion has two parts. First, defining just political participation as locally based peacebuilding will produce clear and realistic postwar goals and forestall postwar problems, advocating for a local consensus rather than imposing democracy and liberal values. Peacebuilding as a central mission of just political participation contributes to the entire *jpb* scheme while serving to protect and rebuild the common good and subsidiarity. This locally led peacebuilding agenda will call actors to think creatively about how they affect change rather than rely on plots that subvert local policies through "elite" military and governmental impositions. Utilizing the World Bank's report proposing the seven functions of local actors in peacebuilding, I will attend to civil society organizations (CSOs)—including FBOs—and the major role they play in promoting attitudinal change for a culture of peace and reconciliation.

In the second part of my suggestion, I will revisit the Niebuhrian approach to *jpb* for civil society peacebuilding. As I begin the second section, I will ensure that Himes's Thomistic approach to *jpb*, along with the principle of establishing civil society, aligns with civil society peacebuilding for just political participation. Although Himes warns that just actors must recognize the limits of *jpb* practices, he does not develop this concern in depth, but as discussed in chapter three, Allman and Winright revisit this issue in their Niebuhrian approach to *jpb* (i.e., *jpb* understood within the frame of Niebuhr's notion of imperfect justice). Accordingly, I will discuss Niebuhr's views on the differences between individual and group morality and how they apply to the relation of love to justice. Through the lens of these two elements of his theology, I will examine the work of CSOs and propose that in the international aspects of *jpb* involving issues of peace and justice, CSOs, especially faith-based ones, have the potential to perform a unifying role by representing the love that is a necessary element to justice.

JUST POLITICAL PARTICIPATION FOR PEACEBUILDING AND RECONCILING FUTURE HOSTILITY

Civil Society Peacebuilding

Defining Local Peacebuilding Actors in Postwar Societies

As Himes emphasized, *jpb* aims to protect the common good, which is only possible through common effort and belongs to no one exclusively, but in which each must participate to rebuild a civil society *post bellum*. This civil society is a political space where governance and development (including peacebuilding) goals are contested. Local peacebuilding actors, as major members of civil society, cannot be analyzed in isolation from classical just actors; they are interdependent. Although local actors' independence from both the state and the international community are a defining feature, they interact closely with the state and/or the international community. Further, they are shaped by the enabling environment *post bellum* largely defined by such classical actors. As previously discussed, classical actors set the legal and regulatory framework for *jpb* and in some cases support civil society activities. In turn, local actors in the postwar society act as a link between the classical actors and citizens by promoting values, accountability, and voice and by channeling information. In particular, while their initiatives and organizations often emerge when states and markets fail, as in the case of a postwar context, they cannot fully replace state functions and formal political processes.[1]

Given the diversity of civil society *post bellum*, it is difficult to categorize local peacebuilding actors in a meaningful or comprehensive way. Despite this limitation, a wide range of these local actor typologies have been developed based on certain characteristics, such as organizational form, purpose, scale, scope, and activities. Therefore, this chapter employs the definition of local peacebuilding actors endorsed by the World Bank report of 2007, titled *Civil Society and Peacebuilding: Potential, Limitations and Critical Factors*. The report defines these actors as civil society organizations, which play roles in public service delivery, improving governance and promoting participatory decision making, influencing policy formulation, peacebuilding, and conflict management. On the one hand, these roles are not limited to ones filled by community-based organizations (CBOs), which are traditionally local actors at the grassroots level. On the other hand, CSOs are also not identical with larger national and international NGOs, which act as donors using local grassroots partners. By definition, CSOs go beyond "the narrower (and to many donors, more familiar) category of development-oriented NGOs, and depict a broad range of organizations" that have a presence in civic life in the local community *post bellum*, "expressing . . . the values of their members or others, based on ethical, cultural, political, scientific, religious or philanthropic considerations."[2]

In particular, employing peace scholar John Paul Lederach's comprehensive transformation-oriented approach, the report argues that strengthening CSOs does not automatically contribute to peacebuilding.[3] In other words, despite the importance of CSOs, their mere existence in a postwar society cannot simply be equated with the existence of peacebuilding actors. Even though they are frequently actors for peace, they can also be actors for violence

---

1 For details, see Thomas Carothers and Saskia Brechenmacher, "Accountability, Transparency, Participation, and Inclusion: A New Development Consensus?," Carnegie Endowment for International Peace, October 20, 2014.

2 Reiner Forster and Mark Mattner, *Civil Society and Peacebuilding: Potential, Limitations and Critical Factors* (Washington, DC: World Bank, 2007), 3–6.

3 Forster and Mattner, 3–10. For John Paul Lederach's comprehensive transformation-oriented approach, see John Paul Lederach, *The Little Book of Conflict Transformation* (Intercourse, PA: Good Books, 2003), 33. Lederach distinguishes his transformation-oriented approach from other conflict resolution approaches. See for comparison: Gary Furlong, *The Conflict Resolution Toolbox* (Mississauga: John Wiley & Sons Canada, 2005).

in the name of justice or peace. Therefore, the report highlights CSO actors' five major tasks in peacebuilding strategies: (i) promoting reconciliation; (ii) engaging in nonviolent forms of conflict management and transformation; (iii) directly preventing violence; (iv) building bridges, trust, and interdependence between groups; and (v) monitoring and advocating in favor of peace and against human rights violations and social injustices.[4]

Further, the report emphasizes that Lederach's approach shifted the focus from top-down actors to the role of local actors within the post-conflict state, which led to a paradigm shift in the field of conflict studies and practices. Until the mid-1990s, top-down actors were mainly asked to support other kinds of top-down actors (i.e., other nation-state and international community actors) in the post-conflict state in order to enhance their peacebuilding capacities. However, since then, an array of local CSO actors, such as NGOs, associations, religious institutions, business and grassroots organizations, and other middle-out/bottom-up local communities or individuals (see the next paragraph for details), are increasingly involved in different peacebuilding activities.[5] These local actor-oriented approaches have been implemented in practice, as their initiatives include peace funds, dialogue projects, peacebuilding training, and capacity building programs for local actors.

Drawn from Lederach's work *Building Peace: Sustainable Reconciliation in Divided Societies*, the World Bank report examines conflict-affected societies, dividing them into three levels requiring different peacebuilding approaches.[6] Top leadership can be accessed by mediation at the level of top-down actors; these actors "can be engaged by Track 1 intervention and outcome-oriented approaches." Mid-level leadership can be reached through more resolution-oriented Track 2 approaches, "such as problem-solving workshops or peace-commissions" with the help of partial insiders, or "prominent individuals in society," such as "leaders respected in sectors, ethnic/religious leaders, academics/intellectuals, humanitarian leaders

---

4 Forster and Mattner, *Civil Society and Peacebuilding*, 9.

5 Forster and Mattner, *Civil Society and Peacebuilding*, 9–10. According to Lederach, peace must be not only a top-down and bottom-up process, but also a middle-out process. Top-down (Track 1) connects capacities that can be mobilized by national elites; bottom-up (Track 3) connects the grass roots to the political projects of elites; and middle-out (Track 2) complements these vertical capacities with horizontal capacities to move back and forth across social divides. For details, John Paul Lederach, *Building Peace: Sustainable Reconciliation in Divided Societies* (Washington, DC: United States Institute of Peace, 1997), 45–46.

6 Cf. Lederach, *Building Peace*, 39.

(NGOs)." The grassroots level represents the majority of the population, as it can be reached through a wide range of peacebuilding approaches. They are engaged through Track 3 approaches, which include community dialogue projects, local peace commissions, or trauma healing. A central wedge of Lederach's three levels for approaching peacebuilding focuses on peacebuilding constituencies, identifying mid-level leadership and empowering the leadership group to build peace and support reconciliation. Empowering the middle level leadership is assumed to influence peacebuilding at both the macro and grassroots levels: "The key role of [the Track 2] intervention is to support local actors and coordinate external peace efforts, requiring an in-depth understanding of local socio-cultural dynamics."[7] In other words, with this empowerment in place, local actors' peacebuilding practice for *jpb* requires both top-down and bottom-up (and middle-out) action in order to conduct a comprehensive human security scheme, or at least to get the classical actors' peace agreements observed in *jpb* practice.

Most importantly, the element of Lederach's peacebuilding approach that focuses on the empowerment of the mid-level leadership actors, as well as their cooperation with the other two leadership groups, signifies that civil society and other nongovernmental peacebuilding initiatives must work together in order to bring comprehensive peacebuilding to the postwar society. This also means that the term "locally based peacebuilding" is too narrow to contain the ultimate meaning of this form of comprehensive and complex peacebuilding work. Therefore, in the interest of precision, the term should be replaced by "civil society peacebuilding." This is also because CSO is a more inclusive term than local peacebuilding actors, since the former not only attends to bottom-up but also to top-down and middle-out actors.[8] In fact, CSO more closely represents Himes's Thomistic approach to *jpb*, which emphasizes "the principle of establishing civil society." As discussed in chapter three, this principle complements the principle of restoration, leading the war-torn society to enjoy and participate in peaceful communal life. In other words, without this principle of rebuilding a civil society, *jpb* would not only fail to repair the destruction of wars but would also unsuccessfully restore the structural components whose absence created the initial need for hostilities.

---

7 Forster and Mattner, *Civil Society and Peacebuilding*, 7.

8 For the sake of clarity, however, I use the terms "locally based peacebuilding" and "civil society peacebuilding" throughout the book, depending on the context of purposes and audiences.

The Peacebuilding of *Jus Post Bellum*:
Distinctions from Just Peacemaking Approach

For the sake of clarity, I must note that this chapter is not about introducing just peacemaking theories. Instead, this chapter is about the peacebuilding of *jpb*, namely, just political participation as civil society peacebuilding. This chapter leans in the direction of a peacebuilding agenda that has been partially shared by just peacemaking approaches: building schools and hospitals and working hard on peacebuilding and reconciliation, as just peace thinkers such as Glen Stassen emphasize. For example, Stassen argues that just peacemaking approaches go beyond the question of whether war is justified or not. Instead, he offers the means of preventing war and creating peace based on conflict resolution, diplomacy, rebuilding, repentance, and other forms of nonviolent action.[9] Lisa Sowle Cahill sees Stassen's work "as a new paradigm that cuts between traditional just war theory and pacifism, combines a biblical faith commitment with political engagement, and aims to unite persons of many faiths and cultures in actually diminishing war and other types of politically motivated violence."[10] In her view, this paradigm is distinguished from pacifism since it does not exclude the entire armed intervention option, nor can it be the same as just war theory since its overriding agenda is nonviolent negotiation and political reconciliation.

However, as emphasized throughout this book, many *jpb* thinkers, such as Himes, are also aware of the importance of (re)building a just political order that promotes the common good. Unlike just peacemaking theorists, who distinguish peacebuilding from JWT, just war thinkers—especially those *jpb* proponents—see the building of the common good through peacebuilding as often associated with *jpb*. Overall, without neglecting the immediate problem of humanitarian crisis and how just actors react to the evil in the world with moral urgency, most *jpb* thinkers, whether they are minimalists or maximalists, argue for peacebuilding practices and strategies for peaceful conflict prevention and resolution.

Despite the shared characteristics between *jpb* and just peacemaking approaches, the phase of just political participation belongs to the JWT. Recall from chapter three that a major distinction is that *jpb* pursues

---

9 For details, see Glen Stassen, ed., *Just Peacemaking: Ten Practices for Abolishing War* (Cleveland: Pilgrim Press, 1998).

10 Lisa Sowle Cahill, "Just Peacemaking: Theory, Practice, and Prospects," *Journal of the Society of Christian Ethics* 23, no. 1 (2003): 195.

postwar justice whereas peacemaking pursues transitional justice. The peacebuilding of *jpb* (i.e., just political participation as civil society peacebuilding) must be distinguished from the just peacemaking practices of transitional justice as the peacebuilding of *jpb* has a limited scope. That is, it has an intervention period of only five to seven years.[11] This is clearly distinct from the long-term peacebuilding agenda of just peacemaking approaches.[12] Most distinctively, regime change is not the main purpose, so making the society democratic, which requires an outsized time commitment and cost, is not necessary.[13] This also means that just actors may consider a democracy as a practical option if (i) it helps the society rebuild the common good, (ii) the local community of the defeated society also agrees, and (iii) these just actors are capable of continuously implementing democracy after the *jpb* period (five to seven years) so they can make a successful move from postwar justice to transitional justice. Distinguishing these three tenets is necessary for developing the idea of just political participation, especially with regard to judging whether and how to spread democracy for civil society peacebuilding.

The Peacebuilding of *Jus Post Bellum*: Just Political Participation in Catholic Social Teaching

With these distinctions in mind, rather than simply laying out what the practice of just political participation would entail, what follows in this chapter is to refine substantive and strategic principles that could be applied to its practice. The first task proposed is to define and characterize just political participation as civil society peacebuilding in light of CST. While we are beginning to look into the CST and how it has influenced the Christian community in the practice of *jpb*, it should not be overlooked that although the papal documents articulate the vision of the Church, the subjects of political participation are the people who are first influenced by their faith commitment working toward the common good and in turn have influenced the CST and its reflection on the practice *post bellum*.

---

11 This distinction was made in nation building scholars' work in chapter four.

12 An exemplary work of transitional justice with emphasis on long-term peacebuilding agenda is Fernado Enns and Annette Mosher's ecumenical project. Fernando Enns and Annette Mosher. *Just Peace: Ecumenical, Intercultural, and Interdisciplinary Perspectives* (Eugene, OR: Pickwick Publications, 2013).

13 This stance was comprehensively articulated in chapter five when addressing nation building for just policing.

First, the word "political," or "politics," within the context of *jpb*, denotes the civil life of the postwar society (*post bellum polis*) and the responsibilities of the local citizen (*polites*) and government (*politeia*). Therefore, politics is concerned with the whole of human life in the postwar society. In other words, postwar politics, or the art of living together in the postwar society, is concerned with the development and adoption of specific postwar policies (just policing), aiming to enshrine them in legislation (just punishment). Furthermore, postwar politics is about the local citizens (re)gaining the right and power for social transformation, working toward rebuilding the common good for their families, jobs, environment, and peace. In CST, politics is not a necessary evil; instead, it has a positive role in society—and here I would advocate for postwar politics to have its proper place in protecting and promoting human flourishing and the common good in postwar political communities. Although there are no CST documents specifically referring to the role of politics in the postwar society or *jpb*, CST emphasizes the vital role of politics as tantamount to protecting the common good.[14]

Second, the pursuit of rebuilding the common good is a demanding process, which includes "participation." In CST, Pope Paul VI reminds us that the theme of participation explains that every member of a society has a right and responsibility to participate in all facets of human society, including culture, education, religion, and political activities, so as to ensure human dignity and equality are fulfilled in the social body.[15] More concretely, I draw attention to Himes's communitarian approach to the common good, which presupposes participation, requires justice, and leads people to social change.[16] I highlight the three qualities (participation, justice, and social change), all of which ought to be pursued in order to rebuild the common good in the context of *jpb*. In other words, all the local citizens, regardless of their values and beliefs, need to respect and accept each other as members of the postwar community, without leaving anyone out.

---

14 See John XXIII, Encyclical Letter *Pacem in Terris* (1963), 63.

15 Paul VI, Encyclical Letter *Octogesima Adveniens* (1971), 24–25.

16 Kenneth Himes, "Catholic Social Teaching on Building a Just Society: The Need for a Ceiling and a Floor," *Religions* 8, no. 4 (2017). Although Himes originally employs these three values when discussing economic justice, I see no reason why I cannot apply them to the context of postwar ethics. Drawn from *Gaudium et Spes*, his communitarian approach attends to the role of participation and its close tie to politics: "Politics can be understood as the art of enabling wider and wiser participation in community . . . to promote and protect the common good."

Further, people in the local community must participate in the postwar politics, while their strategies for action must aim to promote justice and fulfill just requirements and practices. Hence, they can contribute to rebuilding the common good, which is the social condition that gives everyone in the postwar community the ability to pursue their full human potential and fulfill their human dignity. This means that when people in the community are contributing to the common good, they are fully aware of who desperately needs to be included in the postwar society. Finally, social change or transformation presupposes an assessment that both participation and the promotion of justice are not yet fully realized and implemented. This quality of recognizing the limit of transformation is important.[17] As emphasized throughout the book, postwar justice is different from transitional justice or long-term peacebuilding efforts in that postwar justice is conditioned by its narrower scope and objective. Postwar communities in the context of *jpb*, therefore, are not yet fully sharing their human, intellectual, religious, and social capabilities, or fulfilling their obligations to future generations.

Third, one final *jpb* concept must be included for defining just political participation as civil society peacebuilding: subsidiarity. Subsidiarity is a principle of natural law analysis in social ethics, according to which the power to make decisions is given to the lowest level of authority capable of rendering a prudent decision for the common good.[18] Hence, the fundamental aim of subsidiarity is the common good.[19] However, people or certain organizations are not always fully able to contribute to the common good that calls upon subsidiarity. Karen Shields Wright says that in CST subsidiarity aims at promoting the common good in two ways. In the first sense, as Pope Pius XI affirmed in his 1931 encyclical letter *Quadragesimo Anno,* local participation is essential to the principle of subsidiarity as it places responsibility upon individuals and local communities to work toward the common good. Therefore, both individuals and groups at the local level have the right to determine, manage, and fulfill individual and

---

17 Himes. For the sake of clarity, recognizing this limit does not mean that Himes shows a pessimistic or realistic view. Rather, he emphasizes, first, a careful examination and deliberation, and second and more importantly, a Christian community-based vision that brings a deeper understanding of society.

18 Philip Keane, *Catholicism and Health-Care Justice: Problems, Potential, and Solutions* (New York: Paulist Press, 2002), 23.

19 In particular, subsidiarity aims to respect human dignity. Pope Benedict XVI related subsidiarity with human dignity, in order to defend the common good. For details, see Benedict XVI, Encyclical Letter *Caritas in Veritate* (2009), 57.

local needs.[20] In other words, subsidiarity promotes reciprocity between smaller and larger social collectives and sources of civil authorities.[21] Pope Pius XI sought to defend the richness and diversity of human society.[22] Subsidiarity will help guide higher levels of postwar societies to allocate basic resources (land, labor, and capital) in a way that supports engagement and decision-making by the lower level. Moreover, at its best, this principle will enable members of postwar local communities to cultivate the general practice of moral discernment and individual moral agents to make better use of the resources at their disposal.

In the second sense, subsidiarity includes within it a de facto sense of the responsibility of the government for creating the necessary conditions of human flourishing. In his 1961 encyclical letter *Mater et Magistra*, Pope John XXIII affirmed this stance that the higher authority or state governments should intervene to rectify the situation when individuals and local communities are unable or unwilling to fulfill the concrete conditions of justice.[23] Further, Pope Benedict XVI extended the applicability of this principle to global politics; governments or higher authorities, like the UN, have the duty to intervene for the benefit of the local or targeted citizens.[24] For example, when a war refugee camp cannot provide housing to people at the local community level, then the state government or the international community offers the financial assistance to provide shelter. With these two senses of subsidiarity, it is critical to note that the principle of subsidiarity does not simply mean lower levels (i.e., smaller agencies or more local civil authorities) are better. Rather, this principle is about the just and well-ordered society directed toward the common good that requires the international community, the state, local communities, and individuals all to work together in civil society, including postwar society.[25]

---

20 See Karen Shields Wright, "The Principle of Catholic Social Teaching: A Guide for Decision Making from Daily Clinical Encounters to National Policy-Making," *Linacre Quarterly* 84, no. 1 (February 2017). Also see Pius XI, Encyclical Letter *Quadragesimo Anno* (1931), 79.

21 See Christine Firer Hinze, "Quadragesimo anno," in *Modern Catholic Social Teaching: Commentaries and Interpretations*, ed. Kenneth Himes et al. (Washington, DC: Georgetown University Press, 2011), 160–61.

22 Hinze, 160–61. Also see Pope Francis's teaching on subsidiarity: Francis, "Address of the Holy Father," Participation at the Second World Meeting of Popular Movements, July 9, 2015, 3.2.

23 See John XXIII, *Mater et Magistra*, 54. Also see Wright, "The Principle of Catholic Social Teaching."

24 Benedict XVI, *Caritas in Veritate*, 57. See security scholar Geoffrey Garrett's argument for subsidiarity regarding the governance of globalization. Geoffrey Garrett, "Globalization's Missing Middle," *Foreign Affairs* 83, no. 6 (November/December 2004): 84–97.

25 For an extended discussion of this view, see John XXIII, *Mater et Magistra*, 56.

Civil Society Peacebuilding as a Central Project of Just Political Participation

Just political participation and civil society peacebuilding, as an integrated category, are worthy additions to *jpb* because they serve to protect the common good and subsidiarity. This proposal is liable to be critiqued as redundant within the entire body of JWT, and the emphasis on the local population is likely to be criticized as a chaotic alternative that does not always produce equality. At first glance, just political participation and peacebuilding as an integrated category may seem redundant since just war theory already accounts for the postwar situation. However, recent US-led events indicate that not enough thought has gone into war termination and government transformation, putting the United States in risky and vulnerable positions with no clear endgame. In response, I will show that civil society peacebuilding as a central project of just political participation is a move toward clarity.

Just political participation and civil society peacebuilding are an inseparable theme for two reasons. First, *jpb* precedes peace and thus affects the quality of peace. Second, sometimes the transformation of governments or major peacemaking efforts are goals of war. Thus, joining the two terms does not mean that every war must transform governments; civil society peacebuilding needs to be reflected only to the extent that it is an objective of the war being discussed and to the extent it is affected by *jpb* decisions. These two issues are deeply related because *jpb* is the link between war and peace; it influences the quality and longevity of peace—peace that the initial fighting was supposed to secure. As emphasized throughout the book, futile peace agreements that reaffirm the status quo only bring us back to the precarious position that existed before war, and unclear *post bellum* situations deter combatants from standing down.

With that in mind, I advocate that the peacebuilding practice of *jpb* needs to be determined by the local community, and in a larger sense, civil society. Turning to the local community or the entire civil society *post bellum* thwarts the possibility of the victor or the international community imposing governments and laws. Peace and conflict studies scholars Roger Mac Ginty and Oliver Richmond support the "local turn to peacemaking." They first define the term "local" as following.

> By "local" we mean the range of locally based agencies present within a
> conflict and post-conflict environment, some of which are aimed at iden-
> tifying and creating the necessary process for peace, perhaps with or

without international help, and remain in ways in which legitimacy in local and international terms converge.[26]

Building on this notion, Mac Ginty and Richmond propose, "it is a recognition that peace building, state building and development should support their subjects rather than define them."[27] In their proposal, this approach is necessary because the top-down approach is not always efficacious and may have mixed results. They explain that despite international peacebuilding efforts in Cambodia, Ivory Coast, Rwanda, South Sudan, and Tajikistan, those countries were considered "not free" according to the Freedom House in 2012; Burundi, Central African Republic, Guinea-Bissau, Liberia, and Sierra Leone are "partly free," despite efforts by the UN Peacebuilding Commission; and Afghanistan, Angola, Cambodia, Haiti, Iraq, and Nepal have been subjects of international intervention yet were "near the bottom of Transparency International's 2011 Corruption Index."[28] While top-down efforts are seldom effective, local groups alone are often unable to incite transformation, build a burgeoning government, or finance new infrastructure without international support (financial and otherwise). In this way, the turn to the local should not be seen over and against the peacebuilding efforts put forward in documents such as the ICISS's R2P document, but rather as guiding international efforts.[29]

Emphasizing the local also means that classical just actors are duty bound to aid in building governments that the people want, which are not necessarily democracies or supportive of constitutions with liberal values. At times, the rhetoric seems to suggest that these actors are morally obligated to create democracies. However, as emphasized throughout this book, status as a democracy does not make a nation immune to war. Further, Charles T. Call and Elizabeth M. Cousens warn that creating democracies in the postwar society might result in a chaotic and unstable society that is vulnerable to future conflicts or violent threats.[30] Following the conceptual and empirical work conducted by Mansfield and Snyder, Call and Cousens

---

26 Roger Mac Ginty and Oliver P. Richmond, "The Local Turn in Peacebuilding: A Critical Agenda for Peace," *The Third World Quarterly* 34, no. 5 (2013): 769.

27 Mac Ginty and Richmond, 769.

28 Mac Ginty and Richmond, 774.

29 This argument regarding the ICISS's R2P document was discussed in chapter two.

30 Charles T. Call and Elizabeth M. Cousens, "Ending Wars and Building Peace: International Responses to War-Torn Societies," *International Studies Perspectives* 9 (2008): 1–21.

argue, "we know that the process of democratization is itself destabilizing and that this destabilization can contribute to war onset, and we know that while democracies do not go to war often with each other, they do go to war with nondemocracies at relatively high rates."[31] This does not mean that just actors must not aim to set up a democracy in postwar societies. However, it does affirm my argument that creating a democratic government or changing a regime should not be considered a just cause of waging war from the beginning and that creating a democratic government is not a panacea for all postwar communities. Rather, an authentic belief in locally based civil society peacebuilding requires that just actors are prepared to support nondemocratic governments as well as democratic or prodemocratic ones.

In addition, recent events in Iraq illustrate the challenges of implementing democracy. Regarding these challenges, political scientist Melani Cammett—in her article "Democracy in Post-Invasion Iraq"—not only notes that building democracy in the postwar society cannot resolve all of the problems of the postwar conflicts but also finds the cause of the challenge in the absence of local consensus in peace and nation building.[32] Cammett emphasizes:

> A root cause of the poor quality of democratic governance in Iraq was the lack of inclusion in the post-invasion state-building process. Beginning in the immediate aftermath of the US invasion, the processes that generated the new constitution and governing institutions were flawed. . . . The rushed effort to draft the new Iraqi Constitution excluded key stakeholders, most notably representatives from Iraq's Sunni Arab population.[33]

Once the Hussein regime was ousted, Bush aimed to set up a democracy in Iraq and train the Iraqi troops. However, as Cammett describes above, this campaign only further fragmented the Iraqi society, partly because the goals were unclear and contingency plans were nonexistent in the public mind. And the public's skepticism, especially from the Sunni standpoint, is understandable as democracy has yet to flourish in their country. As a result, while the efficacy of the interim postwar government was complicated by the

---

31 Call and Cousens, "Ending Wars and Building Peace," 8.

32 Melani Cammett, "Democracy in Post-Invasion Iraq," *Costs of War*, Watson Institute, Brown University (2014): 4.

33 Cammett, 4–5.

political and economic turmoil they inherited, a majority of the Iraqi people were displeased with their US-led government's democracy-centric policies. These events demonstrate the local people's distrust of the democratic process as they opted to use force rather than votes alone to bring about change. Their resistance to democracy indicates how difficult it is for a nation to forcibly assume democratic principles. Democracy only works, if it does at all, by an organic process led by the local people.[34] Therefore, colonial impulses to impose democracy would be, at best, useless.[35]

Further, one may wonder whether it is pointless or wrong to support governments that do not uphold liberal values. However, the reality of the situation is that classical actors cannot impose their values on the local communities of defeated states without their consent. This means that these actors may have to concede on some issues of equality (but not basic ones concerning human security such as safety and food) in the way other governments are structured. In those cases, the classical actors must cooperate with nonclassical actors and commit themselves together to address inequalities through noncoercive and noninterventionist means, such as public advocacy and education programs. This also means that the classical actors might have to relent on some liberal ideals, such as the direct legal intervention of imposing women's equal rights in a fundamentalist Muslim community, if the nonclassical actors, like local communities, do not desire them. In those cases, however, both actors must not ignore the human rights issues and commit themselves to finding innovative and comprehensive ways to achieve change. For example, the US and local CSOs can opt to fund

---

34 For a similar discussion, see Daniel Byman and Kenneth Pollack, "Democracy in Iraq?," Brookings Institution, June 1, 2003, 2, https://www.brookings.edu/articles/democracy-in-iraq/. In the postwar Iraqi society, the matter was not about the failure of democracy, but the absence of local consensus in that process of building a new government.

35 One controversial case example is Japanese society after WWII. Many *jpb* scholars, such as Brian Orend, James Dobbins, and Dan Caldwell, compared the postwar Iraqi society (after the Second Iraq War) to the postwar Japanese society. They sought to find the reason for the failure of the defeated state to democratize. They emphasized that Japan in 1945 was a highly developed, economically advanced society that was not marred by historical ethnic conflict as in the case of the postwar Iraqi society. However, historians point out that the making of the 1953 Confidential Agreement between Japan and the US reveals how the state leaders concealed the contradictions of needing to prove the successes of US democratization of Japan and celebrate the alliance on one hand, and needing to employ undemocratic and unconstitutional means to veil the de facto asymmetry inherent in the unequal legal relationship between the two sovereign states on the other. See Tahashi Shogimen and Vicki A. Spencer, *Visions of Peace: Asia and the West* (Farnham, Surrey, UK: Ashgate Publishing, 2014); and Yoichiro Sato and See Seng Tan, ed. *United States Engagement in the Asia Pacific: Perspectives from Asia* (New York: Cambria Press, 2015).

female education programs in Iraq and Afghanistan in lieu of imposing equal rights' laws.

The Roles of FBOs in Peacebuilding and Political Reconciliation

For the remainder of this subsection, we will envision a place for political reconciliation within the peacebuilding of *jpb* endorsed by the World Bank report. We will then pay particular attention to FBOs and their roles in peacebuilding and political reconciliation. In this way, hopefully we will have a better understanding of their distinct contributions in the context of *jpb*.

Intermediation and Facilitation for Political Reconciliation

Building on the aforementioned theoretical framework initiated by Lederach's three levels for approaching civil society peacebuilding, the World Bank report proposes seven functions of both middle-out and bottom-up actors in peacebuilding.

(1) Protection of citizens against violence from all parties;
(2) Monitoring human rights violations and the implementation of peace agreements, and issuing early warnings when necessary;
(3) Advocacy/public communication for peace and human rights;
(4) Socialization to values of peace and democracy, along with developing in-group identity of marginalized groups often via peace education;
(5) Inter-group social cohesion by bringing people together from adversarial groups, often in dialogue projects;
(6) Intermediation/facilitation of dialogue at the local and national level between all forms of actors *post bellum*;
(7) Service delivery to create entry points for peacebuilding, i.e. for the six functions listed above.[36]

Most noticeably, while these seven tasks are generally conducted by both the middle-out and bottom-up actors, the sixth task, intermediation/facilitation, is performed and successfully accomplished by intermediary NGOs, CSO networks, and FBOs. Intermediation/facilitation is a practical means of political reconciliation between conflicting parties, within groups and on different levels of the postwar society. In these local actors' peacebuilding practices for *jpb*, "the main activities within this function are

---

36 Forster and Mattner, *Civil Society and Peacebuilding*, 16–23.

facilitation initiatives (formal or informal) between armed groups, and between armed groups and [local] communities or development agencies."[37]

In particular, FBOs play a major role in terms of promoting attitudinal change for a culture of peace and reconciliation.[38] Peace scholars Jacob Bercovitch and S. Ayse Kadayifci-Orellana point out that the involvement of FBOs in intermediation/facilitation for political reconciliation is not a new trend. They argue that in the past, diverse FBOs, including the Catholic Church, monasteries, religious movements, and religiously affiliated state entities, have played a major role in resolving conflicts between states.[39] Another peace scholar, Douglas Johnston, argues for faith-based diplomacy, which refers to the blending of religious concerns in the conduct of international politics. While appreciating the past efforts to resolve conflicts have taken the form of diplomatic efforts by government and intergovernmental bodies, the role of FBOs, especially the ones led by religious leaders in conflict resolution—including popes, local bishops, lay ministry leaders, and faith-based grassroots movement activists—have been overlooked in both the academic and public spheres.[40] However, he believes that because many present-day conflicts overrun the boundary of traditional diplomacy, FBOs at grassroots, national, and international levels are getting increasingly involved in peace and reconciliation.[41] In particular, FBO-led political reconciliation aligned with official and/or unofficial diplomacy is observed by many to offer alternatives for treating identity-based conflicts.

In addition, drawn from Johnston's case study project on the role of the Church in the post-conflict society of Guatemala, the World Bank report concludes that FBOs have comparative advantages over other CSOs and

---

37 Forster and Mattner, 21.

38 This stance is defended by Catholic Relief Services' work. See Mark M. Rogers, Tom Bamat, and Julie Ideh, eds., *Pursuing Just Peace: An Overview and Case Studies for Faith-Based Peacebuilders* (Baltimore: Catholic Relief Services, 2008), https://www.crs.org/sites/default/files/tools-research/pursuing-just-peace.pdf.

39 Jacob Bercovitch and S. Ayse Kadayifci-Orellana, "Religion and Mediation: The Role of Faith-based Actors in International Conflict Resolution," *International Negotiation* 14, no. 1 (2009): 176.

40 Douglas Johnston, "Introduction: Beyond Power Politicism," in *Religion: The Missing Dimensions of Statecraft*, ed. Douglas Johnston and Cynthia Sampson (Oxford: Oxford University Press, 1994), 4.

41 Douglas Johnston, "Faith-Based Organizations: The Religious Dimensions of Peacebuilding," in *People Building Peace II: Successful Stories of Civil Society*, ed. Paul van Tongeren et al. (Boulder, CO: Lynne Rienner Publishers, 2005), 210.

engage in more active roles in intermediation/facilitation for political reconciliation, especially in the following context.

(1) In situations where religion is a significant factor of the conflict or in
    the identity of at least one of the conflict partners;
(2) When religious leaders on both sides of the dispute can be mobilized
    to facilitate peace;
(3) In third-party mediation, when religious leaders or organizations are
    perceived as trustworthy and legitimate by both parties.[42]

The World Bank report provides another example of the role of the
Catholic Church in El Salvador—the Church negotiated with conflict
parties to enact violence-free days in specific regions, which made a vaccination campaign possible, thereby highlighting the common interests of
both conflict parties.[43] In this example, the report concluded that "linking
a service delivery issue (vaccination) with a common interest (health of
children) may have speeded up the peace process."[44] This example illustrates the key roles in which FBOs can represent common interests of the
entire population and thus contribute to opening or widening space for
political reconciliation, whether it be for short-term negotiation or long-
term rapprochement. These FBOs have the potential to facilitate agreement
between conflicting parties and mitigate the impact of violent conflict *post
bellum*. In addition, their initiatives "have symbolic value and can remind
conflicting parties of what they have in common and of the suffering of
the population."[45]

---

42 Forster and Mattner, *Civil Society and Peacebuilding*, 11. Douglas Johnston portrays how the
Catholic Church in Guatemala launched the initiative *Project for the Reconstruction of a Historical
Memory in Guatemala* in the aftermath of the civil war. Begun in 1995, this project enabled victims of the war to tell their stories and provided public ceremonial reburials, so as to both recover
memory and provide closure. For details, see Douglas Johnston, "Faith-Based Organizations,"
239–43. However, strictly speaking, these studies, which deal with civil war, are out of the literature of *jpb* to be considered. As emphasized throughout the book, these cases belong to
transitional justice, which is distinguished from postwar justice. Yet these transitional justice-
oriented case studies at least show the important roles of FBOs in political reconciliation. For
this purpose, I included them in this chapter.

43 For an insightful commentary from a magisterial and theological perspective, see Stephen
Pope, "The Convergence of Forgiveness and Justice: Lessons from El Salvador," *Theological
Studies* 64 (2003): 812–35.

44 Cammett, "Democracy in Post-Invasion Iraq," 21.

45 Cammett, 21.

Civil Society Peacebuilding Practices beyond Intermediation and Facilitation

The World Bank report emphasizes that FBOs' roles in peacebuilding are not limited to political reconciliation reached through intermediation and facilitation. FBOs are also engaged in all seven functions of working toward civil society peacebuilding, as they help both the classical actors and other secular CSO actors. Plainly, they assist the classical actors in undertaking their policing and punishment practices to engage in reconstruction and achieve comprehensive human security while assisting other secular CSO actors in strengthening civil society's contribution to peacebuilding. With respect to this wide sense of civil society peacebuilding, like other secular CSO actors, FBOs are actively engaged at the local level in promoting social cohesion, socialization, dialogue, service delivery, as well as intermediation and facilitation.

However, FBOs are distinct from other CSOs in that they also "usually go beyond these functions, with better access to higher levels and often include some social justice advocacy work."[46] In addition, FBOs, with their religious and spiritual community leaders, often have the potential to access the local community at the individual and the subnational-group levels where inequalities and insecurities are mostly keenly felt. Hence, having access to both top-down and bottom-up actors demonstrates that FBOs play the role of the middle level leadership in peacebuilding and reconciliation. This leadership is key to promoting civil society peacebuilding.

In addition, given the history and structure of the Catholic Church, it is relatively easy to get involved in politics working toward civil society peacebuilding. In his essay from the book *Peacebuilding: Catholic Theology, Ethics, and Praxis*, Lederach argues that the "ubiquitous presence" of the Catholic Church in a civil society provides a basis for making connections for peacebuilding work among a range of sectors within a civil society.[47] This is somewhat different than when he emphasized the importance of mid-level actors in peacebuilding and reconciliation work. I see this not as a different perspective but an evolved version of his mid-level leadership approach since both approaches strive to develop a comprehensive civil society peacebuilding through interactions among different level actors

---

46 Forster and Mattner, *Civil Society and Peacebuilding*, 29.

47 For details, see John Paul Lederach, "The Long Road Back to Humanity: Catholic Peacebuilding with Armed Actors," in *Peacebuilding: Catholic Theology, Ethics, and Praxis*, ed. Robert J. Schreiter, R. Scott Appleby, and Gerard F. Powers (Maryknoll, NY: Orbis Books, 2010).

while overcoming the two established approaches from top-down and bottom-up approaches, which in his eyes are static, ineffective, and polemical. With this attitude, he illustrates how the "ubiquitous presence" of the Catholic Church in a global civil society allows for its unique contribution toward global peacebuilding.[48] He employs the term "ubiquitous presence" to describe the distinctive role that the Catholic FBOs play within the three levels of a leadership-oriented peacebuilding approach.[49] In particular, the Church's presence in Catholic-majority countries creates the potential to cultivate peacebuilding allies among different sectors of a civil society from top-down to bottom-up actors. Many other CSOs, not only secular CSOs but also other FBOs, including the historic peace churches, do not have the power of such a ubiquitous presence.

In my estimation, Lederach's understanding of the ubiquitous presence of the Church is convincing, as it shows positive contributions to peacebuilding in light of its effectiveness in promoting human diversity in the larger civil society. The Vatican has full diplomatic relationships with 176 nations and permanent observer status at the UN (voice and vote at all UN sponsored conferences). Almost all of those conferences work on the basis of consensus that is tantamount to the process of civil society peacebuilding.[50] Further, many national episcopal conferences sponsor organizations such as Catholic Relief Services (CRS) and Pax Christi. After the International Red Cross and World Vision, CRS is the largest global humanitarian organization in the world. When the US government gives goods, it is often through the CRS because they have local contacts and local knowledge. Pax Christi started in Germany and France after World War II and is a global organization for peacebuilding. These agencies partially share the Catholic vision of promoting civil society peacebuilding in nature but are not under the auspices of the bishops. Also, like the Roman Catholic lay group, Sant'Egidio, whose original mission was to help the poor, religious nonprofits and schools that work for justice are already participating in a type of peacebuilding

---

48 For more discussion, see Lisa Sowle Cahill, "Religious Identity, Justice, and Hope: The Case of Peacebuilding," *Criterion* 47, no. 3 (2010): 2–9.

49 For details, see Lederach, "The Long Road Back to Humanity."

50 For a magisterial overview of the vision of peace, see David Smock, "Catholic Contributions to International Peace," Special Report 69 (Washington, DC: United States Institute of Peace, 2001), 1. David Smock notes, "following Vatican II, the establishment of bishops' conferences throughout the world and the establishment of justice and peace commissions have enhanced the church's ability to promote conflict resolution." He sees the Catholic vision of peace in four areas: human rights, development, solidarity, and world order.

activity.[51] Hence, the public significance of these Catholic FBOs is undeniable, particularly in the United States and Latin America.

Scholarly groups and think tanks are another distinct example of FBOs' mid-level leadership. In particular, they are concerned with how the FBOs and interreligious groups can emphasize religious similarities while respecting religious differences that otherwise might have caused conflicts, as observed in many modern postwar societies, such as Bosnia/Serbia, India/Pakistan, and many African and South Asian nations, as well as postwar Iraqi society.

The United States Institute of Peace, a think tank, examines the potential of civil peacebuilding and political reconciliation through religion in "Abrahamic Alternatives to War."[52] The institute acknowledges that Jewish, Christian, and Muslim religions contain scripture verses that both support and curb war and violent behavior. Without mythologizing each religion, this group is able to discuss the potentials and pitfalls of using sacred texts as a peacemaking tool. For example, the Muslim scholars explain that Quran exhortations that permit violence are in reference to self-defense, not to unprovoked violence. They also declare that Islam must "prevail" as a rallying cry to "proclaim" Islam, not as a command for obligatory conversion. To the contested and popularized view of jihad, they explain that "jihad refers to the obligations to strive or exert oneself to follow God's will," and this does not necessarily mean violence or "holy war."[53] In practical terms, each religion offers something distinct: the Jewish scholars stress duties in ethics, the Muslim scholars propose the use of a mediator and forgiveness, and the Christian scholars offer (in addition to mediation and forgiveness) constructive rebuilding and translational cooperation. All scholars assert that their religion supports economic justice. I emphatically endorse their joint opinion that the most authentic, effective, and reliable way to spread local consensus and political equilibrium for civil society peacebuilding "has been by emphasizing human rights, not by imposing [them] through war."[54]

---

51 Smock, 9–11.

52 Their work is comparable to Philpott's *Just and Unjust Peace*. However, while the Institute of Peace mainly deals with issues of postwar justice, Philpott's work is limited to political reconciliation in the context of transitional justice.

53 Susan Thistlethwaite and Glen Stassen, "Abrahamic Alternatives to War: Jewish, Christian, and Muslim Perspectives on Just Peacemaking," Special Report 214 (Washington, DC: United States Institute of Peace, 2008), 4.

54 Thistlethwaite and Stassen, 15.

Finally, reflection on FBOs in political reconciliation and civil society building seems to center around whether and how religion or religious institutions can be used to establish peace. I see religion as a source of peace more than a source of strife.[55] As discussed earlier, CST endorses that the dignity of every human being is inviolable, that the commitment to just political participation for the common good is necessary, and that every member of a society has a right and responsibility to participate in all kinds of human society, including religion, in order to ensure human dignity and equality are fulfilled. This is central to the Catholic moral tradition. Therefore, it is imperative to examine how FBOs' peacebuilding and reconciliation practice relates to the decision-making of post-conflict interim governments and local communities in terms of just political participation.

Refining the Niebuhrian Approach to *Jus Post Bellum* for Civil Society Peacebuilding

As introduced earlier, we will review the Niebuhrian approach to *jpb* for civil society peacebuilding, as it responds to Himes's warning regarding the limitations of *jpb* practices. This recognition of *jpb*'s limitations signifies the incongruity between political ideals and realities, but it also affirms that civil society peacebuilding as part of *jpb* must balance the ideal and the real. In chapter three, we reviewed Allman and Winright on their Niebuhrian Approach to *jpb*. They argued that *jpb* is best understood within the frame of Niebuhr's notion of imperfect justice. Achieving justice in a complete and idealistic sense is unattainable by humans due to their sinful nature and finitude; as a result, there are no perfectly just wars nor perfect *jpb* and only striving for relative justice, the attainable approximation of perfect justice in an imperfect world. While balancing the incongruity between the ideal

---

55 A debate rages regarding the extent to which religion aids peacebuilding or contributes to war or future conflict *post bellum*. Robert J. Schreiter argues that religion does not usually cause violence, even violence that claims religious motives. Robert J. Schreiter, "Future Directions in Catholic Peacebuilding," in *Peacebuilding: Catholic Theology, Ethics, and Praxis*, ed. Robert J. Schreiter, R. Scott Appleby, and Gerard F. Powers (Maryknoll, NY: Orbis Books, 2010). William Cavanaugh also holds this stance. William Cavanaugh, *The Myth of Religious Violence: Secular Ideology and the Roots of Modern Conflict* (Oxford: Oxford University Press, 2009). Scott Appleby takes a different approach. He writes about the ambivalence of religion, which is a way to retrieve the relevance of religion. His question is whether religion has a role in peacebuilding, and he finds that people perceive religion as having a part to play—sometimes people see it as playing a positive and negative role altogether. Scott Appleby, "Religion as an Agent of Conflict Transformation and Peacebuilding," in *Turbulent Peace*, ed. Chester A. Crocker, Fen Osler Hampson, and Pamela R. Aall (Washington, DC: United States Institute of Peace Press, 2001).

and the real, the JWT must be understood within the notion of imperfect justice. Hence, civil society peacebuilding must also be understood with that notion if it is defined as *jpb* and not understood as pacifism or some naïve strands of just peacemaking theories. This section will refine Niebuhr's ethics in two areas: individual and group moral behaviors, and love and justice. I will first highlight Niebuhr's views on the differences between individual and group morality and how that applies to the relationship of love with justice. I will then apply this discussion in a practical, concrete manner to the function of CSOs, primarily that of faith-based ones, in relation to other actors' pursuit of postwar justice and reconciliation.

Individual and Group Moral Behaviors

Essential to this discussion is Niebuhr's view of the rational and moral capabilities of individuals in comparison to the moral capabilities of groups. On the one hand, he believes that individuals, rather than groups, have a stronger capacity to overcome self-interest and look to the needs of others. On the other hand, for Niebuhr, individuals exist in a tension between their finite existence and their ability for transcendence beyond this existence. In this condition of human nature, even if individuals may have consciousness and the ability to reason that allow for this transcendence, this ability for self-transcendence and reason only guarantees an understanding of the needs of others. It does not follow that a human being will automatically act in love to fulfill those needs. Niebuhr continues, "[man's] social impulses are more deeply rooted than his rational life. Reason may extend and stabilize, but it does not create the capacity to affirm other life than his own."[56] Self-transcendence and reason allow for an acknowledgment of others' needs, but the individual requires an element of love to act truly in the interest of others.

That ability "to affirm life other than his own" is endangered by the tension between the individual's finite nature and ability for transcendence. This tension between man's finite and transcendent nature creates anxiety. For Niebuhr, this anxiety created in trying to reconcile the finite and transcendent natures of the individual creates the condition for sin.[57] Niebuhr's

---

56 Reinhold Niebuhr, *Moral Man and Immoral Society* (New York: Charles Scribner's Sons, 1960), 26.

57 Reinhold Niebuhr, *The Nature and Destiny of Man: Human Nature* (Louisville: Westminster John Knox, 1964), 183. The problem one may see in it is that Niebuhr seems to be saying that finitude itself is the cause of anxiety and temptation to sin, which seems to make the Creator responsible for sin, or gets close to it. This is unlike Aquinas. For the sake of focus in this

discussion of sin is exhaustive, but one description that aptly fits this situation describes sin as "the persistent tendency to regard ourselves as more important than anyone else and to view a common problem from the standpoint of our own interest."[58] On that account, the tendency for sin comes as a result of the anxiety between the transcendent and finite nature of the individual, and sin occurs in his or her tendency to value his or her own needs before others. Hence, sin is a result of the anxiety created by humanity's mortality, its finite condition. Within the individual is a capacity to succumb to the insecurities of finite nature and selfishly look after the self at the expense of others. However, the individual also has a capacity to use this transcendence to view the self's need in relation to others and act in a more selfless manner (to be clear, for Niebuhr, that is possible only with God's grace). It is in the capacity for transcendence that the potential for the individual to work for love and justice is found.

In contrast, groups are much less capable of this transcendence. The basic premise is that the larger the group the smaller the capacity for transcendence and a more selfless attitude, or as Niebuhr puts it, "the larger the group, the more certainly will it express itself selfishly in the total human community."[59] Groups by the very nature of their size encourage selfishness.

The first contributing factor to this group selfishness is that as more and more people are added to a group, there is a larger mixture of competing needs and interests. In other words, the tension and anxiety in the individual's struggle for morality is multiplied as more people interact. When the size of a group reaches that of classical just actors—namely that of a victorious nation, or a gigantic international organization—the tendency toward selfishness reaches its pinnacle. To put it another way, a group the size of a nation cannot help but look toward its own self-interests; it is inevitable due to the sheer number of its citizens' conflicting individual needs and self-interests. Niebuhr was adamant about this as he describes the nation as "a corporate unity," which is, in his view, driven more by force and emotion than by reason and self-criticism. Since states lack this

---

book, I will not get into this debate. But to be brief, for Niebuhr, this human finitude is also understood as a result of sin (original sin) while the finite nature of human beings creates the condition of sin.

58 Reinhold Niebuhr, *The Nature and Destiny of Man: Human Destiny* (Louisville: Westminster John Knox, 1964), 259.

59 Niebuhr, *Moral Man and Immoral Society*, 48.

rational ability with self-criticism to transcend themselves, "it is natural that national attitudes can hardly approximate the ethical."[60] Accordingly, nations find it supremely difficult to act in any universal ethical way, as they are governed by coercion and collective self-interest. Niebuhr writes, "perhaps the best that can be expected of nations is that they should justify their hypocrisies by a slight measure of real international achievement, and learn how to do justice to wider interests than to their own, while they pursue their own."[61] Hence, the nation stands in almost complete opposition to the individual in the ability for self-transcendence of its own needs. The nation is almost incapable of self-transcendence that allows for an objective view of needs, and because of this, a nation only pursues its own needs.

One reason the nation becomes so selfish is that it gives the individual the urge to project his or her own selfish interests onto the nation. Niebuhr states, "the man in the street, with his lust for power and prestige thwarted by his own limitations and the necessities of social life, projects his *ego* upon his nation and indulges his anarchic lusts vicariously."[62] This statement implies that the nation acts as an outlet for the selfish desires that one harbors in individual relationships. What people do as part of a group would be morally reprehensible for any individual to do, and the only way people can justify some of the actions of a group is by creating elaborate fictions that justify the groups' actions to themselves, war being an example. The act of one person killing another for simple selfish gain would be almost universally condemned. However, when two nations engage in war with each other, the act of killing has many justifications. This is not to say that war is always morally unjustified, as Niebuhr himself is a just war thinker, but rather to show the ease with which people justify actions undertaken as a group that they would never do as individuals.

Love and Justice

Niebuhr believes the call for justice in society and the call to love are inseparable. He cannot make this clearer when he writes, "In its conception, natural justice is good as far as it goes, but it must be completed by the supernatural virtue of love. The true situation is that anything short of love

---

60 Niebuhr, 88.
61 Niebuhr, 108.
62 Niebuhr, 93.

cannot be perfect justice."[63] As such, all acts of justice must have some measure of love, while love actually transcends justice. Justice, as Niebuhr suggests, has more to do with the balancing of people and groups' self-interests
against each other, while love requires a loss of self-interest in the command
to love the neighbor. This call to love and justice is best interpreted through
the differences between the individual and the group.

Niebuhr defines justice as "an approximation of brotherhood under
conditions of sin."[64] There is an inherent social aspect in justice. Brotherhood suggests a relationship between many sinful individuals, and all
these individuals, as noted earlier, have competing goals and self-interests.
However, the ultimate purpose of justice is to balance these competing goals
and interests through coercion (e.g., just order) to bring about a sense of
harmony. Plainly, justice is an attempt to balance one man's sinful self-interest
against the sinful self-interest of others in society. As Niebuhr writes,
"because of this tendency, all systems of justice make careful distinctions
between the rights and interests of various members of a community. . . .
They set the limits upon each man's Interest to prevent one from taking
advantage of the other."[65] Justice is society's protection from the sinful
nature of men against one another. It acknowledges the claims of each
person's self-interest and attempts to create a social dynamic that keeps all
self-interest in check. This highlights a decided limit to justice, where it is
deficient in some aspects when compared to love. Niebuhr puts forth, "in
so far as justice admits the claims of the self, it is something less than love.
Yet, it cannot exist without love and remain justice. For without the 'grace'
of love, justice always degenerates into something less than justice."[66] In

---

63 Reinhold Niebuhr, *Love and Justice: Selections from the Shorter Writings of Reinhold Niebuhr*,
ed. D. B. Robertson (Cleveland: The World Publishing Company, 1967), 49. For a similar viewpoint
from a Catholic theological perspective, see *ST*, II-II, q.58, a.6. Aquinas believes that charity precedes faith in the order of perfection (while faith precedes charity in the order of occurrence)
and that charity is needed in order for us to fix God as our end and thus to have all our actions
ordered rightly. Admittedly, Aquinas attends to both cardinal and theological virtues, but Niebuhr sees that acting selflessly is possible only with God's grace, not with the cardinal virtues.
For details, see the conclusion of this book, "Lessons Learned and Future Challenges."

64 Niebuhr, 13.

65 Niebuhr, *The Nature and Destiny of Man: Human Destiny*, 252.

66 Niebuhr, *Love and Justice*, 28. To be clear, Niebuhr does not state that the individual has the
capacity to use transcendence to act selflessly and thus to work for love and justice. That is possible only with grace and not with the cardinal virtues. Note that Niebuhr's love is Christian love,
not directly referring to a general ingredient in social action or groups. For further discussion,
see the conclusion to this book.

essence, people tend to pursue their own selfish impulses in groups, and justice is a balancing act attempting to restrain these selfish impulses in order to bring about a sense of brotherhood.

Love, on the other hand, calls not to balance interest against interest but to sacrifice self-interest for the benefit of others. Love also inherently has a more intimate, individual relationship than justice. While it certainly intends to create a sense of brotherhood among men and women, Niebuhr suggests love has a more personal immediacy than justice. He articulates both of these views by stating, "from the perspective of society the highest moral ideal is justice. From the perspective of the individual the highest ideal is unselfishness."[67] The highest ideal in society is justice, the balancing of self-interests, while the highest ideal of an individual is love, the unselfish call of the absolute command to love the neighbor. Love as an act of sacrifice achieves something higher than the achievements of justice and the law. Niebuhr suggests, "Perfect love . . . is a point which stands beyond all law, because the necessity of sacrificing one's life for another cannot be formulated as an obligation, nor can it be achieved under the whip of the sense of obligation."[68] Love calls to a sacrifice that transcends the requirements of the law. It demands a loss of self-interest not expected in the realm of temporal justice. Love does not attempt to create the equality that is the goal of justice, rather, it creates inequality by sacrificing self-interest for the benefit of others.

The reason love is more fitting in personal relationships is that it requires the act of self-transcendence that occurs in the individual, which allows the individual to acknowledge the needs of others in addition to his own needs. Niebuhr clarifies this as a difference between a rational and a religious ethic by stating, "a rational ethic aims at justice, and a religious ethic makes love the ideal. A rational ethic seeks to bring the needs of others into equal consideration with those of self. The religious ethic, insists that the needs of the neighbor shall be met, without a careful computation of relative needs."[69] The requirement of love, the religious ethic, is greater than the requirement of justice, the rational ethic. Once again, Niebuhr regards love as an element required in justice when he acknowledges that "where

---

67 Niebuhr, *Moral Man and Immoral Society*, 257.

68 Reinhold Niebuhr, *The Essential Reinhold Niebuhr: Selected Essays and Addresses*, ed. Robert McAfee Brown (New Haven: Yale University Press, 1986), 150.

69 Niebuhr, *Moral Man and Immoral Society*, 57.

human relations are intimate (and love is fully effective only in intimate and personal relations), the way of love may be the only way to justice."[70] Therefore, justice must have some element of the love that is only achievable in the most intimate relationships for it to be true justice.

However, the selfless love of the individual has its limits, which are reached in two ways. The first limit is reached when more and more people are added to the requirement to love. The larger a group and the more the individual needs of others are added for consideration, the harder it becomes to love all equally, to achieve equality in selfless acts toward all, and to build the common good.[71] The second limit of love is reached in the individual's tension between the finite and the transcendent. The struggle man fights between his transcendence and finitude ensures that no person can act out of pure self-interest. Humanity's sinful nature is essentially what blocks us from perfect love. In Niebuhr's view, if we remain sinners, we must feel the tension between our "self-interest, anxieties and insecurities, and the obligation to forget [ourselves] for the sake of [our] concerns for others."[72] The individual always lives in that anxiety, creating tension and, thus, can never be completely disinterested/unselfish in his actions.

For Niebuhr, love and justice remain intimately connected. When the love of an individual reaches its limit, either through its expansion to groups or in man's sinful nature, it can find an expression in the call to justice, which establishes equality and attempts to protect everyone from each other's sinful nature. Justice is not love since it is a balancing of conflicting interests, but in order to balance them, an element of love is needed. While the disinterested selflessness of love is needed to balance the selfishness of the group, a Christian ethic teaching only love in all situations and failing to acknowledge the limits imposed on love by human finitude and sin is a naïve approach. Niebuhr advises, "a simple Christian moralism counsels men to be unselfish. A profounder Christian faith must encourage men to create systems of justice which will save society and themselves from their own selfishness."[73] The systems of justice that save society are the ones that encapsulate both love and justice in governance.

---

70 Niebuhr, 266.

71 Niebuhr, 74.

72 Niebuhr, *The Essential Reinhold Niebuhr*, 145.

73 Niebuhr, *Love and Justice*, 28.

Faith-Based CSOs as Civil Peacebuilding Actors: Practical Application

After explicating the connection of love and justice and group and individual morality, the next step is to apply this discussion in a practical, concrete manner, to the function of faith-based CSOs—namely, FBOs *post bellum*—in relation to other just actors' pursuit of civil society peacebuilding. As noted earlier, there has been increased discussion of the role of faith-based CSOs in interstate relations and advocacy on an international level. First, faith-based CSOs serve a key role as expert consultants to international organizations, such as CRS's involvement in the UN and the United Nations High Commissioner for Refugees (UNHCR). Second, they serve a purpose of spreading public awareness of situations involving possible human rights violations or peacebuilding and reconciliation issues among other *jpb* topics. Third, they serve as watchdog agencies that work to expose certain violations of international law or diplomacy. By working with the classical just actors and other peacebuilding actors, faith-based CSOs serve the role of the individual and provide the element of love that needs to be found in justice, as Niebuhr proposes. This is accomplished through the independent nature of faith-based CSOs as NGOs and the freedom they have from the restrictions a nation has in international affairs. Essentially, faith-based CSOs are often more insulated from the failures of group morality found in nations and other top-down oriented actors.

CSOs, including faith-based ones, come in many shapes and sizes and work to accomplish varied goals, both foreign and domestic. However, they all share certain key characteristics, enabling general definitions. Political scientist Steve Charnovitz defines CSOs as international NGOs, which are "groups of persons or of societies, freely created by private initiative, that pursue an interest in matters that cross or transcend national borders and are not profit-seeking."[74] This definition addresses a few characteristics. First of all, this indicates that faith-based CSOs are also not for profit organizations, which means if the goals of the CSOs are met, there is no real personal profit to be reaped from their success. Hence, there is less of a chance for self-interested actions in faith-based CSOs compared to the classical actors or for-profit peacebuilding actors. In other words, this separates CSOs from top-down actors, such as nations, that are inherently more selfish in their desired goals. As previously mentioned, for Niebuhr, nations are "not to be

---

74 Steve Charnovitz, "Nongovernmental Organizations and International Law," *American Journal of International Law* 100, no. 2 (2006): 350.

trusted beyond their own interests."[75] In contrast, CSOs, which play roles of international NGOs, are inherently acting out of something other than self-interest, whether it is religiously motivated or not. They try to make the world better in a way from which they may not directly benefit.

However, there are more special benefits to the individual nature of faith-based CSOs and more parallels that can be drawn between them and individual morality and the element of love in justice: the faith-based CSOs' advantage in being independent. Faith-based CSOs operating as NGOs can be more creative than government officials because they are not burdened with the need to champion a particular national or governmental interest.[76] As an individual entity, faith-based CSOs have a freedom from collective interest that sovereign nations cannot achieve. They are more capable of achieving the level of self-transcendence than the individual is, which allows for a more objective calculation of the needs of others. In their freedom from national ties and the group selfishness associated with nations, faith-based CSOs are capable of a more objective, worldwide view of the needs of others.

Another benefit of faith-based CSOs' individuality and freedom is their ability to establish an intimate connection with the local groups for which they advocate. According to security studies scholar Anna Cornelia Beyer, most CSOs have a comparative advantage over the state and the market mainly due to their proximity to their constituency. In particular, they have "a comparative advantage over the private sector and government in relation to poverty alleviation arising out of access to the poor, their relations with intended beneficiaries, and their organizational freedom."[77] As a major body of CSOs, faith-based CSOs also know the people that the policy changes for which they advocate will affect. They have a true knowledge of the unsafe *post bellum* situations of poverty, violence, and injustice, and this gives them expertise on situations of peace and social justice. In addition, Beyer believes that "because of their proximity to the problems they deal with, as well as their closeness to the concerned populations, [these civil society

---

75 Niebuhr, *Moral Man and Immoral Society*, 84. As discussed in the first section, national governments as part of the civil authority in CST are not simply a necessary evil; instead they have a positive role in society (John XXIII, *Pacem in Terris*, 63). However, this does not mean that they do not seek national interests. Niebuhr emphasizes the nation's nature, which is seeking self-interests, while CST does the nation's fundamental goal, which is the common good.

76 Charnovitz, "Nongovernmental Organizations and International Law," 361.

77 Anna Cornelia Beyer, "Non-Governmental Organizations as Motors of Change," *Government and Opposition* 42, no. 4 (2007): 520.

peacebuilding actors] can be experts for specific issues," which are of importance for civil society peacebuilding and politics.[78] With respect to faith-based CSOs, this intimacy with the victims of injustice is reflective of the intimacy required in love. As Niebuhr points out, "where human relations are intimate (and love is fully effective only in intimate and personal relations), the way of love may be the only way to justice."[79] The intimacy faith-based CSOs are capable of is less likely to occur in governments, especially concerning international issues where the interests of one country may conflict with the interests of another. This is why faith-based CSOs are so effective at bringing the element of love into the quest for justice.

However, while faith-based CSOs can be independent organizations capable of the element of love in justice, they are limited in that they have no direct decision-making power over what policies and laws are created. In this regard, faith-based CSOs are dependent on classical just actors, like national governments and international organizations, for the broadest implementations of justice. This lack of lawmaking capabilities is evident in that they are nonclassical actors that are informal and nongovernmental. They do not hold any sort of legislative power; they have no direct means of enacting policy. In essence, faith-based CSOs have no direct role in drafting legislation, hence their role as specialist consultants on specific issues. They are limited in their ability to form and/or enforce concrete laws, as states or the international community are still the main actors when it comes to creating laws and enforcing them for *jpb*. The tools available to faith-based CSOs show these limitations: "The resources they offer are, for example, information about concerned interests, expert knowledge or support with implementation of policies on site or monitoring."[80] These CSOs excel at making policy suggestions to the top-down actors, and once laws have been passed, they excel at monitoring those target postwar societies and ensuring whether laws are faithfully followed, but they still lack an element that allows them to achieve complete *jpb*.

Like other secular CSOs, what faith-based CSOs lack is the coercive force attached to laws, the force that allows interest to be balanced against interest, the amount of coercive power necessary to order civil society in an equal and just manner. As Niebuhr says, "all social co-operation on a

---

78 Beyer, 522.

79 Niebuhr, *Moral Man and Immoral Society*, 266.

80 Beyer, "Non-Governmental Organizations as Motors of Change," 520.

larger scale than the most intimate social group requires a measure of coercion."[81] Some sort of coercive force, whether it be armed or unarmed, is essential for real change to promote the common good in the postwar society. However, the great role that faith-based CSOs as local peacebuilding actors play in bringing awareness to issues of injustice should not be ignored. Niebuhr sees these two factors working together in a pursuit of justice: "So society may move toward the goal of equal justice by gradual and evolutionary processes, in which coercive and educational factors operate in varying proportions."[82] When the coercive powers of the state and the more intimate individual loving actions of faith-based CSOs come together, the pursuit of equal postwar justice moves forward at the greatest speed. These CSOs inform governments as to where force should be used, and Niebuhr is adamant in saying that "the rational use of coercion is a possible achievement which may save society."[83]

An interdisciplinary research project conducted by Amanda M. Murdie and David R. Davis provides a great example of how CSOs, including faith-based ones, serve a role in international relations but still remain, in a way, dependent on the coercive powers of states and international intergovernmental organizations. They attempt to measure the effectiveness of the practice of "shaming and blaming," a practice whereby human rights organizations (HROs) increase awareness in the public forum of countries with human rights violations in an attempt to bring unilateral action against them. As the authors put it, "through their subsequent shaming efforts, HROs both pressure states to change their practices directly and facilitate indirect pressure on the targeted state through third-party states, individuals and organizations." Inherent in this effort to pressure governments is the presence of pressure for change internationally from outside of the country, as well as on a domestic level within the country. The authors suggest that "improvements in human rights can only be expected once pressure is exerted on norm-violating governments from above and below."[84]

Taking a wide sample of NGOs and their shaming actions from 1992 to 2004, Murdie and Davis compared the number of shaming efforts toward

---

81 Niebuhr, *Moral Man and Immoral Society*, 3.

82 Niebuhr, 209.

83 Niebuhr, 235.

84 Amanda M. Murdie and David R. Davis, "Shaming and Blaming: Using Events Data to Assess the Impact of Human Rights INGOs," *International Studies Quarterly* 56, no. 1 (2012): 3.

countries and tried to find a relation to the number of improvements in human rights in those same countries. They found that "without the attention of these third parties, the ability of HROs to work to impact human rights performance may be limited."[85] In particular, the effectiveness of HROs in creating real change is dependent on third-party states and their coercive pressure on countries that make human rights violations. These third-party states have the ability to coerce through economic sanctions or other coercive measures if human rights violations continue. Further, Murdie and Davis note, "these results show that HRO shaming can have a substantial effect on human rights practices even if HROs are not able to have a domestic presence within a state."[86] Thus, even if there is no pressure "from below," sometimes the coercive actions of states and international organizations like the UN "from above" are enough to enact real changes in issues of human rights. Through the shaming and blaming of CSOs, attention is brought to issues of social justice in oppressive countries. With the help of these CSOs, classical just actors are able to rationally use coercive measures to create a situation of increased justice in society.

As noted previously, Niebuhr is convinced that the Christian call to love and the call to justice are inseparable. This dynamic is reflected in the differences in moral capabilities between individuals and groups. While individuals are capable of a transcendence that allows them an objective view of the needs of others in relation to themselves, large groups such as nations are incapable of this transcendence. As a result, individuals remain more capable of the intimate love that Jesus calls for in his command, "love one another as I have loved you" (Jn 13:34). This sacrificial act of love is brought to its completion on the cross. As such, Niebuhr highlights that the highest ideal of individuals is unselfishness—sacrificial love. By contrast, for nations, the highest ideal is equal justice, which uses coercion to balance self-interest against self-interest. Justice is achieved with an element of love when a nation of individuals, empowered by the command of sacrificial love, helps to create justice in the nation and in the world. The individual is the element of love in justice on earth.

In a more international sense regarding *jpb*, faith-based CSOs can serve in the role of presenting the element of love in the international communities' pursuit of equal justice. Their role as individuals, free from the constraints of states within a multinational system, allows them to see the world's

---

85 Murdie and Davis, 10.
86 Murdie and Davis, 11.

problems with an amount of self-transcendent objectivity that allows for the balancing of need against need. Their perspective, combined with the coercive power of countries and international organizations, allows for real progress to be had in the quest for justice in the international community.

However, it might be appropriate to end with an acknowledgment that even though this interaction between individual love and communal justice allows for a great improvement in the world, complete justice and pure love will never be a possibility on earth. The reality of human sin makes the Kingdom of God, the realm of complete justice and perfect love, always beyond any approximation of justice we can achieve here on earth. Niebuhr sees the goodness of the Kingdom symbolized in the cross. He writes that the cross "symbolizes the final goodness which stands in contradiction to all forms of human goodness in which self-assertion and love are compounded."[87] It is in the cross that all the stain of human self-interest is banished and where justice no longer becomes a balance of interest against interest. The Kingdom of God is what we strive for in the pursuit of justice on earth, and it serves as both an encouragement to achieve justice on this earth and a reminder that true justice and love remain only with God.

CONCLUSION

I made four points in the first section of this chapter. First, civil society peacebuilding as a central project of just political participation ought to be implemented because it protects the common good and subsidiarity. My approach to the common good and subsidiarity is drawn from, but does not fully encompass, CST. As emphasized throughout the book, the common good is a notion that *our* goods are shared, which leads to the assertion that the status of the marginalized indicates how the whole is faring. In addition to the common good, subsidiarity is a notion that sets the parameters of the common good, respecting sovereignty at its various levels (personal, subnational, national, international). In theory, the common good ought to include all people, but in practice, reflection on the common good often falls short of the ideal. I hope that the third theme of *jpb*, just political participation, will encourage reflection toward rebuilding the common good *post bellum*.

Second, civil society peacebuilding must be understood as part of *jpb* tantamount to *jus ad bellum*. This agenda must intend to rebuild the

---

87 Niebuhr, *The Nature and Destiny of Man: Human Destiny*, 68.

common good when considering war because it demands that classical just actors account for how the local people in the war-torn country will cope after the war. This requires accounting for how the vanquished people's future will be impacted by war—by the intervention itself and by the devastation of war (financial, infrastructural, emotional, etc.). However, this civil society peacebuilding, as described here, must also fulfill subsidiarity, as it respects local sovereignty. Subsidiarity is predicated on the notion that members of a local community are best suited to determine their own needs.

Third, the local turn to peacebuilding is subject to critique because the method is fraught with problems, as the local community may not possess a consensus on an issue. As this method's proponents point out, "the local turn is characterized by cacophony of thinking."[88] However, a cacophony of thinking also exists amid the top-down approach. Unlike the top-down approach that overlooks mixed public opinion and works against it, the local turn takes dissent seriously and works with it. Mac Ginty and Richmond affirm, "it might be messy but it has the capacity to be vibrant and relevant to the communities from which it emerges."[89] Simply ignoring mixed views does not rid a nation of conflicting opinions.

Fourth, FBOs *post bellum*, or faith-based CSOs, play a major role in promoting attitudinal change for a culture of peace and reconciliation. As I introduced the World Bank's report and its proposal on the seven functions of local peacebuilding actors in peacebuilding, I paid particular attention to FBOs and how they play a major role in promoting attitudinal change for a culture of peace and reconciliation. They are distinguished from other CSOs in that most of their missions are related to political reconciliation reached through intermediation and facilitation. Also, they effectively play the roles of mid-level leadership because of their easier access to both top-down and bottom-up actors. As a result, they are one of the leading actors contributing to civil society peacebuilding.

In the second section, I revisited the Niebuhrian approach to *jpb* for completing civil society peacebuilding. Niebuhr was a theologian engrossed in the quest for justice on earth.[90] Intimately connected to justice is the command to love. He believed that true justice requires an element of Christian

---

88 Mac Ginty and Richmond, "The Local Turn in Peacebuilding," 780.

89 Mac Ginty and Richmond, 780.

90 Though he did not believe the Kingdom of God could be achieved within time, he still thought that the justice characteristic of the kingdom was for Christians to bring about in the world.

love in it and that Christian love contains an element of justice. He also saw a disconnect between people's individual moral behavior and the morality people express within groups. He observed that the larger a group, the more selfish impulses will come to dominate the actions of that group. He stressed that the use of coercion is present in any relationship and saw that the coercive powers of one dominant group often leaves others in a situation of disproportionate justice.[91] I discussed Niebuhr's views on the differences between individual and group morality and how that applies to the relation of love to justice and vice versa. Through the lens of these two elements of his theology, I discussed the work of faith-based CSOs and proposed that in international relations and issues of peace and social justice, these CSOs have the potential to perform a unifying role by representing the love that is an element necessary to justice, especially with regard to postwar justice.

While Himes's Thomistic approach to *jpb*, along with the principle of establishing civil society, offers just actors the ultimate moral and political vision of civil society peacebuilding for just political participation, a Niebuhrian approach to *jpb* helps them recognize the merits and limits of CSOs (faith-based in particular) in civil society peacebuilding in practice. Therefore, just actors ought to consider these two approaches together so as to enable the development of more concrete initiatives to serve people who suffer in the postwar society, especially socially vulnerable and innocent citizens, in a more balanced and comprehensive manner.

---

91 Niebuhr begins with the statement that society and the human person are not the same type of entity. A society requires a balancing of power to change it, whereas a person can change him- or herself.

Conclusion:
Lessons Learned and
Future Challenges

This book challenged the view of those who argue that political reconciliation is the first and foremost ambition of *jpb*. Furthermore, this work attempted to justify the proposition that achieving just policing, just punishment, and just political participation is key to building a just peace, of which the fundamental characteristic must be human security. Reconciliation may not be achievable, but security is, and immediate postwar response is directed to maintaining human security, especially for protecting women, children, minority ethnic groups, and other socially vulnerable populations. This book suggested how reconciliation might occur later on.

As the twenty-first century's postwar conflicts in Afghanistan, Iraq, Syria, the Balkans, central Africa, and elsewhere wind down, we have witnessed that in the immediate aftermath of war, there has been little or no policing, punishment, or avenues for political participation to protect the lives of people, especially those most vulnerable. Furthermore, the need for *jpb* scholars and practitioners across various disciplines to elaborate and apply norms of postwar peacebuilding to assessment of reconstruction policies—of just policing, just punishment, and just political participation—has grown more apparent. Therefore, this project argued (i) that human security is a neglected theme in the discourse of moral and religious intellectual traditions, and (ii) that a more balanced understanding of *jpb* must pay direct attention to the elements comprising human security in a postwar context, as well as the quest for political reconciliation. Certainly, reconciliation ought to be among the norms just actors employ as long as it serves the *jpb*'s primary and foremost mission of human security.

As emphasized throughout the book, *jpb*'s relationship to peace highlights that *jpb* ought to be principally concerned with the immediate time after war. Broad concerns about transforming governments and changing policies are outside the realm of *jpb* (and are often considered just peacemaking). However, peace can be defined in the negative, as an absence of war, or the positive, as the establishment of a just social order. In this book, peace is considered in the positive sense agreed upon by *jpb* and just peacemaking approaches.

My book is an interdisciplinary exercise in applied political ethics—using security studies, international law, and peacebuilding scholarship—to address the topic of postwar justice and sustainable peace as a means of illuminating the moral theological discourse of just war theory. While examining the interrelated challenges of moral and social norms in both political and legal domains, as well as church and faith-based CSO practices, this work proposes an innovative methodology for linking theology, ethics, and social science. In this way, the ideal and the real can inform each other in a postwar ethic and the role of religion therein.

Chapter one focused on the work of the so-called "foundational" *jpb* thinkers. I call them foundational because their works are widely cited across disciplines of *jpb* literature. Each author has contributed important insight to *jpb* thinking: Aristotle's quest for justice in war, Aquinas's systemic outline of the JWT, Walzer's modern attempt to reconstruct the moral norms and practices that constitute the JWT today, and Orend's theoretical foundations for *jpb* in contemporary warfare.

Certain issues overlap while exploring these thinkers. In particular, I refined the three common *jpb* themes for the purpose of constructive discourse: the reconstruction of just policing, just punishment, and just political participation. Based on the three themes, I posed three foundational *jpb* questions: (i) how should just policing be established in the tasks of human and national security to deal with the present injustice? (ii) How should just punishment be enforced by both the laws of war and peace to correct the past wrongdoing? And finally, (iii) how should just political participation balance the tasks of human security and political reconciliation to prevent future violence in the aftermath of war?

Chapter two had three main sections: (i) the discourse surrounding the conventional norm of a right to fight versus the emerging norm of a responsibility to protect people, (ii) the discourse of minimalist versus maximalist positions, and (iii) a redefinition of these two positions to illuminate the three foundational themes of *jpb*. I stressed that these positions are seen as two extremes on either end of a continuum. If we consider the middle ground between them, we can attain a balanced and nuanced view with differences that appear to be of degree rather than type.

In chapters three and four, I observed that within the *jpb* literature, much of the moral theological tradition shares certain commonalities with the moral philosophical tradition. Thus, I proposed that moral theological work should fill the hole that moral philosophical studies of *jpb* has missed or overlooked and that the practical, intrinsically linked commitments of striving to love our neighbors as ourselves and embracing our enemies are essential in working toward rebuilding the common good. In consequence, I developed a distinct discourse in the moral theology of *jpb*: human security and political reconciliation. My argument stated that to deal with these two moral visions together in a thoughtful manner is key to finding the moral compass for reconstructing just policing, just punishment, and just political participation. In particular, I suggested a common-good-seeking approach to justice, the "maxim(um) of ethical minimalism." The norm for *jpb* is achieving the common good to the highest extent possible, with a priority on human security, using nonviolent means insofar as possible and violent means when necessary.

With respect to the scholarship of human security and political reconciliation, I addressed distinctive theological elements, such as an emphasis on establishing a common good to which all have access, that human dignity and rights are reflected in the doctrine of the *imago dei*, and that there be cooperative efforts for social justice flowing from participation in sacramental life. In particular, I proposed four major approaches to the study of human security that emerge from the theological development of *jpb* ethics. They are (i) the Church's response to the norm of R2P; (ii) Schuck's Augustinian *jpb* approach, with emphasis on pursuing right intention; (iii) Himes's Thomistic *jpb* approach thoroughly developed within the JWT, especially right intention, just cause, and legitimate authority; and (iv) Allman and Winright's Niebuhrian *jpb* approach, reflected in a just cause principle signifying imperfect justice.

As far as political reconciliation is concerned, I discussed why Philpott's ethic of political reconciliation is not effectively suitable for postwar justice, or at least why one should not apply it directly to the context of *jpb*. Moreover, I clarified that his ethic can be moderately understood as *a direction* for *jpb,* but should not be understood as *the* direction, as in the case of Scheid's consistent ethics of reconciliation. Scheid's theology's strong adherence to political reconciliation prevents its direct application to a broader range of *jpb* issues (just policing, punishment, and political participation), and thus hinders *post bellum* movements toward human security and peacebuilding efforts in the immediate aftermath of war.

Chapters five through seven attended to policy-oriented and practical concerns in *jpb,* as they returned to the claim of my maxim(um) of ethical minimalism that the establishment of a just peace requires the establishment of a just political order. Just peace, based upon a just political order, provides human security for all and makes it possible to resolve postwar disputes by just and peaceful means. Such a just political order that seeks and maintains peace should exist for all people, not only some individuals or groups. This is especially true for vulnerable people *post bellum*, such as women, children, and refugees, as well as other civilians and military personnel of the defeated nation or party.

It is vital that chapters five and six be viewed in tandem. In chapter five, I showed that just policing must be directed toward the common good, aiming to protect the lives of innocent and vulnerable people. This line of reasoning posited that just actors must undertake moral responsibility to engage in reconstruction and thus achieve a comprehensive version of human security through both armed force (i.e., peacekeeping) and nonviolent means (i.e., nation building). In chapter six, I made a similar claim regarding just punishment: how do armed forces carry out their peacekeeping operations in legal terms? How do nonviolent means, such as international tribunals, contribute to rebuilding the common good? These questions suggest that just punishment be understood within the larger context of just policing. Therefore, just punishment primarily aims to protect innocent and vulnerable populations *post bellum*, when it comes to shaping the status of *jpb* practice from an international legal perspective, especially with regard to both international criminal law and occupation law. These two chapters primarily attend to the role of classical actors.

Chapter seven addressed faith-based CSOs' peacebuilding practices in relation to the decision making of postwar interim governments and to local communities in terms of political participation. In identifying and assessing how the right to political participation operates in a *jpb* context, this chapter highlighted and developed the role of the CSOs (primarily faith-based) as key moral and social institutions, as well as political entities. In particular, I discussed faith-based CSOs' civil society peacebuilding, emphasizing just political participation to prevent future violence in the immediate aftermath of war. I began by reviewing one of the foundational themes and questions in the book: how should just political participation balance the tasks of human security and political reconciliation to prevent future violence in the aftermath of war? I then discussed the just political participation issues embedded in this thematic question. I made the case that this question must be answered alongside another fundamental question: What is just political participation in *jpb*? To answer this question, I considered CST on the common good, understood as the full good of society which entails the ethical responsibility of all members of civil society.

Of course, implementing the common good in postwar societies is challenging. I proposed that the common good must be infused throughout all the political activities of *jpb*. What is the principal goal for just political participation: human security or political reconciliation? This question is vital but answered incompletely if we overlook who the principal agents are. The question is not simply about human security versus political reconciliation. The crux of this question is: who is actually involved in both human security and political reconciliation? While the goals of human security and political reconciliation often seem to conflict with each other, the actual conflict arises when the actors engaged in reconstruction are guided by self-interest rather than selflessness and love. Political reconciliation can be used for human security, but it may be also used for certain group's unjust political interests or other diplomatic agendas. In this regard, as Himes warns, just actors must recognize the limits of *jpb* practices—a point initially put forth by Allman and Winright's Niebuhrian approach to *jpb*. Therefore, I concluded that while Himes's Thomistic approach to *jpb* offers just actors the ultimate moral and political vision of civil society peacebuilding for just political participation, my maxim(um) of ethical minimalism account must incorporate a Niebuhrian approach to *jpb* that helps them recognize the merits and limits of faith-based CSOs in civil society peacebuilding in practice. Taking these approaches together, just actors would be able to develop more concrete initiatives to serve people in the vanquished state, especially the most vulnerable population, in a more balanced and comprehensive manner.

However, one might wonder about the tensions—and perhaps contradictions—between Niebuhrian and Thomistic *jpb* approaches that are suppressed in this final chapter. I intended to strike the right balance between the two positions but may leave theologians or serious religious readers wondering if I could not have presented a more rigorous defense of some of the moral investigations I made in relation to theological questions. For example, they might ask if my use of Niebuhr coheres with my use of CST and Himes's account of *jpb*. Niebuhr (generally in his early work, and especially *The Nature and Destiny of Man*) follows Anders Nygren in his suspicion of all forms of self-love, which can have negative implications toward solidarity and the common good. To be clear, it is (distorted) self-love that has the potential negative implications, not the suspicion of it that has those implications. He defines the common good as the best we can collectively hope for by balancing competing self-interests in a society governed by the state that enforces the rule of law. At least from this point of view, most theologians understand that there is a tension between Niebuhr's Augustinian bent and CST's Thomist, incarnational/sacramental bent. The crux of this matter is that Aquinas agrees with Augustine about the ultimate ends of human life but gives a substantially more optimistic account of human nature and human capacities, which in turn results in significant shifts in opinion on the issue of political order.

In acknowledging this difference, I must clarify two points. The first point informed my attention to faith-based CSOs, as opposed to secular CSOs in the second section. For sure, the main reason I used Niebuhr corresponding to Himes's Thomistic approach to *jpb* was to emphasize that we have to be aware of the limitations and merits of both classical and non-classical just actors. Though, I had to narrow the scope of CSOs to faith-based organizations (especially Christian ones). This is because Niebuhr espouses a different understanding of love and justice than CST and Himes's Thomistic vision. I discussed Niebuhr's understanding of human nature as two poles, freedom and finitude, with anxiety the inevitable outcome. For Niebuhr, anxiety is the condition of temptation to sin, and the only way to resolve the tension between the two poles is through God, Christ, and the theological virtues. There is no natural virtue that can achieve this state and result in justice. This is like Augustine and unlike Aquinas; there is no "natural" virtue alone that can ease this anxiety and result in justice. Niebuhr argues that individuals need God's grace, which allows them to act selflessly and thus work for love and justice. While my quote from Niebuhr's *Love and Justice* sounds more like Aquinas—"natural justice is good as far as it goes," in *The Nature and Destiny of Man*, Niebuhr emphasizes that the highest possibility of history is mutual love and justice and that sacrificial love is a key seed or instigator of them. However, this love is not validated by history itself. It is not a general principle of historical action, nor is it a general ingredient in social action or groups. Plainly, for him, love should be the Christian love.

Therefore, Niebuhr would champion faith-based CSOs over all others, as they introduce Christian sacrificial love into society and have a positive effect toward love and justice. This differs from Aquinas, CST, and Himes's vision of civil society *post bellum*. Of course, like Aquinas, for Niebuhr, the highest ideal of nations is justice. An element of sacrificial love enables this ideal; Niebuhr would not argue that a nation of individuals is empowered by the command to love. Nation-states do not follow the love command. Rather, he is thinking more of Christians acting for the social good, or of churches and faith-based organizations.

The second point addresses that Himes's vision for *jpb* is larger than the Niebuhrian approach to *jpb* in regard to the role of all civil society actors, including both for-profit organizations and nonprofit CSOs. Although the final chapter does not include for-profit actors as part of CSOs, these business actors—specifically social entrepreneurs—play a major role in rebuilding the common good in a postwar society. There is a growing intellectual movement called "peace through commerce" to examine this contribution. With a focus on building global initiatives promoting peace, justice, and fairness through commerce, new business models are emerging from this concept of "peace through commerce" to influence business at every level, from multinational corporations to small, local shops.[1] As Himes emphasized, postwar reconstruction programs without these comprehensive efforts to rebuild a civil society would fail not only to repair the destruction of wars but also would unsuccessfully restore the structural components, the absence of which created the initial need for hostilities.

Nevertheless, there is a reason I did not consider these business actors as civil peacebuilding actors in *jpb* context. Even social entrepreneurs cannot be free from their essential nature as for-profit organizations. Just actors may find a way of promoting human flourishing through economic stability and prosperity; however, given the limited time commitment and cost, the primary agenda must attend to the reconstruction of basic infrastructure, and, to repeat, human security, not human flourishing and economic prosperity, is the heart of *jpb*, as it is key and fundamental in the period *immediately* following war. Likewise, as shown by Charnovitz's analysis of CSOs, for-profit organizations do not appropriately adhere to the *jpb* mission of CSOs. Therefore, business actors must be included in a long-term visionary peacebuilding project, but not for the reconstruction of just political participation in the *jpb* context.

---

1 The intellectual foundations of this movement are relatively recent in academic and professional fields. Nobel economist Amartya Sen; Timothy Fort, Professor of Business Ethics at George Washington University; as well as Kroc Institutes at Catholic research universities have been pioneer leaders in developing the conceptual framework of peace through commerce. See Amartya Sen, *On Ethics and Economics* (New York: Wiley-Blackwell, 1988); Timothy Fort, *Business, Integrity, and Peace* (Cambridge: Cambridge University Press, 2007); and Viva Bartkus, "Business on the Frontlines," in *Understanding Quality Peace: Peacebuilding after Civil War*, ed. Peter Wallensteen and Madhav Joshi (New York: Routledge, 2017).

More crucially, Himes himself recognizes the limit of *jpb* practices that signifies the incongruity between political ideals and realities. Plainly, he sees the difference between a political aspiration of rebuilding a civil society *post bellum* and a realistic sense of the political milieu of *jpb* context. In other words, Himes's approach to *jpb* must aim at human security for post-war justice, *grounded in the JWT*, which is and ought to be engineered by a short term-based nation-building project. This is distinguished from an *extensive* buildup of a civil society scheme, which requires a wider range of peacebuilding efforts, such as exploring transitional justice as a vehicle for social and political transformation in post-conflict states. On that account, Himes's approach to *jpb* must be understood as similar to the Niebuhrian approach to *jpb*. This is true not only in terms of the recognition of the incongruity between political ideals and realities, but also in the acknowledging the effective work of CSOs, excluding for-profit organizations, as, unlike in his aspirational *jpb* vision, such business actors do not belong *in practice* in the immediate aftermath of war. It is also true that my book is limited in addressing his *jpb* vision to the fullest sense in that I focused on faith-based CSOs, not the entire body of CSOs. In addition, I admit that even if Himes's approach to *jpb* needs to be tempered by realism claimed by the Niebuhrian approach to *jpb* in a concrete manner, his approach is more optimistic about the common good and the positive moral possibilities of solidarity. In this sense, my maxim(um) of ethical minimalism account must not only *carefully* incorporate a Niebuhrian approach to *jpb* that helps us recognize the merits and limits of faith-based CSOs, but also needs to find a way to deal with secular CSOs in civil society peacebuilding in practice.

Finally, it must be acknowledged that a number of challenges remain for this *jpb* theory. While the scope of this book was limited to the cases of interstate war as discussed in the introduction, the current and changing landscape of the nature of war presents a challenge to the entire body of traditional just war literature. Lisa Sowle Cahill captures this reality through her examination of the changing global political and economic landscape of war and conflict. She considers the fact that "wars between or among nation-states have actually decreased since the 1980s, but civil, ethnic and communal conflict within nations or across national borders has become the dominant form of warfare since the 1950s." She continues, "While in World War I, fewer than five percent of deaths in war were civilian, today civilians account for seventy-five percent of war dead. Just war criteria

applied prospectively by government officials and elite advisors in the present day are not [quite] as relevant as they once were to the realities of war."[2]
Work needs to be done regarding how the moral and theological norms and
jpb criteria apply to this new situation.

A second challenge to this book arises from many *jpb* theologians
arguing that building a democratic regime is not necessary for postwar justice. They assert that just actors ought to adopt whatever route best guides
them toward securing the vanquished people's civilization and their civility.
In particular, Himes clarifies that the just cause of war excludes regime
change (to a democratic regime). In contrast, the idea of transitional justice
is implicit in an assumption that a post-conflict community is transitioning
to democracy, or at least toward the political culture of democratic government. Despite the recognition of the differences between the two justices, I left room to delineate its application in practice that requires future
case studies.

Third, it is difficult to determine exactly which, if either type of law,
applies to a specific instance in the immediate aftermath of war, especially
in the phase of Low Intensity Conflict. LIC represents a threshold between
war and peace. As a result, it is difficult to determine what criteria should
be used to determine the answer to this quandary.

Lastly, in future work, I hope we will continue to develop the discourse
of *jpb* ethics and approaches to just peacemaking. I will first look into the
roles of religious institutions *post bellum* in terms of public administration.
I am particularly concerned with the role of the Catholic institutions that
have contributed to postwar societies since the events of 9/11—how their
peacebuilding practice relates to the decision-making of post-conflict interim
governments and local communities in terms of political participation. My
ultimate concern is not merely the faith-based institutions and their practices
post bellum but the broader implications for public administration. Examining this issue requires knowledge of how to collaborate with, and even
within, faith groups with respect to their peacebuilding assets. After all, this
is connected with the aforementioned "peace through commerce" project; I
attempt to examine the capacity for business to foster peace even in the most
contentious situations of religious and political conflict.

---

2 Cahill, "How Should War Be Related to Christian Love?," 194. For a similar critique, see Carton
Gentry and Amy E. Eckert, *The Future of Just War: New Critical Essays* (Athens, GA: University of
Georgia Press, 2014).

Several additional issues require future attention. First, current moral theology literature on *jpb* tends to emphasize mercy rather than the moral responsibility of justice. Second, the biggest challenge of *jpb* is that the discourse focuses on nation-states or sovereign political entities, not on the people who suffer from war. Despite my argument for comprehensive human security in this book, most *jpb* literature maintains that state security precedes human security. Lastly, it is important not to overlook the role of the faith-based CSOs in *jpb*. The peacebuilding efforts of faith-based CSOs have contributed greatly to postwar justice and peace, with an emphasis on the delivery and implementation of social services. I hope that this role of the Church and faith-based groups will contribute to a more balanced and sustainable human security for all, especially the most oppressed and vulnerable citizens in postwar societies.

Selected Bibliography

ENCYCLICALS AND OFFICIAL CHURCH DOCUMENTS

All social encyclicals and official Church documents are cited from the Vatican website. Accessed September 25, 2017. http://www.vatican.va.

Benedict XVI. "Address of His Holiness Benedict XVI." Meeting with the Members of the General Assembly of the United Nations Organization. April 18, 2008.

———. *Caritas in Veritate*. Encyclical Letter. 2009.

Francis, "Address of the Holy Father." Participation at the Second World Meeting of Popular Movements, July 9, 2015.

———. "Nonviolence: A Style of Politics for Peace." Message for the World Day of Peace, January 1, 2017.

John XXIII. *Mater et Magistra*. Encyclical Letter. 1961.

———. *Pacem in Terris*. Encyclical Letter. 1963.

John Paul II. *Sollicitudo rei Socialis*. Encyclical Letter. 1987.

———. *Centesimus Annus*. Encyclical Letter. 1991.

———. "Address to the Diplomatic Corps Accredited to the Holy See." January 20, 1993.

———. *Evangelium Vitae*: Encyclical Letter. 1995.

———. "Peace on Earth to Those Whom God Loves." Message for the World Day of Peace, January 1, 2000.

———. "*Pacem in Terris*: A Permanent Commitment." *Origins* 32, no. 29 (January 2, 2003).

Leo XIII. *Rerum Novarum*. Encyclical Letter. 1891.

Paul VI. *Octogesima Adveniens*. Encyclical Letter. 1971.

Pius XI. *Quadragesimo Anno*. Encyclical Letter. 1931.

Pontifical Council for Justice and Peace. *Compendium of the Social Doctrine of the Church*. Washington, DC: USCCB Publishing, 2004.

Vatican Council II. *Gaudium et Spes*. December 7, 1965.

GENERAL BIBLIOGRAPHY

Agger, Inger, and S. B. Jensen. *Trauma and Healing under State Terrorism*. New York: Zed Books, 1996.

Allman, Mark, and Tobias Winright. *After the Smoke Clears: The Just War Tradition and Post War Justice*. Maryknoll, NY: Orbis Books, 2010.

———. "Protect Thy Neighbor: Why Just-War Tradition Is Still Indispensable." *Commonweal*. June 2, 2016.

Appleby, Scott. "Religion as an Agent of Conflict Transformation and Peacebuilding." In *Turbulent Peace*, edited by Chester A. Crocker, Fen Osler Hampson, and Pamela R. Aall, 841–54. Washington, DC: United States Institute of Peace, 2001.

———. *The Ambivalence of the Sacred: Religion, Violence, and Reconciliation*. Lanham, MD: Rowman and Littlefield, 2010.

Aquinas, Thomas. *St. Thomas Aquinas on Politics and Ethics*. Translated and edited by Paul E. Sigmund. New York: Norton, 1988.

———. *Summa Theologica*. Translated by Fathers of the English Dominican Province. New York: Benziger Publishers, 1948.

———. "Whether It Is Always a Sin to Wage War?" In *St. Thomas Aquinas Political Writings*, edited by R. W. Dyson, 239–41. Cambridge: Cambridge University Press, 2002.

Arend, Anthony Clark, and Robert Beck. *International Law and the Use of Force*. London: Routledge, 1993.

Aristotle. *Nicomachean Ethics*. Translated by Terence Irwin. Indianapolis: Hackett Publishing Company, 1999.

———. *The Politics*. Translated by Trevor J. Saunders and T. A. Sinclair. New York: Penguin Books, 1981.

Aron, Raymond. *Clausewitz: Philosopher of War*. Translated by Christine Booker and Norman Stone. New York: Simon & Schuster, 1983.

Arthur, Paige. "How 'Transitions' Reshaped Human Rights: A Conceptual History of Transitional Justice." *Human Rights Quarterly* 31, no. 2 (2009): 321–67.

Asfaw, Semegnish, Guillermo Kerber, and Peter Weiderud. *The Responsibility to Protect: Ethical and Theological Reflections: Geneva, 21–23 April 2005*. Geneva: World Council of Churches, 2005.

Augustine. *The City of God*. Translated by Gerald G. Walsh, Demetrius B. Zema, Grace Monahan, and Daniel J. Honan. Garden City, NY: Doubleday, 1958.

———. "Letter 189: Augustine to Boniface." In *Augustine: Political Writings*, edited by E. M. Atkins and R. J. Dodaro, 30–43. New York: Cambridge University Press, 2001.

Ayers, James. *Military Operations Other Than War in the New World Order*. Wright-Patterson Air Force Base, OH: Air Force Institute of Technology, 1996.

Ball, Nicole. "The Challenge of Rebuilding War-torn Societies." In *Turbulent Peace: The Challenge of Rebuilding War-Torn Societies*, edited by Chester A. Crocker, Fen Osler Hampson, and Pamela R. Aall, 719–36. Washington, DC: United States Institute of Peace, 2001.

Ban, Kimoon. *Implementing the Responsibility to Protect Report*. UN Document A/63/677, January 12, 2009. https://digitallibrary.un.org.

———. *Early Warning, Assessment and the Responsibility to Protect*, UN Document A/64/864, July 14, 2010. https://digitallibrary.un.org.

———. *The Role of Regional and Subregional Arrangements in Implementing the Responsibility to Protect*, UN Document A/65/251, June 28, 2011 https://digitallibrary.un.org.

Bartkus, Viva. "Business on the Frontlines." In *Understanding Quality Peace: Peacebuilding after Civil War*, edited by Peter Wallensteen and Madhav Joshi. New York: Routledge, 2017.

Bass, Gary J. *Freedom's Battle*. New York: Alfred A. Knopf, 2008.

Bay, Chris. *Court-Martial: How Military Justice Has Shaped America from the Revolution to 9/11 and Beyond*. New York: Norton, 2016.

Bellamy, Alex. "The Responsibilities of Victory: *Jus Post Bellum* and the Just War." *Review of International Studies* 34 (2008): 601–25.

———. *Responsibility to Protect*. Cambridge: Polity Press, 2009.

Benvenisti, Eyal. *The International Law of Occupation*. Princeton: Princeton University Press, 2004.

Bercovitch, Jacob, and S. Ayse Kadayifci-Orellana. "Religion and Mediation: The Role of Faith-Based Actors in International Conflict Resolution." *International Negotiation* 14, no. 1 (2009): 175–204.

Beyer, Anna Cornelia. "Non-Governmental Organizations as Motors of Change." *Government and Opposition* 42, no. 4 (2007): 513–35.

Bhuta, Nehal. "New Modes and Orders: The Difficulties of a *Jus Post Bellum* Constitutional Transformation." *University of Toronto Law Journal* 60 (2010): 799–854.

Biggar, Nigel. *In Defence of War*. Oxford: Oxford University Press, 2013.

Boutros-Ghali, Boutros. *Letter Dated 24 May 1994 from the Secretary General to the President of the Security Council*. http://www.un.org/ga/search/view_doc.asp?symbol=S/1994/674.

———. *An Agenda for Peace 1995*. New York: United Nations Publications, 1995.

Boyle, Alan, and Christine Chinkin. *The Making of International Law: Foundations of Public Law*. Oxford: Oxford University Press, 2007.

Brown, Bartram S. "US Objections to the Statute of the International Criminal Court: A Brief Response." *New York University Journal of International Law and Politics* 31 (1999): 855–91.

Brugger, E. Christian. *Capital Punishment and Roman Catholic Moral Tradition*. South Bend, IN: University of Notre Dame Press, 2014.

Byman, Daniel, and Kenneth Pollack, "Democracy in Iraq?" Brookings Institution, June 1, 2003. https://www.brookings.edu/articles/democracy-in-iraq/.

Cahill, Lisa Sowle. *Love Your Enemies: Discipleship, Pacifism, and Just War Theory*. Minneapolis: Fortress Press, 1994.

———. "Just Peacemaking: Theory, Practice, and Prospects." *Journal of the Society of Christian Ethics* 23, no. 1 (2003): 195–212.

———. "Religious Identity, Justice, and Hope: The Case of Peacebuilding." *Criterion* 47, no. 3 (2010): 2–9.

———. "How Should War Be Related to Christian Love?" *Soundings* 97, no. 2 (2014): 186–95.

———. "A Church for Peace? Why Just War Theory Isn't Enough." *Commonweal*, July 11, 2016.

———. *Blessed Are the Peacemakers.* Minneapolis: Fortress Press, 2019.

Caldwell, Dan. *Vortex of Conflict: U.S. Policy toward Afghanistan, Pakistan, and Iraq.* Stanford, CA: Stanford University Press, 2011.

Call, Charles T., and Elizabeth M. Cousens. "Ending Wars and Building Peace: International Responses to War-Torn Societies." *International Studies Perspectives* 9 (2008): 1–21.

Carlson, John D. "Is There a Christian Realist Theory of War and Peace? Reinhold Niebuhr and Just War Thought." *Journal of the Society of Christian Ethics* 28, no. 1 (2008): 133–61.

Carr, Edward H. *The Twenty Years' Crisis 1919–1939: An Introduction to the Study of International Relations.* New York: Palgrave Macmillan, 2001.

Catholic News Service. "Human Dignity, the Common Good, and Solidarity Are 'More than Mere Words,' Bishops say." *America*, November 23, 2016.

Cavanaugh, William. *The Myth of Religious Violence: Secular Ideology and the Roots of Modern Conflict.* Oxford: Oxford University Press, 2009.

Charnovitz, Steve. "Nongovernmental Organizations and International Law." *American Journal of International Law* 100, no. 2 (2006): 348–72.

Chen, Lung-Chu. *An Introduction to Contemporary International Law: A Policy Oriented Perspective.* New Haven: Yale University Press, 2015.

Chesterman, Simon. "Occupation as Liberation: International Humanitarian Law and Regime Change." *Ethics and International Affairs* 18, no. 3 (December 2004): 51–64.

Christiansen, Drew. "Just War in the Twenty-First Century: Nonviolence, Post Bellum Justice, and R2P." *Expositions* 12, no. 1 (2018): 33–59.

Christopher, Paul. *The Ethics of War and Peace.* Upper Saddle River, NJ: Prentice Hall, 2003.

Cicero. *The Republic and the Laws.* Translated by Niall Rudd. Oxford: Oxford University Press, 2009.

Claude, Jr., Inis L. "Toward a Definition of Liberalism." *The Humanist* 17, no. 5 (1957): 259–68.

Clausewitz, Carl von. *On War.* 1832. Edited and translated by Michael Howard and Peter Paret. Princeton: Princeton University Press, 1984.

Collins, Alan. *Contemporary Security Studies.* Oxford: Oxford University Press, 2013.

Comings, Bruce. *The Korean War: A History.* New York: Modern Library, 2010.

Cooley, Alexander. *Base Politics.* Ithaca, NY: Cornell University Press, 2008.

Coomaraswamy, Radhika. *Preventing Conflict, Transforming Justice, Securing the Peace: A Global Study on the Implementation of UNSCR 1325.* New York: UN Women, 2015.

Cortright, David, and George Lopez, eds. *Economic Sanctions: Panacea or Peacekeeping in a Post-Cold War World?* Boulder, CO: Westview Press, 1995.

Crawford, Neta C. "US Budgetary Costs and Obligations of Post-9/11 Wars through FY2020: $6.4 Trillion." *Costs of War,* Watson Institute, Brown University, November 2019.

Crocker, Chester A., Fen Osler Hampson, and Pamela R. Aall, eds. *Turbulent Peace: The Challenges of Managing International Conflict.* Washington, DC: United States Institute of Peace, 2001.

———. *Leashing the Dogs of War: Conflict Management in a Divided World.* Washington, DC: United States Institute of Peace, 2007.

Davies, Brian. *Thomas Aquinas on God and Evil.* Oxford: Oxford University Press, 2011.

DeDominicis, Benedict, and Jaemyung Kim. "Nationalism and Postwar Japanese Society." *Korean Political Science Review* 48, no. 3 (2014): 563–93.

De Gruchy, John W. *Reconciliation: Restoring Justice.* Minneapolis: Fortress Press, 2002.

Dobbins, James. *America's Role in Nation Building: From Germany to Iraq.* Santa Monica, CA: Rand Corporation Publishing, 2003.

Donagan, Alan. *The Theory of Morality.* Chicago: University of Chicago Press, 1977.

Dressler, Joshua. *Understanding Criminal Law.* Durham, NC: Carolina Academic Press, 2022.

Dubois, Heather. "Religion and Peacebuilding: An Ambivalent yet Vital Relationship." *Journal of Religion, Conflict, and Peace* 1, no. 2 (Spring 2008): 1–17.

Durwood, Rosemary, and Lee Marsden, eds. *Religion, Conflict and Military Intervention.* Burlington, VT: Ashgate, 2009.

Elshtain, Jean Bethke. "International Justice as Equal Regard for the Use of Force." *Ethics and International Affairs* 17, no. 2 (September 2003): 63–75.

———. *Just War against Terror: The Burden of American Power in a Violent World.* New York: Basic Books, 2004.

———. "Why Augustine? Why Now?" In *Augustine and Postmodernism: Confessions and Circumfession,* edited by John D. Caputo and Michael J. Scanlon, 244–56. Bloomington: Indiana University Press, 2005.

———. "The Ethics of Fleeing: What America Still Owes Iraq." *World Affairs* 170, no. 4 (Spring 2008): 91–98.

———. "Just War and an Ethics of Responsibility." In *Ethics beyond War's End,* edited by Eric Patterson, 123–44. Washington, DC: Georgetown University Press, 2012.

Enns, Fernando, and Annette Mosher. *Just Peace: Ecumenical, Intercultural, and Interdisciplinary Perspectives.* Eugene, OR: Pickwick Publications, 2013.

Evans, Gareth. *The Responsibility to Protect: Ending Mass Atrocity Crimes Once and For All.* Washington, DC: Brookings Institution Press, 2008.

Evans, Mark. "Balancing Peace, Justice and Sovereignty in Jus Post Bellum: The Case of Just Occupation." *Millennium: Journal of International Studies* 36, no. 3 (2008): 533–54.

———. "Moral Responsibilities and the Conflicting Demands of *Jus Post Bellum.*" *Ethics and International Affairs* 23, no. 2 (Summer 2009): 147–66.

———. "At War's End: Time to Turn to *Jus Post Bellum?*" In *Jus Post Bellum: Mapping the Normative Foundations*, edited by Carsten Stahn, Jennifer S. Easterday, and Jens Iverson, 26–42. Oxford: Oxford University Press, 2014.

Fabre, Cécile. *Cosmopolitan War.* Oxford: Oxford University Press, 2012.

Falk, Richard. *Achieving Human Rights.* New York: Routledge, 2009.

———. "War, War Crimes, Power and Justice: Toward a Jurisprudence of Conscience." *The Asia-Pacific Journal* 10, no. 4 (2012).

Fehr, James. "The Responsibility to Confront Evil: A Pacifist Critique of R2P from the Historic Peace Churches." Unpublished manuscript, accessed October 15, 2020. http://www.dmfk.de/fileadmin/downloads/Responsibility%20to%20Confront%20Evil.pdf.

Feldman, Noah. *What We Owe Iraq: War and the Ethics of Nation Building.* Princeton: Princeton University Press, 2006.

Ferguson, Niall. "Prisoner Taking and Prisoner Killing in the Age of Total War." In *The Barbarization of Warfare*, edited by George Kassimeris, 126–58. New York: New York University Press, 2006.

Fletcher, George. *Rethinking Criminal Law.* Oxford: Oxford University Press, 2000.

Flynn, Jonathan. "No Need to Maximize: Reforming Foreign Criminal Jurisdiction Practice under the U.S.-Japan Status of Forces Agreement." *Military Law Review* 212 (2012): 1–69.

Forster, Reiner, and Mark Mattner. *Civil Society and Peacebuilding: Potential, Limitations and Critical Factors.* Washington, DC: World Bank, 2007.

Fort, Timothy. *Business, Integrity, and Peace.* Cambridge: Cambridge University Press, 2007.

Fox, Gregory H. *Humanitarian Occupation.* Cambridge: Cambridge University Press, 2008.

Freeman, Mark, and Drazan Djukuc, "*Jus Post Bellum* and Transitional Justice." In *Jus Post Bellum: Towards a Law of Transition from Conflict to Peace*, edited by Carsten Stahn and Jann Kleffner, 213–29. The Hague: T.M.C. Asser Press, 2008.

Friedman, Thomas. "Present at . . . What?" Opinion. *New York Times.* February 12, 2003.

Furlong, Gary. *The Conflict Resolution Toolbox.* Mississauga, ON: John Wiley & Sons Canada, 2005.

Galtung, Johan. "Violence, Peace, and Peace Research." *Journal of Peace Research* 6 (1969): 167–91.

Garraway, Charles. "The Relevance of *Jus Post Bellum*: A Practitioner's Perspective." In *Jus Post Bellum: Towards a Law of Transition from Conflict to Peace*, edited by Carsten Stahn and Jann K. Kleffner, 153–62. The Hague: T.M.C. Asser Press, 2008.

Garrett, Geoffrey. "Globalization's Missing Middle." *Foreign Affairs* 83, no. 6 (November/ December 2004): 84–97.

Gentry, Carton, and Amy E. Eckert. *The Future of Just War: New Critical Essays*. Athens, GA: University of Georgia Press, 2014.

George, Robert P., ed. *Natural Law and Moral Inquiry*. Washington, DC: Georgetown University Press, 1998.

Gilkey, Langdon. *On Niebuhr*. Chicago: University of Chicago Press, 2001.

Glennon, Michael. *The Fog of Law: Pragmatism, Security, and International Law*. Stanford, CA: Stanford University Press, 2010.

Grotius, Hugo. *The Law of War and Peace*. Translated by Louise R. Lommis. Roslyn, NY: Walter J. Black, Inc., 1949.

Gustafson, James. *Moral Discernment in the Christian Life*. Louisville: Westminster John Knox, 2007.

Gutierrez, Gustavo. *On Job: God-Talk and the Suffering of the Innocent*. Maryknoll, NY: Orbis Books, 1985.

Hammond, John. "The Bush Doctrine, Preventive War, and International Law." *The Philosophical Forum* 36, no. 1 (2005): 97–111.

Harris, Elise. "The Good Samaritan Isn't Just a Parable, It's a Way of Life, Pope Says." *Catholic News Agency*. July 10, 2016. http://www.catholicnewsagency.com/news/the-good-samaritan-isnt-just-a-parable-its-a-way-of-life-pope-says-85517.

Hass, Richard. *Intervention: The Use of American Military Force in the Post-Cold War World*. Washington, DC: Brookings Institution Press, 1999.

Hayden, Patrick. "Security beyond the State: Cosmopolitanism, Peace and the Role of Just War Theory." In *Just War Theory: A Reappraisal*, edited by Mark Evans, 157–76. Edinburgh: Edinburgh University Press, 2005.

Himes, Kenneth R. "The Morality of Humanitarian Intervention." *Theological Studies* 55, no. 1 (1994): 82–105.

———. "Intervention, Just War, and U.S. National Security." *Theological Studies* 65, no. 1 (2004): 141–57.

———. "Ethics of Exit: The Morality of Withdrawal from Iraq." Excerpted. *The Jesuit Conference*. Fordham University. March 21, 2005. Reprinted, "A Job Half Done." *Foreign Policy* (May-June 2005): 65–66.

———. "Catholic Social Teaching on Building a Just Society: The Need for a Ceiling and a Floor." *Religions* 8 no. 4 (2017).

———. "Humanitarian Intervention and Catholic Political Thought: Moral and Legal Perspectives." *Journal of Catholic Social Thought* 15, no. 1 (2018): 139–69.

———. "The Case of Iraq and the Just War Tradition." The National Institute for the Renewal of the Priesthood. 2002. http://www.jknirparchive.com/himes2.htm.

Himes, Kenneth R., Lisa Sowle Cahill, Charles E. Curran, David Hollenbach, and Thomas Shannon, eds. *Modern Catholic Social Teaching Commentaries and Interpretations.* Washington, DC: Georgetown University Press, 2011.

Hinze, Christine Firer. "Quadragesimo anno." In *Modern Catholic Social Teaching: Commentaries and Interpretations*, edited by Kenneth Himes, Lisa Sowle Cahill, Charles E. Curran, David Hollenbach, and Thomas Shannon, 151–74. Washington, DC: Georgetown University Press, 2011.

Hobbes, Thomas. *Leviathan.* 1651. *With Selected Variants from the Latin Edition of 1668.* Edited by Edwin Curley. Indianapolis: Hackett Publishing, 1994.

Hollenbach, David. *The Common Good and Christian Ethics.* Cambridge: Cambridge University Press, 2002.

Iasiello, Louis V. "*Jus Post Bellum*: The Moral Responsibilities of Victors in War." *Naval War College Review* 57, no. 3/4 (Summer/Autumn 2004): 33–52.

Iké, Fred Charles. *Every War Must End.* New York: Columbia University Press, 2005.

John, Paul II. *Catechism of the Catholic Church.* 2nd ed. Washington, DC: United States Catholic Conference, 2011.

Johnson, James T. *Morality and Contemporary Warfare.* New Haven: Yale University Press, 1999.

———. "The Just War, As It Was and Is." *First Things* (January 2005).

Johnston, Douglas. "Introduction: Beyond Power Politicism." In *Religion: The Missing Dimensions of Statecraft*, edited by Douglas Johnston and Cynthia Sampson, 3–7. Oxford: Oxford University Press, 1994.

———. "Faith-Based Organizations: The Religious Dimensions of Peacebuilding." In *People Building Peace II: Successful Stories of Civil Society*, edited by Paul van Tongeren, Malin Brenk, Marte Hellema, and Juliette Verhoeven, 239–43. Boulder, CO: Lynne Rienner Publishers, 2005.

Kadish, Sanford H., Stephen J. Schulhofer, and Carol S. Steiker. *Criminal Law.* 9th ed. New York: Wolters Kluwer, 2012.

Kant, Immanuel. *Perpetual Peace and Other Essays.* 1795. Translated by Ted Humphrey. Indianapolis: Hackett Publishing Company, 2003.

———. *The Metaphysical Elements of Justice.* 1797. Translated by John Ladd. Indianapolis: Hackett Publishing Company, 1999.

Keane, Philip. *Catholicism and Health-Care Justice: Problems, Potential, and Solutions.* New York: Paulist, 2002.

Kellogg, Davida E. "*Jus Post Bellum*: The Importance of War Crimes Trials." *Parameters* 32, no. 3 (Autumn 2002): 87–99.

Kirchhoffer, David G. "Benedict XVI, Human Dignity, and Absolute Moral Norms." *New Blackfriars* 91, no. 1035 (September 2010): 586–608.

Kwon, David C. "Human Security: Revisiting Michael Schuck's Augustinian and Kenneth Himes's Thomistic Approaches to Jus Post Bellum." *Journal for Peace and Justice Studies* 29, no. 2 (2020): 3–24.

Lederach, John Paul. *Building Peace: Sustainable Reconciliation in Divided Societies*. Washington, DC: United States Institute of Peace, 1997.

———. "Civil Society and Reconciliation." In *Turbulent Peace: The Challenge of Rebuilding War-Torn Societies*, edited by Chester A. Crocker, Fen Osler Hampson, and Pamela R. Aall, 841–55. Washington, DC: United States Institute of Peace, 2001.

———. *The Little Book of Conflict Transformation*. Intercourse, PA: Good Books, 2003.

———. "The Long Road Back to Humanity: Catholic Peacebuilding with Armed Actors." In *Peacebuilding: Catholic Theology, Ethics, and Praxis*, edited by Robert J. Schreiter, R. Scott Appleby, and Gerard F. Powers, 23–55. Maryknoll, NY: Orbis Books, 2010.

———. *When Blood and Bones Cry Out*. Oxford: Oxford University Press, 2010.

Licklider, Roy. "Obstacles to Peace Settlements." In *Turbulent Peace: The Challenge of Rebuilding War-Torn Societies*, edited by Chester A. Crocker, Fen Osler Hampson, and Pamela R. Aall, 697–718. Washington, DC: United States Institute of Peace, 2001.

Love, Maryann Cusimano. "What Kind of Peace Do We Seek?" In *Peacebuilding: Catholic Theology, Ethics, and Praxis*, edited by Robert J. Schreiter, R. Scott Appleby, and Gerard F. Powers. Maryknoll, NY: Orbis Books, 2010.

Luban, David, Julie R. O'Sullivan, and David P. Stewart. *International and Transnational Criminal Law*. New York: Wolters Kluwer, 2010.

Mac Ginty, Roger, and Oliver P. Richmond. "The Local Turn in Peacebuilding: A Critical Agenda for Peace." *The Third World Quarterly* 34, no. 5 (2013): 763–83.

Massaro, Thomas, and Thomas Shannon. *Catholic Perspectives on Peace and War*. New York: Sheed and Ward, 2003.

May, Larry. *War Crimes and Just War*. Cambridge: Cambridge University Press, 2006.

———. *After War Ends: A Philosophical Perspective*. Cambridge: Cambridge University Press, 2012.

———. "*Jus Post Bellum*: Proportionality and the Fog of War." *The European Journal of International Law* 24, no. 1 (2013): 315–33.

———. "*Jus Post Bellum*, Grotius, and *Meionexia*." In *Jus Post Bellum: Mapping the Normative Foundations*, edited by Carsten Stahn, Jennifer S. Easterday, and Jens Iverson, 15–25. Oxford: Oxford University Press, 2014.

———. *Contingent Pacifism: Revisiting Just War Theory*. Cambridge: Cambridge University Press, 2015.

May, Larry, and Elizabeth Edenberg, eds. *Jus Post Bellum and Transitional Justice*. Cambridge: Cambridge University Press, 2015.

McCarthy, Eli S. *Becoming Nonviolent Peacemakers: A Virtue Ethic for Catholic Social Teaching and U.S. Policy*. Eugene, OR: Wipf and Stock, 2012.

McCready, Doug. "Ending the War Right: *Jus Post Bellum* and the Just War Tradition." *Journal of Military Ethics* 8, no.1 (January 2009): 66–78.

Meernik, James. "Victor's Justice or the Law?" *The Journal of Conflict Resolution* 47, no. 2 (April 2003): 140–62.

Miller, Richard B. *Interpretations of Conflict: Ethics, Pacifism, and the Just War Tradition*. Chicago: University of Chicago Press, 1991.

Mueller, John. *Retreat from Doomsday: The Obsolescence of Major War*. New York: Basic Books, 1989.

———. *The Remnants of War: Cornell Studies in Security Affairs*. Ithaca, NY: Cornell University Press, 2007.

Murdie, Amanda M., and David R. Davis. "Shaming and Blaming: Using Events Data to Assess the Impact of Human Rights INGOs." *International Studies Quarterly* 56, no. 1 (2012): 1–16.

Murphy, Colleen. Review of *Just and Unjust Peace: An Ethic of Political Reconciliation*, by Daniel Philpott. *Ethics* 123, no. 3 (April 2013): 577–81.

———. "Political Reconciliation, *Jus Post Bellum*, and Asymmetric Conflict." *Theoria* 62, no. 4 (December 2015): 43–59.

Murphy, Jeffrie. "Legal Moralism and Retribution Revisited." *Criminal Law and Philosophy* 1, no. 1 (2007): 5–20.

Niebuhr, Reinhold. *The Irony of the American History*. New York: Charles Scribner's Sons, 1952.

———. *Moral Man and Immoral Society*. New York: Charles Scribner's Sons, 1960.

———. *The Nature and Destiny of Man: Human Destiny*. Louisville: Westminster John Knox, 1964.

———. *The Nature and Destiny of Man: Human Nature*. Louisville: Westminster John Knox, 1964.

———. *Love and Justice: Selected from the Shorter Writings of Reinhold* Niebuhr. Edited by D. B. Robertson. Cleveland: The World Publishing Company, 1967.

———. *An Interpretation of Christian Ethics*. New York: Seabury Press, 1979.

Notaras, Mark, and Vesselin Popovski. "The Responsibility to Protect." *United Nations University*. April 5, 2011. http://unu.edu/publications/articles/ responsibility-to-protect-and-the-protection-of-civilians.html.

O'Donovan, Oliver. *The Just War Revisited: Current Issues in Theology*. Cambridge: Cambridge University Press, 2003.

O'Keefe, Roger. *International Criminal Law*. Oxford: Oxford University Press, 2015.

Orend, Brian. "Terminating Wars and Establishing Global Governance." *Canadian Journal of Law and Jurisprudence* 12, no. 2 (July 1999): 253–95.

———. "Jus Post Bellum." *Journal of Social Philosophy* 31, no. 1 (Spring 2000): 117–37.

———. *War and International Justice: A Kantian Perspective*. Waterloo, ON: Wilfrid Laurier University Press, 2000.

———. *Michael Walzer on War and Justice*. Montreal: McGill-Queen's University Press, 2001.

———. "Justice after War." *Ethics and International Affairs* 16, no.1 (March 2002): 43–56.

———. "Kant's Ethics of War and Peace." *Journal of Military Ethics* 3, no. 2 (2004): 161–77.

———. "*Jus Post Bellum*: The Perspective of a Just War Theorist." *Leiden Journal of International Law* 20 (2007): 571–91.

———. "*Jus Post Bellum*: A Just War Theory Perspective." In *Jus Post Bellum: Towards a Law of Transition from Conflict to Peace*, edited by Carsten Stahn and Jann K. Kleffner, 31–52. The Hague: T.M.C. Asser Press, 2008.

———. "Justice after War: Toward a New Geneva Convention." Lecture given at *Ending Wars Well: Just War Theory and Conflict's End*, Berkeley Center at Georgetown University, Washington, DC, April 22, 2010. https://berkleycenter.georgetown.edu/events/ending-wars-well-just-war-theory-and-conflict-s-end.

———. "Justice after War: Toward a New Geneva Convention." In *Ethics beyond War's End*, edited by Eric Patterson, 175–96. Washington, DC: Georgetown University Press, 2012.

———. *The Morality of War*. Buffalo, NY: Broadview Press, 2013.

Osterdahl, Inger. "What Will *Jus Post Bellum* Mean? Of New Wine and Old Bottles." *Journal of Conflict and Security Law* 14, no. 175 (June 1, 2009): 175–207.

Paris, Roland. "Wilson's Ghost: The Faulty Assumptions of Postconflict Peacebuilding." In *Turbulent Peace: The Challenge of Rebuilding War-Torn Societies*, edited by Chester A. Crocker, Fen Osler Hampson, and Pamela R. Aall, 765–84. Washington, DC: United States Institute of Peace, 2001.

Patterson, Eric. *Just War Thinking: Morality and Pragmatism in the Struggle against Contemporary Threats*. New York: Lexington Books, 2009.

———. *Ethics beyond War's End*. Washington, DC: Georgetown University Press, 2012.

———. *Ending Wars Well: Order, Justice, and Conciliation in Contemporary Post-Conflict*. New Haven: Yale University Press, 2014.

Pensky, Max. "*Jus Post Bellum* and Amnesties." In *Jus Post Bellum and Transitional Justice*, edited by Larry May, 152–77. Cambridge: Cambridge University Press, 2016.

Petallides, Constantine. "International Law Reconsidered: Is International Law Actually Law?" *Inquiries Journal* 4, no 12 (2012).

Phan, Peter. C. "Catholic Social Thought." *Message of the Fathers of the Church* 20. Wilmington, NC: Glazier, 1984.

Phillipson, Coleman. *The International Law and Custom of Ancient Greece and Rome*, Vol. 2. London: MacMillian, 1911.

Philpott, Daniel. "Lessons in Mercy: Justice and Reconciliation in the Aftermath of Atrocities." *America*. May 4, 2009.

———. "An Ethic of Political Reconciliation," *Ethics and International Affairs* 23, no. 4 (December 2009): 389–407.

———. "Reconciliation: A Catholic Ethic for Peacebuilding in the Political Order." In *Peacebuilding: Catholic Theology, Ethics, and Praxis*, edited by Robert J. Schreiter, R. Scott Appleby, and Gerard F. Powers, 221–39. Maryknoll, NY: Orbis Books, 2010.

———. *Just and Unjust Peace: An Ethic of Political Reconciliation*. Oxford: Oxford University Press, 2012.

———. "An Ethic of Political Reconciliation." Lecture given at *Key Issues in Religion and World Affairs*, Institute on Culture, Religion & World Affairs, Boston University, Boston, MA, January 30, 2015. https://www.bu.edu/cura/files/2013/10/Philpott-Summary-of-CURA-Talk1.pdf.

Philpott, Daniel, and Gerard F. Powers. *Strategies of Peace: Transforming Conflict in a Violent World*. New York: Oxford University Press, 2010.

Plato. *Laws*. Translated by Benjamin Jowett. New York: Prometheus Books, 2000.

Pope, Stephen. J. "The Convergence of Forgiveness and Justice: Lessons from El Salvador." *Theological Studies 64* (2003): 812–35.

Porter, Jean. *The Recovery of Virtue*. Louisville: Westminster John Knox, 1990.

Powers, Gerard F. "Our Moral Duty in Iraq." *America* 198, no. 5 (February 18, 2008): 13–17.

———. "Catholic Peacebuilding." In *A Vision of Justice: Engaging Catholic Social Teaching on the College Campus*, edited by Susan Crawford Sullivan and Ron Pagnucco, 113–37. Wilmington, NC: Glazier, 2014.

Rauter, Thomas. *Judicial Practice, Customary International Criminal Law and Nullum Crimen Sine Lege*. New York: Springer, 2017.

Rawls, John. *A Theory of Justice*. Cambridge, MA: Harvard University Press, 1999.

Reichberg, Gregory M. "Is There a 'Presumption Against War' in Aquinas's Ethics?" In *Ethics, Nationalism, and Just War: Medieval and Contemporary Perspectives*, edited by Henrik Syse and Gregory M. Reichberg, 72–98. Washington, DC: The Catholic University of America Press, 2007.

———. *Thomas Aquinas on War and Peace*. Cambridge: Cambridge University Press. 2019.

Roberts, Adam. "The End of Occupation: Iraq 2004." *The International and Comparative Law Quarterly* 54, no. 1 (January 2005): 27–48.

——. "Transformative Military Occupation: Applying the Laws of War and Human Rights." *American Journal of International Law* 100, no. 3 (2006): 580–622.

Rogers, Mark M., Tom Bamat, and Julie Ideh, eds. *Pursuing Just Peace: An Overview and Case Studies for Faith-Based Peacebuilders*. Baltimore: Catholic Relief Services, 2008. https://www.crs.org/sites/default/files/tools-research/pursuing-just-peace.pdf.

Rorty, Amelie, and James Schmidt, eds. *Kant's Idea for a Universal History with a Cosmopolitan Aim: A Critical Guide*. Cambridge: Cambridge University Press, 2009.

Rose, Gideon. *How Wars End: Why We Always Fight the Last Battle*. New York: Simon & Schuster, 2010.

Royal, Robert. "In My Beginning Is My End." In *Ethics beyond War's End*, edited by Eric Patterson, 65–76. Washington, DC: Georgetown University Press, 2012.

Samaha, Joel. *Criminal Law*. Belmont, CA: Wadsworth, 2011.

Sassoli, Marco. "State Responsibility for Violations of International Humanitarian Law." *International Review of the Red Cross* 84, no. 846 (June 2002): 401–34.

——. "Legislation and Maintenance of Public Order and Civil Life by Occupying Powers." *European Journal of International Law* 16, no. 4 (September 2005): 661–94.

Sato, Yoichiro, and See Seng Tan, eds. *United States Engagement in the Asia Pacific: Perspectives from Asia*. New York: Cambria Press, 2015.

Scheers, Ivar. "Peacekeeping and *Jus Post Bellum*." *The Central European Journal of International and Security Studies* 5, no. 3 (March 2011): 75–119.

Scheid, Anna Florke. *Just Revolution: A Christian Ethic of Political Resistance and Social Transformation*. New York: Lexington Books, 2015.

——. "Just War Theory and Res torative Justice: Weaving a Consistent Ethic of Reconciliation." *Journal of Moral Theology* 5, no. 2 (2016): 99–115.

Schlabach, Gerald, ed. *Just Policing, Not War: An Alternative Response to World Violence*. Collegeville, MN: Liturgical Press, 2007.

Schreiter, Robert J. *Reconciliation: Mission and Ministry in a Changing Social Order*. Maryknoll, NY: Orbis Books, 1992.

——. *The Ministry of Reconciliation: Spirituality and Strategy*. Maryknoll, NY: Orbis Books, 2008.

——. "Future Directions in Catholic Peacebuilding." In *Peacebuilding: Catholic Theology, Ethics, and Praxis*, edited by Robert J. Schreiter, R. Scott Appleby, and Gerard F. Powers, 421–48. Maryknoll, NY: Orbis Books, 2010.

Schreiter, Robert J., R. Scott Appleby, and Gerard F. Powers, eds. *Peacebuilding: Catholic Theology, Ethics, and Praxis*. Maryknoll, NY: Orbis Books, 2010.

Schuck, Michael. "When the Shooting Stops: Missing Elements in Just War Theory." *Christian Century* 111, no. 30 (1994): 982–84.

Sharma, Serena. "Reconsidering the *Jus Ad Bellum / Jus In Bello* Distinction." In *Jus Post Bellum: Towards a Law of Transition from Conflict to Peace*, edited by Carsten Stahn and Jann K. Kleffner, 9–30. The Hague: T.M.C. Asser Press, 2008.

Shogimen, Takashi, and Vicki A Spencer. *Visions of Peace: Asia and the West*. Farnham, Surrey, UK: Ashgate, 2014.

Shore, Megan. "Christianity and Justice in the South African Truth and Reconciliation Commission: A Case Study in Religious Conflict Resolution." *Political Theology* 9, no. 2 (April 2008): 161–78.

Smock, David. "Catholic Contributions to International Peace." Special Report 69. Washington, DC: United States Institute of Peace, 2001.

Sobrino, Jon. *The Principle of Mercy: Taking the Crucified People from the Cross*. Maryknoll, NY: Orbis Books, 1994.

Solis, Gary. *The Law of Armed Conflict: International Humanitarian Law in War*. Cambridge: Cambridge University Press, 2010.

Sonnenberg, Dale, and Donald A. Timm. "The Agreements Regarding Status of Foreign Forces in Japan." In *The Handbook of the Law of Visiting Forces*, edited by Dieter Fleck, 379–420. Oxford: Oxford University Press, 2001.

Stahn, Carsten. "'*Jus ad bellum*', '*jus in bello*' . . . '*jus post bellum*'?—Rethinking the Conception of the Law of Armed Force." *European Journal of International Law* 17, no. 5 (November 2006): 921–44.

———. "The Future of *Jus Post Bellum*." In *Jus Post Bellum: Towards a Law of Transition from Conflict to Peace*, edited by Carsten Stahn and Jann K. Kleffner, 231–38. The Hague: T.M.C. Asser Press, 2008.

Stassen, Glen, ed. *Just Peacemaking: Ten Practices for Abolishing War*. Cleveland: The Pilgrim Press, 2004.

———. Review of *Just and Unjust Peace*, by Daniel Philpott. *Journal of the Society of Christian Ethics* 33, no. 2 (Fall/Winter 2013): 211–12.

Stassen, Glen, Mark Thiessen Nation, and Matt Hamsher, eds. *The War of the Lamb: The Ethics of Nonviolence and Peacemaking*. Grand Rapids: Baker Books, 2009.

Stohr, Mary, and Anthony Walsh, *Corrections: The Essentials*. London: Sage Publications, 2012.

Stokkom, Bas van, Neelke Doorn, and Paul van Tongeren. "Public Forgiveness." In *Public Forgiveness in Post-conflict Contexts*, edited by Bas van Stokkom, Neelke Doorn, and Paul van Tongeren, 1–24. Cambridge: Intersentia, 2012.

Sutch, Peter and Juanita Elias, *International Relations: The Basics*. New York: Routledge, 2007.

Tabensky, Pedro Alexis. "Realistic Idealism: An Aristotelian Alternative to Machiavellian International Relations." *Theoria* 113 (August 2007): 97–111.

Taylor, Sandie. *Crime and Criminality: A Multidisciplinary Approach*. New York: Routledge, 2015.

Teitel, Ruti G. "Transitional Justice Genealogy." *Harvard Human Rights Journal* 16 (2003): 69–94.

Thistlewaite, Susan, and Glen Stassen. "Abrahamic Alternatives to War: Jewish, Christian, and Muslim Perspective on Just Peacemaking." Special Report 214. Washington, DC: United States Institute of Peace, 2008.

Tomasi, Silvano. "Time to Act: Church Teaches Duty to Intervene to Prevent Genocide." *Catholic News Service*, August 12, 2014.

Tutu, Desmond. *No Future without Forgiveness.* New York: Doubleday, 1999.

Villa-Vicencio, Charles. *Walk with Us and Listen: Political Reconciliation in Africa.* Washington, DC: Georgetown University Press, 2009.

Waltz, Kenneth. *Man, the State, and War.* New York: Columbia University Press. 2001.

Walzer, Michael. *Just and Unjust Wars.* New York: Basic Books, 2000.

———. "The Triumph of Just War Theory (and the Dangers of Success)." *Social Research* 69, no. 4: International Justice, War Crimes, and Terrorism: The U.S. Record (Winter 2002): 925–44.

———. "Just and Unjust Occupations." *Dissent.* Winter 2004.

———. "The Aftermath of War: Reflections on *Jus Post Bellum.*" In *Ethics beyond War's End*, edited by Eric Patterson, 35–46. Washington, DC: Georgetown University Press, 2012.

Weiss, Thomas, and David P. Forsythe, eds. *The United Nations and Changing World Politics.* Boulder, CO: Westview Press, 1997.

Westing, Arthur H. *Arthur H. Westing: Pioneer on the Environmental Impact of War.* Edited by Hans Günter Brach. New York: Springer, 2013.

Westra, Joel. *International Law and the Use of Armed Force: The UN Charter and the Major Powers.* New York: Routledge, 2007.

Wetherall, William. "The Girard and Kupski Cases: Extraterritoriality and Jurisdiction in Post-occupation Japan." *Yosha Bunko*, August 20, 2016. Accessed October 15, 2020. http://www.yoshabunko.com/anthropology/Girard_and_Kupsik_cases.html.

Wheeler, Nicholas. *Saving Strangers: Humanitarian Intervention in International Society.* New York: Oxford University Press, 2003.

Williams, Robert E., and Dan Caldwell. "*Jus Post Bellum*: Just War Theory and the Principles of Just Peace." *International Studies Perspectives* 7, no. 4 (November 2006): 309–20.

Winright, Tobias. "Just Policing and the Responsibility to Protect." *The Ecumenical Review* 63, no. 1 (March 2011): 84–95.

Winright, Tobias, and Laurie Johnston, eds. *Can War Be Just in the 21st Century?* Maryknoll, NY: Orbis Books, 2015.

Wogaman, J. Philip. *Christian Ethics: A Historical Introduction.* Louisville: Westminster John Knox, 1993.

Wright, Karen Shields. "The Principle of Catholic Social Teaching: A Guide for Decision Making from Daily Clinical Encounters to National Policy-Making." *Linacre Quarterly* 84, no. 1 (February 2017): 10–22.

Index

A

accountability, 29, 59, 65, 111, 132, 169, 190, 202, 227

actors, just, 100–108, 111–20, 151; in Aquinas, 185–86; classical, 196–97; in Fehr, 92–93; good and, 151–52; imperfect, 184; maximalism and, 138; meionexia and, 66; minimalism and, 83; moral principles and, 82; nonclassical, 196–97; overreach by, 97; peace and, 46; in Philpott, 134–35; policing and, 163–64, 163n4, 182–87; political participation and, 78; punishment and, 73; repentance and, 98; reprisals and, 27n38; in Scheid, 139; scope of, 146–47; security and, 68; types of, 145–46

Afghanistan, 2, 38, 40–41, 43, 54, 85, 168, 171–72, 186n57, 221, 237, 240, 261

Aftermath, The (film), 1

Allman, Mark, 24, 81, 83, 85, 107, 107n70, 108–19, 121–23, 132–33, 138–39, 145, 151, 156–57, 189, 246, 263, 265

America's Role in Nation Building (Caldwell), 172

anarchy, 69

Appleby, Scott, 246n55

Aquinas, Thomas, xi, 13, 19–26, 20n19, 24n32, 26, 32, 41–44, 44n73, 65n40, 83, 99, 104–8, 185–87, 187n60, 250n63, 266

Arend, Anthony Clark, 193

Argentina, 122

Aristotle, 13–18, 41, 43–44, 151, 218, 262

arms control, 9, 163–66, 170, 175, 183

asymmetric warfare, 8, 71n53, 239n35

Augustine, 13n1, 19–20, 23–25, 63, 83, 94, 94n32, 96–99, 118, 145, 266

authority, 20–21, 25–26, 36–38, 53, 99–108, 162, 177, 179, 192, 195–96, 198n26, 219–20, 234–35

Ayers, James, 165–66, 175, 175n31, 194n17

B

Ban, Kimoon, 53n8

Beck, Robert, 193

Bellamy, Alex, 49, 52, 54–56, 60–61, 68

Benedict XVI, Pope, 89, 234n19

Benvenisti, Eyal, 200–202

Bercovitch, Jacob, 241

Beyer, Anna Cornelia, 254–55

Bhuta, Nehal, 202–4, 206

Biggar, Nigel, 184, 185n51

Boniface, 96

Building Peace: Sustainable Reconciliation in Divided Societies (Lederach), 229

Bush, George W., 238

C

Cahill, Lisa Sowle, 84, 231, 268

Caldwell, Dan, 73n55, 170–73, 176, 180, 205

Call, Charles T., 237

Cammett, Melani, 238

Carlson, John D., 117

Catholic Social Teaching (CST), 154–55, 232–35, 246

CBOs. See community-based organizations (CBOs)

Challenge of Peace, The (US Catholic Bishops), 108

charity, 24n32, 154–55, 158, 250n63

Chen, Lung-Chu, 191n4

Chesterton, G. K., xi

Christiansen, Drew, 2

citizenship, 74

civil society organizations (CSOs), 226–30, 239–42, 244, 253–58, 266–68

civil war, 8, 38, 136, 203, 242n42

Clausewitz, Carl von, 175n32

closure, 28–31, 242n42

communitarianism, 32, 35–36, 61, 74, 233, 233n16

community-based organizations (CBOs), 228

Compendium of the Social Doctrine of the Church, 164

compensation, 29–31, 37–38, 45, 74–75, 112

conservation, 197–200, 222

Cousens, Elizabeth M., 237

crimes against humanity, 51, 51n3, 52, 78, 136, 208n56, 219, 220n91

CSOs. *See* civil society organizations (CSOs)

CST. *See* Catholic Social Teaching (CST)

Cusimano Love, Maryann, 84

D

Davis, David R., 256–57

death penalty, 219

demilitarization, 38–39, 76–77

democracy, 28–29, 51, 70, 79, 84, 135, 200n35, 232, 238–39

Deuteronomy, book of, 134n26, 153

dignity, 44, 88–89, 93, 95, 105n62, 106, 152, 155, 185, 194, 224, 233–34, 234n19, 246

discrimination, 27, 30, 33, 36–37, 75, 77, 82, 97, 192

Djukuc, Drazan, 218

Dobbins, James, 172–73, 175–76, 179–80, 205

Donagan, Alan, 65n40

E

East Timor, 168, 199, 222

Elias, Juanita, 35

El Salvador, 242

Elshtain, Jean Bethke, 58–60, 70–71, 75–76, 79, 140, 184–85

Emperor (film), 1

empiricism, 115

Enns, Fernando, 232n12

environmental threats, 95

ethnic cleansing, 51–52, 51n3, 78, 208n56

Evans, Mark, 4n3, 46, 49, 56–57, 61–65, 78

evil, 20, 22, 63, 98, 116, 118–19, 126–27, 127n10, 133–34, 144, 153, 185–86, 214, 231, 233, 254

evil peace, 19

F

faith-based organizations (FBOs), 226, 240–46, 253–58

Falklands War, 122

Fehr, James, 91–93

Feldman, Noah, 173–80, 205, 219

Fletcher, George, 215n75

forgiveness, 18, 62, 64–65, 67, 83, 99, 126, 129–32, 134, 138–39, 245

"Forming Consciences for Faithful Citizenship," 164

Fox, Gregory, 200, 206n52

Francis, Pope, 2, 89–90, 154

Freeman, Mark, 137n30, 217–18

free will, 98, 184

Friedman, Thomas, 57n19

functionalism, 71

G

Galtung, Johan, 14n3

Garraway, Charles, 194, 194n17

Gaudium et Spes (Second Vatican Council), 164, 233n16

Genesis, book of, 127, 190

Geneva Convention, 31, 38–39, 45, 189–90, 192, 197, 204, 221n93

genocide, 8, 27n38, 51–52, 51n3, 52n3, 78, 92, 134n25, 136, 208n56, 209n61, 219

Germany, 135, 173, 213n67, 219–20, 223

God: evil and, 126–27; good and, 22, 105; image and likeness of, 155; mercy and, 126; neighbor love and, 186–87; peace and, 183n46; reconciliation with, 182–87; right relationships and, 134n25; will and, 21–22

Golden Rule, 153

good: in Aquinas, 24; God and, 22, 105; in Himes, 100; just actors and, 151–52; minimalism and, 147–53; policing and, 175–76, 178–87; war and, 17

Good Samaritan, 154

Grotius, Hugo, xi, 14, 14n3, 54

Guatemala, 241–42, 242n42
Gulf War, 30. *See also* Iraq

H

Hague Convention, 103n54, 190, 190n1, 192, 197–98, 198n26
Haiti, 101–2
Hart, H. L. A., 214, 215n72
Hass, Richard, 177
Hayden, Patrick, 195
Hehir, Thomas, xi
Herodotus, 15
Himes, Kenneth, 13n1, 83, 90, 99–108, 119–20, 135–36, 145, 148, 150–51, 181, 187–88, 227, 233, 233n16, 234n17, 246, 265, 268–69
Hobbes, Thomas, 57
holistic approach, 108–12
HSU. *See* Human Security Unit (HSU)
hubris, 58–59
human rights, 33–34, 72–73, 130, 169, 193–96
Human Security Unit (HSU), 1–2
Hussein, Saddam, 219

I

Iasiello, Louis, 155
ICC. *See* International Criminal Court (ICC)
idealistic realism, 128n14
Iké, Fred Charles, 175n32
intention, 21, 43, 94, 96, 98–100, 105–7, 105n62, 109, 115–16, 119–20, 139, 186–87, 263
International Commission on Intervention and State Sovereignty (ICISS), 51–53
International Criminal Court (ICC), 51n3, 208, 219, 221–22
International Criminal Tribunal for Yugoslavia (ICTY), 209n61
International Law of Occupation, The (Benvenisti), 200
Iraq, 2, 30, 85, 87, 89, 94, 102–5, 108, 135, 174, 199, 219–20, 222, 238–39, 261

Isaiah, book of, 154, 183n46
Islam, 65, 153, 239, 245
Islamic State (ISIS), 89
Israel, 183n46

J

Japan, 135, 173, 211, 213n67, 219, 223, 239n35
Jeremiah, book of, 134n25
John Paul II, Pope, 87–88, 119, 122, 155
Johnson, James Turner, 22
Johnston, Douglas, 241
John XXIII, Pope, 235
jpb. See jus post bellum
Judaism, 152–53
jus ad bellum, xi, 2; intention and, 43, 98; *jus post bellum vs.*, 149; just cause and, 103; in Orend, 32, 113–15; peacemaking and, 110; punishment and, 210–12; Responsibility to Protect and, 52; in Schuck, 94; violation of, 42, 117, 210–12; in Walzer, 27
jus in bello, xi, xii, 2; intention and, 43; *jus post bellum vs.*, 149; in McCready, 95n32; in Orend, 32, 115; punishment and, 210–12; in Schuck, 94; violation of, 42, 117, 210–12; in Walzer, 27; war crimes and, 75
jus post bellum (jpb), 2; Aquinas and, 19–26; Aristotle and, 13–18; ethical minimalism and, 7; foundational questions in, 47; foundational sources in, 13–41; foundational themes of, 41–47, 68–80; Himes and, 101–8, 119–20, 150–51; holistic approach to, 109–11; *jus ad bellum vs.*, 149; *jus in bello vs.*, 149; justice *vs.*, 8n5; liberal foundation of, 50–53; moral philosophy of, 49–80; moral theology of, 81–157; Niebuhrian approach to, 116–19; Orend and, 31–41; peace and, 46; peacebuilding of, 231–35; phases of, 111–12; Philpott and, 124–36; political reconciliation and, 121–57; precedent for, xi; Scheers and,

167–68; Scheid and, 137–40; Schuck and, 94–99; scope of, 210–22; security and, 7; as third element of just war theory, 41–45; transformative, 199; transitional justice *vs.*, 122; Walzer and, 26–31

Just and Unjust Peace (Philpott), 125

Just and Unjust Wars (Walzer), 26

just cause, 21, 26–27, 60, 99–103, 106–9, 111–16, 139n36, 148–49, 238, 263, 269

justice: in Aquinas, 24–25; battlefield, 42–43; common-good-seeking, 154–57; criminal, 212–13; democracy and, 28–29, 135; general, 24n34; imperfect, 108–9; *jus post bellum vs.*, 8n5; just war tradition and, 7; love and, 249–52; maximalism and, 72; in Orend, 39–40; particular, 24n34; peace and, 20, 23; in Philpott, 125–26, 152; political reconciliation and, 121–24; postwar, xii–xiii, 67, 84, 121–24; rectificatory concept of, 57; religious basis as not required for, 105n62; restorative, 65, 127, 132, 136; retributive, 138, 214–15; transitional, xii–xiii, 66–67, 84, 121–24, 232n12; utilitarian, 213–17; victor's, 75, 218

just war: norms and, xii; verification phases for, 42

just war theory: in Carlson, 117; in Elshtain, 58–59; *jus post bellum* as third element of, 41–45; pacifism *vs.*, 109; peace and, 110–11; peacebuilding *vs.*, 231; in Scheid, 141

just war tradition (JWT), 2; in Aquinas, 21–22; development of, 6; justice and, 7

K

Kadayifci-Orellana, S. Ayse, 241

Kant, Immanuel, xi, 34–35, 35n59, 50n2, 63, 65n40, 70–71, 78–80, 115–16, 215n76

Kellogg, Davida, 213–14

Kent, James, 1

Korean War, 178, 211n64

Kosovo, 168, 199, 222

L

law: in Aquinas, 20, 20n19, 25; defined, 20; eternal, 20; humanitarian, 191–96, 206–7; human rights, 193–96; international, 190–97, 194n15, 206–9, 221; natural, 20–21, 65n40, 88, 217, 217n83, 224, 234; occupation, 190, 197–206; rule of, 191–222

Lederach, John Paul, 228n3, 229–30, 229n5, 243–44

Leebaw, Bronwyn, 137n30

legitimacy, local, 28–29, 45

Leo XIII, Pope, 154–55

Leviathan (Hobbes), 57, 69

Leviticus, book of, 153

liberal foundation, 50–53

LIC. *See* Low Intensity Conflict (LIC)

Locke, John, 50n2

love, 96, 126, 152–53, 184–87, 187n60, 249–52

Low Intensity Conflict (LIC), 165–66, 194, 269

Luke, Gospel of, 19, 153–54

M

Mac Ginty, Roger, 236–37, 259

Matthew, Gospel of, 19, 134n25, 152, 154

maximalism, 49, 119; in Allman and Winright, 118–19; in Bellamy, 54–56; just policing and, 175; limits of, 72; minimalism *vs.*, 82–83; redefining, 56–68; in Scheid, 138–39; in Walzer, 60n26, 148n44

May, Larry, 4n3, 64–66, 73, 83

McCarthy, Eli, 84, 110

McCready, Doug, 95n32

meionexia, 65–66, 73, 216

mercy, 83, 111, 121, 125–26, 132–34, 137–38, 140, 270

Military Operations Other Than War (MOOTW), 9, 165–66

Miller, Richard, 23n28

Milosevic, Slobodan, 219
minimalism: in Bellamy, 54–56, 61, 67–68; defining, 82; in Elshtain, 70; good and, 147–53; loose, 148n44; maximalism of, 143–57; in moral philosophy, 54–68; in Orend, 60, 67, 79; in Patterson, 69–70; redefining, 56–68; in Walzer, 31, 33–34, 60–61, 60n26, 67
mission creep, 63, 166
Moore, Michael, 215n72, 215n76
MOOTW. *See* Military Operations Other Than War (MOOTW)
moral philosophy, 49–80
Moral Responsibilities and the Conflicting Demands of Jus Post Bellum (Evans), 61–62
moral theology, 81–157
Mosher, Annette, 232n12
multinational operations, policing and, 178–81
Murdie, Amanda M., 256–57
Murphy, Colleen, 133, 137n30
Murray, John Courtney, xii

N
nation-building, 161–64, 167–68, 170–82, 187–89, 197, 226, 232, 238, 264, 268
natural law, 20–21, 65n40, 88, 217, 217n83, 224, 234
Nature and Destiny of Man, The (Niebuhr), 265–66
Nicomachean Ethics (Aristotle), 17
Niebuhr, Reinhold, 83, 108–9, 113, 156, 227, 246–58, 247n57, 250n66, 260n91, 265–66
noncombatant immunity, 27n38
Noriega, Manuel, 101–2
norms, xii, 50–51, 68–69, 81–82, 147–53
Nuremberg trials, 14
Nygren, Anders, 265

O
occupation, 30, 39, 55, 62–63, 171, 174, 190–92, 196–207, 210–11, 222–23

order, 58, 70–71, 174
Orend, Brian, 4, 4n3, 13, 30–43, 36n61, 40n68, 50, 60–61, 67–68, 70–71, 73n55, 75–77, 79, 107–8, 112–15, 117–18, 129–30, 140, 148n45, 189–90, 214–15, 214n70
Osterdahl, Inger, 204–6

P
Panama, 101–2
participation, political, 3–5, 7, 9, 26, 41, 47; in Aquinas, 25; Catholic Social Teaching and, 232–35; civil society peacebuilding and, 236–40; future hostility and, 227–58; just actors and, 145–46; peace and, 46; peacebuilding and, 227–58; in Philpott, 134–35, 142–43, 144n42, 145; punishment and, 158; reconstruction of, 77–80, 225–58; theoretical ground for practice, 225–26; in Walzer, 28
Patterson, Eric, 57–60, 69–71, 75
Paul VI, Pope, 101n49, 155, 233
Pax Christi International, 84
peace: Abrahamic concepts of, 126; in Aristotle, 15, 17; attainability of, 168; evil, 19; God and, 183n46; in Hobbes, 69; intention and, 43; *jus post bellum* and, 46; justice and, 20, 23; just war theory and, 110–11; in Kant, 34–35, 35n59; losing, xi; love and, 96; negative, 14n3; in Patterson, 69; positive, 14n3; with reconciliation, 139–40; stability of, 62; in Walzer, 60n26
Peacebuilding: Catholic Theology, Ethics, and Praxis (Lederach), 243
Peace of Westphalia, 91
Pensky, Max, 215–16, 216n81
Petzold, Christian, 1
Philpott, Daniel, 64–67, 65n40, 73–74, 83–84, 122–36, 127n10, 133n24, 137n30, 140–44, 144n42, 152, 152n51, 155, 157n62, 158, 216n77, 245n52, 263
Phoenix (film), 1

Pius XI, Pope, 155, 234–35
Pius XII, Pope, 101n49
policing, just, 3–5, 7, 25–26; arms control
    and, 164–65; challenges of, 175–87; for
    common good, 178–87; costs of, 176–
    78; establishment of, 47; as foundational
    theme, 68–73; from, to punishment,
    189; for injustice, 163–87; international
    community and, 172–73; just actors
    and, 163–64, 182–87; multinational
    operations and, 178–81; nation-build-
    ing and, 170; peace and, 145; peace-
    keeping and, 164–65; in Philpott,
    134–35, 144n42; political reconciliation
    and, 144; practical challenges in, 175–
    87; punishment vs., 146; reconstruction
    of, 46, 161–87; security and, 162–63,
    181–82; self-determination and, 173–
    74; self-governance and, 173–74; as
    state practice, 175–76; theoretical
    ground for practice of, 161–63; from
    theory to practice, 161; time commit-
    ment in, 176–78; victor's obligation and,
    170–72
Pontifical Council for Justice and Peace, 84
"Pottery Barn Rule," 57, 57n19
Powers, Gerard F., 82n3
POWs. See prisoners of war (POWs)
prisoners of war (POWs), 76
proportionality, 27n38, 36, 44, 66, 82,
    107n70, 111, 139, 148, 149n46, 192
Protestantism, 90–93
Psalms, book of, 134n25
punishment, just, 66; for amending past
    wrongdoings, 191–222; in Aquinas, 41,
    186; conservation and, 197–99; defined,
    130; fair trials and, 213–22; Geneva
    Convention and, 45; good and, 180;
    humanitarian law and, 191–96;
    humanitarian occupation law and, 199–
    206; international law and, 191–97,
    206–9; just actors and, 146; justice and,
    111–12; occupation law and, 197–206;
    in Orend, 37, 76; peace and, 46; in Phil-

pott, 124–25; from policing to, 189;
    political reconciliation and, 131–32,
    157n62; proportionality and, 82; recon-
    struction of, 73–77, 189–224; rehabilita-
    tion and, 145; rule of law and, 191–222;
    scope of, 210–22; sovereignty and, 200–
    202; theoretical ground for practice of,
    189–91; war crimes and, 43

Q
Quadragesimo Anno (Pius XI), 234

R
R2P. See Responsibility to Protect (R2P)
Rahner, Karl, 105n62
realism, 8, 29, 108, 116–18, 127, 128n14,
    156–57, 268
realistic idealism, 128n14
reconciliation: facilitation for, 240–42;
    faith-based organizations and, 240–46;
    with God, 182–87; horizontal, 183;
    intermediation for, 240–42; peacebuild-
    ing and, 240–46; political, xii–xiii, 44,
    58, 66, 71, 83–84, 121–57, 212–13; ver-
    tical, 183
reconstruction: as core theme, 45; in
    Himes, 104; justice and, 7; of just poli-
    cing, 68–73; of just political participa-
    tion, 77–80; of just punishment, 73–77;
    revenge and, 76; as term, 4n4; in
    Walzer, 29
rehabilitation, 31, 38, 43, 61, 76–77, 82–83,
    105, 120, 145, 178, 213, 215
reparation, 44, 46, 65–66, 74–77, 112, 124,
    130, 138, 181, 209, 212–13, 215
repentance, 94–96, 94n32, 97–99, 182–87,
    231
responsibility: in Elshtain, 58–59; in Kant,
    50n2; in Locke, 50n2; norm of, 81–83;
    shift of norm from right to, 50–51
Responsibility to Protect (R2P), 49, 51–53,
    51n3, 64, 78, 85–119, 92n26, 137,
    208n56, 237
restitution, 37, 66, 74, 111, 169

restoration, 95, 133, 136. *See also* justice, restorative

retribution, 1, 66, 132, 138, 214–15, 214n70, 215n72, 217

revenge, 36–37, 43, 76–77, 105, 181

Richmond, Oliver, 236–37, 259

righteousness, 125–26, 134n25, 152, 152n51

right relationships, 57, 65, 106, 126–32, 134n25, 140–41, 152

right to fight, 51, 56

right to intervene, 51, 56

Roberts, Adam, 198–99

Rome Statute, 51n3, 208n56

Rose, Gideon, 177n34

Royal, Robert, 30

rule of law, 191–222

S

Scheers, Ivar, 165, 167–70

Scheid, Anna Floerke, 84, 121, 124, 137–44, 144n42, 155, 157n62, 158

Schlabach, Gerald, 157n62

Schreiter, Robert, 122, 246n55

Schuck, Michael, 13n1, 83, 94–99, 94n32, 106, 109, 118, 145, 148, 184

Schwarzkopf, Norman, 94

Second Vatican Council. *See* Vatican II

security, 7, 44, 137; comprehensive, 162, 162n1, 189; as fundamental aspect, 150; in Himes, 106; as human right, 33; justice and, 29–30; in moral theology, 81–120; national, 68; order and, 58, 70; in Orend, 71; in Patterson, 71; policing and, 162–63, 181–82; as principal concern, 158; reconciliation and, 143–47; theology and, 85–94

Security Council. *See* United Nations Security Council (UNSC)

self-defense, 6, 27, 86, 101, 101n49, 107, 141, 184–85, 187, 193, 245

self-determination, 173–74

self-governance, 173–74

Smock, David, 244n50

SOFA. *See* Status of Forces Agreements (SOFA)

solidarity, 86, 91, 155, 265, 268

Sollicitudo rei Socialis, 155n56, 164

Sonnenberg, Dale, 178

sources, foundational, 13–41

South Korea, 178, 211, 211n64

sovereignty, 28, 31, 68–69, 71, 169, 195, 200–202

Soviet Union, 1

Special Working Group on the Crime of Aggression (SWGCA), 213n67

Stahn, Carsten, 202–4, 206

Stassen, Glen, 84, 108, 231

state practice, 175–76

Status of Forces Agreements (SOFA), 210–12

Stephen, James Fitzjames, 214n70, 215

Suárez, Francisco, xi

subsidiarity, 53, 226, 234–35, 234n19, 236, 258–59

Summa theologiae (Aquinas), 19nn13–16, 20, 20nn20–21, 21nn22–24, 23n28, 24nn33–34, 25n35, 44n73, 100n46, 105n64, 106n65, 156nn59–60, 157n61, 183n44, 185nn54–56, 186n58, 187n61, 250n63

Sutch, Peter, 35

SWGCA. *See* Special Working Group on the Crime of Aggression (SWGCA)

synderesis, 20

T

themes, foundational, 41–47, 68–80

Thessalonians, Second, 86

Thomas Aquinas. *See* Aquinas, Thomas

Tojo, Hideki, 219

Tomasi, Silvano, 87–88

To Perpetual Peace (Kant), 34–35

Torrance, Alan, 122

trials, war crimes, 29–30

Truth Commission, 146, 155, 197

U

UDHR. *See* Universal Declaration of
   Human Rights (UDHR)
United Nations Charter, 190, 193, 193n11
United Nations Security Council (UNSC),
   53, 121, 191, 193, 196, 200, 202–4, 221,
   223
Universal Declaration of Human Rights
   (UDHR), 195

V

Vatican II, 105n62, 244n50
victor's justice, 75
Villa-Vicencio, Charles, 122–23
Vinjamuri, Leslie, 133, 137n30
virtue, 17–18, 24n32, 249, 250n63, 250n66,
   266
Vitoria, Francisco de, xi
Volf, Miroslav, 122
*Vortex of Conflict, The: US Policy towards
   Afghanistan, Pakistan, and Iraq* (Cal-
   dwell), 171

W

Walzer, Michael, xi, 4, 4n3, 13, 26–32, 34–
   35, 41–44, 50, 60–61, 60n26, 67–68, 73–
   75, 78–79, 113, 129, 140, 148n44,
   162n2, 189, 218, 220n92
war: in Aquinas, 22–23; in Aristotle, 14–18;
   asymmetric, 8, 71n53, 239n35; in

Augustine, 25; in Elshtain, 59; good and,
   17; in Grotius, 14; in Hobbes, 69; intention in, 43, 94, 96, 99–100; in Kant, 35;
   as last resort, 26n37; as natural, 16; in
   Orend, 32–33; phases of, 97; presump-
   tion against, 23n28; realism and, 117–
   18; virtue and, 17–18; in Walzer, 26–28
war crimes, 29–30, 51n3, 52, 64, 66, 73, 75–
   78, 112, 124–25, 136, 168, 190, 207–9,
   208n56, 214, 217–23, 220n91, 221n93
War Crimes and Just War (May), 64
WCC. *See* World Council of Churches
   (WCC)
Webber, Peter, 1
Weiss, Thomas, 163n3
*What We Owe Iraq: War and the Ethics of
   Nation Building* (Feldman), 174
Williams, Robert E., 34, 73n55, 170
Winright, Tobias, 24, 81, 83, 85, 88, 107–
   19, 107n70, 121–23, 133, 138–39, 145,
   151, 156–57, 189, 246, 263, 265
World Council of Churches (WCC), 90–91
World War I, 37, 73
World War II, 1, 37, 40n68, 73–74, 77, 173,
   213n67, 219–21, 220n94, 223, 239n35,
   244
Wright, Karen Shields, 234

Y

Yugoslavia, 209n61